في ذكرى

مارك لينز

Hijab

Three Modern Iranian Seminarian Perspectives

Lloyd Ridgeon

GINGKO

First published in 2021 by
Gingko
4 Molasses Row
London SW11 3UX

Cover image: Hengameh Golestan, *Untitled* (*Witness* '79 series), photograph, March 1979, Anatole France (Neuphle le-Chateau) Street, opposite the USSR (Russian) Embassy, Tehran; © Hengameh Golestan, Courtesy of Archaeology of the Final Decade.

A CIP catalogue record for this book is available from the British Library.

ISBN 978-1-909942-56-1
e-ISBN 978-1-909942-57-8

Typeset in Times by MacGuru Ltd
Printed in the United Kingdom

www.gingko.org.uk
@GingkoLibrary

In gratitude to my parents,
and my sisters, Evie, Barbara and Fiona,
and my wife Jessica, and our children, Boo, Hattie and Felix,
for countless happy times and acts of kindness.

Contents

Part 4: Hijab Depending on Time and Place: The Views of Muhsin Kadivar

List of Illustrations

Acknowledgements

I am extremely grateful to so many friends and colleagues who have provided inspiration or else given valuable information and sources for this work. Without their help this book would not have been started. My greatest debt is to Farhad Shafti who suggested that I investigate the thought of Ahmad Qabil, and introduced me to his website. I also need to express my thanks to Muhsin Kadivar, as during the course of writing this book he generously directed me to many pertinent works of his, and patiently answered my questions on matters related to jurisprudence. Others worthy of mention include Ali Ansari, Naser Ghobadzadeh, Paul Luft, Mohammad Mesbahi, Ziba Mir-Hosseini, Andrew Newman, Magdalena Rodziewicz, Eskandar Sadeghi-Borujerdi, and Fatima Tofighi.

I should also thank the staff at Gingko and Barbara Haus Schwepcke for facilitating the publishing process, both financially and professionally.

Several images illustrate the nature of the hijab in this work, and I would like to acknowledge the assistance of Bita Pourvash of the Aga Khan Museum for permitting the reproduction of Shaykh Safi al-Din, @ The Aga Khan Museum, AKM264. Likewise, Jennifer Berry offered much help in securing the right for the photographs in Chapter 2 taken by Antoin Sevruguin, held by the Freer Gallery of Art and Arthur M Sackler Gallery. Monica Park was also kind to offer advice on securing the rights for Figure 5. I would also like to thank Charla Wilson of Northwestern University Library and Daniel Meyer, Director, Special Collections Research Center, University of Chicago Library. I am also extremely grateful to the Makhmalbaf Film House, in particular to Maysam Makhmalbaf for giving me the right to reproduce two images in chapter five (Figures 17 and 18).

I am also grateful to the Leverhulme Trust who partly financed the project by enabling me to buy-out my undergraduate teaching for two years at Glasgow University, during which time I was able to stay at home to engage in research for this work.

Transliteration

The system of transliteration in this book operates on the basis of the IJMES method for technical terms. Some of these have been Anglicised and are commonly recognisable. These include words such as Qurʾan, hadith, sharia, ulama and hijab. For the sake of consistency, the word hijab becomes *ḥijāb* when placed in the title of a Persian or Arabic book, or when in a Persian compound, e.g. *bad-ḥijāb*.

Following the recommendations of the publisher, except for *ayn* and *hamza*, I have removed diacritical marks from all names of individuals. In addition, some names appear in the way that they have been rendered in English by the individuals themselves, or in the fashion that they are commonly recognised, e.g. Hassan Rouhani (which according to the IJMES system would normally be Ḥasan Rūḥānī), Soroush and Eshkevari.

Introduction

> Let me be as blunt and direct as I can be. Western civilization is in a war. We should frankly test every person here who is of a Muslim background, and if they believe in Sharia, they should be deported. Sharia is incompatible with Western civilization.

So claimed Newt Gingrich in 2016, former Speaker of the House of Representatives in the US (1995–99), who also ran a presidential campaign in 2012. Gingrich's comments in an interview with Fox News came in the wake of a terrorist attack in Nice which left 84 people dead. The act had been perpetrated by Mohamed Lahouaiej-Bouhlel who hailed from Tunisia but lived in France, and responsibility for his act was taken by ISIS. Gingrich's reaction to the atrocity needs to be seen in the context of populist politics which had been making inroads in many parts of the West, resulting in electoral successes in Europe and North America for candidates who were unsympathetic to either Islam, or Muslims or states where Islam is entwined with the constitution. The list of leading political figures who have espoused such ideas includes the following: Viktor Orbán in Hungary (prime minister since 2010), who referred to refugees as 'Muslim invaders' who were not welcome in his country;[1] Donald Trump (elected president of the United States in 2016), who famously instituted a 'Muslim ban' on nationals from seven predominantly Muslim states from entering the US;[2] Marine le Pen in France, 'campaigning under the threat of two "totalitarianisms" – economic

1 Emily Schultheis, 'Viktor Orban: Hungary does not want "Muslim Invaders"', *Politico* 1 August 2018, https://www.politico.eu/article/viktor-orban-hungary-doesnt-want-muslim-invaders/.

2 Moustafa Bayoumi, 'The Muslim Ban ruling legitimates Trump's bigotry', *The Guardian* 27 June 2018, https://www.theguardian.com/commentisfree/2018/jun/27/muslim-ban-ruling-trumps-bigotry.

globalisation and Islamic fundamentalism',[3] who was narrowly defeated in the first round of the presidential elections in 2017, scoring 21.53% compared with Emmanuel Macron's 23.75%.[4] To this list we may also add fringe parties and individuals, such as the leading figures of the British National Party which wants to 'ban shariah law'.[5] Populist politics and increasing nationalist sentiment have been concomitant with anti-Islamic and anti-sharia views in recent times, especially since the events associated with 9/11. Sharia in the Western popular imagination is arguably associated with the amputation of limbs, stoning of homosexuals, flogging for adultery, etc., and in the words of one British political journalist, 'most non-Muslims in the West seem united with hardline Islamists in the misguided belief that there is one monolithic, unchanging sharia.'[6] Such a view of the 'misguided' interpretation of sharia is echoed in Islamic lands too, typified by the comments of the reformist Iranian theologian Muhammad Mujtahid-Shabistari, who observed,

> Europeans tend to regard the sharia as a solid edifice. But the sharia is not a solid edifice. It is dependent upon the *fuqahā*, Islamic legal scholars, who are allowed to issue a *fatwa*, i.e. an Islamic legal pronouncement. When these legal scholars are free-thinking individuals, then they can interpret Islamic law in such a way to present no hurdles to the establishment of democracy. Those who venture even further could say, 'We can find passages in the Koran, the Sunna and the sharia that encourage us to adapt a democratic system.'[7]

This book expands upon the idea promulgated by Shabistari through assessing the claim of an interpretation of sharia that is 'liberal, progressive and broad-minded'.[8] The sharia is a complex subject, indeed the argument should more

3 Chloe Farand, 'Marine le Pen launches presidential campaign with hardline speech', *The Independent* 5 February 2017, https://www.independent.co.uk/news/world/europe/marine-le-pen-front-national-speech-campaign-launch-islamic-fundamentalism-french-elections-a7564051.html.

4 Henry Samuel, 'French election 2017: Emmanuel Macron and Marine Le Pen through to presidential run off', *The Telegraph* 24 April 2017, https://www.telegraph.co.uk/news/2017/04/23/french-election-live-results-exit-polls.

5 https://bnp.org.uk/policies/reversing-islamisation/.

6 Mehdi Hasan, 'It's time to lay the sharia bogeyman to rest', *New Statesman* June 2011, https://newstatesman.com/religion/2011/06/islamic-law-sharia-british.

7 Jan Kuhlmann, interview with Muhammad Mujtahid-Shabestari (© *Qantara.de 2012),* 'Why Islam and democracy go well together', https://en.qantara.de/content/interview-with-mohammad-mojtahed-shabestari-why-islam-and-democracy-go-well-together.

8 This is the claim made by Hassan Rouhani, who wrote his PhD thesis under the name

specifically be one about *fiqh*, or jurisprudence, and this will be examined herein through the prism of a contemporary and controversial case study: how modern Iranian seminarians (the jurists, or *fuqahā*) have arrived at very different opinions about the necessity of women wearing a head-covering or hijab since the Iranian state demands that women's head hair should be concealed. Understandings of the 'clerics' have been chosen because the opinions emanating from the seminary (typically the establishments in Qum or Mashhad) frequently carry significant weight.[9] Of course, this is not to say that all seminarian views are the same or hold equal significance, and this study clearly shows there is great diversity.

Sharia is often understood as the pristine divine law that has been set out by God, traditionally interpreted by the religious authorities, or the seminarians. This human appreciation is known as *fiqh* (jurisprudence) and it has been considered an accumulation of opinions of individual scholars in the *hawza*s (seminaries). Following the success of the Islamic Revolution in 1978–79, there emerged a new configuration of interpreters and organisations (overseen to a large extent by the Leader (*rahbar*)), and composed of members of parliament (*majlis*), supervised by certain bodies (dominated by seminarians) appointment to which was restricted to those with the appropriate Islamic credentials. These bodies included the Guardian Council, the Expediency Council, and the Society of Seminary Teachers of Qum. In other words, *fiqh* is now contested within the Iranian Parliament and its political structures, which are informed by the reasoning and declarations made by specific factions of senior figures in the seminaries.[10]

Hassan Feridon, which is his birth-name. His father was called Haj Asadollah Feridoun. Hassan Feridon, 'The Flexibility of Shariah (Islamic Law) with Reference to the Iranian Experience', PhD thesis, University Glasgow Caledonian University 1998, 392.

9 The word cleric/clerics is a translation of the Persian and Arabic term *ʿalim*/ulama that denotes an individual or body of individuals who have trained in the seminary, and still maintain seminary methods and belief in Twelver Shiʿi Islam. Despite this, some of the contemporary ulama have expressed 'radical' and 'modern' views which depart significantly from 'traditional' understandings. The word ulama is an umbrella term that includes theologians (*mutakallimūn*), jurists (*fuqahā*), philosophers (i.e. Islamic philosophers), hadith scholars (*muḥaddithūn*) and Qurʾanic exegetes (*muffasirūn*). It might be argued that the broadness of the term is too loose to fit comfortably over the main scholars in this study (Murtaza Mutahhari, Ahmad Qabil and Muhsin Kadivar). Certainly, Qabil and Kadivar have considered themselves as *mujtahid*s (private email from Muhsin Kadivar, dated 7 November 2018). And yet categorising other leading scholars in this study poses other problems; Mutahhari was a theologian and philosopher, while Muhammad Mujtahid Shabistari considers himself a theologian. The difficulty of bunching this group together within a single term is recognised, and although ulama has its limitations, it is the best term that can be employed.

10 Behrooz Ghamari-Tabrizi, 'Women's Rights, Shariʿa' Law, and the Secularization of Islam in Iran', *International Journal of Politics, Culture, and Society* 26.3, 2013, 237–53.

So it is here that the dilemma facing the Islamic Republic of Iran becomes apparent: on the one hand, the governmental machinery of the state and certain factions within the seminaries are the ultimate arbiters of Islam and *fiqh*, but traditionally jurists from the seminaries have remained independent from governmental structures, and therefore have enjoyed the freedom to express autonomous views on the religious legality of specific issues. The institutionalisation of Islam in Iran through executive, legislative and judicial organisations has in practice reduced this independence, but nevertheless some within the ulama have fiercely guarded and demanded the right to express views that have sometimes been contrary to that of the state (such as the necessity for women to wear the hijab). A contemporary group from the seminaries known as the 'New Religious Thinkers' have rejected the univocality of *fiqh* interpretation and implementation. They have set out diverse methods which promote a pluralist approach, as set out in chapter one of this book, which serves as the key to subsequent chapters.

As such the research and primary significance of this book is the demonstration of '*fiqh* plasticity', and its responsiveness to the needs of the time. The book also informs the debate of 'religious secularity' (here indicating the separation of religion and state – not necessarily the decrease of religious sentiment) and shows how the imposition of state sponsored religiosity and piety has been challenged. Juristic hermeneutics are guided by the interplay between traditional ways that sacred scripture has been understood and the demands and customs of a society which in the 20th–21st centuries has witnessed change at an unprecedented speed. This book also shows how the jurists of the modern period have been influenced by the 'ethical turn' (in addition to the 'linguistic turn')[11] in which the 'literal' understanding of sacred texts, the practice of reading verses in isolation from the overall message of the Qur'an, and the foregrounding of rights and duties over ethics have been challenged.[12] In practice this has resulted in arguments over how to define piety and the nature of an 'Islamic' way of life.[13] The 'ethical turn'

11 The influence of the 'linguistic turn' is most obvious in the ideas of Muhammad Mujtahid Shabistari, discussed in Part One.

12 Marion Katz observes this phenomenon in the Sunni tradition and says, 'I would argue that one discernible and little-noticed phenomenon is that in some cases ethical themes have taken on a distinctly more prominent role in legal argumentation since the beginning of the twentieth century.' See *Ethics, gender, and the Islamic Legal Project*, Yale Law School, Occasional Papers, 2015, 25.

13 Lara Deeb makes the pertinent point that a way forward in understanding Islamic societies is to trouble 'or at least ethnographically unpack … our understandings of the boundary between what counts as piety or the pious and what does not, and by beginning to conceptualize that boundary itself as a moving target that is part of Muslims' own ongoing

has resulted in interpretations that are diverse and contradictory, ranging from an understanding of piety and ethics that witnesses minute observance of every act being grounded in law to that which regards sacred texts and law as providing general guidance, allowing believers more freedom to choose from a range of 'pious' options. However, the relationship between law and ethics is not a simple binary one, and as Katz has astutely observed the dynamic between them is very complicated and defies simplistic categorisation. This being so, it is best just to 'complicate the received narrative about Islamic law and ethics and draw attention to the wide range of relationships between these two fields before and after the advent of modernity'.[14]

The degree of *fiqh* plasticity and the influence of the 'ethical turn' among some modern Iranian seminarians are demonstrated in this book with reference to a case study of the hijab in Iran. In recent years the opinions about the hijab made by the ulama cover a range of possibilities for women, from the necessity to wear a head-covering, to the desirability to don the hijab, and finally to permitting women freedom of choice. And anyone who has been to Iran, or who has seen images of modern Iranian women, will know that the hijab is worn in different ways and that the law to cover all the hair is often flouted. Thus, the case study of the hijab offers an excellent illustration of *fiqh* in practice, and it is a good example of the dilemmas facing a people who hold a variety of perspectives, ranging from the 'traditionalists' who favour the hijab, to 'modernists' who do not feel any contradiction about adopting 'Western' fashions and norms. The analysis in this book does not focus on the motivations of women for wearing or not wearing the hijab, as these are notoriously problematic to identify. Religious, cultural, and political factors are all relevant considerations, which are not necessarily mutually exclusive, especially as definitions of these terms inevitably melt into one another.

The hijab represents a major point of discussion with regard to *fiqh* because the Iranian state's policy of mandatory hijab and the imposition of punishments for non-observance typifies an approach that has been censured by Muslims and non-Muslims in contemporary times.[15] As indicated at the very start of this

---

discussions'. Lara Deeb, 'Thinking piety and the everyday together: A response to Fadil and Fernando', *Hau: Journal of Ethnographic Theory* 5.2, 2015, 95.

14 Katz, *Ethics, gender, and the Islamic Legal Project*, 29.

15 Article 638 of Islamic Penal Code states that women who appear in public not wearing the hijab will receive a prison sentence of between 10 days to two months and a fine of between 50,000 to 500,000 rials (between $1.50 and $15 at the time of writing). (See 'Iran's Prosecutor Dismisses Hijab Protesters as Childish and Ignorant', *Iranwire* 31 January 2018, https://iranwire.com/en/features/5136.)

introduction, sharia has been the focus of attention in the West, where not only does it provoke emotions such as fear, outrage and disgust, but it has in recent times been the subject of constructive criticism from Muslims living in the West. That is to say, the criticism by reforming Western Muslims is levelled at specific interpretations of *fiqh*, rather than censure of sharia as God's ideal law, referring to 'the universal, innate, and natural laws of goodness'.[16] Khaled Abou El Fadl, Professor of Islamic Law at UCLA in the US, has referred to the implementation of *ḥudūd* punishments (corporal punishment, stoning, the death penalty, etc.) and has made associations with Iran, Saudi Arabia, Pakistan, Nigeria and Afghanistan, remarking that these countries 'have at different times and circumstances committed injustices that could only be described as thoroughly ugly'.[17] In a similar fashion Tariq Ramadan, who was Professor of Contemporary Islamic Studies at the University of Oxford, declared publicly that 'the application of the sharia today is used by repressive powers to abuse women, the poor and political opponents with a quasi-legal vacuum. Muslim conscience cannot accept this injustice.'[18] Although both of these Muslim scholars follow Sunni Islam, it is just as easy to discover Muslim academics in the West who critique certain interpretations of *fiqh* and who adhere to Shiʿi Islam (making their evaluations more relevant to the Iranian case, which has been a Shiʿi majority region since the sixteenth–seventeenth centuries). For example, Abdulaziz Sachedina, Professor of Islamic Studies at George Mason University, Virginia (who has been visiting lecturer in seminaries in Iran),[19] speaks of an 'epistemological crisis' faced by jurists when it comes to legal matters pertaining to women, who have had restricted access to learning. Women's voices are simply not heard when matters such as purity, equality or modesty are discussed. Sachedina observes, 'There is no doubt that the tone of the rulings is set by the powerful male jurist who, in most cases, ignores the female evaluation of her

16 Khaled Abou El Fadl, *Reasoning with God*, London 2017, xxxii.

17 El Fadl, *Reasoning with God*, 291.

18 Tariq Ramadan, 'We must not accept this repression', *The Guardian* 30 March 2005.

19 Sachedina himself makes the following claim:

> In Qom, among the traditional scholars, I have now given lectures about human rights, religious pluralism and the academic methodology I apply in my studies in Islamic law and ethics. I have lectured on bioethics and the methodology I use. And Iran has published my studies in those fields in Persian. Since I have been teaching in Persian, Iran has published my lectures and my specific take on Islamic texts as a guide to teach new students of seminary – the modern methodology.

See 'An interview with Abdulaziz Sachedina on His Life and Scholarship', *Maydan* 13 September 2017, https://www.themaydan.com/2017/09/interview-abdulaziz-sachedina-life-scholarship/.

own social situation.'[20] Another Western Shiʿi academic who advocates reform is Liyakat Takim, who has the Sharjah Chair in Global Islam at McMaster University in Canada. Takim discusses the 'failure of *ejtehad*',[21] which is basically the jurists' inability to provide adequate solutions, based on rational investigation that does not contravene sacred scripture, to the challenges of modern situations and circumstances. These observations and criticisms by Western Muslim scholars reflect the concerns of the so-called 'New Religious Thinkers' among the ulama in Iran. Not only are the major issues the same, but the language used by the Western-based scholars mentioned above is similar to that of their Iranian counterparts who speak of the cruelty and the ugliness of recent applications of *fiqh*.

*

The present work is divided into four parts. Part One provides an illustration of the most significant of the inventive methods that the aforementioned New Religious Thinkers among the seminarians have utilised in their interpretations of *fiqh*. It demonstrates the facile Western understandings of sharia to which this introduction has alluded by discussing the radical implications that these new interpretations of the key components of *fiqh* have for jurisprudence, theology and politics. The most controversial of the seminarians among the New Religious Thinkers, namely Hasan Yousefi Eshkevari,[22] Muhsin Kadivar, Ahmad Qabil and Muhammad Mujtahid Shabistari are taken as examples, although these examples are not exhaustive of the movement.

The Second, Third and Fourth parts of this book share a symmetry in basic structure; they all contain sections which outline a chronological perspective of the main contours of the hijab controversy in Iran. Part Two deals with the premodern period and encompasses the impact of Western thought and orientalism in the nineteenth century, and the adoption of the 'modernising' meta-narrative of the Pahlavi monarchy which led up to the Islamic Revolution in 1978–79. Part Three concentrates on how the regulations on the hijab were established in Iran, and it highlights the challenges faced by the Islamic government between the

20 Abdulaziz Sachedina, 'Woman, half-the-man? The Crisis of Male Epistemology in Islamic Jurisprudence', *Intellectual Traditions in Islam*, ed. Farhad Daftary, London 2000, 175.

21 Liyakat Takim, 'Islamic Law and Post-Ijtihadism', unpublished paper, http://www.ltakim.com/Post-Islamism.pdf.

22 Hasan Yousefi Eshkevari is the spelling that is given on his own website, so in this work the same spelling is used (http://yousefieshkevari.com/).

years 1979–2005. Part Four concludes the historical survey examining the period from 2005 to the present, and it shows that the range of seminarian thinking is not limited to a single understanding, but continues to offer interpretations that may be considered 'conservative' to those that are regarded as radical and 'liberal'.

After the historical-contextual sections in each of Parts Two, Three and Four, there are two further sections. The first of these sections investigates the general religious and theological perspectives of a seminarian chosen to represent that particular era. The subsequent section in Parts Two, Three and Four include translations of the works of the selected seminarian on the topic of the hijab. Part Two focuses on Ayatollah Murtaza Mutahhari (d. 1979), who is regarded by the Islamic regime as a great champion of the ongoing revolution and battle against the non-religious forces that struggled against the regime. Mutahhari's theology provided an alternative to both the left-wing ideologies in Iran during the 1960s and 1970s, and also to the secularising and 'modernising' forces of the Shah. Whilst he was prepared to tackle many of the 'traditional' patterns of thought among the ulama, his writings on women and the hijab still betray a certain degree of conservatism in his thought. He is representative of those mullas who believe that the hijab is compulsory (*vājib*). Part Three focuses on the ideas of Ahmad Qabil (d. 2012), a seminarian who is virtually unknown in the West, but who achieved considerable fame in Iran because of his political opposition to the Leader, ʿAli Khamenei, and also due to his fatwa of 2004 in which he declared that the hijab was not compulsory, but desirable. This shift in the legal status of the hijab reflected Qabil's larger theological perspective, built upon the exercise of reason. Part Four turns to the ideas and thinking of Muhsin Kadivar, who, like Qabil, has become known as a staunch opponent of Khamenei and his clique who rule Iran. And both Qabil and Kadivar share many of the same principles for reforming the ways in which seminarians think about jurisprudence. Nevertheless, there is great difference of opinion between them when it comes to the hijab, for Kadivar does not believe that the hijab is either necessary or desirable. Instead he holds that its use depends on the 'time and place' (a major jurisprudential principle), which allows for the setting aside of religious commands. Kadivar even goes as far as to say that there is no Qurʾanic imperative for women to wear the hijab.

Seminarians have responded to their changing socio-political contexts by utilising traditional jurisprudential methods that provide 'legitimate' ways to interpret sacred scripture and narrations. The three seminarians selected as case studies here were specifically chosen because of their different opinions. I would have liked to have studied female voices within the ulama on the topic of the hijab, but this has not been possible due to the fact that I have been unable to identify any female seminarian who has voiced an influential opinion about the hijab.[23] Female voices, seminarian or otherwise, that articulate views about the hijab must have their place in the general discussion. However, at present it seems that the women's voices are reflected more in their actions rather than in theological and jurisprudential writing.

The New Religious Thinkers among the Iranian ulama have yielded substantial scholarship in Persian, but much of the English and European scholarship tends to focus on the views of the non-seminarian trained scholar Abdolkarim Soroush.[24] Studies on the seminarians among the New Religious Thinkers in Iran comprise a drop in the ocean of the literature on Shiʿi Islam that more usually concentrates on the ideas and policies of Khomeini, or politicians such as Ahmadinejad.[25] This work is the first to analyse the responses of the New Religious Thinkers on a specific issue that not only assesses their original approach to interpretations of *fiqh*, but also highlights the context in which they composed their answers to these challenges. More specifically, it provides an essential window through which to understand and assess debates around the hijab (seemingly a 'simple piece of cloth'[26]) which in Europe appears to many quite unfathomable, but which to Muslims in Europe and in Islam-majority states is of critical importance. Surprisingly, the

---

23 There are very few females who have reached the level of *mujtahid* and are therefore recognised as being qualified to issue jurisprudential opinions. Mirjam Künkler and Roja Fazaeli look at two women who have reached this level. See 'The life of two mujtahidahs: Female religious authority in 20th century Iran', *Women, Leadership and Mosques: Changes in Contemporary Islamic Authority*, ed. Masooda Bano and Hilary Kalmbach, Leiden 2010, 127–60. This work notes that the *mujtahida*s take on the hijab falls in line with that of Mutahhari (see Part One), and indeed, it is not a topic to which they accord much attention. See also Keiko Sakurai, 'Shiʿite women's seminaries (*howzeh-ye ʻelmiyyeh-ye khahran*) [sic] in Iran: Possibilities and limitations', *Iranian Studies* 45.6, 2012, 727–44.

24 One of the most celebrated of Soroush's early works is his *Qabz o Bast-i Tiʾurik-i Sharīʿat* [*The Theoretic Expansion and Contraction of the Sharia*], Tehran 1995. Some of his works have appeared in English, such as *Reason, Freedom, and Democracy in Islam: Essential Writings of Abdolkarim Soroush*, Oxford 2000, and *The Expansion of Prophetic Experience; Essays on Historicity, Contingency and Plurality in Religion*, trans. Nilou Mobasser, Leiden 2009. There are many secondary works on Soroush, see for example Behrooz Ghamari-Tabrizi, *Islam and Dissent: Abdolkarim Soroush, Religious Political and Democratic Reform*, London 2008.

25 The scholarship on Khomeini is vast, and a list of works that investigates the various dimensions of his thought (including the jurisprudential, political and mystical) would be exceedingly long and out of place here. The few articles that have been published on the ulama among Iran's New Religious Thinkers are referenced in Part One of this book.

26 The term is used by Professor Linda Woodhead, 'The Muslim Veil Controversy and European Values', *Swedish Missiological Themes* 97.1, 2009, 89–105.

English language literature on the hijab in Iran is minimal, despite the abundance of general and introductory literature in the West about the veil.[27] The most active scholar in the field is the feminist anthropologist Ziba Mir-Hosseini whose articles on gender and the hijab have provided inspiration on many occasions for this study. In several articles Mir-Hosseini has mentioned and highlighted 'conservative' thinking, typified in the writings of Mutahhari.[28] Her analysis also focuses on how this was developed by the likes of the non-seminarian ʿAli Shariʿati (d. 1977), and has been advanced by some of the ulama themselves in more recent years. Mir-Hosseini's focus on the New Religious Thinkers is brief since most of her work has been in the form of articles or book chapters, and does not permit jurisprudential or contextual backgrounds in great depth. The kinds of responses to the hijab that attempt to highlight the dangers of patriarchal seminarian thinking (including Mir-Hosseini's understanding) have been criticised by Minoo Derayeh who warns of the dangers of cultural relativism, which unwittingly endorses 'fundamentalist conservatism' that 'fails to expose the reality of life and experiences of those Muslim women whose voices are silenced' by post-modern relativism. (Derayeh includes Mir-Hosseini in her list of culprits, and she also talks of 'over-generalized apologetic works consolidating patriarchy'.[29]) Other authors have focused on various aspects of the hijab in Iran, such as Rebecca Gould whose work looks mainly at the hijab as a commodity form. Although she notes that her article focuses on the negative consequences of mandatory veiling, she cites Hoodfar who claims that 'women have used the same social institution to free themselves from the binds of patriarchy'.[30] A cursory glance at these above mentioned articles demonstrates that the hijab is not a simplistic topic. What is missing from these works, however, is an in-depth study that examines the range

---

27 One of the best introductions is Sahar Amer, *What is Veiling*, Edinburgh 2014. Also worthy of note is Katherine Bullock, *Rethinking Muslim Women and the Veil*, Hendon VA, 2002.
28 The most useful of these is Ziba Mir-Hosseini, 'Hijab and Choice: Between Politics and Theology', *Innovation in Islam: Tradition and Contribution*, ed. Mehran Kamrava, Berkeley 2011, 190–212. The reader is advised to look at Mir-Hosseini's website where there is a list of her publications (books, articles and chapters from books), many of which are available to download. See http://www.zibamirhosseini.com/.
29 Minoo Derayeh, 'The myth of creation and *hijab*: Iranian women, liberated or oppressed', *Pakistan Journal of Women's Studies: Alam-e-Niswan* 18.2, 2011, 1–21.
30 Rebecca Gould, 'Hijab as commodity form: Veiling, unveiling, and misveiling in contemporary Iran', *Feminist Theory* 15.3, 2014, 221–40.

of seminarian thinking, the theological underpinning of such perspectives, and the contexts in which they emerge.[31]

It is surprising that the issue of the hijab has not been considered in any profundity in a monograph by Western scholars, or even among Iranian academics who write in English. In an otherwise excellent survey of contemporary thinking among the ulama, Naser Ghobadzadeh writes, 'the raising of sensitive subjects such as the hijab and the consumption of alcohol has been side-stepped by reformist scholars at the current stage of Iran's political trajectory to avoid conflict.'[32] But it will be demonstrated in this book that the issue of the hijab has in fact enjoyed a considerable degree of attention among reformist ulama.[33]

*

In the course of writing this book, a social media campaign was initiated that encouraged women in Iran to put on a white head scarf or veil instead of the usual black.[34] This campaign mushroomed following events of 27 December 2017, when a young Iranian woman stood bareheaded in a busy main road – Inqalab Street in Tehran – and waved her hijab at the end of a wooden stick. Images of this event went viral on the internet and it was widely reported in the media.[35] The

31 The context is provided in some writings including Nima Naghibi, 'Bad Feminist or Bad-Hejabi?', *Interventions: International Journal of Postcolonial Studies* 1.4, 2006, 555–71; Homa Hoodfar, 'Veil in their minds and our heads', *Resource for Feminist Research* 22.3/4, 1994, 5–18; Faegheh Shirazi, *The Veil Unveiled: The Hijab in Modern Culture*, Gainesville 2001; Ashraf Zahedi, 'Concealing and Revealing Female Hair: Veiling Dynamics in Contemporary Iran', *The Veil: Women Writers on its History, Lore, and Politics*, ed. Jennifer Heath, Berkeley 2008, 250–65.

32 Naser Ghobadzadeh, *Religious Secularity: A Theological Challenge to the Islamic State*, Oxford 2015, 6.

33 The term 'reformist' is a little misleading here, because it is difficult to classify the ulama by such terms. For example, is it possible to include the 'dissident' jurist Ayatollah Montazeri in this group? Certainly, he has been very critical of the Islamic Republic subsequent to his 'dismissal' in 1989, and yet he produced a number of guidelines for his followers on the topic of the hijab which were very 'conservative' and stood at odds with the thinking of the so-called 'New Religious Thinkers' (see the discussion in Part Four of the present work). The terms 'reformist' and 'conservative' must always be treated with the utmost caution in the Iranian context.

34 The campaign was initiated by Masih Alinejad on Facebook.

35 'The Girls of Enghalab Street: Iranian woman who stood in Tehran street without a hijab released from custody says lawyer', *The Independent* 29 January 2018, https://www.independent.co.uk/news/world/middle-east/girl-of-enghlelab-street-iran-woman-tehran-street-no-hijab-headscarf-custody-release-nasrin-sotoudeh-a8183716.html. See also Kate C. Hashemi, 'The Girls of *Enghelab* Street: Women and Revolution in Modern Iran', https://

'Girls of Inqalab Street' became a household term. Similar bareheaded protests proliferated throughout Iran, causing great concern among leading governmental figures from the ulama. Even the Leader of Iran, ʿAli Khamenei, referred to these events in a recent speech in which he accused Iran's 'enemies' (the West, and those Iranians living there in exile) of cultivating the campaign to remove the veil. He said:

> Several months ago, the enemies of Iran sat down in a room together, and over the past three months they schemed. In their imagination [they believed] they would finish-off the Islamic Republic by February or March (*Isfand*). [They have busied themselves with] so much expenditure, planning and propaganda, but in conclusion they have [merely] deceived a few girls who take off their head-covering in some corner or alley, and all their effort ends in this. [It is] trivial and insignificant. It is not a problem, but I think that the issue about 'mandatory veiling' is being articulated by several elites. [Some of them] are journalists, enlightened thinkers and even turbaned clerics (*ākhūnd-i muʿammam*).[36] They follow the same policy that the enemy could not bring to fruition, even with all of [their] expenditure.[37]

---

www.academia.edu/37994754/The_Girls_of_Enghelab_Street_Women_and_Revolution_in_Modern_Iran.

36 The term *ākhūnd* (rendered in the translation as 'cleric') is a more derogatory word for an individual member of the ulama.

37 'The excellence of the term "hijab": the Islamic government is duty bound to stand against "social taboos"', Speech of ʿAli Khamenei, 08 March 2018, reported in the chapter of al-Khattab, 'Hijab: The Islamic Government is obliged to stand against "the social prohibition"', http://ijtihadnet.ir/%D9%81%D8%B5%D9%84-%D8%A7%D9%84%D8%AE%D8%B7%D8%A7%D8%A8-%D8%AD%D8%AC%D8%A7%D8%A8%D8%9B-%D8%AD%DA%A9%D9%88%D9%85%D8%AA-%D8%A7%D8%B3%D9%84%D8%A7%D9%85%DB%8C-%D9%85%D9%88%D8%B8%D9%81-%D8%A7/.

The accusation against the enemies is a common trope in the discourse of the supportive 'state' ulama in the Islamic Republic. For example, Ayatollah Safi Gulpaygani writes:

> The solid and noble pillar of 'hijab' is fundamental and essential for Muslim women to be distinguished in the world, and it is a privilege and an honour to show pride in it. It is the same principle to which the enemies of Islam gave such importance, to the extent that one of the former prime ministers of Britain wrote clearly in a note: 'For as long as the Kaʿba, the Qur'an and the hijab exist in Islamic societies we cannot have lordship and mastery over them. We must burn the Qur'an, destroy the Kaʿba (they have brought Wahhabism into Arabia to achieve that purpose) and take away the chastity and the hijab from Muslim women.'

See *Ḥijāb: Imtiyāz-i Zanān* [*Hijab: The Privilege for Women*], http://ijtihad.ir/NewsDetails.aspx?itemid=11466. This page has been taken down recently. The prime ministers to whom Gulpaygani refers seem to have been Gladstone and Lord Salisbury. See Barry Rubin and

Of particular interest is Khamenei's claim that some among the ulama support the anti-mandatory hijab movement. It is to be wondered to whom Khamenei is referring; it is unlikely that he is making oblique references to those outside of Iran, such as Muhsin Kadivar who now resides in the US. However, there has been disquiet among the ulama about the use of force to implement the hijab. For example, President Rouhani has often issued a veiled argument that the strict enforcement should not be observed.[38] Moreover, in the middle of the recent controversy of the 'Girls of Inqalab Street', Rouhani chose to release an opinion poll from 2014 conducted by the Centre for Strategic Studies, a government research group, that found in a survey of 1167 people (including both men and women) that 49.8% of Iranians consider the hijab a private matter and think the government should have no say in it.[39] It can only be speculated why Rouhani decided to have the findings of the poll released at such an incendiary moment. Rouhani is not alone, as Ayatollah Muhammad ʿAli Ayazi[40] opposed mandatory veiling even before the recent outbreak of public disquiet, citing senior figures responsible for the establishment of the Islamic Republic (such as Ayatollah Mutahhari) and maintaining that they did not support compulsory veiling. He also believes that such a policy is against the sharia.[41] There are other influential

Wolfgang G. Schwanitz, *Nazis, Islamists, and the Making of the Modern Middle East*, London 2014, 42. The authors of the aforementioned book mention that in 1915 several fatwas were 'engineered' by the Germans to appeal to the Muslim world. The fatwa in question was composed by an Iraqi Shiʿi scholar Hibat al-Din Muhammad al-Shahrastani (1884–1966). Rubin and Schwanitz mention how he lists some of the sins of the Allies 'some of them fabricated' and then they summarise his accusations (cited above).

38 See 'Rouhani clashes with Iranian clergy over women arrested for "bad hijab"', *The Guardian* 27 May 2015, https://www.theguardian.com/world/iran-blog/2015/may/27/iran-hijab-rouhani-versus-senior-clergy-enforcement.

39 Thomas Erdbrink, 'Compulsory Veils? Half of Iranians Say "No" to Pillar of Revolution"', *New York Times* 4 February 2018, https://www.nytimes.com/2018/02/04/world/middleeast/iran-hijab-veils.html.

40 Ayatollah Muhammad ʿAli Ayazi was one of three middle ranking seminarians who were chosen by Ayatollah Montazeri to take responsibility for answering questions sent to his website. See the electronic book, *Dar Mahzar-i Faqīh-i āzādāna: Ustād Ḥusayn ʿAlī Muntazarī Najafābādī* [*In the Company of the Noble Faqih: The Master Husayn ʿAli Muntazari Najafabadi*] (1392/2013), 34–5, https://kadivar.com/category/1-books/14-b/0-b-14/.

41 See 'Sayyid Muhammad ʿAli Ayazi: Ḥijāb amri-yi ijtimāʿī nīst ki mujazat dashta bashad' [Sayyid Muhammad ʿAli Ayazi: Hijab is not a social matter that is punishable], *Intikhab* website, 2 July 2012. He says, 'My belief is that the hijab, like prayer, fasting, [and paying] religious taxes (*khums va zakat*) are a personal legal matter. The hijab is like the use of people's property; it is not a social issue that entails punishments. In truth, our religious teachings are of two kinds. In one group there is a personal religious responsibility, and the other kind is social for which punishments have been passed. Naturally, the Islamic

seminarians who share Ayazi's view. A lower ranking member of the ulama and former editor of the popular newspaper *Hamshahri*, Hujjat al-Islam Muhammad Riza Zaʾiri has remarked, 'I strongly believe the policy of mandatory hijab has been totally wrong.'[42] In addition to Zaʾiri, another reformist member of the ulama, Abu Fazl Najafi Tihrani, uploaded a number of tweets seemingly in support of the 'Women of Enqelab Street'. He has also tweeted photographs of the famous bareheaded female poet, Forough Farrokhzad (d. 1966), and of the Iranian *faqīh* who found fame in Lebanon, Musa Sadr, who, we are informed, did not mind having his photograph taken with a group of bareheaded women.[43] Clearly the Iranian regime has been rankled by the issue of the hijab and by Masih ʿAlinejad's attempt to maintain momentum by posting film clips of bareheaded women walking in urban areas of Iran. This is evidenced by the threat from Tehran's Revolutionary Court of a ten-year jail sentence for those appearing in these videos.[44]

The significant point is that this diversity of opinion, ranging from mandatory veiling to freedom to choose, demonstrates the fallacy of a fixed and unchanging body of law called 'sharia' and represents the correct way of understanding Islamic law. The Islamic Republic has attempted to paper over such diversity, and in the opinion of Muhsin Kadivar it has done so for political reasons: 'the case of the hijab is not a religious or legal one. It is completely political. The hijab has

---

Government can give teachings about the hijab and encourage people to follow it, but there has never been any command (*dastūrī*) for retributive clashes.' Ayazi considers hijab compulsory for believers, but command cannot be enforced by the state, https://www.entekhab.ir/fa/news/69889.

42 Ibid. Riza Zaʾiri spoke out against the mandatory hijab as early as 2015. It seems that he eventually bowed to the authority of Khamenei:

> … when Zaeri learned that Khamenei opposed even having a discussion on the issue, he wrote: 'I let the matter drop because, although my opinion has not changed, I believe that [the Leader] must be obeyed in actions, not just in beliefs.'

See Reza Haghighatnejad, 'Khamenei dismisses hijab protesters as "insignificant and small"', 12 March 2018, http://www.trackpersia.com/khamenei-dismisses-hijab-protesters-insignificant-small/.

43 See https://twitter.com/najafi_tehrani?lang=en. Tweets posted between 31 January and 8 February. On 30 January, he tweeted,

> As the number of women of Enqelab Street increases, the failure of the 40-year cultural policies of the regime becomes clearer. The only path is a new view on cultural macro-policies and accepting diversity, variety, and the cultural colourfulness of Iranians among all [of their] people, religious schools, and refraining from compulsion, and respect for individual freedom.

44 Maya Oppenheim, 'Iranian women defy threat of decade-long jail sentence by taking photos of themselves without headscarves', *The Independent* 1 August 2019.

been a matter of maintaining face for the regime. The mandatory veil was born with the Islamic Republic and it will die with the Islamic Republic.'[45]

*

Given the trajectory in the contents of this book (a movement from endorsement of the hijab, to the recommendation to adopt this custom, to a final rejection of compulsion to wear head-covering), it might be assumed that I have similar sympathies with the 'progressive, broad-minded and liberal' understanding. My own perspective on the Qur'anic verses relating to the hijab are that they are all concerned with modesty and piety, and believing Muslim women are encouraged to cover themselves in some form which is not sufficiently clear to determine whether head-covering is absolutely necessary. From a historical perspective, this issue becomes more complex once the narratives of the Shiʿi imams are considered. It is for Shiʿi believers themselves to decide on how to understand these statements; whether to abide and respect the opinions of the imams, or to regard them as representative of their times and consider valid changes in conformity with the demands of the times and conditions of the contemporary period. Having said this, I believe that the issue for contemporary female believers concerns agency; if women feel comfortable wearing a hijab, and their decision is informed and intelligent, then surely there can be little meaningful objection to such sartorial choices. As Saʿdiyya Shaikh has observed,

> Ultimately in any study of dress and *hijab* among Muslim women, it is necessary to look at the complexity of the varying narratives and to treat Muslim women as subjects instead of objects of research. Such an approach will prioritize Muslim women's self-understandings, it will look at the varying ways in which veiling operates in relation to women's agency, it will recognise sites of resistance as well as contradictions and ambivalence within the discourses, instead of treating veiling as evidence of the monolithic victimization of women.[46]

The extent to which the three sources used in this book have observed the kind

---

45 Muhsin Kadivar, '*Sanjaq kardan-i hijāb-i ijbārī bi hayāt-i niẓām*' [The linkage of the mandatory hijab to the regime's life], 09 March 2018, http://kadivar.com/?p=16476.
46 Saʿdiyya Shaikh, 'Transforming Feminism', *Progressive Muslims: On Justice, Gender and Pluralism*, ed. Omid Safi, Oxford 2003, 153.

of advice offered by Shaikh is left up to the reader to decide. However, sufficient historical contextualisation is given throughout to enable the reader to reach an informed conclusion. More difficult questions surround the *niqāb*, or the face-covering, but that is a completely different issue. As a male scholar writing on the topic, I do feel that it is wrong for me to offer any definitive statements. As much as possible I have tried to follow the advice of the famous Persian poet Hafiz, who said:

حجاب راه تویی حافظ از میان بر خیز

خوشا کسی که در این راه بی حجاب رود.

Hafiz, you are the hijab in the path. Get up out of the way!
How fortunate is the person who walks on this path without a hijab.[47]

47 *Dīvān-i Ḥāfiż*, ed. Parviz Natil Khanlari, Tehran 1984, 432 (ghazal, no. 216).

Part 1

1

Sharia, *Fiqh*, and the New Religious Thinkers

Introduction

The challenges of day-to-day life in Iran in the wake of the Islamic Revolution of 1978–79, which instituted a legal system based on many of the accepted norms of the early years of Islam in 7th–9th centuries, threw into sharp relief the contrast between early medieval standards established in Arabia and the Near East with the requirements of a modern society that was evolving and developing politically, economically and socially at an unprecedented rate. This apparent discrepancy is not a new problem when seminarians are concerned. For a hundred years, Shiʿi scholars have been criticised for being unable to bridge adequately the laws derived from sacred scripture to pressing, modern questions. One of the most famous advocates of political and social reform in Iran and the Middle East, Jamal al-Din al-Asadabadi (known popularly as al-Afghani [d. 1897] and famous for promoting 'pan-islamism') commented on the deficiencies of seminarians in his age:

> The science of principles consists of the philosophy of the sharia, or 'philosophy of law'. In it are explained the truths regarding right and wrong, benefit and loss, and the causes for the promulgation of laws. Certainly, a person who studies this science should be capable of establishing laws and enforcing civilization. However, we see that those who study this science among the Muslims are deprived of understanding the benefits of laws, the rules of civilization, and the reform of the world.[1]

---

1 'Answer of Jamal ad-Din to Renan', *Modernist Islam 1840–1940*, ed. Charles Kurzman, Oxford 2002, 110.

Afghani may have been saying what his audience wished to hear, considering how in other letters and addresses he reflected on the potential that jurisprudence holds for Islamic societies. But he clearly despaired of the ability of the *mujtahid*s (or the *faqīh*s) to carry out the ideal role he envisaged for them. Since Afghani's criticisms, there has been a frequent and regular call for reform, or a demand to modernise the way of thinking in the seminaries. At this point it is useful to define some recurring terminology in order to avoid confusion. There is a subtle difference between sharia and *fiqh*. The former is 'the utopia, the immutable, the normative, and the ideal Islam'.[2] In contrast, *fiqh* (or jurisprudence) is substantive law, and 'the changing and mutable domain of legislation because it is only an approximation of the sharia arrived at by the use of the human cognitive process'.[3] Many individuals who have been vocal in seeking changes to sharia have actually been speaking about *fiqh*. The appeal to make jurisprudence 'relevant' has come from senior figures within the seminaries and political structures of Iran, such as the former Leader, Ayatollah Khomeini (d. 1989), who in November 1988 said:

> Today, fortunately, owing to the Islamic Revolution, the words of the jurists and opinion holders are heard on the radio and television [and read] in the newspapers because there is a practical need for these discussions on the [following] matters: on the issue of ownership and its limit; on the issue of land and its division; on governmental property the profits of which must be distributed to the public and public wealth; on complicated financial issues and foreign exchange and banking; on taxation, on internal and foreign trade; on share cropping and silent partnerships, and rent and mortgages; on Islamic punishments and blood-money; on civil laws; on cultural issues and artistic encounters with public spirituality, including photography, painting, sculpture, music, theatre, cinema, calligraphy, and others; on environmental issues and the care of nature and preventing the cutting down of trees even on private lands; on issues of food and drink, prevention of childbirth in necessary situations or establishing a period of time between births; solving medical complications such as the grafting of human limbs and other bodily parts like this to other humans; on the issue of subterranean and open mines, and national [mines]; the changing of what is prohibited and permitted, and the expansion and contraction of specific commands (*aḥkām*) at various

2 Hamid Mavani, 'Paradigm Shift in Twelver Shiʿi Legal Theory (*uṣūl al-fiqh*): Ayatullah Yusef Saanei', *The Muslim World* 99.2, 2009, 341.
3 Mavani, 'Paradigm Shift in Twelver Shiʿi Legal Theory', 341.

> times and places; on legal issues and international laws and their conformity with Islamic commands, the constructive role of women in Islamic society and their destructive role in corrupt and non-Islamic societies; the limits of individual and societal freedom, the encounter with unbelief (*kufr*) and associating gods with God (*shirk*) and selective interpretation (*intiqāt*) by the block of followers of *kufr* and *shirk*, and how to perform [Islamic] duties in the air or in space, and make movement contrary to the direction of the Earth, or in conformity with it, with a velocity more than its speed, or in rising up and neutralising the Earth's gravity; and most important of all of these, the delineation and establishment of rulership of the *vilāyat-i faqīh* in the government and society, because all of these are one among thousands of issues of concern to the people and the government which the great jurists have discussed.[4]

The complexity of modern life demands answers to all these problems. The difficulty of providing answers to such daunting questions is typified in the simplistic claim that Islam offers solutions to the issues that the contemporary world presents. However, more sophisticated responses argue that the belief that sharia is immutable and unchanging does not mean that Islam cannot respond to these changes, because *fiqh* offers a human interpretation of divine law, comprehended as a general and ethical ideal. Problems arise, however, if *fiqh* is understood as inflexible, fixed and invariable, and thereby unable to provide an adequate answer to the ever-evolving demands and needs of modern life.[5] A problem facing schol-

---

4 See Khomeini's reply to the letter of Muhammad ʿAli Ansari, dated 1 November 1988. The reply has become commonly known as the 'Brotherly Charter' (*manshūr-i barādarī*). See *Ṣaḥīfa-yi Imām*, vol. 21, 2010, 177–80, http://www.imam-khomeini.ir/fa/page/210/.

5 In his work *Vilāyat-i Faqīh*, written in Najaf in 1970, Khomeini rejected the idea of changing commands, and argued that the Qur'anic *aḥkām* were all immutable and permanent: 'According to one of the noble verses of the Qur'an, the ordinances of Islam are not limited with respect to time and place; they are permanent and must be enacted until the end of time' (*Islam and Revolution*, trans. Hamid Algar, London 1985, 41). On noting this point, I contacted Muhsin Kadivar and asked him if he knew which verse Khomeini might have been thinking of when he wrote this sentence, since Khomeini's text did not specify which verse this was. Kadivar kindly pointed out that in a subsequent Persian edition of *Vilāyat-i Faqīh*, the publishers have added in footnotes several verses, e.g. 14:52, 10:2, 22:49, 33:40 and 36:70 (see Imam Khomeini, *Vilāyat-i Faqīh: Hukūmat Islāmī*, Tehran 1377/1998, 18, fn. 21). These verses do not explicitly or implicitly indicate the permanent nature of the *aḥkām*. The position of Khomeini in the early 1970's may be understood in the light of his attempt to show that Muhammad's prophethood set up a government and had specific verses and commands that assisted him in this respect. However, the practical difficulties of

ars, indeed, all concerned, is that sharia and *fiqh* are often conflated by Western observers and by Muslims themselves.

The attempt to use *fiqh* in responding to the challenges that are thrown up by modern life has not proved an easy matter in modern Iran, in spite of the establishment of the Islamic Republic in 1979. Some thirty years later, Hasan Yousefi Eshkevari, a modern reformist member of the ulama, listed ten different methods that have been offered as *fiqh*-based solutions to such challenges that have been formulated during this same period.[6] The ten-fold taxonomy that Eshkevari presented can be simplified into two groups: the first includes interpretations that encourage reform and which are open to debate and discussion, while the other group does not promote or encourage alternative views.

The first kind of interpretation is typified in a PhD thesis held at Glasgow Caledonian University, submitted by Hassan Rouhani (the President of the Islamic Republic since 2013), titled 'The Flexibility of Shariah (Islamic Law) with Reference to the Iranian Experience'. The main argument of the thesis is that 'Islamic law enjoys a series of dynamic features and judicial instruments which objective analysis would define as liberal, progressive and broad-minded'.[7] Rouhani's conception of flexibility has been advanced to a far greater degree by the so-called New Religious Thinkers (*naw-andīshān-i dīnī*) among Iranian ulama. Indeed, some advocate a separation of religion from the state, what others have called 'religious secularity',[8] a term that does not necessarily remove religion from politics or society. A common feature in the writings of these ulama is a plea for an open and tolerant society that engages in unrestricted discussion of religion and politics.[9] The ideas of New Religious Thinkers are a direct challenge to those

government experienced by the Islamic Republic may have persuaded Khomeini to change his mind, as he is known to have endorsed the necessity to pay attention to time and place, and how they impact the necessity to enforce the *aḥkām*, e.g. he mentioned that discussions must be had about 'the changing of what is prohibited and permitted, and the expansion and contraction of some of commands (*aḥkām*) at various times and places'.
Liyakat Takim posits this question in his 'Maqāṣid al-Shari'a in contemporary Shi'i jurisprudence', *Maqāṣid al-Sharī'a and Contemporary Reformist Muslim Thought*, ed. Adis Duderija, New York 2014, 101.

6 Hassan Yousefi Eshkevari, 'Rethinking men's authority over women', *Gender and Equality in Muslim Family Law*, ed. Ziba Mir-Hosseini, Kari Vogt, Lena Larsen and Christian Moe, London 2009, 199–201. The ten-fold classification is discussed in greater detail in Persian in 'Ḥuqūq-i bashar va aḥkām-i ijtimā'ī-yi Islām' [Human Rights and the social commands of Islam], 7 May 2010, http://yousefieshkevari.com/?p=751.

7 'The Flexibility of Shariah (Islamic Law) with Reference to the Iranian Experience', 392.

8 This term is coined by Naser Ghobadzadeh, *Religious Secularity.*

9 For example, the call for an open discussion on different jurisprudential perspectives is a

established in state institutions, and it is for this reason that many of the reformists have faced virulent criticism, incarceration and exile.

In this chapter, some of the methods advocated by several members of the ulama among the New Religious Thinkers are described and assessed, concentrating on the thought of four of the most radical and well-known ulama, namely Hasan Yousefi Eshkevari, Muhsin Kadivar, Ahmad Qabil, and Muhammad Mujtahid-Shabistari. As mentioned above, many of the reformists have encountered opposition and campaigns of intimidation aimed to silence them. Eshkevari was arrested in 2000 and faced charges such as 'waging war against God',[10] and after spending a long time in jail, he now resides in Europe.[11] Muhsin Kadivar was arrested in 1999 and spent 18 months in prison before he was able to leave Iran and take up teaching posts in the US. He is currently a Research Professor of Islamic Studies at Duke University. Ahmad Qabil, a student of Ayatollah Montazeri, was also arrested and served prison sentences between 2001 and 2012 for his criticisms of the Iranian regime before he died of a brain tumour in 2012. Shabistari, a seminarian, had also been professor at Tehran University but in 2006 he 'fell victim to the purges of the Ahmadinejad regime … [and] was forced into retirement'.[12] It might have been possible to describe the views and philosophies of other individuals who are often included among the new generation of thinkers, such as Abdolkarim Soroush or Mustafa Malikiyan. However, the former has no formal seminary training, and indeed his writings do not focus on jurisprudential questions. The latter was associated with the Madrasa Radhawiya seminary in

recurrent theme in the writings of Ahmad Qabil (d. 2012), one of the Iranian reformist jurists. He states, 'We recognise the necessity to maintain respect for those whose ideas are criticised and whose method of opposition we consider unscientific.' Ahmad Qabil, *Sharīʿat-i ʿAqlānī* [*Rational Sharia*], 57. Despite Qabil's plea for toleration and free and open discussion for his opponents, hoping no doubt that it would be reciprocal, he was imprisoned for 'spreading propaganda against the regime' and for 'insulting Iran's supreme leader'. See RadioFreeEurope, 'Iranian Religious Scholar Jailed on Propaganda, Insult Charges', 16 December 2010, https://www.rferl.org/a/2250328.html.

10 Ziba Mir Hosseini and Richard Tapper, *Islam and Democracy in Iran: Eshkevari and the Quest for Reform*, London 2006, 38, 173.

11 Ghobadzadeh, *Religious Secularity*, 52.

12 Katajun Amirpur, *New Thinking in Islam: The Jihad for Freedom, Democracy and Women's Rights*, London 2015, 188. On Muhammad Mujtahid Shabistari, see Katajun Amirpur, *New Thinking in Islam*, 168–98; Farzin Vahdat, 'Post-revolutionary Islamic modernity in Iran: the inter-subjective hermeneutics of Mohammad Mojtahed Shabistari', *Modern Muslim Intellectuals and the Qur'an*, ed. Suha Taji-Farouki, Oxford 2006, 193–224; Ashk P. Dahlén, *Islamic Law, Epistemology and Modernity*, London 2015, 163–85.

Mashhad in 1984 where he taught elementary Arabic,[13] and has found a considerable following, especially among university students, as a philosopher who does not utilise 'Islamic' argumentation. Indeed, his works have become 'increasingly devoid of anything that might be deemed exoterically Islamic, let alone identifiably Shiʿi'.[14] And Soroush's influence in Iran on the topic of religious reform cannot be denied, and reference is made to his contributions to the debate on reform when appropriate.

The second kind of interpretation to appreciate or discover the sharia opposes that of the New Religious Thinkers. It advocates a method that accepts the codification and reification of traditional ways of understanding law, to the extent of regulating minute aspects of the lives of believers through such means as 'the reinforcement of compulsory hijab, obligatory prayer observance in the workplace, the official prohibition of eating and drinking during Ramadan, and various methods of rewarding those who effect a religious mien such as wearing a beard or wearing one's shirt outside of one's trousers'.[15] Shabistari classifies such an approach under the rubric of the 'official reading of religion', and maintains that 'the supporters of this reading say … the religion of Islam has permanent and eternal political, economic and legal structures. The form of government is deduced from the book [i.e. the Qurʾan] and Sunna, and [the form of government] is not a rational matter. The duty of the government is to execute the Islamic commands among the Muslims'.[16] Shabistari further argues how the official reading has been entangled in a crisis because it has opposed democratic methods and utilised violence which it justifies as a way to both enforce Islamic commands and protect Islam. Moreover, it can lay no claim to scientific learning and its whole *raison d'être* has been disliked.[17] Another common criticism of such 'official readings' is the claim of its irrelevance to the practical problems encountered in modern life. One of the new class of reformist *mujtahid*s, Kadivar has observed that, 'Constantly rehearsing fatwas that have been issued in the past and glorifying

13 I am grateful to Muhsin Kadivar who informed me of this in email exchanges in late August–September 2018.

14 Eskandar Sadeghi-Boroujerdi, 'Mostafa Malekian: Spirituality, Siyasat-Zadegi and (A) political Self-Improvement', *Digest of Middle East Studies* 23.2, 2014, 284.

15 Naser Ghobadzadeh, *Religious Secularity*, 84.

16 Muhammad Mujtahid-Shabistari, *Naqdi bar Qirāʾat-i Rasmī az Dīn* [*Criticism of the Official Reading of Religious*], Tehran 1381/2002–3, 30. He cites Taqi Misbah Yazdi as an example of a seminarian who espouses such a view.

17 Mujtahid-Shabistari, *Naqdī bar Qirāʾat-i Rasmī az Dīn*, 31.

constantly-recurring opinions as the best amounts to nothing more than the imitation of our predecessors in formulating opinions.'[18]

In summary, the official reading of religion is criticised by the New Religious Thinkers on two very basic counts. The first is its rigid hermeneutical approach, which denies any kind of legitimacy to views other than its own. The New Religious Thinkers have advocated the use of a range of methods to address the 'crisis' that jurisprudence faces, and these methods are the focus of the present chapter. The second criticism, related to the first, is that the official reading of religion promotes only a single hermeneutical approach, which has been advocated by the state. This problem was outlined in the introduction to this work. As a result of such a rigid official reading of religion, it is often argued that the demands for the welfare (*maṣlaḥa*) of society have not been satisfied. This concept, in association with the aims of the sharia, is one of the most significant features in the hermeneutical approach adopted by the New Religious Thinkers.[19]

Traditional understandings of sharia have been based on interpreting four sources of law: the Qurʾan; the sayings of the Prophet (hadith) and narrations of the imams; the consensus of the wise (*ijmāʿ*); and reason. Those with specialist knowledge of the sources emerged as religious leaders to be obeyed and emulated (*marjaʿ taqlīd*), and the decentralised nature of pre-modern Iranian society meant that there existed several *marjaʿ* at any one time (some of whom resided in the cities of what is now Iraq). With the centralisation of Iran from the nineteenth century onwards, this position increasingly became focused on a few, eminent jurists. With the establishment of the Islamic Republic in 1978–9, the final say in the codification of *fiqh* under state law has been overseen by the Leader (*rahbar*), although other *marjaʿ taqlīd* continue to carry out their function of guiding the community through their understandings of *fiqh*. This structure of centrifugal religious authority in which all power and rules emanate from the centre carries with it the potential for tension between the state and the *Rahbar* on the one hand, and on the other dissenting ulama who advocate a multi-centred model of power and authority.[20] The Society of Seminary Teachers of Qum, which has emerged as one of the most authoritative 'state' associations for determining *fiqh*, has been instrumental in this centralisation, and in 1994 it issued a list of seven ayatollahs whom it regarded as suitable *marjaʿ*s. In the first decade of 2000s, the Society

---

18 Mohsen Kadivar, 'Human Rights and Intellectual Islam', *New Directions in Islamic Thought: Exploring Reform and Muslim Tradition*, ed. Kari Vogt, Lena Larsen and Christian Moe, London 2009, 72–3.

19 See Liyakat Takim, 'Maqāsid al-Sharīʿa in Contemporary Shiʿi Jurisprudence'.

20 See: http://kurdane.com/article-19206.html.

announced that any ayatollah seeking to publish his own *Tawżīḥ al-Masāʾil*, thus declaring his claim to be a *marjaʿ*, had to obtain the Society's approval.[21] Of interest too is how there has been a reaction against increasing centralisation; in 2003 a Regular Meeting of Professors of Qum Seminary was formed with 'the announced goal of achieving the seminary's independence from politics, financially and intellectually'.[22] And most recently in 2019, a dispute arose between the Society of Seminary Teachers and Ayatollah Burujirdi when the latter, a nephew of the celebrated *marjaʿ* of the same name who died in 1961, declared himself *marjaʿ*. This elicited a strong response from the Society's leading representative, Ayatollah Yazdi, who suggested that nepotism and attempts to bask in the glory of one's family were not proper criteria for becoming a *marjaʿ*. Regardless of the particulars of this case, it is significant that it highlights a tendency towards increased centralisation. Yazdi said:

> If someone is not verified in possessing scientific ability, yet enters the arena, I will be obliged to publicly announce that he does not have the right to claim *marjaʿiyat* … if such a person puts up his credentials, I will take them down … We have four or five *marjaʿ*s, who are legally *marjaʿ*s (*az ṭuruq-i sharʿī*). They are sufficient, not everyone must be a *faqīh* and *marjaʿ*. It is necessary to protect the office of *marjaʿiyat*, the Commission for the Protection of *Marjaʿiyat* is approved by the Society of Seminarians and is ratified by five *marjaʿ*s, one of which is the office of Leadership.

Examples of the tension over the decentralisation versus centralisation of power erupt with a degree of regularity in the Islamic Republic and are often coupled with economic grievances and disillusionment with political rights – typified in the Green Movement of 2009, or in the demonstrations that occurred in Iran in 2017–18. Indeed, it is difficult to envisage how a state-directed *fiqh* could exist alongside independent *marjaʿ*s who may not necessarily be sympathetic with the state's interpretation. Many of the New Religious Thinkers among the ulama foreground an ideal utopia (sharia) which transcends the particularistic concerns of *fiqh*, and which does not necessitate the kinds of detailed and intimate personal rulings to be enforced at a state level. The aims of the sharia (*maqāṣid al-sharīʿa*)

21 Rohollah Faghihi, 'Self-proclaimed marja riles other Iranian Ayatollahs', *Al-Monitor* 24 September 2019, https://www.al-monitor.com/pulse/en/originals/2019/09/iran-hardliners-opposition-new-marja.amp.html.
22 Rohollah Faghihi, 'Self-proclaimed marja riles other Iranian Ayatollahs'.

are to lead the individual to God and the promotion of a harmonious life among the believers, necessitating a less rigid and fixed implementation of *fiqh*.

This chapter explores how the ulama among the New Religious Thinkers have offered 'radical' interpretations of law which lead to a largely flexible and ethical worldview. The diversity of their methodologies is bewildering and defies simple classification. As mentioned above, what Rouhani considers a 'liberal, progressive and broad-minded' perspective is seen as the barest minimum, or the starting point. Many of the ulama discussed herein have pushed the boundaries of interpretation to the very limits of what is deemed acceptable in the Islamic Republic, and as such they may not be considered as 'representative' or 'orthodox' of current Twelver Shiʿi understandings in Iran, or at least 'state Shiʿism'. Nevertheless, their thoughts have staked out new boundaries of religiosity through the dissemination of such ideas in newspapers, journals and websites, and the state is largely unable to prevent the circulation of these ideas. Although a comprehensive survey of how *fiqh* may be considered as a suitable system upon which to base a country's laws is beyond the scope of the present work, at least it is possible to focus on how the four sources of jurisprudence have been understood by these Shiʿi ulama. Therefore, this chapter outlines the most radical ways that have been offered in recent years. The sections in this chapter are structured around the four sources of *fiqh*, which as mentioned previously are: i) the Qurʾan; ii) the Sunna (and sayings of the imams); iii) *ijmāʿ*; and iv) reason – the latter two are grouped together in this chapter. It would have been convenient if the New Religious Thinkers who are covered in this chapter dealt with each of these four sources of *fiqh* in an equal fashion. But of course each of the thinkers stresses his own specific perspective, so that it is impossible to get a balance of views of all thinkers on each of the four categories. For example, Eshkevari is known for foregrounding the concept that 'the command follows the subject matter' (*ḥukm tābiʿ mawżūʿ*),[23] while Ahmad Qabil is concerned with the principle of rational permission (*iṣālat al-ibāḥat al-ʿaqliyat*),[24] Kadivar elaborates on the conditions of time and place, and Shabistari emphasises how individuals emerge with different readings (*qirāʾat*) of revelation and sacred texts as a result of their background

23 This is discussed in more detail in Part Three. According to Eshkevari, this is a common principle discussed in *fiqh*. See Mir-Hosseini and Tapper, *Islam and Democracy in Iran*, 165. Eshkevari also discusses the relationships between commands and subject matter in his 'Ḥuqūq-i bashar va aḥkām-i ijtimāʿī-yi islām' [Human rights and the social commands of Islam].

24 This is discussed in Part Three.

and individuality.[25] Each of these is examined in their appropriate places in this book.

The Qur'an

The Qur'an is the starting point to any investigation about the nature of the sharia; to use the Qur'an's own words, 'We sent down to you the book as a clarification for all things, and as a guidance and a mercy for those who submit' (Q. 16.89), and 'Then We placed on you a sharia of the affair, so follow it' (Q. 45.18). Murtaza Mutahhari (d. 1979), who has been called 'the chief ideologue of the [Islamic] revolution',[26] observed that Islamic teachings have been divided into three main categories: the first is with realities and beliefs (such as the unity of God, the resurrection, etc.); the second is morality and self-perfection; and the third is the laws and issues of action. It is this third prescribed teaching that he terms jurisprudence (*fiqh*) in contrast to a more expansive application.[27] Mutahhari mentions common discussions about the interpretation of the Qur'an and its application to *fiqh*, and these include deliberations about: i) abstract (*mujmal*) and clear (*mubayyan*) verses; ii) abrogating (*nāsikh*) and abrogated (*mansūkh*) verses; iii) imperatives (*ʿawāmir*) and prohibitions (*nawāhī*); iv) generalities (*ʿāmm*) and particularities (*khāṣṣ*); v) tacit meanings (*mafāhīm*); and vi) unconditional (*muṭlaq*) and conditional (*muqayyad*) verses.[28] It will become clear by the end of this section on the Qur'an how much (though by no means all) of the New Religious Thinking parallels many of these discussions, and as such it is a legitimate claim that the New Religious Thinkers argue from within the tradition. This, in fact, demonstrates their commitment to the tradition as well as to their creativity and inventiveness in yielding new ways to read the text and understand *fiqh*. The New Religious Thinking on the Qur'an is extensive, indeed it deserves a monograph of its own, however, in order to fit the description and analysis into the parameters of this chapter, a summary is made of four elements of Qur'anic studies: first,

---

25 This is discussed later in this chapter, see section on the topic of revelation.

26 Hamid Dabashi, *Theology of Discontent*, New York 1993, 147.

27 Mutahhari, *Jurisprudence and its Principles*, New York n.d., 28. This work is available at: http://www.iranchamber.com/personalities/mmotahari/works/jurisprudence_and_its_principles.pdf. *Fiqh* is related to the common Qur'anic term found in various forms of the Arabic root f.q.h., such as, 'Behold how We vary the signs, that they may understand (*yafqahuna*)', (Q. 6.65); 'And why should not a party from each group go forth to gain understanding (*tafaqquh*) in religion and to warn their people when they return to them that haply they will be aware?' (Q. 9.122).

28 Mutahhari, *Jurisprudence and its Principles*, 15–19.

the classification of Qurʾanic verses (or what Mutahhari terms abstract and clear verses); second, abrogation (which includes a discussion of Mutahhari's conditional verses); third, the commands (or the imperatives and prohibitions); and fourth, the nature of revelation.

Diversity in the types of Qurʾanic verses

The various ways in which the Qurʾan has been understood by jurists reflects the reality that on a whole range of jurisprudential issues there have existed differences of opinion (known as *ikhtilāf*). Ayatollah Khomeini recognised this in the 'Brotherly Charter' (*manshūr-i barādarī*) of 1988 in which he observed:

> The books of the great jurists of Islam are full of differences of opinion, styles and understandings on various military, cultural, political, economic, and worship affairs to the extent that on a [single] issue on which a consensus has been claimed, there are different sayings, and even on consensual matters too it is possible to find contradictory sayings.[29]

The study of *ikhtilāf al-fuqahā* (disagreement among the jurists) has been discussed frequently in jurisprudential circles, 'yet current studies of Islamic law generally ignore its implications for the development of *fiqh* and its relevance for law reform in the modern context'.[30] The point, however, is that differences of opinion about Qurʾanic interpretation and juristic conclusions are not uncommon, and is an indication that perceived in the correct fashion, they have the potential to lead to flexible and dynamic understandings. Idealistic as it may be, this sentiment has been echoed by Muslim scholars.[31] One of the New Religious Thinkers from Iran who is studied in depth in this book is Ahmad Qabil. When asked what was the fundamental difference between his inclusive approach and the official approach current in the Islamic Republic of Iran, he alluded to the difficulty in promoting various juristic approaches. His reply referred to two jurisprudential maxims: 'In answer to this question I need only mention [the idioms] "[just] *one*

---

29 Khomeini, 'Manshūr-i baradarī', *Ṣaḥīfa-yi Imām*, vol 21, 2010, 175.

30 Muhammad Khalid Masud, 'Ikhtilaf al-Fuqaha: Diversity in Fiqh as a Social Construction', *Wanted: Equality and Justice in the Muslim Family*, ed. Zainah Anwar, Malaysia 2009, 65.

31 'The existence of *ikhtilāf* as a well-developed and cognised branch of Fiqh is naturally indicative of a healthy climate of tolerance among the leading "ulamā" and scholars of Islam.' Muhammad Hashim Kamali, '"Ikhtilāf": juristic disagreement in the Shariʿah', *Islamic Studies* 37.3, 1998, 332.

approach is all [that is needed]" and "*some of the jurists' conclusions are different*" to show that different claims are not foolish.'[32]

The possibility of diverse and sometimes conflicting readings of the Qur'an is all too clear with reference to Q. 3.7, which states:

> He it is who has sent down to you the book, therein are clear signs (*muḥkamāt*); they are the mother of the book, and others similar/allegorical (*mutashabihāt*).[33] As for those whose hearts are given to swerving, they follow the *mutashabihāt*, seeking temptation and seeking its interpretation and none knows its interpretation save God and those firmly rooted in knowledge ...

The first part of Q. 3.7 classifies two kinds of verse which are the clear (or stable) and the similar/ambiguous. The subsequent part of Q. 3.7 allows interpretation or understanding only to God and Muhammad's household.[34] With the occultation of the Twelfth Shiʿi Imam, the jurists were very cautious about giving definitive rulings, let alone producing any interpretation of the *mutashabihāt*.[35]

32 Ahmad Qabil, *Sharīʿat-i ʿAqlānī*, 50. This difference in opinions is one of the major themes in Qabil's works, perhaps because he despaired of attempts to silence divergent opinions. For example: 'The different fatwas of Shiʿi jurists are so many that ʿAllama Hilli in his book *Differences of the Shia* allocated nearly four thousand pages (in the new edition), quoting some of the issues [where there are] differences among the Shiʿi jurists from the fourth century to the eighth century (10th–14th centuries). Surely, if someone wants to set out a collection of the differences in opinions among the Shiʿi jurists from the second to the fifteenth century (8th–21st centuries) with all of their details he will get head-spinning results.' See *Sharīʿat-i ʿAqlānī*, 85.

33 The implications of how this term is translated has been highlighted by Leah Kinberg, 'Muḥkamāt and mutashābihāt (Koran 3/7): Implication of a Koranic pair of terms in medieval exegesis', *Arabica* 35.2, 1988, 143–72.

34 The Sunni tradition holds that Q. 3.7 should be read in the following way: '... none knows its interpretation save God. And those firmly rooted in knowledge, they say "We believe in the book ...".' Thus, interpretation is limited to God. A popular Shiʿi interpretation, recognising that there were no full-stops in the early Qur'anic manuscripts made the following plausible reading: '... none knows its interpretation save God and those firmly rooted in knowledge, they say "We believe in the book ...".'

35 Dahlén, *Islamic Law, Epistemology and Modernity*, 94. The jurisprudential principle of caution (*iḥṭiyāt*) has a long history. It has continued to be practised to the present day, and was explained by the Iraqi *marjaʿ*, Muhammad Baqir al-Sadr, who says that if there is a probable command (i.e. it is not known if the command is definite) then believers exercise caution. 'This we do by refraining from whatever is probably forbidden and fulfilling whatever is probably obligatory.' Muhammad Baqir al-Sadr, *Principles of Islamic Jurisprudence: According to Shiʿi Law*, London 2003, see lesson twenty-two.

But the identification of which verses are *muḥkamāt* and which are *mutashabihāt* has been questioned, and as a result a large body of literature has emerged which has attempted to clarify what verses are open to interpretation. An in-depth classification of such an attempt is impossible in this small space, but the significance of these efforts has been highlighted by Abdolkarim Soroush, the 'doyen' of intellectual Islamic reform and leading non-seminarian religious thinker, who was one of the first intellectuals in post-revolutionary Iran to formulate the kinds of questions that probed the boundaries of 'acceptable' discourse. Soroush regards the efforts of scholars to classify the *muḥkam* and the *mutashabihāt* as futile because 'the whole history of Islam clearly shows that virtually every verse of the Qurʾan has been suspected at one time or another of being *mutashabihāt*'.[36] This has serious implication for the investigation into Qurʾanic commands and controversies on issues such as the mandatory hijab. This manner of questioning renders the Qurʾan unstable of any fixed meaning; all of its verses, the word of God, are bequeathed to human interpretive authority, to exercise its investigative scalpel in order to analyse and perhaps remould the verse, influenced by the preferences, prejudices and persuasions of the time. The hermeneutics of Qurʾanic study that were developed over many centuries channelled the interpretive process to avoid temporal considerations of interpreters as much as possible and direct the act of interpretation towards the 'original' understanding of the time of revelation. However, the recognition of the unavoidability of human input into reading the Qurʾan has been acknowledged by many modern Iranian ulama, and is just one of the elements in their armoury when defending a more open and diverse understanding of sharia.

The possibility that Q. 3.7 opens up new vistas for interpreting the Qurʾan was rejected by the *marjaʿ taqlīd* Grand Ayatollah Khuʾi (d.1992) who argued that *mutashabihāt* are clear in meaning, although they refer to verses in which there is a word or expression which bears two or more meanings. In such cases, judgement about the meaning of the verse should be suspended until it is clear which meaning is intended. An expression which is understood as literal cannot be considered *mutashabihāt*.[37] Khuʾi's interpretation is neither new, as it can be discovered in the arguments of Sunni medieval commentators, nor does it sufficiently

36 Abdolkarim Soroush, 'The evolution and devolution of religious knowledge', *Liberal Islam*, ed. Charles Kurzman, Oxford 1998, 249; see also Soroush, 'Islamic revival and reform', *Reason, Freedom, and Democracy in Islam: Essential Writings of Abdolkarim Soroush*, Oxford 2000, 35. See also Hussein Abdul-Raof, 'On the dichotomy between the muḥkam and mutashabih', *Journal of Qurʾanic Research and Studies* 3.5, 2008, 47–70.
37 Al-Khuʾi, *The Prolegomena to the Qurʾan*, trans. Abdalaziz Sachedina, Oxford 1998, 184.

address the various ways in which scholars have understood the *mutashabihāt*, nor indeed does it consider the implications of Soroush's observation. Such views demonstrate how traditionalist claims may be regarded as 'conservative' when considered by the criteria of opening the sharia to new and fresh investigative analysis.

In spite of Khuʾi's distaste for the kinds of understanding offered by Soroush, Western non-Muslim scholars have pointed out that the Qurʾan contains several verses, even words, that by themselves are ambiguous, and have been understood within the Islamic tradition with reference to other sources of jurisprudence, such as the hadith. The term 'seal of the prophets' which occurs once in the Qurʾan in 33.40, is such an example. While tradition holds this term to mean that Muhammad is the last prophet, thereby rendering post-Islamic religions false and innovations, recent scholarship has questioned the assumption that the 'last of the prophets' pointed to this very significance at the time of revelation. David S. Powers has argued that the term simply meant that Muhammad confirmed the previous divine revelations, but that as a result of a 'thought experiment' later generations of Muslims speculated that had Muhammad been a father to a son, the latter would also have become a prophet, following the Judeo-Christian tradition.[38] So the meaning of the term shifted somewhat to indicate that he was the very last and final prophet, which ensured that the reforms and traditions established by Muhammad would outlast the claimants to prophecy that emerged after him.

Soroush's claim concerning Q. 3.7 may not be acceptable to the modern New Religious Thinkers,[39] but his views are significant if only because they demonstrated the extent to which such topics were open for discussion. His views may also have encouraged scholars to start thinking about the 'changeability' of certain verses – a topic that is discussed further in the next section. 'Changeability' is clearly an important theme in Soroush's works: 'it becomes evident that the categories of certainty and ambivalence themselves are subject to change. It is not as though a verse would remain certain or ambivalent forever.'[40]

38 David S. Powers, *Zayd*, Philadelphia 2014.

39 Kadivar has confirmed to me in a private email (22 June 2020) that he completely disagrees with Soroush on this point.

40 Soroush, 'Islamic Revival and Reform', *Reason. Freedom, and Democracy in Islam: Essential Writings of Abdolkarim Soroush*, ed. M. Sadri and A. Sadri, Oxford 2000, 35.

Abrogated verses

Another method employed for determining the meaning of Qur'anic verses involves the concept of abrogation, or *naskh*, a term that like the *muḥkamāt* and *mutashabihāt* appears in the Qur'an.[41] The case of *sakar* (in Q. 16.67, derived from the fruits of the date palm), understood as an intoxicating or strong drink by some scholars, provides a good example.[42] Q. 16.67 permits believers to imbibe this drink. (Indeed, intoxicating drinks are allocated to the believers in the hereafter, see Q. 47.15 on rivers of wine – *anhar min khamr* – and Q. 83.22 on nectar – *rahiq*.) But drinking wine is prohibited, according to some scholars, by Q. 2.219 and Q. 5.90, which refer specifically to *khamr*. Such seeming 'inconsistencies' regarding intoxicating drinks were explained with reference to the concept of *naskh*.[43] But *naskh* only makes sense if there is a clear chronology of the verses revealed, so that a late verse might abrogate an earlier verse. Since the Qur'an was not compiled (in book form) on the basis of such a chronology, believers resorted to the hadith to determine when a verse was revealed. The authenticity of the hadith has been a major source of dispute among scholars, East and West. However, Q. 16.67 which permits believers to drink date wine was not abrogated according to Grand Ayatollah Khu'i, who argues that this is so because *sakar* (date wine) and *khamr* (grape wine) are not the same, and the verse does not state what those who produce *sakar* do with it (the inference being that they may not drink it).[44] In Khu'i's study of the Qur'an, a whole chapter is devoted to abrogation, and he is of the opinion that aside from the abrogation of previous sharia (the Torah and the Gospel) not one verse of the Qur'an has been abrogated. He cites the opinion of Ahmad al-Nahhas (d. 949) to the effect that there are 137 abrogating verses, but he then adds, 'We have undertaken this discussion to examine these verses that are claimed to have been abrogated, and to demonstrate that, in reality, not even one of them has been abrogated.'[45] Khu'i's approach, as far as modern Shi'i thought is concerned, has been described as a 'radical stance [which] seems to be somewhat exceptional', and may be related to the concern that there is a very

41 Hossein Modarressi, 'Early debates on the integrity of the Qur'an: A brief survey', *Studia Islamica* 77, 1993, 5–39.
42 For more on the Qur'anic perspectives on wine see J. D. McAuliffe, 'The wines of earth and paradise: Qur'anic proscriptions and promises', *Logos Islamikos*, ed. Roger M. Savory and Dionisius A. Agius, Toronto 1984, 159–74.
43 The most extensive study of *naskh* within the Sunni tradition is Louay Fatoohi, *Abrogation in the Qur'an and Islamic Law*, London 2013.
44 Al-Khu'i, *The Prolegomena to the Qur'an*, 235.
45 Ibid., 186.

short distance between *naskh* and *taḥrīf* (falsification), a position Shiʿi scholars would wish to avoid at all costs.[46]

Khuʾi's refusal to endorse abrogation is also reflected in a discussion by Mutahhari, typified in his writing on the topic of jihad.[47] Jihad has been a focus of attention for scholars interested in abrogation,[48] but Mutahhari considered that a verse that advocates jihad in an unconditional manner (such as Q. 9.29, 'Fight against those who believe not in Allah nor the Last Day, nor hold that forbidden which has been forbidden by Allah and His messenger, nor acknowledges the religion of Truth'), must be interpreted in parallel to conditional verses. Conditional verses in this respect are Q. 2.190, which instructs Muslims to fight only with those who fight them, and Mutahhari also relied upon the famous verse Q. 2.256 ('There is no compulsion in religion') – which some scholars believed was abrogated (as Khuʾi reminds us).[49] In this fashion, Mutahhari presented an interpretation of jihad for the twentieth century which may be understood as non-aggressive, and appropriate for the time. He did not explicitly address the issue of abrogation, but it is an unstated element that runs throughout his treatise.[50]

The refusal of some scholars to utilise abrogation reflects the idea that the Qurʾan speaks of *naskh* only in reference to the abrogation of previous sacred scriptures. Such a perspective among modern scholars may be a result of their commitment to the view that the text of the Qurʾan is perfect and the idea of abrogating any verse in some fashion reduces the miraculous nature of God's word, which through *naskh* is limited by temporal changes. Khuʾi's perspective on abrogation and that of Mutahhari are alternatives to the views of other 'established'

---

46 Rainer Brunner, 'Abrogation and Falsification of Scriptures', *Approaches to the Qurʾan in Contemporary Iran*, ed. Alessandro Cancian, Oxford 2019, 234.
47 Murtaza Mutahhari, *Jihad: The Holy War of Islam and its Legitimacy in the Qurʾan*, trans. Mohammad Salman Tawhidi, Tehran 1985.
48 Q. 9.5, which for centuries has been at the centre of the dispute, commands: 'Then when the sacred months have passed, slay the idolaters wherever you find them, capture them, besiege them, and lie in wait for them at every place of ambush. But if they repent, and perform the prayer and give the alms, then let them go their way.' Some scholars have claimed that this verse abrogates all the verses that commanded believers towards harmonious and peaceful relations with the *ahl al-kitāb*; Ibn Jawzi (d. 1200) claimed that it abrogated 124 verses, see Reuven Firestone, *Jihad: The Origins of Holy War in Islam*, Oxford 1999, 63.
49 Al-Khuʾi, *The Prolegomena to the Qurʾan*, 205. He claims that some believed this verse had been abrogated by 9.73: 'O Prophet! Strive against the disbelievers and the hypocrites', which Mutahhari considers unconditional, and therefore in need of interpretation through a conditional verse.
50 Mutahhari, *Jihad and the Holy War of Islam and its Legitimacy in the Quran*.

seminarians, such as ʿAllama Tabatabaʾi (d. 1981),[51] and also the New Religious Thinkers. Typifying this trend is Ahmad Qabil who claimed that: 'In the glorious Qurʾan, there are both permanent commands and also temporary and impermanent [commands]. This topic is the subject of agreement of *all* the wise people [believing in] the Islamic sharia; the [Qurʾanic] verses are given to the Prophet of God and some have been abrogated and a new command has replaced them.'[52] Qabil was one of the modern Iranian jurists pressing for reform in society, which he believed could occur with the correct interpretation and application of *fiqh*, and the above quote suggests he considered abrogation as a part of this process. Of particular relevance are his comments in *Sharīʿat-i ʿAqlānī*, in which he attempted to legitimise his claim with reference to previous Shiʿi scholars:

> Shaykh Tusi (d. 1067) uses rational (*ʿaqlī*) and empirical proof to explain the reason for the abrogation (*naskh*) of the previous sharias by the Muhammadan sharia. He writes, 'The sharia of our Prophet is the abrogator (*naskh kunanda*) of previous sharias because human welfare changes according to the conditions of time and with people, just as a medical operation for each sick person is different according to his/her constitution and sickness.'[53]
>
> We know that 'rational proofs do not depend upon [people's] understanding', so if the 'change in human welfare according to the condition's time and people' is sufficient proof for [both] 'abrogating previous sharias' and setting aside the commands of that sharia, [then] it is possible for [the change in human welfare] to apply also within one sharia, and for it to be the cause of 'changing the commands of the [same] sharia'.[54]

On this topic, it is worthwhile to also mention the views of Ayatollah Maʿrifat (1931–2007) who advocated the idea of 'preparatory abrogation' (*naskh-i tamhīdī*). He believed that some verses of the Qurʾan (such as those related to the permissibility of slavery and the mistreatment of women) were incompatible with certain ethical goals. Therefore, although such institutions and practices were not

51 See Muhammad Husayn Tabatabaʾi, *Shining Sun* [*Mihr-i Tābān*], trans. Tawus Raja, London 2011, 319–24.

52 Qabil, 'Thābit va mutaghayyir dar Qurʾan', *Fiqh, Karkard-hā va Qābiliyat* [*Jurisprudence, Applications and Potentialities*], 276.

53 Qabil cites his source for the quote as *Javāhir al-Fiqh*, 248–9.

54 Qabil, *Sharīʿat-i ʿAqlānī*, 83. There is a work of this name composed by Ibn al-Barraj (d. 1088) who studied under Tusi and was his representative in Syria. See A. Sachedina, *The Just Ruler in Shiʿite Islam*, Oxford 1988, 13, n. 3.

abolished in the Qur'an, the ground was prepared by limiting their harm or practice, and so the eventual abrogation of these verses at a later stage (either by the Prophet himself or by the imams) was made that much easier.[55]

A further step was taken by Muhsin Kadivar who considers abrogation 'one of the most important topics of discussion in Qur'anic studies, theology and the principles of *fiqh*'.[56] He has proposed a systematic method for a contemporary abrogation that he has termed 'rational abrogation'.[57] Kadivar argues that changing most commands in the Qur'an is permissible if it is based on the promotion of welfare, including the implementation of human rights, the abolition of slavery and the removal of all forms of discrimination whether based on gender or religious affiliation. But abrogation must not be based on 'state expediency' or the decision of a ruling *faqīh* or his appointees, since this will give only temporary sanction to the abrogation in question. A more permanent solution is to be discovered outside of 'state' *fiqh* by referring to the criteria for establishing whether a command can be changed (abrogated), which is to be found in the attributes of justice, rationality and morality. If a Qur'anic command does not meet these standards, then it is clear it has served its life term; it was not meant to be a permanent ruling. However, Kadivar respects the jurisprudential ways, and establishes a methodology to discover replacements (or abrogating verses) for those that are abrogated. The abrogating verses must have been revealed after the abrogated verse, the case for the abrogating verse must be stronger (meaning that a weak hadith cannot abrogate a Qur'anic verse), and the abrogating verse must be clear and explanatory of the context of the arguments present in the abrogated verse.[58] Moreover, he holds that definite reason, or a reason-based precept can abrogate verses that are understood as temporary. He says, 'If reason is qualified to discover sharia precepts, it is undoubtedly also qualified to discover when a sharia precept has reached the end of its term. The idea that the ruling of reason can serve as an abrogator simply means that reason is capable of imposing time limits on sharia precepts.'[59] Like many other representatives of the New Religious Thinkers, Kadivar considers reason as intrinsic to revelation, so that there is no real contradiction between the two.

55 Eshkevari, 'Rethinking men's authority over women', 207. See also Mihdi Sultani Ranini, 'Naskh az dīdgāh-i Ayatollah Maʿrifat', *Majalla-yi Takhassusī Ilāhiyat va Ḥuqūq* 46, 1386/1997, 91–2. I am grateful to Dr. Farhad Shafti for acquiring this article for me.

56 Mohsen Kadivar, 'Human rights and intellectual Islam', 68.

57 Kadivar, 'Ayzāḥ-i naskh-i ʿaqlī' [Explaining rational abrogation], 5 September 2015, https://kadivar.com/?p=14660.

58 Kadivar, 'Ayzāḥ-i naskh-i ʿaqlī'.

59 Kadivar, 'Human rights and intellectual Islam', 69.

Regardless of the strengths and weaknesses of the arguments put forth by Khuʾi, Mutahhari, Qabil, Maʿrifat and Kadivar on abrogation, the significant point lies in that from very different methodological perspectives, they ultimately reach a 'compassionate' understanding of Islam. It is a perspective that arguably responds to the challenges of modernity, and which might be considered more compatible with modern universal standards as opposed to the medieval version which endeavoured to assert the supersessionist nature of Islam.

Just as the Shiʿi tradition offers diverse understandings of *naskh*, Sunni scholars too in the contemporary period have provided differing perspectives, although it has been argued that the general tendency in modern times has been to reject the medieval reliance on abrogation to render the Qurʾan meaningful to the circumstances of Muslim communities.[60] For example, Sir Sayyid Ahmad Khan (d. 1898), the famous Indian reformer, claimed that there was only one abrogating verse in the whole of the Qurʾan, which referred to the abrogation by Islam of Judaism and Christianity.[61] This refusal to accept the principle of abrogation should probably be considered in the context of 19th-century Christian criticisms of *naskh*, based on the claim that a 'change' in God's word implied a change of mind, a seeming inconsistency for the Divine.[62] The Egyptian 'radical' Sayyid Qutb (d. 1966), associated with the Muslim Brotherhood, accepted the possibility of *naskh* in the Qurʾan, although he used different terms to denote change such as *taʿdīl* (alteration), *taqyīr* (change) and *rafʿ* (lifting).[63] In recent times, and in complete contrast to Ahmad Khan and Sayyid Qutb, a far-reaching and radical approach has been advocated by Mahmoud Taha (d. 1985) and his student ʿAbdullahi Ahmed An-Naʿim who claim that the Qurʾan contains verses that do not uphold the principle of reciprocity, and they point to specific verses on slavery, disparities in gender equality and freedoms between Muslims and non-Muslims.[64]

60 Daniel Brown, 'The triumph of scripturalism: The doctrine of *naskh* and its modern critics', *The Shaping of an American Islamic Discourse: A Memorial to Fazlur Rahman*, ed. Earle H. Waugh, Frederick Mathewson Denny and Fazlur Rahman, Atlanta 1998, 49–66.

61 The sole case of abrogation was the replacement by Islam of previous scripture. Khan examines sura 2 (not just the specific verse 2.106 [the verse is mistakenly given as 2.100]) and concludes that the *aya* refers not to specific verses, but rather the Qur'an which abrogates the Gospel and the Torah. See Ernest Hahn, 'Sir Sayyid Ahmad Khan's "The controversy over abrogation (in the Quran)"', *The Muslim World* 64.2, 1974, 124–33.

62 Hahn, 'Sir Sayyid Ahmad Khan's "The controversy over abrogation (in the Quran)"', 124–33.

63 Thameem Ushama, 'The phenomenon of al-naskh: a brief overview of the key issues', *Jurnal Fiqh* 3, 2006, 120.

64 Mahmoud Mohamed Taha, *The Second Message of Islam*, trans. ʿAbdullahi Ahmed An-Naʿim, New York 1987; ʿAbdullahi Ahmed An-Naʿim, *Toward an Islamic Reformation:*

Their background in Sudan where Muslim-Christian tension and conflict has been rife was no doubt an influence upon these scholars' beliefs. They have advanced the idea that the Qur'an's universal message is contained in the Meccan verses in contrast to the later Medinan verses which are more specific and particular to the issues of the Medinan context. And so, An-Naʿim argues for the abrogation of all of those Medinan verses that deny the principle of reciprocity.

The belief that the contemporary understandings of abrogation is a 'deeply conservative principle'[65] must be taken with some caution, and certainly within the modern Shiʿi circle it seems to be the exact opposite. Shiʿi ulama are not ignorant of the writings of their Sunni counterparts. Muhsin Kadivar has responded to the theory of Taha and An-Naʿim, rejecting their proposals for reform largely on the jurisprudential procedure mentioned above.[66] He writes that according to the laws of *fiqh*, the verses being abrogated must historically precede the verse that is the abrogator, but in Taha's and An-Naʿim's scheme the reverse is the case. Moreover, the classification of verses as Meccan and Medinan itself is problematic. Instead, Kadivar set out his alternative to Taha and Naʿim's theory, which reaches the same goal but with different methods.

Aḥkām *(commands or precepts)*

Mention was made earlier of Mutahhari's classification of Qur'anic verses into three groups, reflecting realities and beliefs, morality and self-perfection, and laws and issues of action.[67] According to Mutahhari, it is the last of these that scholars have termed *fiqh*, or jurisprudence.[68] This third group, containing the commands, is often considered the smallest category. Mutahhari estimated that about one-thirteenth of the Qur'an pertains to laws, that is about 500 verses from a total of 6660,[69] and 'the commands and regulations of Islam have not been explained by the Qur'an or by the Prophet and the imams in such a way that each and every

---

Civil Liberties, Human Rights, and International Law, New York 1990.

65 Massimo Campanini, professor of the History of Arab Countries at the Oriental University in Naples states, '… abrogation can be seen as one of the pillars of the conservative readings of the Qur'an in the present day.' See his *The Qur'an: Modern Muslim Interpretations*, London 2011, 63.

66 Kadivar, 'Ayzāḥ-i naskh-i ʿaqlī'.

67 Mutahhari, *Jurisprudence and its Principles*, 28.

68 Ibid. It is worthwhile noting the observation of Sachedina that abrogation (discussed in the previous section) was introduced only in connection with the legal injunctions (*aḥkām*). See Sachedina, 'The Qur'an and other religions', 302.

69 Mutahhari, *Jurisprudence and its Principles*, 8.

particularity has been expressly dealt with.'[70] This necessitates the science of *fiqh*, or jurisprudence. The person with knowledge of the science of jurisprudence is a *faqīh*. The New Religious Thinkers express views similar to those of Mutahhari, but they limit the realm of *fiqh* even further. Thus, Ahmad Qabil argues that 'a majority of more than 90% of the verses (most of which do not explain the commands) have no use in the [everyday] life of humans'.[71] And Muhsin Kadivar has claimed that only 2% of Qur᾿anic verses concern non-worship sharia commands.[72] Although the sharia commands comprise a small proportion of all the verses in the Qur᾿an, another of the New Religious Thinkers, Muhammad Mujtahid-Shabistari, has observed that throughout Islamic history *fiqh* has been recognised as the noblest of sciences, because the commands and prohibitions had both an individual dimension, based on personal faith and religion, and also a social aspect.[73] He adds that *fiqh* subsequently became separated from the spiritual dimension of religion, and the explanation of God's commands and prohibitions was related only to the forms of behaviour, or in the words of Ghazali, the towering medieval theologian, *fiqh* became a purely worldly concern.[74]

For some it may seem that there is a paradox here. On the one hand the commands comprise the smallest element in the Qur᾿an. Yet on the other hand the understanding and implementation of *fiqh* was the noblest of Islamic sciences, and as Muhsin Kadivar states, the *fiqh* of social transactions 'has gained indescribable importance, to the point where it has overshadowed the parts of religion that relate to faith, morality and worship'.[75] The historical significance of *fiqh* has resulted in scholars according it particular attention, and the sheer volume of study devoted to jurisprudence has resulted in scholars voicing diverse and often contradictory opinions. This has had important consequences in the politics of the Islamic Republic of Iran, where it was considered during the 1980s that political divisions within the parliament (*majlis*) were harmful to the regime. One of the topics that had caused disunity in the *majlis* was the issue of the *ta῾zīrat* laws.[76]

70 Ibid., 6.
71 Qabil, 'Thābit va mutaghayyir dar Qur'an', *Fiqh, Karkard-hā va Qābiliyat*, 276.
72 Kadivar, 'Human Rights and Intellectual Islam', 65. The Persian original is 'Ḥuqūq-i bashar va rawshanfikr-i dīnī', *Aftāb* 3.27, 2003, 54–9, and 3.28, 2003, 106–15.
73 Shabistari, *Naqdī bar Qirā᾿at-i Rasmī az Dīn*, 163.
74 Shabistari, *Naqdī bar Qirā᾿at-i Rasmī az Dīn*, 163.
75 Kadivar, 'Human Rights and Intellectual Islam', 66.
76 Azadeh Niknam, 'The Islamization of Law in Iran', *Middle East Research and Information Project*, (MER212). See http://www.merip.org/mer/mer212/islamization-law-iran. The *ta῾zīrat* laws were criminal laws covering *ḥudūd* and *qiṣāṣ*. The scope of *ta῾zīrat* expanded as the nature and complications of modern life grew, resulting in more and more

Ayatollah Khomeini sought to quell dissention in his aforementioned 'Brotherly Charter' by pointing to the need for diversity:

> In the Islamic government the gate of *ijtihād* (juristic reasoning) is always open and the nature of the revolution and the regime always requires this because juristic-*ijtihādī* opinions should be freely aired on various topics even if they contradict one another, and no one has the power or right to prevent this.[77]

Khomeini also referred to two kinds of jurisprudential approaches, the traditional jurisprudence (*fiqh-i sunnatī* or *fiqh-i jawhari*) and the dynamic jurisprudence (*fiqh-i pūyā*), which is often taken as the reformist variety, although he tried to minimise the difference, locating them squarely within the seminary:

> But on the topic of the seminary's programmes for education and research, I believe in traditional jurisprudence and *ijtihād-i jawharī*, and I do not consider divergence from it as permissible. *Ijtihād* is correct in that manner, but this does not mean that Islamic jurisprudence is not dynamic (*pūyā*).[78]

Khomeini's declaration had significant consequences. On the one hand, the traditionalists claimed that they too were simply interpreting Qur'anic commands with *fiqh-i pūyā*. In other words, 'In light of the effort of implementing Islamic law within the structure of the modern nation state, *fiqh-i pūyā* is essentially interpreted by Islamic traditionalists to be the practical implementation of the eternal shariat into changing human conditions.'[79] On the other hand, Khomeini's endorsement of the permissibility of different interpretations of Islamic law, including *fiqh-i*

crimes being adjudicated by the government. *Ta'zīrat* in effect became part of the *ḥukm-i ḥukūmatī* or governmental law. In short, the dispute was about the expanding role of government (necessitating a form of expansion of interpretation). In contrast, opponents advocated for a limited and 'literal' application of sharia. Of course, *ḥukm-i ḥukūmatī* may be applied or interpreted in a 'liberal' fashion, or a more severe and strict fashion.

77 Khomeini, 'Manshūr-i Barādarī', *Ṣahīfa-yi Imām*, vol. 21, 80. The New Religious Thinkers also point to the diversity of opinions within the tradition of *fiqh*, see, for example, Shabistari who refers to 'changes in opinion and in juristic fatwas in the course of the history of *fiqh*, and countless differences in the opinions of the *faqīh*s in each epoch'. 'Fiqh-i siyāsī bi-satr-i 'uqalā'i-yi khud-rā az dast dāda ast', *Naqdī bar Qirā'at-i Rasmī az Dīn*, 165.

78 Khomeini, 'Payām bi-rūḥāniyat, mudarrisīn, ṭullāb …' [Message to the spiritual leaders, religious teachers and religious students, known as the 'Manshūr-i Rūḥāniyat' (Charter for Spiritual Persons)], 3 Isfand 1367 (22 February 1988), *Ṣahīfa-yi Imām*, vol. 21, 288.

79 Dahlén, *Islamic Law, Epistemology and Modernity*, 117.

pūyā, resulted in several prominent thinkers, seminarian and non-seminarian, arguing for a more dynamic understanding of law, by which they meant more democratic, open, pluralist interpretations that respected individual rights. One of the many and most common elements of *fiqh-i pūyā* is the classification of *aḥkām* into immutable and changing commands, a topic that has been discussed by many of the New Religious Thinkers. They claim that the commands should reflect the basic ethical imperative of the Qur'an (as reflected by the *maqāṣid al-sharīʿa*). This stands in contrast to the traditional jurisprudential perspective that focuses specifically on the legality (permissibility or otherwise) of individual commands in isolation from the more general context of revelation. The view of commands that are constant and variable has been the most popular of perspectives over the past one hundred years.[80] This time span corresponds to the increasing presence of Western science, knowledge and culture in the Middle East, and it became apparent to many that the new circumstances posed a challenge to certain traditional Islamic values and Qur'anic commands, such as those which appeared to discriminate on gender and on religious affiliation, and which endorse slavery, demonstrating their 'incompatibility' with life in the modern world.

The approach that challenges traditional understandings is foreshadowed in the writings of Shariʿat-Sangalaji (d. 1944), whose Islamic reformation was based on a reading of the Qur'an unencumbered by superstition and excessive reliance on hadith. Moreover, he rejected a dry, formulaic and static reading of the Qur'an, recognising that human understandings of even single words change depending on circumstances and time.[81] Moreover, as Rahnema notes, it is possible to infer from his writings that the emphasis he placed on reason might lead to the conclusion that he saw religion as ultimately preparing believers for a time when they would 'freely regulate their relations with God and pursue their lives'.[82] In the generation after Shariʿat-Sangalaji, the idea of change in Islamic practice without destroying the spirit of Islam was advanced by Mutahhari, whose *Islām va Muqtażiyāt-i Zamān* (published in 1973) called for believers to recognise that different times required diverse responses to the challenges of life.[83] He offered examples of how the prophetic Sunna and the lives of the imams contrasted with how believers should conduct their own lives, not necessarily imitating the exact and precise

80 Mohsen Kadivar, 'From traditional Islam to Islam as an End in Itself', *Die Welt des Islams* 51, 2011, 462.

81 Ali Rahnema, *Shiʿi Reformation in Islam*, London 2015, 71–3.

82 Rahnema, *Shiʿi Reformation in Islam*, 111.

83 Mutahhari, *Islām va Muqtażiyāt-i Zamān* [*Islam and the Necessities of Time*], Tehran 1370/1991–2.

model that was offered by sacred texts. By way of illustration, he related a story from the *Nahj al-Balāgha* in which Imam ʿAli was asked why he had not dyed his beard, since the Prophet had commanded people to colour their white beards. In reply ʿAli said that this command was for the Prophet's time and not for his generation, and he explained that the number of Muslims in the Prophet's time was small, and many of them were old and served in the Prophet's army. This gave a psychological advantage to the enemy army, whose soldiers saw a proportionately large number of white beards in the opposing army and assumed the men to be weak. And it was for this reason that the Prophet commanded the men to dye their beards. The purpose was not a permanent command to die beards, but rather it was a command to carry out action that would strengthen the Muslims' position vis-à-vis their opponents.[84] Mutahhari argued how 'a variable need [the colouring of beards] is linked to a permanent one [strengthening Islam], and it requires a *mujtahid* to discover this relation, and then explain the command of Islam'.[85] Such a position resembles Mutahhari's views on abrogation, mentioned above, for he did not uphold abrogation as permissible *per se*, but advocated the discovery of Qurʾanic verses that place conditions on an outdated verse. Writing at a time when Muhammad Riza Shah's secularising and 'modernising' reforms were sweeping the country, and when left-wing ideas were becoming increasingly popular, Mutahhari's concerns were very different from those of the present generation of New Religious Thinkers, whose calls for reform must be seen in the context of Iran post-Khomeini, when increasing awareness of international 'norms' became more evident with the advances in IT technology and greater roles for women in society. Nevertheless, Mutahhari is an important figure in identifying how the interpretation of Qurʾanic commands changed in the 20th century. Consider, for instance, his statement: 'The spirit of Islam is a permanent one. At all times it is just like a human body that changes, although the spirit is unchanging. This resemblance does not mean that the necessities of time demand that the Islamic commands are deficient.'[86] He likewise gives another example of the changing circumstances of time: 'If the Prophet lived in my time he would dress like me, and if I too had lived in the Prophet's time I would have dressed like him.'[87]

Without a doubt, the New Religious Thinkers owe a debt to Mutahhari, evidenced by their practice of citing passages from his works in their writings. But

84 Mutahhari, *Islām va Muqtażiyāt-i Zamān*, 239.
85 Mutahhari, *Islām va Muqtażiyāt-i Zamān*, 239–40.
86 Mutahhari, *Islām va Muqtażiyāt-i Zamān*, 236.
87 These words are attributed to Imam Sadiq Jaʿfar, see Mutahhari, *Islām va Muqtażiyāt-i Zamān*, 221.

the New Religious Thinkers have pushed *fiqh* plasticity further than Mutahhari ever did, demonstrating the flexibility or the adaptability of Qur'anic commands with reference to abrogation (as argued above), and also through referring to the overriding principle of ethics and reason to determine which command is changeable and which is permanent. Eshkevari offers an interesting example in an article in which he discusses the abhorrence of all forms of social and religious discrimination.[88] He attempts to associate Muhammad with a dislike for *jizyah*, a tax on non-Muslims (a practice that is endorsed in the Qur'an) by citing a hadith from the time of the death of Muhammad's son Ibrahim, whose mother was Coptic: 'If Ibrahim had lived, I would have removed the *jizyah* tax from all the Copts.' Some of the New Religious Thinkers adopt the seemingly extreme view that there are no Qur'anic laws that can be considered eternal. For example, Shabistari argues that the jurists imagine the word of God (*kalām*) to be human-like, and they use the same criteria to understand it that they would employ for understanding human speech. He then adds a significant point in relation to Islamic laws (commands or prohibitions, or *aḥkām*): 'It is impossible to conceive of timeless (*farā-tārīkhī*) duties or commands and prohibitions (*amr va nahī*) in language – which is a human phenomenon.'[89] The full implications of Shabistari's views, and how he deals with the linguistic difficulties concerning language, are the subject of the following section on revelation.

The nature of revelation

The election of Muhammad Khatami as President of Iran in 1997 seemed to herald a new liberal era in the country's politics. Given that a proportionately large percentage of votes was cast by women and the young, it appeared that the time was ripe and opportune for new perspectives of *fiqh* to deliver social reform in favour of such a large voting block. It is perhaps no surprise that it was during Khatami's two terms as president that systematic and challenging responses to traditional jurisprudence were published in newspapers and journals by the New Religious Thinkers among the ulama who were inspired by the efforts of Soroush. He had been advocating for a more open society in the years after Khomeini's

88 Eshkevari, *Ḥuqūq-i Bashar va Aḥkām-i Ijtimāʿī-yi Islām.* (It is worth pointing out that the second and longest section of this article in entitled *Islām va Muqtażiyat-i Zamān* – a clear nod to Mutahhari.)

89 Shabistari, 'Rāh-i dushwār-i mardumsālārī' [The difficult path of democracy], *Aftāb* 4.22, 2003, 32. I am exceedingly grateful to Dr Naser Ghobadzadeh for sending me a PDF of this important article.

death. Just one year after Khomieni's comments on dynamic jurisprudence, a series of articles by Soroush were published in book form in 1990 under the title *Qabż o Basṭ-i Ti'urīk-i Sharī'at* (*The Theoretic Expansion and Contraction of the Sharia*).[90] Although he has denied that this work was an attempt to resolve the dispute between traditional and dynamic jurisprudence,[91] Soroush's observation that there has always existed diverse interpretations of Islam implicitly endorsed dynamic jurisprudence, and his preoccupation with the human understanding of religion and the human reception of revelation inevitably have implications related to how the Qur'an is read, and therefore how the law is comprehended. Soroush criticises interpretations that focus primarily on law, and it is here that he is different from many of the ulama, as he argues for a new approach outside of jurisprudence to the challenges of religion in modern Iran:

> When the scholarly-juristic perspective begins to operate, the government's first endeavour is to give the society a countenance that conforms to the religious law. It will start to employ the *hadd*-punishments, to collect blood money, to insist on veiling, etc. But the perspective that relies on faith does not start from this point but saves these matters (that is, introduction of Islamic law) for later and makes people devout through wisdom, sermons and discussions.[92]

More recently, Soroush argues in favour of the temporal nature of the divine word through Muhammad, and he distinguishes 'between essential and accidental aspects of the religion'. He cites the example of corporal punishment in the Prophet's day, which was culturally determined and is not appropriate for the present age, and he doubts whether such laws would be part of the message if the Prophet were still alive.[93] The larger question is to determine which verses of the Qur'an denote essential aspects of religion and which are accidental, or in other words, should the Qur'an be viewed as culturally determined, and if so, is it appropriate to provide the basis for a universal religion?

---

90 Abdolkarim Soroush, *Qabż o Basṭ-i Ti'urīk-i Sharī'at* [*The Theoretic Expansion and Contraction of the Sharia*], Tehran 1995.
91 Soroush, *Reason, Freedom, and Democracy in Islam*, 34.
92 Abdolkarim Soroush, 'Taḥlīl-i mafhūm-i ḥukūmat-i dīnī' [Analysis of the understanding of religious government], *Kiyān* 6, 1996, 32–3. Cited in Amirpur, *The New Thinking in Islam*, 154–5.
93 Abdulkarim Soroush, 'The Word of Mohammad', *The Expansion of Prophetic Experience; Essays on Historicity, Contingency and Plurality in Religion*, trans. Nilou Mobasser, Leiden 2009, 275.

Similar questions have been asked by Shabistari, who spent his formative years as director of the Islamic centre of Hamburg between 1968–77. On returning to Iran in the wake of the revolution, he was elected to the first parliament, and thereafter he was a professor at Tehran University until 2006. The influence of his exposure to Christian and postmodern philosophy whilst in Germany is apparent in his writings, as he has frequently cited Paul Tillich, Karl Barth and Hans Georg Gadamer among others. Shabistari's hermeneutical approach accepts that a contextual and historical analysis of the Qurʾan is necessary, and that any understanding of a text is ultimately limited and framed by the preconceptions of the reader. During the 1990s, Shabistari was sufficiently cautious not to correlate such principles with the Qurʾan.[94] However, by 2007, he published an article in which he showed no such reservations, and which he considered to be 'the pinnacle of his intellectual activity'.[95] This article, 'Qirāʾat-i nabawī az jahān' (A prophetic reading of the world) was published in a journal called *Madrasa*, which was forced to suspend publication soon after.[96] In the first part of the article Shabistari is at pains to emphasise the human contribution of the Prophet Muhammad to the Qurʾan. He states in the opening paragraph:

> His [Muhammad's] experience was that he was chosen and stimulated (*bar-angikhta*) by God. And an external aid, which has been understood as 'revelation', came to him. And with the effect of this help, he became powerful in this speaking (*takallum*), in other words, in the expression of spiritual and meaningful sentences, and because of this, it was the *ayat* (the phenomenon) of God that was recited in this speaking.[97]

In the subsequent paragraph the revelation is described as being secret and hidden from the usual intellectual faculty of humans, otherwise all humans would have been able to comprehend it easily, the inference being that Islam would have been accepted without a challenge, and of course it was not. Shabistari then is able

94 Amirpur, *New Thinking in Islam*, 177.
95 Amirpur, *New Thinking in Islam*, 189.
96 'Qirā'at-i nabawī az jahān' [A Prophetic Reading of the World], *Madrasa* 2.6, 2007, 92–6. The article is also available on Shabistari's website, see: http://mohammadmojtahedshabestari.com/category/%D9%86%D9%88%D8%B4%D8%AA%D9%87/%D9%82%D8%B1%D8%A7%D8%A6%D8%AA-%D9%86%D8%A8%D9%88%DB%8C-%D8%A7%D8%B2-%D8%AC%D9%87%D8%A7%D9%86/.
97 I have not seen or used the article as it appears in *Madrasa*, but I have used the web version throughout. All subsequent citations are from this text.

to claim that the utter difference between revelation and normal linguistic communication meant that Muhammad was compelled to convey the revelations in a comprehensible fashion, meaning that the verses of the Qur'an were spoken in his tongue. He states:

> The Prophet did not make the claim that the Qur'anic verses, as they appear at present in the noble scripture, came to him in words and meanings from God, and he merely recited it for the people. Both words and meanings came from him, although he experienced God [as] his teacher (*mu'allim*), which he understood as revelation.

This historicising and 'humanitising' of the Qur'an, making it more specific to Muhammad's time through the use of linguistic forms and through his immediate experience of revelation, reflects his social reality.

> The experience [of the Prophet] about which the Qur'an informs us, is that the Prophet discovered an interpretive, religious understanding (*fahmī tafsīrī-dīnī*) of the world. In his experience the understanding of the world was either prior to the interpretation of the world or the same as it.

Shabistari returns to this point in his text and makes it clear that the Prophet's understanding is the same as his interpretation. This is a crucial and subtle point (*nukta-yi ẓarīf*) because of the contrast of his portrayal of Muhammad with the more conventional and traditional perspectives that view the Prophet as immaculate, implying his perfect knowledge. In such a traditional understanding, there is no room for interpretation, which by definition is fallible. Shabistari was influenced by the German Catholic theologian Richard Schaeffler (b. 1926) who sees interpretation beginning not when the individual asks about the meanings of the experience but with the 'howness' of the experience. In other words, what the individual brings to the experience in terms of expectations, fears, hopes, prejudices and suppositions. In effect, this removes God further from the Qur'an, even if He is the original teacher. Shabistari continues:

> The text of the Qur'an says that the Prophet was involved with things, not that he made his audience aware of things. It says he saw the world, not how the world is. He made his understanding clear. He 'read' the world. The Qur'an (the verse of the noble scripture) is the reading (the interpretive understanding of the Prophet) of the world.

So, for Shabistari, the Qur'an no longer is the literal word of God, a doctrine so essential for pre-modern, and many modern, understandings of the Qur'an. As the word of Muhammad, it is a text that is an interpretation of the revelation that came to him, and interpretations are simply human and there can be no guarantee that they are correct. Traditionally, the Qur'an is understood as the literal word of God, and Muhammad is simply the channel by which this word is communicated to humans. But Shabistari completely rejects this:

> His prophethood was the same as his being stimulated [by God]. If his claim was that he was a channel for the sounds [of the Qur'an] this would have had no relation [to his being] inspired [by God]. A loudspeaker is not inspired.

And as a human, Muhammad reflected on his experiences and revelation within the confines of seventh-century Arabia, meaning that the reading had to be delivered in a form that made sense to the people around him. This historical situatedness of the speaking (*qirā'at*) holds significant ramifications for Qur'anic commands (*aḥkām*):

> The legal commands of the Qur'an were established upon the interpretive understanding of the truth (*vāqī'at*) and existing social relations of society in the Hijaz, and upon human devotional relations with God in that society. And the aim of that interpretation of social truths was in accordance with God's wishes. The revelation of these commands did not mean the establishment of commands for all societies and all times.[98]

Shabistari spelled out the implications of this in more detail during an interview in 2008:

> … well, of course, there is no mention of wearing of veils in the Koran. There is an expression in the Koran that says that one should keep a dignified appearance. That refers to a way of life for a particular society and the Prophet's precepts were intended to be appropriate for that society at that

98 Muhsin Kadivar, 'Ta'amulī darbara-yi naw andīshī-yi dīnī dar irān-i mu'asir' [Reflections on the New Religious Thinkers in Contemporary Iran], 10 November 2015, http://kadivar.com/?p=14729.

time. But that does not mean that these precepts with regard to ritual or the other points mentioned belong to the core of the faith.[99]

The significance of this message of Shabistari needs to be viewed in light of the similar opinions expressed by the Pakistani scholar of Islam, Fazlur Rahman (d. 1988), and the Egyptian Nasr Hamid Abu Zayd (d. 2010). Fazlur Rahman was director of the Central Institute of Islamic Research in Pakistan but was 'forced' to leave following translations of his book *Islam*, in which he problematised the nature of revelation by calling into question the tradition of Muhammad simply being a channel for God's word.[100] Called a disbeliever in the Qur'an and facing death threats, Rahman left Pakistan and settled in the US.[101] Abu Zayd was an academic at Cairo University who treated the Qur'an as a literary text. In 1995, he was put on trial and convicted of apostasy, resulting in forced separation from his wife (as a Muslim woman cannot be married to an apostate, a non-Muslim), and he went into exile in the Netherlands for his own security.[102] It is surprising that Shabistari has been left relatively unmolested in Iran since his 'retirement' from university teaching, for in addition to his views on revelation, some of his other works are a very thinly veiled critique of the regime.

Although Shabistari's views are highly controversial, even among the New Religious Thinkers, it is hard to disagree with Kadivar's generous assessment of the contributions made by Shabistari to post-revolutionary thinking. These include the spread of critical thinking in religious circles in Iran, a historical approach to religion, accelerating the process of secularisation (the separation of religion from the state) in Iran, and laying out the possibility of reaching different understandings from a single text. In Kadivar's words, 'Muhammad Mujtahid-Shabistari …

99 Interview with Mohammad Mujtahid Shabistari (Part 1): 'Islam Is a Religion, Not a Political Agenda.' See https://en.qantara.de/content/interview-with-mohammad-mujtahid-Shabistari-part-1-islam-is-a-religion-not-a-political.

100 Rahman links revelation very closely with the person of Muhammad. He says, 'But orthodoxy (indeed, all medieval thought) lacked the necessary intellectual tools to say both that the Qur'an is entirely the Word of God and, in an ordinary sense, also entirely the word of Muhammad.' Fazlur Rahman, *Islam*, Chicago 1966, 31.

101 Farid Panjwani, 'Fazlur Rahman and the search for authentic Islamic education: A critical appreciation', *Curriculum Inquiry*, 42.1, 2012, 35.

102 Much has been written by and about Nasr Hamid Abu Zayd. But for the accusation of apostasy levelled against him see Fauzi Najjar, 'Islamic Fundamentalism and the Intellectuals: The Case of Nasr Hamid Abu Zayd', *British Journal of Middle Eastern Studies* 27.2, 2000, 177–200. For a more general study of his ideas see Katajun Amirpur, 'Nasr Hamid Abu Zayd: Who's the Heretic Here?', *New Thinking in Islam*, London 2015, 35–65.

has engaged in distinctive and distinguished activity that one must not belittle or be unaware [of].'[103]

Shabistari's ideas provoke a range of questions related to divine revelation, and it is not difficult to comprehend why his writing is so problematic for many Muslims. If revelation is not the exact word of God and instead reflects the culture and time of Arabia, how is it possible to know with certainty that the precise words that appear in the Qur'an are those intended by God? And building upon this line of argumentation, what happens in situations when Muhammad's cultural make-up and belief system differed from that of the revelation he received? Of particular relevance in this respect is Q. 4.34, which permits men to beat their wives if they remain obstinate after their husbands have admonished them and refused to share their beds. The verse was supposedly revealed after a woman had complained to Muhammad that her husband had unjustly beaten her. According to some exegetes, Muhammad had sympathy with the woman and adjudicated in her favour. However, Q. 4.34 was revealed some time afterwards, suggesting that Muhammad's initial reaction was incorrect. Ayesha Chaudhry asks pointedly, 'How could Muhammad be so out of sync with his Lord that he would offer a legal opinion that was the exact opposite as that intended by God? Would he not have intuitively anticipated a ruling somewhat closer to the divine intention?'[104] The issue assumes greater significance in light of the Sunni tradition concerning the influence that Umar ibn Khattab had upon revelation, which is known as the *muwafaqat-i Umar* (agreement of Umar). The argument runs that Umar in some way anticipated some Qur'anic verses with which Muhammad was less than enamoured.[105] Such positions foreshadowed to a certain degree the views of Shabistari and completely humanise Muhammad, rendering prophecy as something that is intimately involved in the context and culture of the time. Indeed, the *muwafaqat-i Umar* is not just an arcane and interesting academic discussion, as it formed the basis of Fatima Mernissi's thesis, *The Veil and the Male Elite*, the Persian translation of which was banned in Iran in 2002 (see Part Three). The demystification of sacred scripture, 'humanising' Muhammad, and foregrounding the culture and history of seventh-century Arabia raises questions that for some undermine the foundations of how Islam has been understood traditionally. For others it opens up the possibility of fresh and creative ways to comprehend the relationship between the divine and creation.

---

103 Kadivar, 'Taʿamulī darbara-yi naw andīshī-yi dīnī dar Irān-e muʿasīr'.

104 Ayesha S. Chaudhry, *Domestic Violence and the Islamic Tradition*, Oxford 2013, 34.

105 Avraham Hakim, 'Context: Umar b. Al-Khattab', *The Blackwell Companion to the Qur'an*, ed. Andrew Rippin, Oxford 2006, 205–20.

The Sunna and Sayings of the Prophet and Imams

The difficulty of understanding and interpreting the Qur'an has led many Shi'i Muslims to refer to the sayings of Muhammad and the imams to elucidate on ambiguous or unclear points. The problematic nature of relying on hadith is well-known, and Muslims themselves have devised ways to weed out those sayings and reports that have been considered forgeries or inauthentic. Nevertheless, the distrust felt by some of the ulama for the application of human reason to comprehend the wisdom behind divine message has resulted in movements to foreground the 'literal' understanding of sacred scripture in determining the correct course of action for the believer. Sacred scripture here includes not just the Qur'an but also the hadith and the sayings of the imams. One such movement is typified by the Akhbari school of thought which emerged under the leadership of Mulla Muhammad Amin ibn Muhammad Sharif Astarabadi (d. 1624 or 1627). Reflecting the dependence on sacred scripture, and in particular the sayings of the imams, the encyclopaedia of traditions known as the *Biḥār al-Anwār* of Baqir Majlisi (d. 1699–1700), is the most salient example of the comprehensive nature of Akhbari thought. Majlisi's work assembled virtually all reports attributed to the imams, resulting in a collection that in its modern printing comes to 110 volumes and some forty-thousand pages.[106] This blanket coverage placed the hadith and narrations in a privileged position to the extent that it was only through these narrations that the Qur'an could be understood. The problem for modern scholars who emphasise rational scholarship is that the narrations included by Majlisi are representative of a time when extreme beliefs were prevalent in Shi'i circles. 'Ali Rahnema observes, 'Majlesi's *Bahar al-Anvar* certainly provides a very rich and diverse treasure chest of phantasmical, non-rational and superstitious accounts that has throughout time been injected into the Shi'i community.'[107]

The differences between the Akhbari school and the Usulis (who accepted rational argumentation as one of the four sources of law) has been discussed elsewhere and cannot be developed here. However, from the 19th century onwards, Usulis still felt the need to remind their followers of the dangers of Akhbari thought. One of the most critical opponents of the Akhbari thought in the 20th century was the aforementioned Shari'at-Sangalaji, whose attempts to advance a more rational version of Shi'i Islam were even criticised by Usuli scholars.[108]

---

106 Ali Rahnema, *Superstition as Ideology in Iranian Politics: From Majlesi to Ahmadinejad*, Cambridge 2011, 171.

107 Rahnema, *Superstition as Ideology*, 188.

108 Rahnema believes that Ayatollah Khomeini singled out Sangalaji (though not by name) in his work of 1944 entitled *Kashf al-Asrār*. See Rahnema, *Shi'i Reformation in Iran*, 37.

Shariʿat-Sangalaji was not alone in criticising the tendency to rely on spurious hadith and sayings of the imams.[109] Ahmad Kasravi (d. 1946), who had trained in the seminary before voluntarily defrocking, was not hesitant in expressing his opinion about the shortcomings of the Shiʿi tradition. In particular he referred to 'exaggerated fabrications' found in Shiʿi books related to matters of belief, and he argued that there had even been cases of additions of chapters and sentences to the Qurʾan.[110]

Shariʿat-Sangalaji and Kasravi were most likely reacting in part to the excesses they witnessed in Shiʿi thought, which was a legacy of the Akhbari tradition. Opposition to such a legacy continues even in the present day, typified in the thought of Ayatollah Sayyid Kamal Haydari (b. 1956). He believes that the existence of a large number of fabricated narrations among Shiʿis and Sunnis have brought about 'narrative rationality' (*ʿaqlāniyat-i ravāʾī*), which is not the same as Qurʾanic rationality. In the same breath he mentions the need to investigate Majlisi's *Biḥār al-Anwār* which has had a great influence on Shiʿi culture.[111] Kamal Haydari is also disturbed by the amount of 'Israʿiliyat' or stories deriving from non-Qurʾanic sources, such as those from ancient Jewish and Christian literature.[112]

The New Religious Thinkers have also pointed to the care that is needed to be taken with narrations. Ahmad Qabil considered himself an expert in the study of hadith – indeed he claimed to be among the best ten Iranian hadith scholars.[113] Qabil recognised many of the long-standing criticisms directed at hadith and narrations, and he acknowledged 'deviations' (*taʿrīf*), and forged narrations (*ravāyat-i majʿūla*),[114] while describing how it was necessary to 'review selected texts, popular among religious scholars, based upon common rationality of contemporary humans and upon contemporary scientific findings'.[115] A good example of such a text, not mentioned by Qabil, but which has been at the centre of much controversy is found in the *Nahj al-Balāgha*, commonly ascribed to Imam ʿAli, but which was collected and assembled by Sharif Razi (d. 1015) in the 10th century. The offending part of ʿAli's sermon advises, 'Do not consult women

109 For Shariʿat-Sangalaji's criticisms of Majlisi, see Rahnema, *Shiʿi Reformation in Iran*, 80, 82, 102–3, 142.

110 Ahmad Kasravi, 'Shiʿism', *On Islam and Shiʿism*, trans. M. R. Ghanoonparvar, Costa Mesa 1990, 149, 155, 157.

111 See Rahnema, *Superstition as Ideology in Iranian Politics*, 159–92.

112 See ews.com/fa/news/59325. This page had been removed since I last checked in July 2020.

113 Reported by Eshkevari in *Sharīʿat-i ʿAqlānī*, 276.

114 Qabil, *Sharīʿat-i ʿAqlānī*, 93.

115 Qabil, *Sharīʿat-i ʿAqlānī*, 93–4.

because their view is weak and their determination is unstable.' Ziba Mir-Hosseini has discussed this text with Soroush, whose talks in Tehran in 1992 focused on the passage in question.[116] Soroush recognised the problematic nature of the text, but responded to criticisms of it by saying that subsequent portions attempt to argue why women should not be consulted. Soroush explained, 'If Imam ʿAli reasons with us, he invites us to reason back, to use our critical faculties.'[117] He also pointed to a sharia principle that holds that maxims 'speak of their time and thus we need a reason for extending them to other societies or times'.[118] The same narration from *Nahj al-Balāgha* has been the subject of investigation by the New Religious Thinkers among the ulama.[119] Muhsin Kadivar cites this saying of Imam ʿAli in an article about women's rights, and he resolves the discriminatory nature of what he calls 'deserts-based' justice with a method that recalls the 'preparatory abrogation' that was discussed previously in relation to Ayatollah Maʿrifat. Kadivar advances the idea that Islam promoted women's rights, 'but not as far as full equality'. However, on the basis of the inherent qualities of justice and rationality that he witnesses in the Qurʾan, Kadivar concludes that the '[l]awgiver adopted a policy of gradualism to reach the desired conditions … deserts-based justice was the first half-step and egalitarian justice the second'.[120] In effect, Kadivar believes ʿAli's narration is an impermanent ruling and may be abrogated by Qurʾanic verses which describe the genderless nature of the single soul that is the 'origin of male and female humans'. He adds that human souls have duties and rights, the foundation for which is equality.[121]

The attempts of Soroush and Kadivar to interpret ʿAli's recommendation about not consulting with women fit squarely within Qabil's purview of material to be

116 Ziba Mir-Hosseini, *Islam and Gender: The Religious Debate in Contemporary Iran*, London 1999, 222–37.
117 Mir-Hosseini, *Islam and Gender*, 239.
118 Mir-Hosseini, *Islam and Gender*, 225.
119 A discussion on a very similar topic appears in the works of Mutahhari who discussed ʿAli's claim that women are lacking in faith. He rejected the simple acceptance of this claim by saying that deficient in faith in the time of ʿAli meant a deficiency in performing actions. As such then, women were not lacking in faith compared to men if faith is simply construed as confirming something in the heart. See Sareh Ardeshir Larijany, 'Mutaharri and His Approach to Women's Social Life', PhD submitted to University of Birmingham, July 2020, 103.
120 Muhsin Kadivar, 'Revisiting Women's Rights in Islam: "Egalitarian Justice" in Lieu of "Desert-based Justice"', *Gender and Equality in Muslim Family Law: Justice and Ethics in the Islamic Legal Tradition*, ed. Ziba Mir-Hosseini, Lena Larsen, Christian Moe and Kari Vogt, London 2013, 227.
121 Kadivar, 'Revisiting women's rights in Islam', 226.

re-assessed, even if such narrations are deemed appropriate by 'traditional' and eminent scholars of the modern period such as ʿAllama Tabatabaʾi (d. 1981).[122] And just as inappropriate narrations must be re-assessed, material that has long been forgotten and left unseen must be brought into the daylight. What might have been considered incompatible with previous generations may be well-suited in the contemporary age.[123] In fact, Qabil's attempt at re-evaluating narrations should be seen in the context of his wider efforts to reform jurisprudence through ethics, which is grounded on reason. Humans of a sound mind should be allowed greater freedoms to choose:

> Narrations from the infallible [imams] (peace be upon them) have stated that Muslims have three approaches to narrations … 1). acceptance; 2) not putting into practice the narration (*imtināʿ*); 3) [outright] rejection. Of course, it has been recommended that [Muslims] prohibit rejection and permit acceptance or not putting into practice. In other words, each Muslim has the right to accept the narration from the Prophet of God or from the imams, and to act on that. Or the Muslim [does] not accept it and does not act on it. [But] the only thing that has been considered forbidden is the non-scholarly rejection of narrations.[124]

Ijmāʿ and Reason

The third source of law within Islamic jurisprudence is consensus (*ijmāʿ*), which traditionally is the agreement of all scholars on a specific ruling. Ahmad Qabil considers the understanding of traditional Shiʿi scholars of the concept of *ijmāʿ* as a proof for deducing law behind the Qurʾan, Sunna and sayings and example of the imams.[125] However, his own formulation of the concept raises it from its comparatively low status to one that is on a par with sacred scripture. *Ijmāʿ* was not an issue of concern as long as an imam was alive to offer guidance to the community, but the situation changed with the occultation of the Twelfth Imam in 941CE. Henceforth it fell to the learned scholars to offer their views on topics that demanded attention, and their answers could only represent the probable will of the Hidden Imam. And with the institutionalisation and increasing centralisation

122 The description and assessment are Kadivar's. See his 'Revisiting women's rights in Islam', 218.
123 Qabil, *Sharīʿat-i ʿAqlānī*, 95.
124 Qabil, *Sharīʿat-i ʿAqlānī*, 85–6.
125 Qabil, *Mabānī-yi Sharīʿat* [*Foundations of the Sharia*], 248.

of the system of such learning, the practice of following a learned, living scholar (or *marjaʿ taqlīd*) became established in Shiʿi societies. Over time seminarians made claims to *ijmāʿ* that conflicted with strong rational and narrated proofs, and they issued fatwas opposing reliable proofs, the only basis for which was the 'proof' of *ijmāʿ* itself. In this sense, according to Qabil, *ijmāʿ* became a very conservative tool that did not respond to changing circumstances. And rather than issuing relevant fatwas, many jurists responded cautiously, reconfirming the out-dated status quo. Ahmad Qabil quoted the view of Mutahhari,

> The tendency in humans to conform is very strong. Among the jurists this problem is [also] strong. One jurist produces an inference on a case, but he does not have the bravery to express it. He goes and looks to find whether there are like-minded jurists of [his] time with the same opinion. There are few jurists who after going and looking and [finding] that no-one has said the same thing, have the bravery to declare their fatwas. In other words, the jurist is scared when he sees he is alone on the path.[126]

Qabil played on the same theme in his chapter on *ijmāʿ* in *Mabānī-yi Sharīʿat*, arguing:

> A study and critique of the *faqīh*s' understanding is required since their well-known approaches or their consensual opinions on some subjects do not conform to scientific and empirical human approaches. Contemporary human rationality does not see the benefit of some of [their] approaches, and the waste of time and resources on a path [where] the wise are forgotten, the product of which does not attain its aim, is a futile endeavour.[127]

The well-known approach mentioned above refers to the jurists' penchant for caution (*iḥtiyāṭ*),[128] which has been discussed by a number of New Religious

---

126 Qabil, *Mabānī-yi Sharīʿat*, 248, citing Ayatollah Mutahhari, *Taʿlīm va Tarbīyat*, 285. He cites the same passage in *Sharīʿat-i ʿAqlānī*, 87–8.
127 Qabil, *Mabānī-yi Sharīʿat*, 249.
128 See Vikør Knut, *Between God and the Sultan: A History of Islamic Law*, London 2005, 133; Oliver Leaman claims that Shaykh Ansari (d. 1864) was instrumental in consolidating the practice of caution within contemporary Shiʿi jurisprudence. See his article 'Ansari, Murtada bin Muhammad Amin', *The Biographical Encyclopaedia of Islamic Philosophy*, ed. Oliver Leaman, London 2015. For an examination of caution (or doubt) in the Shiʿi tradition, see Intisar A. Rabb, *Doubt in Islamic Law: A History of Legal Maxims, Interpretation, and Islamic Criminal Law*, Cambridge 2015, 260–315. Rabb discusses two groups that she calls

Thinkers. Kadivar criticises those jurists who lean towards traditional interpretations, commenting on how '[t]raditional *fiqh* is very cautious', typified by jurists who have reservations about reaching definitive conclusions even if these would accord with the decisions of the Hidden Imam, based on rational analysis.[129] But the importance of Qabil's observations, as outlined above, lie in the recognition that *ijmāʿ* has the potential to be a dynamic tool that can respond to modern challenges. His own understanding of *ijmāʿ* in fact departs from the traditional view that limited its role behind the Qurʾan and Sunna, and the sayings and examples of the Imams. He stated,

> Of course, a point that must not be put to one side is the possible connection in the debate about *ijmāʿ* with the way of reasonable people (*sīra-yi ʿuqalā*). If someone considers the 'validity of the way of reasonable people' as the foundation for the validity of *ijmāʿ*, and proposes *ijmāʿ* as 'justification for the way of reasonable people', it is possible to make [the connection between] the subject of discussion and study, and examine all of its angles.[130]

What is interesting in the quote above is how Qabil linked *ijmāʿ* (which in the Usuli tradition has traditionally been the preserve of the jurists) with the wider

the rationalists and traditionalists. She concludes, 'In criminal law, rationalist and traditionalist approaches to interpretation revealed thoroughly informed conceptions about the scope of human discretion to resolve doubt in this most contentious area of law. These different approaches resulted in a back-and-forth between stances favouring punishment avoidance based on the recognition of doubt and those favouring enforcement out of strict adherence to understandings of foundational texts', 312.

129 Kadivar, 'Human rights and intellectual Islam', 59. Typifying this tendency for caution in decision making is Al-Shaykh al-Ansari (d. 1864) who was one of the most eminent 19th-century jurists and who divided his major work, *Farāʾiż al-Uṣūl* into three epistemological sections (certainty, opinion and doubt). As Gleave notes, 'The emphasis is firmly on the unobtainability of knowledge,' and the aim of *fiqh* for him became how people fulfil their obligations to God (carrying out precepts) rather than finding out God's law. See Robert Gleave, 'Imami Shiʿi Legal Theory', *The Oxford Handbook of Islamic Law*, ed. Anver M. Emon and Rumee Ahmed, Oxford 2018, 18–19 of vol. 25. Momen makes the following assessment of Ansari's contribution to *fiqh*: 'Whereas previously the mujtahids had restricted themselves to ruling on points where there was the probability or certainty of being in accordance with the guidance of the imams, the rules developed by Ansari allowed them to extend the area of their jurisdiction to any matter where there was even a possibility of being in accordance with the imam's guidance. This effectively meant that they could issue verdicts on virtually any subject. Ansari's own strict exercise of *iḥtiyāṭ* (prudent caution) severely restricted this freedom but other mujtahids allowed themselves a freer hand.' Moojan Momen, *An Introduction to Shiʿi Islam*, New Haven 1985, 187.

130 Qabil, *Mabānī-yi Sharīʿat*, 251.

domain of the reasonable people who are composed not simply of jurists, but include non-seminarians. The topic of *sīra-yi ʿuqalā* has been understudied by academics in the West,[131] while it has been a hermeneutical tool among the seminarians for some time and was utilised by Muhammad Husayn Tabatabaʾi (d. 1981).[132] A number of seminarians, including Tabatabaʾi and Qabil, believed that *sīra-yi ʿuqalā* was a tool that did not refer only to the wise in the generation of the Prophet's community, whose customs and tradition were endorsed and verified by Qurʾanic revelation. Rather, the *sīra-yi ʿuqalā* referred to the way of the reasonable people in subsequent generations. For the New Religious Thinkers, some Qurʾanic commands are known as *imżāʾī*, or validating commands, because they sanction Jewish or Christian practices, or those practices that had been agreed upon by the reasonable people. Such validating commands reflected the levels of reason among the wise at the time. [133] Qabil maintained,

> The main reason for the validation of those commands was the spread and circulation of those methods among the wise people in Arabian society or among the Meccans and Medinans … To use another expression, Islam's commands of validation are 'customary commands' (*aḥkām-i ʿurfī*) because they witnessed the rational power of humans of that time.[134]

The *sīra-yi ʿuqalā* has been considered 'normative' and it carries weight for the reason given by Muhammad Baqir Sadr, who referred to it in the following manner: 'The universal practice of the human race in a particular matter is evidence unless there has been a RULING to the contrary from an INFALLIBLE PERSON.'[135] The crucial point here is the conditional application of the *sīra-yi ʿuqalā*, and as Takim points out: 'In Shiʿi legal theory, the concept of the conduct of reasonable

131 An exception is found in the works of Liyakat Takim. See his 'Custom as a Legal Principle of Legislation for Shiʿi Law', *Studies in Religion/Sciences Religieuses* 47.4, 2018, 481–99. See also his 'Privileging the Qur'an: Divorce and the Hermeneutics of Yusuf Saniʿi', *Approaches to the Qurʾan in Contemporary Iran*, ed. Alessandro Cancian, Oxford 2019, 89. Takim shows how the concept of *sīra-yi ʿuqalā* has been used by Saniʿi to establish a way whereby a woman can legally initiate a divorce from her husband.

132 Seyfeddin Kara, 'Rational-analytical Tafsīr in Modern Iran: The Influence of the Uṣūlī School of Jurisprudence on the Interpretation of the Qurʾan', *Approaches to the Qurʾan in Contemporary Iran,* ed. Alessandro Cancian, Oxford 2019, 29–31.

133 Muhammad Baqir al-Sadr, *Lessons in Islamic Jurisprudence*, trans. Roy Parviz Mottahedeh, Oxford 2005, 222.

134 Qabil, *Sharīʿat-i ʿAqlānī*, 78.

135 al-Sadr, *Lessons in Islamic Jurisprudence*, 124. (The capitalisation is included in the original text.)

people replaces the need for a written text and becomes a binding sunna *if there are no textual proofs that repudiate a particular mode of behaviour*.'[136] However, the New Religious Thinkers like Qabil and Kadivar differ on the understanding of the way of reasonable people, by extending it to times after those of the Prophet in order to dispense with the need to apply the principle only in the absence of written texts. Qabil's understanding, however, is worth considering at this point:

> There is no reason that we should consider 'human rational power in the present age' to be out with the commands in the Muhammadan [divine] law, and that we should be content with 'stiff outer appearances'.[137]

The application of the *sīra-yi ʿuqalā* as a means to respond to new circumstances, thereby placing it on a par with *ijmāʿ*, is a method that opens extensive discussions that previously had solely been in the domain of the seminarians. Not all scholars agree that *sīra-yi ʿuqalā* may be an appropriate jurisprudential method for the contemporary age, and some have argued that the *sīra-yi ʿuqalā* pertains only to the time of the Prophet and the infallible imams.[138] Kadivar seems to acknowledge this, noting that in traditional jurisprudence, the way of reasonable people has been interpreted as unchanging and stable.[139] However, he considers that the current way of reasonable people can justify the abrogation of legal commands (*ḥukm-i sharʿī*) and explain their time-bound and historical nature, the relevance and application of which has come to an end.[140] He cites the specific examples of slavery, treatment of women and cruel punishments that modern reasonable thinking rejects. Kadivar outlines a significant point: 'One of the clear points [showing] the difference of historical Islam and New-Thinking Islam is the opposition of the way of reasonableness (contemporary, not having precedent at the beginning of Islam) with the validating commands of the beginning of Islam.'[141] Put plainly, the New Religious Thinkers foreground reason and its application

136 Takim, 'Privileging the Qur'an: Divorce and the Hermeneutics of Yusuf Saniʿi', 89. (The italics are mine.)
137 Qabil, *Sharīʿat-i ʿAqlānī*, 78.
138 M. Alipour, 'Shiʿi a neo-traditionalist scholars and theology of homosexuality: review and reflections on Muhsin Kadivar's shifting approach', *Theology and Sexuality* 24.3, 2018, 214, n. 39.
139 Kadivar, 'Pursish va pāsukh-i ḥuqūq-i bashr va rawshanfkikrī-yi dīnī' [Question and answer about human rights and the religious intellectuals], 1387/2008, https://kadivar.com/1066 1387/2008.
140 Kadivar, 'Pursish va pāsukh-i ḥuqūq-i bashar va rawshanfkikrī-yi dīnī'.
141 Kadivar, 'Pursish va pāsukh-i ḥuqūq-i bashar va rawshanfkikrī-yi dīnī'.

to Qur'anic verses and abrogation, and this is the basis for an ethical imperative in making religious decisions,[142] hence raising the status of *ijmā'* from being an influential source of law-making (behind the Qur'an and Sunna and sayings and examples of the imams) and the way of reasonable people to a legitimate mode of authority in its own right, enjoying parity, perhaps even with priority, over the other sources.

For the New Religious Thinkers law must be based on reason, which may then be understood as *ijtihād*. Mutahhari defended *ijtihād* as 'putting in utmost effort in discovering the laws of the sharia from its reliable sources'.[143] In another work he associated *ijtihād* with reason; 'the employment of careful consideration and reasoning in reaching an understanding of the valid proofs of the sharia.'[144]

Even before the Islamic Revolution there were attempts to modernise the seminary and to make *ijtihād* more relevant to the everyday life of believers. In the early 1970s, Mutahhari pointed to the general perception that *ijtihād* was limited to arcane and abstruse matters such as whether believers had to take one or two handfuls of earth when performing *tayammum*.[145] He insisted that such issues were of no major importance, and that jurists should instead focus on topics that

142 Qabil, *Mabāni-yi Sharī'at*, 189.
143 Murtaza Mutahhari, *The Role of Ijtihad in Legislation*, trans. Mahliqa Qara'i, https://www.al-islam.org/al-tawhid/vol4-n2/role-ijtihad-legislation-ayatullah-murtadha-mutahhari.
144 Murtaza Mutahhari, *The Principle of Ijtihad in Islam*, trans. John Cooper, https://www.al-islam.org/al-serat/vol-10-no-1/principle-ijtihad-islam-ayatullah-murtadha-mutahhari. Reason and *ijtihād* are the distinguishing features of the Usuli school which sets it apart from the Akhbaris within the Shi'i jurisprudential tradition. Usulis look back to the very early history of Shi'i doctrine and theory, and such jurists foreground the application of reason and justice in discovering law. This is due to the belief that Imam 'Ali and subsequent imams were deprived of their 'legitimate' right to lead the Islamic community, and denying the imams their right (i.e. giving them justice) can only be comprehended with the criterion of reason to distinguish between right and wrong. This emphasis on reason and justice dovetailed with the emerging school of the Mu'tazila among the Sunnis who emphasised these two attributes for other reasons related to their rational and systematic theological perspective of an allegorical interpretation of the 'anthropological' verses of the Qur'an. Shi'i beliefs are often considered to be aligned closer to Mu'tazilite thinking than other Sunni perspectives, such as the Ash'arite, which focuses in general upon God's power and ability rather than justice. (The literature on Mu'tazili thinking is vast. Good surveys include W. Montgomery Watt, *The Formative Period of Islamic Thought*, Oxford 1988. A modern take on the Mu'tazilis is offered in Richard C. Martin, Mark R. Woodward and Dwi S. Atmaja, *Defenders of Reason in Islam*, Oxford 1997.) The New Religious Thinkers frequently mention the Mu'tazilite school with approbation (see for example, Kadivar, 'Human rights and intellectual Islam', 50; Qabil, *Sharī'at-i 'Aqlānī*, 90).
145 *Tayammum* is the practice of using dry sand or earth for performing ablutions in place of water.

were new and original.[146] Yet despite this, Mutahhari's works also demonstrated the kind of conservatism within jurisprudential circles which is apparent in a discussion about the command for abstaining from consuming pork.[147] He outlined that some Islamic commands have no cause or reason given in the Qur'an, and so the *faqīh* is obliged to deduce a cause. He was reluctant to accept the argument that the definite rational cause for the prohibition on eating pork was the existence of tapeworms, and he asked rhetorically if this was the only reason for observing the prohibition on consuming pork, or if perhaps there was another reason. He assumed that there would be doubt and hesitancy in the answer, and so he argued rather defensively:

> We cannot find fault with today's *faqīh* when you say [to him], 'Reason is a proof based on deduction, so [in light of] today's discoveries why do you not give a fatwa permitting [the consumption] of pork?' He replies, 'We ask reason, "Oh reason! Oh learning! Do you have definite proof (*dalīl*) that other than this there is nothing else, and nothing will be discovered in the future?"' Or he says, 'We have discovered this now, perhaps there may also be something else.'[148]

It is worth pointing out that the New Religious Thinkers have traditionally been shy of applying their ethical and rationalising worldviews to the domain of worship and its rituals (such as the five daily prayers). And laws of food and drink are a part of the laws on worship, but Mutahhari did not frame his rejection of consuming pork on this principle. Instead it was simply based on the 'inadequacy' of reason, which in the passage above is hardly convincing. Had he framed the argument around reason and the rituals of worship he might have been able to offer a firmer argument. Mutahhari's deference to reason-based future discoveries, giving due respect to caution, smacks of a defensive and conservative jurisprudential position, one that he himself argued against in other places, and one of which the New Religious Thinkers too were highly critical, despite their obvious attachment and affection for Mutahhari himself.

146 Mutahhari, *Islām va Muqtażiyāt-i Zamān*, 233.
147 The command not to consume pork is of course a very serious one for Muslims. It is not an arcane issue, and to understand how large it looms for many Muslims one can point to the sepoy 'Mutiny' in India in 1857, which was supposedly triggered by the introduction of cartridges which were greased with lard (pig fat), and the Indian soldiers had to bite open the lard-lined package to get access to the cartridge.
148 Ibid., 57.

In any case, the tendency to be cautious among the ulama was also challenged by Khomeini in 1988, just before he died, when he insisted on the exercise of *maṣlaḥat*, or expediency, in promoting and implementing the policies of Islamic government.[149] The extent to which Khomeini considered the government had the legitimacy to exercise *maṣlaḥat* resulted in his public declaration that government could even enforce laws that could temporarily cause the non-observance of some Islamic duties:

> I must declare that government is a branch of the absolute governance of God's Prophet; it is one of the primary commands of Islam. It has priority over all derivative commands (*aḥkām-i furū'ī*), even prayer, fasting and hajj. The ruler can destroy a mosque or a building in the path of a road, and he may compensate the owner of the building. The ruler can close a mosque at a necessary time and he can [even] destroy it in cases where the harm is in not destroying it. The government can annul legal treatises that it has made with the people in situations when those treatises oppose the welfare (*maṣāliḥ*) of the country and Islam. It can prevent any action, whether based on worship or non-worship, the performance of which opposes the welfare of Islam. The government can temporarily stop hajj, which is one of the divine and important duties in situations that it considers against the welfare of the Islamic country.[150]

Some have seen the principle of *maṣlaḥat* as contradicting traditional Shi'i jurisprudential methods.[151] This is because it seems to override the explicit and specific

149 'But in an Islamic government, the gate of *ijtihād* must be open, and the nature of the revolution and the regime always necessitates the free expression of *ijtihādī*-juristic judgements on different topics even if they oppose one another. No-one has the ability and right to prevent this. But it is important for the correct understanding of government and society that on the basis of this, the Islamic order can [establish] a programme for the welfare of the Muslims that [promotes] unity of conduct and necessary action. Because of this the current *ijtihād* in the seminaries is insufficient, indeed, if there is one person, the most knowledgeable in the customary sciences of the seminaries, but who cannot discern the best interest (*maṣlaḥat*) of society, or cannot discern a good and useful person from an unsound one, and in general, lacks correct insight and power of decision-making on social and political matters, [then] this person is not a *mujtahid* on social and governmental matters and he cannot take the reins of society' (See Khomeini, *Ṣaḥīfa-yi Imām,* vol. 21, 177–80).

150 Khomeini, *Ṣaḥīfa-yi Imām*, vol. 20, 450–1.

151 Godfrey Jansen, 'Khomeini's heretical delusion of grandeur', *Middle East International* 317, 1988, 18–19. Jansen states that Khomeini's ideas have 'no basis whatsoever in the Qur'an and [there] is an artificial construct by Khomeini which he tailored to fit his own personal ambitions'.

rulings of the Qur'an and Sunna. Traditionally *maṣlaḥat*, *ijtihād* and the use of reason are exercised when a clear ruling from the Qur'an or the Sunna is unavailable. Khomeini's view has been endorsed by the New Religious Thinkers from the perspective that it permits a ruling to be abrogated if it contravenes justice and the way of reasonable and rational people and the general ethical spirit of Islam, and it has opened wide interpretive strategies which in practice obviate the paramount standing of scripture over reason and its supports.[152] However, his views have also been criticised because first, the new rational ruling can only be temporary, not permanent, and when the 'crisis' has been resolved, the old ruling must be reaffirmed. Second, the *fiqh* of *maṣlaḥat* appears to give the ruling *faqīh* too much power at the expense of the opinions of other *faqīhs*.

In contrast to criticisms of Khomeini's use of *maṣlaḥat*, it should also be considered that from the perspective of justice and reason, his arguments for the application of *maṣlaḥat* have the potential to correspond with the 'spirit of Islam'. Indeed, Khomeini's declaration of 1988 was not the innovation it is generally assumed to be, as he was hardly the first of the modern generation of ulama to discuss the need for applying *maṣlaḥat*. Mutahhari had argued that in the absence of specific Qur'anic and Sunna based guidance, the command of reason (*ḥukm-i ʿaql*) discovers either the expediency (*maṣlaḥat*) or corruption (*mafsada*) in an action.[153]

Despite the attempts by some of the ulama to foreground reason and *maṣlaḥat* and a progressive form of *ijtihād*, some academics speak of the 'failure of *ijtihād*'.[154] This is because it was formulated in the medieval era and it cannot respond to modern circumstances. For example, the Canadian based Shiʿi scholar, Liakat Takim blames the textual nature of *fiqh*, and although he acknowledges that reason is included as an independent source of law, he claims that 'it is hardly ever invoked to generate new laws when the other sources fail to produce an effective ruling'. He also points to the failure of Shiʿi ulama to utilise other devises that Sunnis use like analogy, *maṣlaḥat*, *maqāṣid al-sharīʿa*, and *istislāḥ*. The textual basis for Shiʿi *fiqh* is of course understandable, especially as the reports from and about the imams provide the essence of Shiʿi identity. Undermining these sources robs the Shiʿi ulama of their legitimacy to comprehend the probable will of the Hidden Imam, and it also strips them of their identity vis-à-vis Sunni

152 See, for example, Kadivar, 'From traditional Islam to Islam as an end in itself'.
153 Mutahhari, *Islām va Muqtażiyāt-i Zamān*, 37.
154 Liyakat Takim, 'Islamic Law and Post-Ijtihadism', unpublished paper, 3 (See http://www.ltakim.com/Post-Islamism.pdf).

ulama. And despite the warnings given by Khomeini and Mutahhari about the need to examine contemporary issues, Takim argues that current legal treatises do not discuss issues such as 'human rights, the ecology, social welfare, justice, forms of government, … unemployment, [and] bio-medical ethics' and preference is given to 'topics like *kurr* (the amount of water that is required to purify an object), [and] details of distance traveled to pray *qasr* (shortened prayers)'.[155] Takim's analysis also calls into question Rouhani's 'liberal, progressive and broad minded' methods to determine law. However, Takim recognises that the growing body of reformist scholars is beginning to question the stereotype. In addition to the limited number of New Religious Thinkers included in this chapter as exemplars of this tendency, he mentions Ayatollah Saniʿi, Ibrahim Jannati, Muhaqqiq Damad, Mahdi Shams al-Din and Muhsin Saʿidzada as advocates of a new form of jurisprudence.[156] The establishment of the Islamic Republic has not resulted in a dramatic change on many social issues. Interestingly, Ahmad Qabil provides a list of thirty-one contemporary social issues on which he thinks discussions should take place (see Part Three). While *fiqh* clearly has the potential to blossom through employing a range of methodologies suggested by the New Religious Thinkers, in practice it is still embedded in traditional ways of thinking. And it is not just academics like Takim who see the crisis in *fiqh*. The New Religious Thinkers too, as demonstrated above, argue that the problem is deep-rooted, reflected in a reluctance to engage with rational thinking to its full extent. The views of Eshkevari are representative in this respect:

> We know that in Shiʿi jurisprudence, from the fifth century (13th century) onwards, reason was one of the four proofs of *ijtihād*, but there have been various thoughts and ideas about the definition and boundaries of rationality in the programme of jurisprudence and *ijtihād* (the kind of relation between reason and narration). In general, one can say that … human reason was not accorded much credit in the *ijtihād* of the Shiʿi *mujhtahid*. When the noble principle of '*ijtihād of the sacred text is forbidden*' was accepted, in practice, rationality and argumentation based upon reason and independent human wisdom lost currency and authority (*ʿitibār va ḥujjiyat*).[157]

155 Takim, 'Islamic Law and Post-Ijtihadism', 6–7.

156 Takim, 'Islamic Law and Post-Ijtihadism', 9.

157 Eshkevari, 'Qabil, shahrvand-i mudirn-i mūʾmin-i musalmān būd' [Qabil was a modern, believing Muslim citizen], 28 October 2012. Contained in Qabil, *Yād-nāma*, 466.

Likewise Muhsin Kadivar appears exasperated by the observation of the most senior Iraqi Shiʿi scholar, Sayyid Muhammad Baqir Sadr, who commented about his fatwa handbook: 'I did not use reason, although I believe in it, because after sufficient verbal sources, I do not need it at all.'[158]

Conclusion

The call to reform jurisprudence is not a recent phenomenon in Iran. However, in recent years the scale and scope of such demands has increased. Exemplifying this trend is the work of Muhammad Mujtahid-Shabistari who has lamented that the realm of juristic commands is limited to the kinds of arcane questions that are included in the practical treatises (*risāla-hā-yi ʿamaliya*) and 'explanation of problems' (*tawżīḥ al-masāʾil*).[159] Shabistari's views of jurisprudence and jurists are typical of many of the New Religious Thinkers, who desire reform and restructuring, but at the same time are aware of the need to preserve the jurisprudential heritage and its role of guiding believers in the performance of correct behaviour (albeit with a wider circle of specialists).[160]

Over the past century there have been calls for reform, and the urgency of such demands is reflected in the approaches advocated by the New Religious Thinkers.

158 Muhsin Kadivar, 'Ijtihad in Usul al-Figh: Reforming Islamic Thought through Structural Ijtihad', *Iran Nameh* 30.3, 2015, xxvi.

159 *Risāla-ya ʿamaliya* is a 'practical treatise' produced by a senior *ʿalim*, and which contains his fatwas. For the importance of this *risāla* in becoming a senior *ʿalim*, see Linda Walbridge, 'The counter reformation: Becoming a Marjaʿ in the modern world', *The Most Learned of the Shia: The Institution of the Marjaʿ Taqlid*, ed. Linda Walbridge, Oxford 2001, 231–2. Likewise, the *tawżīḥ al-masāʾil* genre contains the fatwas of leading ulama in which the general contents or themes are fixed. For an example of such a work, see Ruhollah Khomeini, *A Clarification of Questions: An Unabridged Translation of Resaleh Towzih Al-Masael*, trans. J. Borujerdi, London 1984. The forward to this work summarises the genre, see Michael M. J. Fischer and Mehdi Abedi, 'Forward', ix–xxvii. The relevance of such works to modern Iranians, to which Shabistari alludes, may be witnessed in the kinds of fatwas included in Khomeini's work. Consider the following: 'If a fly gets into the throat of one who is fasting it is not necessary to pull it out in case that it goes down so far that the swallowing of it is not called eating, and his fast is correct. But if it does not go down by that amount he must take it out even if it causes vomiting and voids the fast. And if swallowed, his fast becomes void and he must, as an obligatory caution, practice a cumulative expiation', 219.

160 Qabil talks of establishing a think-tank and engaging specialists in humanities, which is mentioned in Part Three. He castigates the juristic practice of being too cautious in giving fatwas, and following the opinions of other jurists. Kadivar balances criticisms of traditional *fiqh* ('Human right and intellectual Islam', 71), with the need for a 'new' jurisprudence to be led by suitably qualified jurists ('Human right and intellectual Islam', 73).

This chapter has demonstrated how the New Religious Thinkers have advanced a series of reform programmes, by focusing on the following: assessing the suitability of Qur'anic verses with modern circumstances (looking at the diversity in the types of verses, abrogation, *aḥkām* and the nature of revelation); reviewing the authenticity of the Sunna and the sayings of the Prophet and imams; and the foregrounding of *ijmāʿ* and reason as the criteria to determine the *maqāṣid al-sharīʿa*, exercising *maṣlaḥat*. In short, the following approach of Ayatollah Saniʿi typifies the methods used by the New Religious Thinkers:

> In the works of Ayatullah Saanei [sic], one observes a major epistemological shift in the Twelver Shiʿi theory by privileging the Qur'an, empowering reason as a legitimate source to discover the rationale or *ratio legis* of a legal directive and mindful that legal rulings were issued based on a particular concept of time (*zamān*) and space (*makān*) and, as such, lack universal applicability for all times and places.[161]

But there are also differences among the New Religious Thinkers. For example, Shabistari's views about Muhammad's active involvement of the revelatory process has not elicited great support among the New Religious ulama, indeed the response has been very muted, suggesting that it is regarded as problematic. It is fair to conclude that the sheer breadth, range and daring of the New Religious Thinking among the ulama is breathtaking, and to say that some of these ideas are radical is an understatement. Ahmad Qabil's use of reason and *ijmāʿ*, for example, follows in a long line of ulama who have stressed the role of reason. But Qabil stood the four sources of *fiqh* on their head by situating reason, *sīra-yi ʿuqalā* and rational *ijmāʿ* as principles that were equal to, if not more significant than both the sayings of the Prophet and the imams, and also the Qur'an. Eshkevari and Kadivar too hold very similar views about the rationality of the commands and how these must be filtered through a rational lens.

Indeed, the stress that some of the ulama among the New Religious Thinkers place upon reason and justice in their thought implicitly questions the very nature, the necessity and sufficiency of traditional Shiʿi thought in their reforms. The concern for some is that this reliance on reason and justice is not specific to Shiʿi worldview, but may be equally and enthusiastically embraced by secularists. Seminarians such as Kadivar are wary that the non-seminarian perspective

161 Mavani, 'Paradigm Shift in Twelver Shiʿi Legal Theory', 341.

of thinkers such as Soroush smacks too keenly of relativism.[162] The ulama among the New Religious Thinkers, however, ensure that their ideals and methods are not mistaken for secular doctrines, and their methodologies are frequently clothed with Shiʿi references and traditional Shiʿi methods.

This chapter has demonstrated how the New Religious Thinkers have employed tools to offer what some may consider a flexible and progressive sharia. The following parts in this book take the hijab as a case-study to illustrate this claim. The views of only three seminarians are contained in detail in the following chapters, but they demonstrate the breadth of seminarian thinking, and how they have responded to the concept of 'time and place'. Thus, Mutahhari, although writing a generation before the New Religious Thinkers, not only paved the way for rethinking the hijab, but he also established the groundwork for a new seminarian hermeneutics. Although his views on the hijab appear conservative – he considers the hijab compulsory – in his time his argumentation for its use in society was a cause of great unease among 'traditional' seminarians. The second thinker considered in this book, Ahmad Qabil, utilised traditional practices but came up with the view that the hijab was merely desirable. And Muhsin Kadivar offers

162 Kadivar criticises Soroush's ideas about revelation (*vaḥī*) being the product of Muhammad's experiences and his dreams. See 'Nukātī darbāra-yi mubāḥith-i vaḥī-yi pazhūhān-i akhīr' [Some points about the controversy of revelation by recent researchers], 17 March 2008, https://kadivar.com/2995; see also 'Tāʾamulī dar-bāra-yi vaḥī' [Reflections on Revelation], 14 May 2017, https://kadivar.com/15964. Kadivar's rejection of Soroush's reforms are long standing, typified by a debate between the two in 1999. At issue is the starting point of reform. For Kadivar it is *fiqh*, whereas Soroush refuses to contemplate this, basing his ideas on philosophy, ethics, and *ʿirfān*. The differences between the two are a recurrent theme in Naser Ghobadzadeh, *Religious Secularity*. In addition, Kadivar seems to have held that Soroush's position fostered relativism, as he remarked in 1999:

> What I wanted to show is that believing in antinomies in religious matters is incompatible with the core of our Shiʿi beliefs. Also, when we speak of the text it isn't true that all parts of the text have many interpretations. Some do but one cannot argue that all verses do. It is not possible to beat everything in the Book and Sunna with the same stick of inextricable ambiguity *(ibhām-e nāzudūdanī*). To be able to say that everything in Islam is a text and that, as a result, it can be read multiple ways just opens the door to absolute relativism.

See Banafsheh Madaninejad, 'New Theology in the Islamic Republic of Iran: A Comparative Study between Abdolkarim Soroush and Mohsen Kadivar', PhD thesis, submitted at the University of Texas at Austin, 2011, 119. This thesis has been placed on Kadivar's website. See https://en.kadivar.com/2011/08/09/new-theology-in-the-islamic-republic-of-iran-a-comparative-study-between-abdolkarim-soroush-and-mohsen-kadivar/. Put more succinctly, at one point Kadivar warned Soroush not to move from 'the plurality in the comprehension of the truth to the plurality of truth itself' and 'from critical realism to absolute relativism'. See Behrooz Ghamari-Tabrizi, *Islam and Dissent*, 234.

a more 'radical' understanding that the Qur'an does not argue for the adoption of the hijab, instead it advocates for general modesty, and therefore the hijab is neither compulsory nor desirable. The views of other seminarian thinkers discussed in Part One (in this chapter), such as Eshkevari and Shabistari, have not been included in the rest of the book, because their views on the hijab have either been considered elsewhere (as is the case of Eshkevari) or they have not produced any systematic and lengthy discussion on the topic.

Part 2

HIJAB AS MANDATORY (*VĀJIB*): THE VIEWS OF MURTAZA MUTAHHARI

2

The Hijab in Iran from Pre-Modern Times to the 1960s

Introduction

Head-covering, or more specifically head-hair covering, in Iran is generally known under the term 'hijab', and often in contemporary times it is effected with a scarf and sometimes with a '*chādur*' which is an all-enveloping cloak that is thrown over the head and wrapped around the body. It is unfortunate that in the jurisprudential and academic literature (Western and Iranian) concerning head-hair covering, the term has been, and is, rather vague and ambiguous. Indeed, the word 'hijab' does not appear in the Qur'an in the sense of a head-covering. Ayatollah Murtaza Mutahhari admitted: 'I do not know the reason why the terms *hijab* and *purda* and *purdagī* (seclusion) became widespread in the current age in place of the common juristic expressions, in other words, *sitr* and *pūshish*.'[1] Whilst the term 'hijab' has become common parlance since the Islamic Revolution of 1978–9, denoting a simple head-covering, prior to these years the practice of covering included the face, the neck and the body. The varieties of Iranian face- and head-covering from pre-modern times until the 1960s are illustrated in this chapter. The ambiguity of the word 'hijab' as used in this chapter is intentional, referring to both the generic notion of covering, and also the specific sense of head-hair covering. This ambiguity is intended to demonstrate the usage of nineteenth- and early twentieth-century writings on the topic.

The hijab has been an element of female apparel in Iran for many centuries, although the reasons for its use, whether it was specific to certain regions, or if it was adopted among certain classes of women, or among urban as opposed to rural

1 Murtaza Mutahhari, *Mas'ala-yi Ḥijāb*, Tehran 1348/1969, 76.

women, requires a survey more extensive than that offered in this chapter. Yet it is clear from looking at a variety of pre-modern sources that it was customary for many Iranian women to wear not only the hijab in front of *nā-maḥram* individuals (i.e. those with whom it was possible to marry), but there are frequent references to *niqāb*s (face veils), as well as coverings that shrouded the whole of the head and face. It would seem that Iranians considered wearing the hijab, and varieties thereof, as normative, and it was not until the emergence of European powers in the region that alternative discourses appeared. At the same time, the development of Babism, an indigenous religious tradition in Iran in the nineteenth century, gave rise to different views related to hijab.[2] Thus, by the turn of the twentieth century, questions relating to the hijab were being posed by those who considered the old traditions as backward, hindering the progress of Iran in the quest to establish a modern nation state.

The first part of this chapter fleshes out some of the themes mentioned above, subsequently focusing on the sartorial reforms carried out by Riza Shah, who famously instigated the compulsory unveiling of women in 1936, and reflects on the basis for the support or general unpopularity of the policy. While the directive on unveiling was not observed or enforced after the abdication of Riza Shah in 1941, the general trend among the ulama was to advocate modesty and strict Islamic clothing, which was typified in the most popular of all modern Islamic treatises on the topic, that of the aforementioned Mutahhari. Thus, chapter two will conclude by highlighting the context of Iran from Riza Shah's abdication until the late 1960s when Mutahhari published his work on the hijab.

The Hijab in Pre-Modern Iran

The hijab is a ubiquitous feature of women's clothing that appears across literary, artistic and decorative genres, from late antiquity onwards. In terms of literary references, the hijab appears as soon as modern Persian became a literary language in the tenth–eleventh centuries, and by the medieval period of the thirteenth and fourteenth centuries it is not difficult to discover texts that include passages wherein the hijab features. Many good examples of stories about women and their hijab appear in hagiographical literature, such as in the Persian *Manāqib-i Awḥad al-Dīn Kirmānī*, which relates a number of tales about the well-known thirteenth-century Sufi. One anecdote describes how the people of Konya participated in a

2 On Babism, see Abbas Amanat, *Resurrection and Renewal: The Making of the Babi Movement in Iran, 1844–1850,* Ithaca 1989.

samāʿ gathering where devotional poetry was recited and sung, during which the participants sometimes cast off their outer garments and turbans. The women of Konya decided to go along to the *samāʿ*, and in agreement with one another they took off their head-coverings (*sar-band*). The Sufi shaykh was none too pleased at this turn of events, and he chastised the women, saying that women who joined the *samāʿ* along with unknown men should instead conform to the model of modesty exemplified by the Prophet's wives, and not fall into iniquity.[3] Konya enjoyed the Persianate culture of the medieval times when its geographical range was greater than that of the contemporary period. An example that is located within the heartlands of the geographical boundary of contemporary Iran is the illustration of the famous Moroccan traveller, Ibn Battuta (1304–69), which provides a perfect case of how Iranian women observed the hijab. He wrote how the women of Shiraz 'when out of doors are swathed in mantles and head-veils, so that no part of them is to be seen'.[4]

Another literary genre worthy of investigation is poetry, and here again it is not difficult to find references to the hijab. For example, Awhadi Maraghaʾi (d. 1338) remarked, 'A veiled wife is like a candle for the house / A coquette is a calamity at all times.'[5] Persian Sufi poets and men of letters frequently played with images of the veil that either revealed or concealed the beloved (or God), and to illustrate their message they employed the allegory of the veil of a beautiful woman. For instance, in his prose work Rumi warns men not to describe to others the beautiful faces of the brides of heavenly truth. He remarks that it is not proper to parade such maidens in the bazaar, thus inviting others to look upon them.[6] Such allegories would only have made sense if the women of Rumi's time covered and concealed themselves from the non-*maḥram* individual.

Persian painting also provides a valuable tool for assessing how women observed the hijab. From the Safavid period onwards (1501–1722) there are many examples of hijab-clad women in paintings. For example, the famous Chehel Sotun Palace in Isfahan contains frescoes of female musicians and dancing girls, and they are all appropriately attired. And with regard to miniature painting, the great majority of images depict women with some kind of head-covering. A good example from the Safavid period is a miniature of Shaykh Safi dancing in ritualised Sufi fashion (painted circa 1582), where of interest are four women sitting in

3 Lloyd Ridgeon, *Awḥad al-Dīn Kirmānī and the Controversy of the Sufi Gaze*, London 2018, 204.
4 *The Travels of Ibn Battuta, II*, trans. H. A. R. Gibb, Delhi 1999, 300.
5 *Jām-i Jam* [*Dīvān-i Awḥadī*], ed. S. Nafisi, Tehran 1340/1961, 548.
6 Rumi, *The Discourses of Rumi* [*Fihi ma Fihi*], trans. A. J. Arberry, London 1961, 81–2.

attendance in white *chādur* and face-covering (**Figure 1**).[7] Tile work too from this period reveals the same concern to depict women with the hijab, as is evident in the 'picnic' tile panel of a garden scene of a woman and her attendants held in the Vitoria and Albert Museum.[8] These are not isolated examples, as there are similar tile images dating into the Qajar period (1795–1925).[9]

Female head- and face-covering are also mentioned in the reports of European travellers to Iran. Foreign travellers to Iran are useful sources of information on the hijab, keen as they appear to be to highlight differences in sartorial preferences and activities between Iranian men and women on the one hand, and between Iranian women and European women on the other. Jean Chardin (1643–1713) provided a chapter on clothes and household goods in the second volume of his *Travels in Persia*, detailing information about veiling. He remarked:

> Their Head is very well cloath'd, and over it they have a Vail that falls down to their Shoulders, and covers their Neck and Bosom before. When they go out, they put over all, a great white Vail, which covers them from Head to Foot, not suffering anything to appear, in several Countries, but the Balls of their Eyes. The Women wear four Vails in all; two of which they wear at Home, and two more when they go Abroad. The first of these Vails is made like a Kerchief, falling down behind the Body, by way of Ornament: The second passes under the Chin, and covers the Bosom: The third is the White Vail, which covers all the Body: And the fourth is a sort of Handkerchief, which goes over the Face, and is fasten'd to the Temples. This Handkerchief or Vail, has a sort of Net-work, like old point, or Lacc, for thcm to scc through [(**Figure 2**)].[10]

Whether this is a general observation about women in urban settings, or in certain locations, or among particular classes, cannot be ascertained. It would certainly be wise to question blanket assumptions of Iranian women adopting the hijab during the Safavid period. Instructive in this regard is a work composed by a theologian

7 At times, the situation of women demanded that they were depicted without a hijab; images of a bareheaded Shirin bathing – in an episode that is found in Nizami's famous poem – were common during the Safavid period. See the image by Shaikh Zada, *Khusrau Catches Sight of Shirin Bathing*, Folio from a *Khamsa* (*Quintet*) of Nizami, c. 1524–5, ink, opaque watercolour, and gold on paper, page: 32.1 x 22.2 cm (Metropolitan Museum of Art).
8 See http://www.vam.ac.uk/content/articles/e/explore-the-picnic-tile-panel/.
9 See http://collections.vam.ac.uk/item/O113643/tile-unknown/.
10 Sir John Chardin, *Travels in Persia*, New York 1988, 215–6.

and judge, Aqa Jamal Khunsari, entitled *The Beliefs of Women*, in which he discussed the folk practices of the women of Isfahan. Notwithstanding the desire to entertain, the possibility of hyperbole, or wishing to castigate through exaggeration, it is noteworthy that Khunsari stated that women believed they should veil before anyone in a turban, and in particular, theology students, and that in contrast the hijab might be relaxed in front of Jewish peddlers, grocers, cloth merchants, physicians, fortune-tellers, exorcists and minstrels.[11]

Like any other item of clothing in the Middle East during the pre-modern period, covering served a multitude of purposes. What Donald Quataert has observed in relation to the Ottoman Empire and its clothing habits, customs and regulations is equally true of Iran; sartorial habits were not just about religion, piety and chastity; they also held deep significance for those wishing to display their status (religious, class and ethnic or otherwise).[12] Nevertheless, during the nineteenth century the increase in European influence in the Middle East resulted in a movement that cast covering in a negative fashion, as a symbol of backwardness and decline. Indeed, jurists and theologians have pointed out that the hijab was never a controversial issue until the appearance of Europeans in the Middle East, which is demonstrated by the absence of a specific category for the hijab or head-covering in their books. In more recent times, if the hijab or covering was discussed, it was placed by a jurist in his book about prayer or marriage (*kitāb al-salwāt wa kitāb al-nikāḥ*).[13]

Despite physical and intellectual pressures from Europe, which no doubt impacted on how Iranians perceived covering, it is also the case that there were indigenous pressures that do not seem to have been directly influenced by European thinking, and which advocated for the removal of head-covering. Of note is the 'infamous' case of the unveiling of Qurrat al-ʿAyn,[14] one of the leading figures

11 See the translation of Khunsari's text by James Atkinson, *The Customs and Manners of the Women of Persia*, London 1832. Cited by Hasan Javadi, 'Women in Persian satire', *The Education of Women and the Vices of Men*, ed. Hasan Javadi and Willem Floor, New York 2010, 150.

12 Donald Quataert, 'Clothing Laws, State, and Society in the Ottoman Empire, 1720–1829', *International Journal of Middle East Studies* 29.3, 1997, 403–25.

13 Mutahhari, citing his own *Mas'ala-yi Ḥijāb* in his *Pāsukh-hā-yi Ustād bi Naqd-hā-ī bar Kitāb-i Mas'āla-yi Hijāb*, Tehran 1370/1990–1.

14 For Qurrat al-ʿAyn see Amanat, *Resurrection and Renewal*, 295–331. Also worthy of note is Farzaneh Milani, *Veils and Words: The Emerging Voices of Iranian Women Writers*, London 1992, 77–99; Milani's chapter, titled 'Becoming a presence: Tahereh Qorratol-ʿAyn', investigates Qurrat al-ʿAyn as a poetess. Qurrat al-ʿAyn's poetry has been translated into English, see John Hatcher, *The Poetry of Tahirih*, Oxford 2002.

of the Babi movement that challenged the 'orthodoxy' of Twelver Shiʿi thought towards the end of the first half of the nineteenth century (before its leaders made the claim that it was a brand new religion, distinct from Islam). By 1848, the Babi movement had gathered at Badasht, when one of its leaders, Fatima Baraghani, also known as Qurrat al-ʿAyn (who was the daughter of a well-respected mulla from Qazvin), is supposed to have appeared before her supporters unveiled. While there is some dispute about the event of this public unveiling, it is clear that subsequently for Iranian religious classes, and perhaps in the popular imagination, Babism is linked so inextricably with Qurrat al-ʿAyn's unveiling that it is difficult to determine whether or not the opposition to the movement was more concerned with the doctrinal and ritual challenges to 'normative' Twelver Shiʿi Islam,[15] or if its primary worries centred around the corruption of a single public unveiling witnessed by a handful of individuals. Although the unveiling is popularly associated only with Qurrat al-ʿAyn, Sayyid Muhammad ʿAli (or the Bab himself) seems to have advocated uncovering too, which was noted by reformers of a Westernising ilk (such as Akhundzada, d. 1878).[16]

Another well-known voice of reform in this period came from Mirza Aqa Khan Kirmani, who published the newspaper *Akhtar* ('The Star') from the safe distance of Istanbul. Kirmani was a Babi, although it seems he distanced himself from Babism towards the end of his life, and his calls for reform included the values espoused by the European Enlightenment thinkers,[17] and also the removal of the hijab. He remarked, 'Since the Arab invasion, Iranian women have been buried alive under hijab. And have been interned and locked-away in seclusion. Hijab has deafened and blinded women.'[18] Other reformers who advocated for Western-style change and also pointed to the evils of veiling included the aforementioned Akhundzada who made associations between the hijab and men's rough character, and the detriments caused by segregation which led men to seek homoerotic relationships.[19] It is of interest that many of the Persian writings criticising the hijab were composed outside of Iran. Yet there was also an 'indigenous' movement

15 The doctrinal issues endorsed by Qurrat al-ʿAyn included the abrogation of primary ritual ordinances, including prayer and fasting. She also held to the belief that the Bab, Sayyid ʿAli Muhammad, was the recipient of a new sharia.
16 See Afsaneh Najmabadi, *Women with Moustaches and Men without Beards: Gender and Sexual Anxieties of Iranian Modernity*, Berkeley 2005, 148.
17 Pejman Abdolmohammadi, 'The influences of western ideas on Kermani's political thought', *Iran* LIV.I, 2016, 23–38.
18 Cited in Parvin Paidar, *Women and the Political Process in Twentieth Century Iran*, Cambridge 1995, 47.
19 Najmabadi, *Women with Moustaches*, 55–6.

within Iran which was perhaps influenced by the presence of European schools for girls.[20]

The nineteenth-century reformers were most likely directing their frustration about the lack of development in Iran not so much at the hijab that simply covered the hair, but at the practice of seclusion and at sartorial covering which impeded more free movement for females. It was the tradition in nineteenth- and early twentieth-century urban Iran, at least amongst the higher classes of women, to cover the face with a *rū-band* veil, a rectangular piece of cloth in which a lace lattice permitted women to see in front of them (seemingly similar to the description of the face-covering mentioned by Chardin, but which prevented others from witnessing the woman's face).[21] This custom of covering the face was criticised by some Western observers such as the British diplomat F. B. Bradley-Birt, who called the *niqāb* 'the most unpicturesque, ungraceful costume that the most jealous of husbands could devise. No stranger may look upon the Persian woman and see the beauty that many a poem and romance would lead one to believe lies behind those close-drawn veils'.[22] In addition to the *rū-band*, women's heads and bodies were concealed by a *chādur*, 'a cloak which descends from the head to the feet'.[23]

During the late Qajar period the tendency towards less covering of the face became increasingly conspicuous, particularly among the upper classes and the educated, where Western influence was at its greatest. There was also a tendency not to wear a veil within rural and tribal society where head- and face-covering were not conducive to agricultural work, among other activities.[24] In such societies, the absence of covering had not resulted in higher levels of immorality and debauchery, a criticism that was and still is levelled against Western societies. The point, however, is that the practice of uncovering in Iran was simply not class-bound, as the reasons for lack of veiling were diverse and depended upon contexts that defy simple categorisation. Despite this, it does appear that the advocates of reform and vocal supporters among the anti-covering group were numerous among the educated and upper classes, who were aware of the same

20 Rasul Ja'fariyan, 'Muqaddama-yi baḥth' [Introduction to the Topic], *Rasā'il Ḥijābiya*, ed. Rasul Ja'fariyan, Tehran 1380/2001–2, 43.

21 Jennifer Scarce, *Women's Costumes of the Near and Middle East*, London 2002, 175–6, provides excellent images of the *rū-band*.

22 F. B. Bradley Birt, *Through Persia from the Gulf to the Caspian*, London 1909. Cited in Katherine Bullock, *Rethinking Muslim Women and the Veil: Challenging Historical and Modern Stereotypes*, London 2007, 10.

23 Firoozeh Kashani-Sabet, *Conceiving Citizens*, Oxford 2011, 148.

24 Janet Afary, *Sexual Politics in Modern Iran*, Cambridge 2011, 44–5.

anti-covering sentiments among the educated Westernised classes of neighbouring Muslim countries.

By the close of the nineteenth century, some Iranians would have been aware of the female emancipation and suffragette movements in the West and also in parts of the Middle East, where important individuals often held negative views of female covering.[25] For example, many scholars claim that Lord Cromer, the Governor General of Egypt between 1883–1907 connected the backward situation of Egypt and Islam with seclusion, of which female sartorial covering was an outward manifestation.[26] Some of the elite and influential individuals of the Middle East had experience of living in European cities during the second half of the nineteenth century. One of these, the Egyptian reformer Qasim Amin had studied at the University of Montpellier and composed a response to an anti-Islamic tract entitled *L'Egypt et les Egyptiens*, written in 1894 and depicting Egypt as a backward country, which reflected on the low status of women and the use of the veil.[27] In his initial response Amin defended current Islamic practices such as veiling, but subsequently he published two works called *The Liberation of Women* (written in 1897) and *The New Woman* in which he supported unveiling. The controversy about Amin's books in the Egyptian context has been discussed elsewhere, but it also had significance in other regions of the Islamic world.[28] The book was translated into Persian in 1900, only one year after its publication in Arabic in Cairo. However, the Persian version, entitled *Tarbiyat-i Nisvān* (*Education of Women*) omitted the second chapter of Qasim Amin's original, that

25 In this regard it is instructive that it was fashionable for Iranians to decorate the interior of their houses with images of unveiled Western women. This practice may have been widespread, and not just confined to the rich who were able to afford paintings. The introduction of lithograph prints and also of photographic images meant that the relatively less well-off were able to afford such images. See Parviz Tanavoli, *European Women in Persian Houses: Western Images in Safavid and Qajar Iran*, London 2015.
26 Despite the claims of many scholars (see Karen Armstrong, 'My life in a habit taught me the paradox of veiling', *The Guardian* 26 October 2006) about Cromer and the veil, he never makes an explicit connection. In his publication, *Modern Egypt*, New York 1908, 539, Cromer describes the social position of women as a 'fatal obstacle' to their progress. An important work tracing the changing nature of Western views about Muslim women through the centuries is Mohja Kahf, *Western Representations of the Muslim Woman*, Texas 1999.
27 Mansoor Moaddel, *Islamic Modernism, Nationalism and Fundamentalism: Episode and Discourse*, Chicago 2005, 94.
28 See Leila Ahmed, *A Quiet Revolution: The Veil's Resurgence, from the Middle East to North America*, New Haven 2011, 19–45; Margot Badran, *Feminism in Islam: Secular and Religious Convergences*, Oxford 2011, 55–64. For an English translation of Qasim's works, see Qasim Amin, *The Liberation of Women & The New Women: Two Documents in the History of Egyptian Feminism*, trans. Samiha Sidhom Peterson, Cairo 2000.

is, the chapter on the veil. Afsaneh Najmabadi argues that the central reason for this was due to the translator's regard for education as the pivotal issue relating to women's reform, and 'there was no fixed connection between the issue of veiling and women's education'.[29]

In Middle Eastern countries veiling remained a complex issue that defied simplistic analysis. On the one hand, the anti-veiling group criticised the practice because it simply endorsed the orientalist claims about the inferiority and subordination of women within Islam. On the other hand, anti-colonialists approved of covering because it was more than just sartorial choice, and reflected resistance to the oppressive colonial and neo-colonial meta narratives. Such perspectives were articulated by successive generations in Iran, and also across the Middle East. Hifni Nasif in Egypt (d. 1918) pointed to the 'damned if we do and damned if we don't' conundrum surrounding the issue, arguing furthermore that the problem was not necessarily associated with orientalism, or religion, but was one of patriarchy:

> The majority of us women continue to be oppressed by the injustice of man, who in his despotism commands and forbids us so that now we can have no opinion even about ourselves … If he orders us to veil, we veil, and if he demands that we unveil, we unveil.[30]

Veiling in the specific Iranian context was just one of the issues related to gender, and as mentioned above it transcended class, the urban/rural divide, and the category of educated/uneducated (examples of Qajar era veiling are shown in **Figures 3–6**). As Najmabadi indicates, the question of hijab surpassed the simple binary of traditionalists (supporters of Islamic covering) versus modernists (advocators of the removal of covering) that has been described by Tavakoli-Targhi.[31] Despite the trend that has often associated unveiling with better education and modernity, in Iran the arguments became increasingly complex, typified in a treatise composed by Shaykh al-Raʾis, entitled *Ittiḥād-i Islām* (*The Unity of Islam*) in 1895–6. Rather than advocating for the removal of covering and for an end to separation, which would permit women the complete freedom of movement enjoyed in foreign countries, Shaykh al-Raʾis proposed that girls should be taught that observing religious chastity and legal commands are not an obstruction to

29 Najmabadi, *Women with Moustaches*, 135.
30 Cited in Amer, *What is Veiling*, 141.
31 Najmabadi, *Women with Moustaches*, citing M. Tavakoli-Targhi, *Refashioning Iran: Orientalism, Occidentalism, and Historiography*, New York 2001, 54.

human progress. He reminded his readers of the hadith which states that seeking wisdom is the duty of each believer, male and female, implying that religious education would be adequate to meet the requirements of the modern age for girls, and this would not necessitate covering.[32] The discussion about unveiling continued in Iran during the Constitutional period, and in 1911 the first treatise on the subject of hijab entitled *Aḥkām-i Ḥijāb va Niqāb az Kitāb-i Muqaddas* (*Commands on the Hijab and the Niqab from the Sacred Book*) was composed by Fakhr al-Islam, a supporter of the Constitutionalist movement.[33] However, he was not an advocate of unveiling, as he remarked that the opponents of the constitution desired that women would remove their veils in order to put the blame on the reforming Constitutionalists.[34] Jaʿfariyan has observed that what makes the work significant is the emphasis on reason to persuade the reader, rather than relying simply on citing scripture.[35] While the Qurʾan is cited, it is novel that the verses in question are explained in a fashion to satisfy the increasingly informed and educated Iranian about the reasonable nature of the revelations.[36] The early years of the twentieth century witnessed an increasing number of publications about the hijab. Jaʿfariyan's collection (*Rasāʾil Ḥijābiyya*) includes over twenty short compositions on the topic, critical of unveiling, that were published by seminarians between 1924–9. This was a period when freedom of expression was still relatively allowed, and the reign of Riza Shah had not yet become the authoritarian and dictatorial regime it was characterised by from the mid-1930s onwards.

The debate concerning the hijab was fuelled no doubt by the verses of well-known poets such as ʿIshqi (d. 1924) and Iraj Mirza (d. 1926). In the early years of the twentieth century, such poets and many reformers referred to the hijab in derogatory terms. Farzaneh Milani observes, 'Calling the veil a "shroud", a "sack", or a "jail", and a veiled woman a "walking bundle", a "black crow",[37] or an "ink pot", they maintained that the veil had prevented women from developing their fullest potential.'[38] But for many of the advocates of unveiling, covering was not simply a woman's problem, for it had effected Iranian men and caused

32 Jaʿfariyan, 'Muqaddama-yi baḥth', 34–5.
33 Jaʿfariyan, *Rasāʾil Ḥijābiyya*, 58.
34 Jaʿfariyan, *Rasāʾil Ḥijābiyya*, 59; Najmabadi, *Women with Moustaches*, 136.
35 Jaʿfariyan, *Rasāʾil Ḥijābiyya*, 59
36 The whole of the short treatise is provided in ibid., 60–70.
37 The comparison with black crows has a long history. There is a hadith narrated by Abu Daʾud (in his *al-Sunan*) that Umm Salama said: 'When the aya [33.59] "... to draw their cloaks over themselves..." was revealed the women of the Ansar came out looking as if there were crows on their heads, because of their clothing' (Sunan Abi Daʾud, *Kitāb al-Libās*).
38 Milani, *Veils and Words*, 29.

moral depravity. Although Persian culture has a long history and tradition that has approved of homoeroticism,[39] by the nineteenth century such practices, under the glaring light of Western and Christian morality of the Victorian era, were frowned upon. Najmabadi demonstrates how attempts were made to place the blame of homosocialisation and homoeroticism on women and the veil.[40] Even so, Sprachman has indicated that Iraj Mirza's work, for instance, does not simply portray the negative dimensions of the hijab. The *chādur* (or veil) can paradoxically heighten the sexual appetite of the spectator: 'It is the "rustling sound" or "suggestive movement" … accentuated by the veil that stirs his passion initially.'[41]

These Persian poets would have been well aware of the increasing trends of anti-veiling that were taking place across the Middle East, and news focused on the mainly aristocratic and privileged women usually educated in the West, who were unveiling and advocating women's rights. Examples include: Nazira Zayn al-Din, a Druze scholar who composed a work titled *al-Sufūr wa'l-Ḥijāb* (*Veiling and the Hijab*) in 1928;[42] and Huda Shaʿrawi, an Egyptian nationalist who also opened a girls' school in 1910, and publicly removed her face veil in 1923, a gesture which provoked similar acts among Egyptian women.[43] During the 1920s, Turkish women in major urban areas such as Istanbul were likewise removing their face veils, inspired perhaps by the Westernising reforms of Kemal Ataturk. Changes in veiling in the Anatolian region had been ongoing for a number of years prior to the Iranian experience, but the veil was never officially banned in Turkey, although the ruling elite strongly encouraged women to adopt European clothing,

39 See, for example, chapter 16 of *Qābūs-nāma*, where the author states that a man's desire should incline towards women in the winter and to men in the summer. See Kai Kawus ibn Iskandar ibn Vashmgir, *Qābūs-nāma*, ed. Ghulam Husayn Yusufi, Tehran 1345/1966–7, 87.

40 Such an accusation was made by Mirza Aqa Khan Kirmani in his *Sih Maktūb*. It continued into the post-Constitutional period, typified in the following verse by Iraj Mirza:

> Until our tribe is tied up in the veil
> This very queerness is bound to prevail.
> The draping of the girl with her throat divine
> Will make the little boy our concubine.

See Paul Sprachman, 'The poetics of *hijab* in the satire of Iraj Mirza', *Iran and Iranian Studies: Essays in Honor of Iraj Afshar*, ed. Kambiz Eslami, New Jersey 1998, 349.

41 Sprachman, 'The poetics of *hijab* in the satire of Iraj Mirza', 350.

42 For a general survey see Miriam Cooke, *Nazira Zeineddine: A Pioneer of Islamic Feminism*, London 2010. Sections of Nazira Zayn al-Din's work has been translated into English. See Nazira Zein-ed-Din, 'Unveiling and veiling', *Opening the Gates: A Century of Arab Feminist Writers*, trans. and ed. Margot Badran and Miriam Cooke, London 1990, 272–6.

43 For a general survey see Huda Shaʿrawi and Margot Badran, *Harem Years: The Memoirs of an Egyptian Feminist (1879-1924)*, New York 1987.

which also meant the removal of the veil.[44] Most significant of all, perhaps, was the public appearance in Tehran, without a veil, of Queen Soraya of Afghanistan in June 1928. The royal couple were representative of the small Westernising elite in Afghanistan, but they were unable to persuade their subjects to embrace their reforms.[45] In 1929, King Amanullah was deposed; nevertheless, Queen Soraya's removal of the face veil is said to have left a deep impression on Riza Shah.[46]

It was in such a context – of the unveiling of educated upper classes and royal elites – that an event took place in 1928 which in retrospect served as a precursor to the decree that banned the veil in 1936. During Ramadan of 1928, Riza Shah's female royal relations visited the holy shrine in Qum, and according to some their heads were covered only by a 'light *chādur*'[47] which was 'transparent'.[48] Some have claimed that the women were bareheaded,[49] and others have said they wore European hats.[50] One of the leading seminarians, Ayatollah Bafqi was made aware of the situation and he sent a message to the ladies, asking why they had visited, attired as they were. News of these events were wired to Riza Shah, and Bafqi was dragged out of the shrine and publicly insulted and humiliated. Algar has claimed that Bafqi's opposition to Riza Shah was one of the reasons for the delay in banning the hijab.[51] These events surely encouraged the educated female elite who felt sufficiently comfortable to appear unveiled in public. One of these was Sidiqa Dawlatabadi, a French-educated psychology student and activist for women's rights, who refused to wear the veil in public from 1927.[52] Dawlatabadi

44 See Serap Kavas, '"Wardrobe modernity": Western attire as a tool of modernization in Turkey', *Middle Eastern Studies* 51.4, 2015, 515–39.
45 For Queen Soraya and the Westernising reforms in the context of women in modern Afghanistan see Huma Ahmad-Ghosh, 'A history of women in Afghanistan: Lessons learnt for the future or yesterdays and tomorrow: Women in Afghanistan', *Journal of International Women's Studies* 4.3, 2003, 1–14.
46 J. Rostam-Kolayi, 'Family law, work and unveiling', *The Making of Modern Iran: State and Society under Riza Shah, 1921–1941*, ed. Stephanie Cronin, London 2003, 171.
47 Shireen Mahdavi, 'Reza Shah and women: A re-appraisal', *The Making of Modern Iran*, ed. Stephanie Cronin, London 2003, 188.
48 Houchang E. Chehabi, 'Banning of the veil and its consequences', *The Making of Modern Iran*, ed. Stephanie Cronin, London 2003, 196.
49 Hamid Algar, 'Bafqi, Mohammad-Taqi', *Encyclopedia Iranica* III.4, 392.
50 Paidar, *Women and the Political Process in Twentieth-Century Iran*, 107.
51 The significance of the event extends beyond the focus on unveiling. At issue too was the power of Riza Shah and his manly honour as head of the royal family. The event should also be considered in the larger context of Shah-ulama relations.
52 Paidar, *Women and the Political Process in Twentieth-Century Iran*, 94. For more on Dawlatabadi, see Mansoureh Ettehadiyeh, 'Sediqeh Dowlatabadi: An Iranian feminist', *Religion and Politics in Modern Iran*, ed. Lloyd Ridgeon, London 2005, 71–98.

was made director of the *Kānūn-i Bānūvān* (Women's Society) in 1935, which was a state-promoted educational and vocational school for females, the main function of which 'was to prepare public opinion for generalized unveiling'.[53] This preparation was facilitated by discussions in popular women's literature, such as the *ʿAlam-i Nisvān*, the aforementioned bi-monthly magazine, which from 1931 contained discussions about veiling and unveiling in 'almost every issue'.[54]

Events such as the overthrow of the King of Afghanistan in 1929, and the desire not to further antagonise the clergy, as well as his personal reluctance to unveil members of his own family,[55] may be among the reasons that help explain Riza Shah's delay in banning the hijab. The anti-veiling campaign was 'focused on the removal of the *chādur*, the face veil, and headscarf and the adoption of European-American dress and hats'.[56] The implementation of *kashf-i ḥijāb* followed Riza Shah's trip to Turkey in the summer of 1934, during which, as many scholars have indicated, he was impressed with the advances Ataturk had made in modernising and Westernising the country.[57] From 1935, the Shah prepared the way for the subsequent unveiling as 'state organs issued decrees in an authoritative fashion';[58] thus, ministers were ordered to appear alongside their unveiled wives on a weekly basis at various official functions, and in the spring of the same year the Ministry of Education announced that female teachers who wore the *chādur* or *pīcha* (face veil) would not receive their salaries.[59]

In January 1936, the Queen and the princesses appeared publicly unveiled at graduation ceremonies of the first Women's College, and Riza Shah delivered an oft quoted speech in which he expressed his pleasure to see Iranian women 'coming alive to their condition, rights and privileges'. It appears that the decree was aimed primarily at face-covering, so that for example, police were 'ordered to abstain from "violently [removing] this kind of hijab [i.e. hair-covering] from the

53 Chehabi, 'Banning of the veil and its consequences', 198–9.
54 Rostam-Kolyani, 'Family law, work and unveiling', 168.
55 Chehabi, 'Banning of the veil and its consequences', 200.
56 Jasamin Rostam-Kolayi and Afshin Matin-Asgari, 'Unveiling ambiguities: revisiting 1030s Iran's *kashf-i hijab* campaign', *Anti-Veiling Campaigns in the Muslim World: Gender, Modernism and the politics of Dress*, ed. Stephanie Cronin, London 2014, 123.
57 A. Marashi, 'The Shah's official visit to Kemalist Turkey', *The Making of Modern Iran*, ed. Stephanie Cronin, London 2003, 99–119. In particular, the press in Iran made much of the 'co-ed schooling, female scouting, and un-hejabed women' (Ibid.,108). Kashani-Sabet has argued against the inspiration for the decree as deriving from Turkey. See Firoozeh Kashani-Sabet, *Conceiving Citizens: Women and the Politics of Motherhood in Iran*, Oxford 2011, 156.
58 Rostam-Kolayi and Matin-Asgari, 'Unveiling ambiguities', 124.
59 Chehabi, 'Banning of the veil and its consequences', 198.

head'".[60] But the decree was enforced by the security forces, sometimes brutally, with veils being publicly torn from the faces of women who appeared covered in public.[61] The police targeted certain streets to enforce the law, and taxi drivers, restaurant owners, public-bath keepers and chemists were forbidden to trade with veiled women.[62]

The reluctance to obey the decree appears to have been widespread, and ingenious ways were thought of to avoid acceding to the decree; some men even contracted temporary marriages which enabled them to take their temporary wives to official functions so that their permanent wives would not have to attend unveiled.[63] In the provinces, many local officials appealed for leniency and more time to implement the decree. One of the major obstacles that women faced in obeying the decree was poverty, seeing as they were unable to afford the cost of buying new European fashions and hats.[64] Despite the general unpopularity of *kashf-i ḥijāb*, it remained in force until the Shah was compelled to abdicate in 1941.[65]

The seminaries opposed the sartorial reforms. Reference has already been made to the 1928 incident in Qum, when Riza Shah chastised the ulama for insulting his family. More tragic and severe was the Gawharshad mosque incident in 1935, when the Shah's forces fired on, and killed, demonstrators in Mashhad after they had protested in mass, instigated by a local preacher who publicly opposed the Shah's sartorial plans for Iran from the pulpit.[66] Amanat states that

60 Rostam-Kolyani, 'Family law, work and unveiling', 167. Rostam-Kolyani observes, 'Ironically, the actual physical appearance of women in public after Kashf-e Hejab, according to this dress-code [of 1936], was not fundamentally different from the present Islamic dress enforced in the Islamic Republic' (168).

61 See the documents cited in F. Shirazi, 'Iran's Compulsory Hijab: From politics and religious authority to fashion shows', *The Routledge International Handbook to Veils and Veiling*, ed. Anna Mari Almila and David Inglis, London 2017, 103.

62 Kashani-Sabet, *Conceiving Citizens*, 158.

63 Chehabi, 'Banning of the veil and its consequences', 203. Chehabi offers other examples of the reaction and resistance to the decree (202–4).

64 Shirazi, 'Iran's compulsory hijab: From politics and religious authority to fashion shows', 101.

65 The unpopularity of the decree has caused much myth-making and erroneous accusation. For example, in a novel set in the times of Riza Shah by Kader Abdolah a claim is made that at the Shah's orders the lips of the poet Farrukhi were sewn closed because he had written about women who stumbled and could not walk without their *chādur*s. See Kader Abdolah, *My Father's Notebook*, trans. Susan Massotty, Edinburgh 2007, 27. This seems to be a mistake, as Farrukhi's lips had been sewn together decades earlier in 1909 by Zayqum al-Dawla Qashqa'i, the Governor of Yazd. See Ali Gheissari, 'The poetry and politics of Farrokhi Yazdi', *Iranian Studies* 26.1/2, 1993, 35.

66 Chehabi, 'Banning of the veil and its consequences', 199; Kashani-Sabet, *Conceiving*

the indiscriminate firing of the security forces on the protestors resulted in more than a dozen fatalities, injuring a few hundred more.[67] Other sources claim over a thousand people were killed.[68] From Qum, the head of the seminary, Ayatollah Haʾiri, sent a letter in 1936 to the monarch, expressing his 'extreme concern' at the *kashf-i ḥijāb* because it contradicted the laws of Islam.[69] In the wake of unveiling Ayatollah Haʾiri is reported to have said: 'Until now, I have not intervened in anything. But now I hear that steps are being undertaken which are flagrantly opposed to the Jaʿfari school of thought and the law of Islam. Henceforth restraint and forbearance will be difficult for me.'[70] His death in January 1937 removed the need for the Shah to take retaliatory action. Reflecting Haʾiri's position, another very senior leader in the *ḥawza*, Ayatollah Hujjat, sent a message to the Shah, warning against the implementation of un-Islamic practices in the country.[71]

Many among the ulama must have been terrified of antagonising the Shah, however, as they had been cowered by the violence and brutality that the monarch had exercised in implementing his policies. It is in this light that it is possible to understand the reticence of many Iranian seminarians to speak out against the Shah.[72] Typifying this attitude was the major reforming mulla from Tehran, Shariʿat Sangalaji (d. 1943). Rahnema has observed how Sangalaji 'believed that

Citizens, 155; see also Parvin Qudsizad, 'The Period of Pahlavi I', *Pahlavi dynasty: An Entry from Encyclopaedia of the World of Islam*, ed. Ghulam Ali H. Adel and Mohammad J. Elmi, London 2012, 41; Said Amir Arjomand, *The Turban for the Crown: The Islamic Revolution in Iran*, Oxford 1988, 82. In the wake of the Gawharshad incident, according to Mahmood T. Davari 'all the leading ulama of the city [of Mashhad] were arrested … religious schools were closed and the tullab [students of religion] were forced to change their clerical dress'. See his *The Political Thought of Ayatullah Murtaza Mutahhari*, London 2005, 13.

67 Abbas Amanat, *Iran: A Modern History*, New Haven 2017, 482.

68 Yvette Hovespian-Bearce cites two Iranian sources that claim between 2,000–5,000 people were killed by the Shah's forces. See her *The Political Ideology of Ayatollah Khamenei: Out of the Mouth of the Supreme Leader of Iran*, Abingdon 2016, 44, n. 4.

69 Muhammad Sharif-Razi, *Aṯhār al-ḥujjah: yā tārīkh va dāʾirat al-maʿārif-i ḥawza-yi ʿilmīyya-yi Qum*, Tehran 1953, 51.

70 Hamid Algar, 'Haʾerī, ʿAbd al-Karim Yazdi', *Encylopedia Iranica*, December 15, 2002.

71 ʿAbd'ul Rahim ʿAqiqi-Bakhshayishi, *Yakṣad sāl-i mubārazah-i rūḥānīyat-i mutaraqqī*, Tehran 1982, vol. 3, 62; Hamid Basiratmanish, *ʿUlamā va rizhīm-i Riżā Shāh: naẓarī* bar ʿamalkard-i *siyāsī-farhangī-i rūḥānīyūn dar sālhā-yi 1305-1320*, Tehran 1997, 503. The text of the telegram sent by Ayatollah Hujjat is extant, but its date is unclear. It is assumed to be 1936, when Ayatollah Haʾiri was still alive (private email with Dr Muhammad Mesbahi, dated 22 June 2020).

72 For a general overview of the relationship between the Shah and the clergy see Shahrough Akhavi, *Religion and Politics in Contemporary Iran: Clergy-State Relations in the Pahlavi Period*, Albany 1980, 23–60. Unfortunately, Akhavi's work does not address the *kashf-i ḥijāb* episode.

in time, given socio-economic development, the people would come to pose fundamental questions regarding certain practices and that it was best for the clergy to initiate the reform process in order to guarantee the faith of the people in the future'.[73] To this end he employed *ijtihād* to offer contemporary understandings on a whole range of issues, so that they confirmed to the rational understandings of the day.[74] It is unclear what his views on unveiling were.[75]

Riza Shah's unveiling policy was part of an attempt to modernise society which must be seen in the context of the reforms that were sweeping through much of the Middle East and beyond. The suffragette movement had spread across Europe in the early part of the century, and nationalism, in which all members of society were to contribute, had similarly been a major factor in European politics. Riza Shah would have been aware of these developments, and it was his goal to allow women to participate in such a nationalistic drive towards modernity (although they did not have the right to vote). However, unveiling was not to be instituted without regulation; what was required was an orderly unveiling so that the women could serve the state and nation. As Najmabadi observes, 'Before the physical veil was discarded, it was replaced by an invisible metaphoric veil, *ḥijāb-i ʿiffat* (veil of chastity), not as some object, a piece of cloth, external to the female body, but a veil to be acquired through modern education, as some internal quality of self, a new modern self, a disciplined modern body that obscured the woman's sexuality, obliterated its bodily presence.'[76] In other words, there were some women (and men) who did not consider Riza Shah's reforms as inherently anti-Islamic or devoid of spirituality, because the foregrounding of new roles for women (motherhood, education, service to society, etc.)[77] were inherent within Islamic sacred texts. It was women's modesty (this new form of *ḥijāb-i ʿiffat*) that was of significance. Najmabadi claims that this sense of modesty motivated her mother to turn her face to the wall when walking to work once the unveiling decree was made,

73 Rahnema, *Shiʿi Reformation in Iran*, 168.
74 On Sangalaji see also Yann Richard, 'Shariʿat Sangalaji: A reformist theologian of the Rida Shah period', *Authority and Political Culture in Shiʿism*, ed. S. Amir Arjomand, New York 1988, 159–77.
75 In private email exchange with Rahnema, who has studied Sangalaji's writings and thought in detail, I was informed that Sangalaji did not express any opinions on the topic of unveiling, perhaps reflecting his common sense, political quietism, and desire not to alienate the Shah.
76 Afaneh Najmabadi, 'Veiled discourse – unveiled bodies', *Feminist Studies* 19.3, 1993, 489.
77 Kashani-Sabet, *Conceiving Citizens*, 121–46.

in order to avoid the gaze of men. At the same time, she soon also realised the possibilities that the new circumstances opened up.[78]

The abdication of Riza Shah in 1941 resulted in the relaxing of the law. Mahdavi has stated that the return of Iranian women 'back to the veil' reflects the brevity of the time (only five years) since the decree was in place: 'Such a period was not by any standards long enough for centuries of indoctrination to be erased.'[79] And she also points to the role of the ulama, who started to advocate the reuse of the *chādur*, and for men to keep their daughters out of school where the hijab was forbidden. Influential seminarians such as Ayatollah ʿAbu'l-Qasim Kashani immediately clamoured for women to wear the hijab, and Ayatollah Husayn Qumi asked the government to make the issue one of choice.[80] Ayatollah Tabatabaʾi and religious groups advocated the freedom for women to wear the veil without fear of being punished, and the government agreed to this demand.[81] On 3 September 1943 it was made official that the adoption of the veil was an issue of free choice. It is worth noting that in the wake of Riza Shah's abdication, the young Khomeini wrote a work titled *Kashf al-Asrār* (*Unveiling of Secrets*) in which he castigated the Shah for his edict on the hijab:

> A government which, contrary to the laws of the land and everything considered just, appoints a group of predatory animals as police in every town and city to fall upon chaste Muslim women, who have committed no crime, and by force of the bayonet to tear their veils from their heads and confiscate them, to kick these defenceless women causing some of the pregnant ones amongst them to miscarry their innocent, unborn babies, we call a tyrannical government, and say assisting or working with it in any way is tantamount to blasphemy. We say a dictatorial government is an oppressive one, and those who work for it are tyrants and oppressors. If you have anything to say on this matter do so, so that their infamy may be added to.
>
> The oppressed masses of Iran today also abhor the agents of the dictatorial regime of that day who so mistreated their innocent women and children the

78 Najmabadi, 'Veiled discourse – unveiled bodies', 512–13, n. 9.
79 Mahdavi, 'Reza Shah and women', 189.
80 Chehabi, 'Banning of the veil and its consequences', 205; Said Amir Arjomand, 'Traditionalism in Twentieth Century Iran', *From Nationalism to Revolutionary Islam*, ed. Said Amir Arjomand, Oxford 1984, 204; Muhammad H. Manzur al-Ajdad, *Marjiʿīyat dar ʿarṣah-i ijtimāʿ va siyāsat: asnād va guzārish-hā-yī az Āyāt-i ʿizam Naʾini, Isfahani, Qumi, Haʾiri va Burujirdi*, Tehran 2000, 269.
81 Kashani-Sabet, *Conceiving Citizens*, 161.

> way they did, and perpetrated such shameful injustices against them. Indeed, whoever regards them as decent, honourable people is himself devoid of honour and justice. Those newspapers that back the oppressive actions of the runaway dictator, the most painful of which is the unveiling of women, are actually aiding the savage principles of dictatorship and should be burnt in public.[82]

The secular intelligentsia, however, maintained their support for the principle of unveiling even after the abdication of Riza Shah. Such was the perspective of the influential secular thinker, Ahmad Kasravi, who was educated within a seminary, and who in 1944 published a work entitled *Khāharān va Dukhtarān-i Mā* (*Our Sisters and Daughters*). The first chapter of this work was called 'On veiling', where Kasravi traced the custom of veiling back to pre-Islamic Iran, pointing out that women did not cover their faces in Muhammad's community. He wrote how it was a result of the Iranian influence that the early Arab Muslims adopted the veil, and it was promoted by the religious classes. Kasravi was keen to demonstrate that the harm of veiling lay in its power of preventing women from engaging in an active role in society. However, he advocated a cautious approach to permitting unveiled women to appear in society, as they were to be seen only when it was safe and should mix at parties when accompanied by a male relative or husband. He viewed the excesses of European society as dangerous and inappropriate for Iranian society.[83]

*

Photographs from Iran in the 1950s and 1960s, such as those found in *Iṭṭilāʿāt* and *Zan-i Rūz* show that it was not just female members of the royal family that continued to remain bareheaded, but university students sat in mixed classes with female students attending without hijab, and middle class types adopted Western style clothing. However, there was also a dimension to Iran that made the ulama even more uncomfortable than the more modest forms of Western clothing. Typifying this trend were the annual beauty pageants held in Iran from the mid-1960s

---

82 Khomeini, *Kashf al-Asrār*, 239, see: http://www.imam-khomeini.com/web1/english/showitem.aspx?pid=-1&cid=2139.

83 Carol Regan, 'Ahmad Kasravi's views on the role of women in Iranian society as expressed in *Our Sisters and Daughters*', *Women and the Family in Iran*, ed. Asghar Fatehi, Leiden 1985, 60–76.

onwards.[84] The name of this pageant changed several times in the 1960s, but the glamour and *raison d'etre* of the event ran against seminary principles on modesty. Photographs of the event reveal how young women in the 1960s were 'conservatively' dressed (**Figure 7**); for instance, there were no swimwear shots that were common in beauty contents in the West during the 1970s.

The images associated with these beauty contents were much more modest than the pictures used to advertise the Persian film industry, which produced a genre of movies known as *film fārsī*, in which elements of Western culture became increasing evident. As Naficy observes, from the late 1960s onwards there was an increase in the 'production of more violent and sexually charged but politically safe, escapist, and melodramatic commercial movies ... which in a few years would bring revolutionary wrath down on the movie houses as emblems of decadent western influences'.[85] **Figure 8** represents the kinds of pictorial representations of young attractive women in film that appeared in Iran during the 1960s. The image is of a poster from the 1968 movie, *Haft Shahr-i ʿIshq* (*Seven Cities of Love*), and it is an example of the salacious advertising that was employed to entice viewers into the cinemas. The main female star of the film, Furuzan, is depicted in her underwear, and another female character lies underneath a lusting male. Whilst the Iranian film industry produced some artistic successes during the 1960s, such movies also included scenes that the seminarian authorities would not tolerate. The hugely successful film *Qayṣar,* directed by Masʿud Kimiaʾi, included a rape scene at the beginning of the movie, and so it is unsurprising that Ayatollah Khalkhali banned the film in Tehran in June 1980.[86]

Such images reflect the modern and Westernised image of women that presented them as both sexually alluring, socially powerful and seemingly free agents of their own destiny and sexuality. Others would reject such interpretations and categorise such images as degrading for women and belittling their attempts to attain equality. It is at this time, in 1967, that there ensued a lively public discussion concerning women's rights. Davar cites the example of a judge, Ibrahim Mahdawi Zanjani, who participated in this debate by publishing forty articles in favour of reforming the Civil Code.[87] In the same year, the Shah introduced the Family Protection Law, which was an attempt to give Iranian women similar

84 See the images and information at: http://missosology.info/forum/viewtopic.php?f=79&t=60723.

85 Hamid Naficy, *A Social History of Iranian Cinema*, Durham 2011, vol. 2, 195.

86 Ali Reza Haghighi, 'Politics and cinema in post-revolutionary Iran', *The New Iranian Cinema*, ed. Richard Tapper, London 2002, 112.

87 Davar, *The Political Thought*, 50.

rights to those enjoyed by women in many Western countries. The Law was designed to limit arbitrary divorce (initiated by males), restrict polygamy and limit the male right to custody of children. In these cases, the legislation provided for the secularisation of decisions relating to the family, which in many instances had reverted to the seminary since the legislation of the Civil Code promulgated during the reign of Riza Shah.[88] Paidar has argued that the state reforms in the 1960s reflected a contradictory mix of values. On the one hand, women were promoted as sex-objects through the mass media, contrasting with the regulation of female sexuality (through the Family Protection Law) which retained elements of patriarchy and adherence to traditional understandings of sharia law. And at the same time, the state provided some provision for 'emancipatory potential for women'.[89]

The promotion of modernisation propagated by the Shah was not left unanswered or passively consumed by all Iranians, as aside from the many seminarians, sizeable numbers of students and intellectuals began to espouse a nativist doctrine that leaned heavily on Iran's Islamic heritage and rejected the superficial changes that were being implemented in political, economic and social spheres by Muhammad Riza Pahlavi. The most well-known work of this kind was *Gharbzādagī*, written in 1964 by Jalal Al-i Ahmad.[90] In terms of changes on the position of Iranian women Al-i Ahmad noted that the only real changes were the forceful removal of the veil and the opening of schools. He remarked, 'What have we really done? We have simply given women permission to display themselves in society. Just a display. That is exhibitionism … We've brought them into the streets, to exhibit themselves, to be without duties, to make up their faces, to wear new styles every day and to hang around.'[91] The religiously tinged nativist discourse of Al-i Ahmad was extremely popular in Iran, and no doubt it made the ulama aware of the urgent need to address similar issues in a way that would appeal to the burgeoning educated classes. It was of no use simply to compose treatises and fill them with arcane jurisprudential terminology or to cite passages from the Qur'an or include statements from the imams. What was needed was a more sophisticated rhetorical discourse that was both modern, adapting concepts

88 Paidar, *Women and the Political Process in Twentieth-Century Iran*, 153.
89 Paidar, *Women and the Political Process in Twentieth-Century Iran*, 157–8.
90 See Rochelle Terman, 'The piety of public participation: The revolutionary Muslim woman in the Islamic Republic of Iran', *Totalitarian Movements and Political Religions* 11.3/4, 2010, 289–319.
91 Jalal Al-i Ahmad, *Gharbzadegi* [Weststruckness], trans. John Green and Ahmad Alizadeh, Costa Mesa 1980, 80.

and terminology from the West, and which demonstrated the compatibility of such a discourse with traditional learning.

This discourse was indeed forthcoming, as Murtaza Mutahhari responded to Zanjani's articles (mentioned previously), and the mulla's views were subsequently published as *The System of Women's Rights in Islam* in 1974–5.[92] This work was representative of a traditionalist perspective that endorsed the complementarity of the sexes, and rejected equality. According to Dabashi, it supported an essentialist difference between men and women,[93] in which there was a strict binary between rights and duties. The argument endorsed temporary marriage and the general privileging of men over women. From a twenty-first century perspective the text appears exceedingly dated, although as Mir-Hosseini states, 'His arguments … are the most refined among those that give the concept of gender equality no place in Islam.'[94] To appreciate the stance adopted by Mutahhari, the secularising tendencies of the Shah and the modernists must be borne in mind. It is in this context that the contribution of Mutahhari assumes significance regarding the general jurisprudential perspective and the more particular issue of the hijab. Caution needs to be exercised of painting a rampant misogyny in Mutahhari's compositions, however, because he also held very progressive views against the grain of 'conservative' seminarian thinking, as has been indicated by Ardeshir Larijani, such as how women should have the right to issue fatwas and also to participate in politics, even taking high political positions.[95]

92 This is a work of some volume, being over 400 pages in the English translation. See Murtaza Mutahhari, *The Rights of Women in Islam*, Tehran 1981.
93 Hamid Dabashi, *Theology of Discontent*, New York 1993, 208.
94 Ziba Mir-Hosseini, 'Islam and gender justice', *Voices of Islam*, vol 5: *Voices of Change*, ed. Vincent Cornell, Omid Safi and Virginia Gray Henry, Westport 2007, 85–113.
95 Ardeshir Larijani, 'Mutahhari and His Approach to Women's Social Life'.

3

The Life and Thought of Murtaza Mutahhari

The Life of Mutahhari

One of the most prolific seminarian authors in the pre-revolutionary period, Murtaza Mutahhari composed both short and long tracts on the various religious, socio-political and economic issues prevalent in Iran during his lifetime. His work has elicited a range of responses. Negative responses come predominantly from academic commentators who are now based in the West, such as Mir-Hosseini who considers Mutahhari's approach 'defensive and apologetic', leaving scholars like him 'in an intellectual cul-de-sac',[1] and Abrahamian who maintains that Mutahhari's analysis of Marxism and class amounted to little more than 'half-baked and third-hand conservative arguments designed to preserve the socioeconomic status quo while implicitly questioning the political power structure'.[2] On the other hand, there are academics who have recognised the significant role Mutahhari played in Iran in the second half of the twentieth century. Martin claims that he was 'an outstanding political theorist, reformer and radical activist',[3] and Dabashi regards Mutahhari as wielding together an intellectual constituency among the traditional seminarian classes and in universities and middles classes, writing: 'The massive orchestration of social groupings and religious sentiments by all these ideologies considerably paved the way for the Islamic Revolution.'[4] Mutahhari's detractors and sympathisers agree on his role in both formulating an Islamic response to the

---

1 Mir-Hosseini, 'Islam and gender justice', 103.
2 Ervand Abrahamian, review of Hamid Dabashi, 'Theology of Discontent', *International Journal of Middle East Studies* 28.2, 1996, 300.
3 Vanessa Martin, *Creating an Islamic State*, London 2000, 75.
4 Dabashi, *Theology of Discontent*, 214.

Western ideologies that were becoming popular in Iran, and in developing ideas that were adopted in the country in the wake of the Revolution. It is noteworthy how Mutahhari is held in such esteem by the Islamic Republic, demonstrated at his funeral in 1979 when Ayatollah Khomeini wept openly and called him 'a part of my flesh' and a 'dear son'.[5] And the Islamic reformist president, Muhammad Khatami, acknowledged his respect for Mutahhari by dedicating to him a substantial section of his book, *Bīm-i Mawj* (*Fear of the Wave*).[6]

Born in 1920 into a seminarian family, Mutahhari pursued a religious education and participated in lessons delivered by both Ayatollahs Burujirdi and Khomeini (also becoming close friends with Montazeri). These associations, lessons and discussion groups provided the basis for Mutahhari's writings on a host of Islamic topics, including prophethood, ethics, justice, and the *Nahj al-Balāgha* among others. Aside from their dislike of the Shah's reforms, the seminarians were wary of the popularity of left-wing reform proposals, and Mutahhari composed numerous works and delivered speeches that refuted socialist and communist ideologies.[7]

During the 1960s, a wide spectrum of political groups engaged in propagating panaceas for Iran's malaise and identity crisis. The Tudeh Party, formally established in 1941, represented a radical socialist, secular solution.[8] Other left-wing groups included a nucleus of individuals who were to coalesce later into the Fidaʾyan-i Khalq in 1971, a Marxist-Leninist urban group. These individuals, inspired by Latin American revolutionaries, were busy forming cells and affiliated groups in Tehran, Tabriz and Mashhad.[9] Another solution to Iran's difficulties was

5 See Hamid Algar, 'Introduction', *Fundamentals of Islamic Thought: God, Man the Universe by Ayatullah Murtaza Mutahhari*, trans. R. Campbell, Berkeley 1985, 19.

6 Sayyid Muhammad Khatami, *Bīm-i Mawj* [*Fear of the Wave*], Tehran 1372/1993, 47–93. In the preface to the book Khatami comments that these compositions comprise speeches delivered at universities around 1370/1991. The title of the chapter on Mutahhari, 'Enlightened thought and splendour of religion', is reflective of Khatami's attitude towards Mutahhari and his thought.

7 See Dabashi, *Theology of Discontent*, 151–6. Mutahhari published the first and second volumes of *The Principles of Philosophy and the Realistic Method* in 1953 and 1954. Another influential work was *The Causes of Attraction to Materialism*, which was published in 1971, and reflects his lectures of the late 1960s. Until the end of his life he continued to debate such issues. For example, he published *A Criticism of Marxism* in 1977, and *Society and History* (a critique of the Marxist position) remained unfinished.

8 The Tudeh Party is dealt with extensively in Ervand Abrahamian, *Iran between Two Revolutions*, New Jersey 1982, 281–415.

9 Peyman Vahabzadeh, 'Fedāʾiyān-e Khalq', *Encyclopaedia Iranica*, 2015, http://www.iranicaonline.org/articles/fadaian-e-khalq.

provided by a range of groups and parties with various attachments to Islam. One element of this has been termed nativist, and is best typified in the aforementioned work, *Gharbzādagī*,[10] which combined a critique of the Westernising policies of the Shah and the excesses of modernisation with a desire to return to an 'authentic' Iranian culture and belief system which the author located in Islam.[11] Elements within the ulama were also active in promoting their own responses to Iran's situation under Muhammad Riza Pahlavi. The resistance of the ulama was led by Ayatollah Khomeini, who had emerged as a leader opposed to the Shah following the quiescent stance adopted by Ayatollah Burujirdi, the senior authority in Qum.[12] Khomeini rejected the apolitical approach, and he vehemently opposed the Shah's 'White Revolution' in 1963.[13] After launching a series of stinging criticisms against the Shah, he was arrested on 5 June 1963. Khomeini was not a lone figure in his fierce opposition to the Pahlavi regime. The Fidaʾyan-i Islam, which had existed since 1945, advocated an Islamic state in Iran and full implementation of sharia law, and it employed terrorist operations and assassinations against its un-Islamic opponents.[14]

Mutahhari's compositions reflect the context in which the struggle to represent a modern but 'authentic' Iran was being waged. In addition to writing on 'contemporary' topics, Mutahhari was among a group of mullas who wished to update seminarian structures. An initiative had been taken by Ayatollah Burujirdi to reorganise the *ḥawza* (seminarian establishment), and to this end he had established a small committee which included Khomeini. When the committee published its findings, Burujirdi realised that if the update was implemented, 'his authority concerning decision-making in the seminary' would have been severely compromised. The findings were never acted on, and Mutahhari's involvement resulted

10 Al-i Ahmad, *Gharbzadeghi*.

11 For a critical appraisal of Al-i Ahmad's views see Dabashi, *Theology of Discontent*, 39–101; see also Mehrzad Boroujerdi, *Iranian Intellectuals and the West: The Tormented Triumph of Nativism*, New York 1996, 65–76.

12 'During the fifteen years in which he was sole *marja*ʿ, Borujerdi maintained an almost unwaveringly quietist stance, remaining more or less neutral in the stormy political contests of the post-war period.' Hamid Algar, 'Borūjerdī, Ḥosayn Ṭabāṭabāʾī', *Encyclopaedia Iranica* 4.4, 377.

13 Ostensibly Khomeini disliked clauses within the White Revolution which did not include references to the adherence to Islam of voters and candidates in elections. The White Revolution also extended the vote to women, which was problematic to some seminarians. See Fakhreddin Azimi, 'Khomeini and the "White Revolution"', *A Critical Introduction to Khomeini*, ed. Arshin Adib-Moghaddam, Cambridge 2014, 19–42.

14 Farhad Kazemi, 'Fedāʾīān-e eslām', *Encyclopaedia Iranica* 9, Fasc. 5, 2012, 470–4; see also Davari, *The Political Thought of Ayatullah Murtaża Muṭaharri*, 20–3.

in a cooling of relations with Burujirdi.[15] Mutahhari's commitment to reform and modernisation was not quenched, however, and after Burujirdi's death he participated with a number of other leading mullas in a series of seminars focusing on the leadership of the seminary. Mutahhari submitted several papers, the main points of which have been summarised by Ann Lambton.[16] He called for the responsible use of *ijtihād*, and for believers to follow a *marjaʿ* who was a specialist in the appropriate field of knowledge.[17] In addition, he reflected on the funding that religious students receive from the *marjaʿ*, by which the religious establishment preserved its independence from the state, but which also meant that religious scholars lost some of their intellectual freedom, as they were dependent on the people who donated their religious taxes.

Whilst working as a reformist seminarian, Mutahhari was also employed in state structures of education, as in 1955 he was appointed Associate Lecturer of Philosophy in the Faculty of Theology in the University of Tehran. This new post must have placed Mutahhari in an awkward position in the light of his continuing support for his friend and mentor, Ayatollah Khomeini, who had opposed the Shah's White Revolution. Certainly, the Shah and state authorities must have regarded him with considerable suspicion, and Mutahhari was arrested on the same night as Khomeini (5 June 1963) by SAVAK, the infamous secret police, and put in prison for 43 days.[18] His application for promotion at the university was also denied.[19] But there was no doubt where Mutahhari's sympathies lay. Dabashi has observed, 'Between June 1963 and the advent of the revolutionary movement in 1977–79, Mutahhari was in constant contact with Ayatollah Khomeini, and, in fact, through a religious edict, became his sole representative in Iran in charge of collecting and dispensing religious taxes due to the exiled Ayatollah.'[20] In order to spread the message of the reformed version of Islam that was to meet challenges posed by left-wing secular ideologies and the kind of modernism espoused by the Shah, Mutahhari became instrumental in establishing a religious teaching and propagation institute, the Husayniyya Irshad, in north Tehran. It is of interest to see how Mutahhari intended to utilise the Irshad, especially as the following

15 Davari, *The Political Thought*, 29.

16 Ann K. S. Lambton, 'A reconsideration of the position of the Marjaʿ Al-Taqlīd and the religious institution', *Studia Islamica* 20, 1964, 115–35; Davari, *The Political Thought*, 34–5; Dabashi, *Theology of Discontent*, 161–2.

17 Lambton, 'A reconsideration of the position of the Marjaʿ Al-Taqlīd', 127.

18 Davari, *The Political Thought*, 38.

19 Dabashi, *Theology of Discontent*, 150.

20 Dabashi, *Theology of Discontent*, 150.

citation reflects also the perspectives of the two other jurist-theologians (Ahmad Qabil and Muhsin Kadivar) studied in this book:

> My objective is to use this Institute as an organisation for disseminating and researching Islam at a high level, in order to respond to the theoretical needs of the present volatile society. I want this Institute to be shaped in such a way as to provide a true picture of Islamic ideology, in contrast to the current ideologies of the present world. Naturally, I believe the message transmitted from this Institute, be it in writing or in a lecture, must be based on logical reasoning and not on emotions.[21]

Mutahhari's contribution to the Husayniyya Irshad was significant as he sat on the directors' board, lectured there and submitted several works to be published.[22] Despite the success of the institution in attracting large crowds to its functions, Mutahhari withdrew from the Husayniyya Irshad, largely because of differences with ʿAli Shariʿati, who also used the base to deliver his own brand of reformed Islam. Algar claims that the difference between the two was centred on the seminarian tradition; whereas Mutahhari had a deep respect for Shiʿi institutions and their particular jurisprudential methodologies, Shariʿati did not share this esteem.[23] There is no doubt that Shariʿati's work was immensely popular and could reach and motivate large numbers of young Iranians through its emotive messages and his direct rhetorical style.

Although Mutahhari withdrew from the Husayniyya Irshad, he continued lecturing elsewhere and publishing on Islamic jurisprudential and philosophical issues during the 1970s. He continued to criticise materialism and its supporters in Iran, some of whom had formed militant organisations. With the onset of the Islamic Revolution in 1978, Mutahhari flew to Paris to consult with Khomeini, and subsequently set up the Revolutionary Council to prepare the way for the new Islamic regime. When Khomeini was denied entry to Iran by Prime Minister

21 Murtaza Mutahhari, *Sayrī dar Zindigānī-yi Ustād Mutahharī*, Tehran 1991, cited by Davari, *The Political Thought*, 42,

22 Algar, 'Introduction', 15.

23 Algar, 'Introduction', 16. For Shariʿati's criticism of the clergy see Ali Rahnema, 'Ali Shariati; Teacher, Preacher, Rebel', *Pioneers of Islamic Revival*, ed. Ali Rahnema, London 1994, 232–3. Mutahhari too was not entirely enamoured with the seminarian institution and had been involved in proposals for reform. However, Shariʿati's virulent language and bluntness far surpassed any of Mutahhari's utterances. It is to be wondered how much of the difference between the two was choice of words, and how much was actual substance. The Mutahhari-Shariʿati relationship is also discussed by Davari, *The Political Thought*, 38–49.

Shapur Bakhtiyar, Mutahhari took sanctuary in protest in University of Tehran's mosque. On Khomeini's eventual return to Iran, Mutahhari had not yet taken up any official position when he was gunned down and killed by Furqan, a Marxist military group, on 1 May 1979.

The Jurisprudential Writings of Mutahhari

One of Mutahhari's major pre-occupations was to address the secular philosophies taking root amongst the young generation of Iranians from the 1950s and into the 1970s. The Shah's implementation of secularism increased during this period, but his dictatorial methods only strengthened the appeal of various left-wing ideological groups. Much of Mutahhari's writing reflects a deep desire to combat both. His scholarly activity in the 1960s took place following the death of the politically quiescent Ayatollah Burujirdi, when the seminary in general went through a period of soul searching, seeking to find methods to attract Iranians to their cause. Many of Mutahhari's speeches and published writings were directed at audiences that were not steeped in a jurisprudential milieu, but were graduates of a secular education, albeit interested in Iran's Islamic heritage. Therefore, Mutahhari was obliged to reach his new audience by employing the kind of terminology they would understand and appreciate, and by demonstrating his familiarity with the names and theories of popular Western philosophers and thinkers, thereby gaining a reputation as an Islamic thinker who could readily engage with modern thought. Many of his works contain scattered comments about and references to the British philosopher Bertrand Russell (d. 1970) and the American historian and philosopher Will Durant (d. 1981). This penchant to engage in debate with Western philosophies was not carried out in great depth, and suggests that he was either aware of the basic ideas and names of philosophers from the West, or else he was targeting his works at an elementary academic level. For example, in his work on the hijab, there is no mention of leading feminists in Europe such as Simone de Beauvoir, who in 1949 published *The Second Sex*, which was translated into English in 1953. Nevertheless, Mutahhari 'preferred to be generally known as a philosopher … [even though his] works seem to be more those of a modern theologian'.[24] Underpinning these 'philosophical' works is a firm commitment to traditional Islamic jurisprudence, and in particular the role of reason (*'aql*) in formulating responses to challenges posed by modernity.

As mentioned earlier, in the early 1960s, many within the seminarian

24 Davari, *The Political Thought*, 31.

establishment were reviewing their own position and function, and this resulted in a series of seminars, the outcome of which was a publication in 1962, titled *Baḥthī Darbarā-yi Marjaʿiyat va Rūḥāniyat* (*A Discussion about Leadership and Spiritual Authorities*).[25] Mutahhari offered two short essays in this book on the theme of *ijtihād*.[26] Another important work is *Islām va Muqtażiyāt-i Zamān* (*Islam and the Requirements of the Time*), which he published in the early 1970s.[27] In addition to these theoretical works, Mutahhari published a number of shorter essays dealing with more practical and specific issues, such as *Masʾala-yi Ḥijāb* ('The Question of the Hijab') and *Niẓām-i Ḥuqūq-i Zan dar Islām* ('The System of Women's Rights in Islam').[28]

In Mutahhari's 'The Principle of *Ijtihād* in Islam' (a short essay of some nineteen pages in the English translation), *ijtihād* is defined as 'the employment of careful consideration and reasoning in reaching an understanding of the valid proofs of the sharia'. In the Shiʿi tradition, the resources for such an investigation are the Book (Qurʾan), the Sunna (the life of the Prophet as replicated in the hadith and sayings of the imams), *ijmāʿ* (consensus of opinions from the jurists) and *ʿaql* (reason). But Mutahhari pointed out that deriving truths from the proofs of the sharia is not the task for any rational person. It required 'competence and expert technical knowledge' of Qurʾanic Arabic and the various fields of Qurʾanic studies (such as matters relating to abrogation, the clear and ambiguous verses, the science of hadith, the history of transmission, and so on). In other words, *ijtihād*, and the use of reason to ascertain an understanding of sharia is the domain of the expert jurisprudent alone. The need for the qualified jurist had become increasingly evident in the modern world because of the enormous advances and developments of various sciences. Mutahhari seemed to believe that an exchange of ideas was necessary, although it is not exactly clear whether he meant between specialities of 'secular' sciences, or consultation and dialogue within the science of *fiqh*. However, it is clear that he favoured the reduction of an individualistic approach among the ulama, and preferred the creation of councils in the seminaries for decision-making to be made on the basis of consensus.

In an even shorter essay titled 'The Role of Reason in *Ijtihād*',[29] he endorsed reason in accepting religious laws and cited the well-known narration from Imam

25 Mutahhari, *Baḥthī dar barā-yī Marjaʿiyat va Rūḥāniyat*, Tehran 1341/1962.

26 These chapters have been rendered into English as *The Principle of Ijtihad in Islam*, and *The Role of Reason in Ijtihad.*

27 Mutahhari, *Islām va Muqtażiyāt-i Zamān.*

28 Mutahhari, *Niẓām-i Ḥuqūq-i Zan dar Islām*, Tehran 1370/1991.

29 Mutahhari, 'The Role of Reason in Ijtihad'.

Kazim that recognises reason as an 'inner proof' and an 'internal prophet', and he accepted the definite judgements of reason as enjoying the approval of the Divine Lawgiver.[30] He rejected the alternative of considering 'the aim and purpose of the sharia as entailing mere obligation and acts of absolute servility devoid of any objective, and clos[ing] all the doors on research and intellectual inquiry'. While appearing to argue from a logical, rational, scientific perspective, and framing thought-provoking questions such as whether human rights precede social existence, or whether the rights of the individual in society are posterior to society, it is unfortunate that in this brief essay Mutahhari did not provide specific examples of how reason should be understood in light of modern human rights. According to traditional Islamic thought, such arguments are irrelevant in any case, as the individual has no real intrinsic right, which belongs to God and society. In comparison, freedom and equality for all has been more commonly associated in modern Western philosophical circles with perspectives that have not been tied to religious tradition. However, Mutahhari's careful rhetorical skills enabled him to avoid such questions, although they are given an Islamic veneer in statements such as: 'The aim is to stress the scientific study of problems which are covered in the great scope of the teachings of Islam.' It is a language that both encouraged the inquisitive and educated youth of Iran, who were attracted by modern ideologies to investigate such issues but also to include Islam and its heritage in that discussion.

Mutahhari's jurisprudential writings and his ideas about the role of reason in jurisprudence are further elaborated in his *Fiqh va Uṣūl-i Fiqh* (*Jurisprudence and the Principles of Jurisprudence*). As one of the four sources of jurisprudence, reasoning necessarily accorded with what is contained in the other sources. Indeed, Mutahhari even observed that no proof other than reason was necessary in some cases because of its binding testimony. There could be no contradiction between revelation and narrations on the one hand and reason on the other. This was due to the belief that both the sharia and reason ensured the best interests of human beings, and prohibited those things that were in their worst interests. Mutahhari offered the example of opium, the use of which is not explicitly mentioned in the Qur'an or hadith. However, reason demonstrated its harm and corruption, and its use is clearly not in the best interests of humans. Mutahhari also offered conclusions on topics of debate that were not so clear cut, and he deviated from traditional juristic understandings, thereby providing himself with space in which he could reach out to both seminarian readers and modern secular

30 Mutahhari, 'The Role of Reason in Ijtihad'.

audiences. Dabashi points to Mutahhari's arguments related to music and the plastic arts. In *Taʿlīm va Tarbiyat* (*Education and Training*), Mutahhari prohibited certain forms of music because it dulled the mind, in a similar way that wine and gambling have the same effect. Thus, based on jurisprudential traditions and 'rationality', Mutahhari attempted to provide a ruling to satisfy two audiences; the traditional Shiʿi ulama by referring to the views of past scholars, and the modern generation seeking satisfying 'rational' answers. Dabashi argues that Mutahhari deliberately left himself space to legitimise certain kinds of music, as his was not a blanket prohibition, covering only music that dulled the mind.[31] Dabashi also points to Mutahhari's jurisprudential/rational prohibition of sculpture. Mutahhari's argument was counterfactual, and it betrays a rather negative perspective of society and its lack of intellectual development, which is challenged by subsequent jurist-theologians, as we shall see in the following sections of the book. Indeed, if reason is universal, then one wonders if Mutahhari would have understood Western Europe, China and Japan as idolatrous because of the very long and rich history of sculpture (both for secular and sacred purposes). Dabashi claims that Mutahhari's rejection of the plastic arts was not a blanket ban, as he wished to leave himself some wriggle-room for 'future negotiation' between the secular intellectuals and the seminarians. And Dabashi concludes that 'this glorification of rationality, however rooted in canonical sources, is the necessary and inevitable preface for engagement in contemporary social issues ... no-one did more than Mutahhari in legitimating this updated Shiʿi juridical discourse'.[32]

Yet the difficulty of equating Mutahhari's traditional Shiʿi understandings with reason has been highlighted by Mir-Hosseini. She has shown how Mutahhari upheld the complementarity approach to gender, which foregrounded the innate differences between men and women in society. This necessitates different rights and duties, which for the traditional seminarian were enshrined in revelation, and which accorded with the 'nature of things' and reason. Mutahhari's essentialisation of male and female emotions and love appears rather antiquated, even though Mir-Hosseini considers his views as 'the most refined among those that give the concept of gender equality no place in Islam'.[33] Mutahhari states,

> Man wants the woman herself, and yet woman wants the heart of man and his self-sacrifices. For man, insofar as he possesses the woman herself, he does

31 Dabashi, *Theology of Discontent*, 202–3.
32 Dabashi, *Theology of Discontent*, 201.
33 Mir-Hosseini, 'Islam and gender justice', 99.

> not care if he loses her heart. Thus, man does not care that on polygyny he loses the heart and the sentiments of the woman. But for woman, the heart and the sentiments of man are essential. If she loses that, she loses everything.[34]

Mutahhari's defence in *Niẓām-i Ḥuqūq-i Zan dar Islām* of certain practices fails to convince readers whose criterion of acceptability is reason. He defends polygamy, temporary marriage, the practice of giving a dowry, believes that 'women are "essentially" more prone than men to conspicuous consumption',[35] defends the Qur'anic imbalance in inheritance laws, and accepts the male prerogative to initiate divorce, although he admits there are some circumstances when a woman too can commence divorce proceedings.

The linkage of sharia with reason in a specific way, however, does not mean that such understandings need to be fixed, as Mutahhari himself was an advocate of linking rulings to the inevitable developments and transformations that unfold in society over time. This makes the above kinds of essentialist positions in *Niẓām-i Ḥuqūq-i Zan dar Islām* appear out of date. Mutahhari advanced these ideas in the 1960s and 1970s when women's rights, intellectual perspectives on gender issues, and the societal changes that took place in Iran after the Islamic Revolution (and in particular, after the Iran-Iraq war, which in many ways offered women different opportunities) had yet to result in new articulations of women's rights in Islamic society. Although he argued for essentialist and from biologically determined perspectives, Mutahhari also advocated the kind of jurisprudence that demands flexibility and the need to respond to the requirements of the times, which he considered as the most important social issue of the age.[36] He discussed this idea in his *Islām va Muqtaẓiyāt-i Zamān* which was published in 1973, a few years after his writings and lectures on the hijab. Some scholars, typified by the contemporary seminarian, Mahdi Mihrizi, claim that if jurists adopted the same kind of rational methodology as Mutahhari, then many of the problems (especially those relating to women) would be solved – which is a same kind of claim made by Ahmad Qabil about his own thought.[37]

---

34 Dabashi, *Theology of Discontent*, 208, citing Mutahhari, *Niẓām-i Ḥuqūq-i Zan dar Islām*, 350. Ardeshir Larijani also cited Mutahhari's comments, that men are the slaves of passion and need to love and protect, while women need to be loved and protected. See Larijani, *Mutahhari and His Approach to Women's Social Life*, 145, citing *Niẓām-i Ḥuqūq-i Zan dar Islām*, 159–165.

35 Dabashi, *Theology of Discontent*, 208.

36 Mutahhari, *Islām va Muqtaẓiyāt-i Zamān*, vol. 1, 11.

37 See Sareh Ardeshir Larijany, 'Mutahhari and his approach to Women's Social Life: with

Mutahhari's position on reason often frustrates the reader because of the dissonance between his theoretical perspectives and the practical implementation of rulings with social relevance. On the one hand, he claimed that there was no contradiction between reason and the divine books or Sunna, and that reason was to be regarded as a source for deducing Islamic commands, and the latter were related to human expediency (*maṣlaḥat*). Necessary acts were followers of necessary expediency for humans, and forbidden acts were followers for necessary corruptions. So confident was Mutahhari in the efficacy of reason that he maintained it was not necessary for there to be a reason given for a Qur'anic or Sunna based command. He said, 'We understand the apparent meaning of the Qur'an and the Sunna through the command of the definite proof of *'aql*. There is no contradiction between the Qur'an and *'aql*.'[38] Mutahhari simply asked his opponents to produce an example of such contradictions, which he obviously believed was beyond the realm of possibility. On the other hand, he qualified the previous perspective by stating that this did not mean that reason had free reign in determining the correct course of action, as the application of such reason became active when there was a lack of guidance in the Qur'an or Sunna.[39] Only in this situation could the command of reason discover the expediency or corruption in an act.[40] It is on this point that the next generation of Islamic jurists and theologians advance further than Mutahhari and make explicit their beliefs that reason determines any interpretation of sacred scripture, even if it seems to contradict the specific commands of a particular case.

Mutahhari and the Hijab

Mutahhari discussed the charges to sartorial preferences which had been so controversial in Iran throughout the twentieth century in *Islām va Muqtażiyāt-i Zamān*, which he hoped would demonstrate the flexibility of his jurisprudential perspectives. He raised the particular issue of whether the *kulāh shāpaw* (or the Western style hat for men) was *ḥarām*.[41] The Western style brimmed hat had been a contentious matter ever since Riza Shah introduced a decree in 1928 enforcing

special reference to Political Participation and Issuing Fatwas', PhD thesis submitted to the University of Birmingham, July 2020, 49.

38 Mutahhari, *Islām va Muqtażiyāt-i Zamān*, 37.

39 Mutahhari, *Islām va Muqtażiyāt-i Zamān*, 37.

40 Mutahhari, *Islām va Muqtażiyāt-i Zamān*.

41 Mutahhari, *Islām va Muqtażiyāt-i Zamān*, 241.

Western sartorial styles on men, except clergymen.[42] Of significance was that men were obliged to wear the so-called Pahlavi hat, cylindrical in shape and sporting a brim at the front, replacing the traditional fur hat and turban. Chehabi has observed how 'objection to the Pahlavi hat centered on its visor, which impeded touching the ground in prayer. Some Tehran ulama took sanctuary in Qom, and the bazaars closed in protest'.[43] Seven years later in May 1935, the Shah introduced the chapeau as part of the process of Westernisation and modernisation. And so, on 8 July 'the fedora was made obligatory by cabinet decree. All state employees were ordered to wear the new hat or be put on unpaid leave'.[44]

The Qur'an is silent on the requirement to wear a turban, although hadith literature contains several examples of Muhammad advocating its use, explaining how it is 'the crown of the Arabs'; 'the turban is the boundary between faith and infidelity'; and, 'The same distance separates the turban from the hat as separates us from the polytheists'.[45] In pre-modern Iran, it was never made obligatory to wear a turban, although according to Islamic law, as Algar states, it was either *mandūb* (highly recommended) or *mustaḥabb* (desirable), and wearing it was particularly encouraged during prayer.[46] The removal of the turban was not meant to leave Iranian heads naked, as its replacement by the hat ensured that the male head was covered, which was one of the important functions of the turban.

As a scholar trained in the seminaries, and as a student who grew up during the 'modernising/Westernising' periods of Riza Shah, it is inconceivable that Mutahhari would have been unaware of the hadith literature related to the turban. At the same time, he must also have realised that to insist on wearing the turban would have been tantamount to 'swimming against the tide'. Perhaps the reality that the turban was still only current in the seminaries – that it provided the ulama with some kind of differentiation from non-seminarians – in addition to the non-obligatory nature of the turban according to Islamic law, persuaded him that it was an issue that could indeed reflect the changing tastes and requirements of the times. In his work of 1973, he argued in the following manner:

42 Ali-Akbar Saidi Sirjani, 'Clothing xi. In the Pahlavi and post-Pahlavi periods', *Encyclopaedia Iranica* V.8, 2011, 808–11, http://www.iranicaonline.org/articles/clothing-xi.
43 Houchang E. Chehabi, 'Staging the emperor's new clothes: Dress codes and nation-building under Reza Shah', *Iranian Studies* 26.3/4, 1993, 212.
44 Chehabi, 'Staging the emperor's new clothes', 215.
45 These hadiths are cited in Hamid Algar, ''Amāma', *Encyclopaedia Iranica*, originally published 15 December 1989, updated 2 August 2011. This article is available in print: vol. I.9, 919–21
46 Algar, ''Amāma', *Encyclopedia Iranica*.

> If they ask, 'Is the brimmed hat *ḥarām* or not, is the suit and tie *ḥarām* or not?' We say, 'At one time these have been *ḥarām*, but now they are not *ḥarām*, although there was a time when the brimmed hat was quite foreign. It was, indeed, a foreigner's hat. If someone wore this hat, it meant that he was a Christian. Wearing the brimmed hat carried this sense. For as long as [men put on] this hat, it signalled that any Muslim who wore it was performing forbidden acts. But when [wearing] this hat became customary throughout the whole world, the people of each religious school (*madhhab*) and each religious community (*millat*) accepted it, and that particular signification was dropped, and since the signification was forgotten, today that [sartorial] garment no longer has the meaning that it had in previous times. And a new prophet does not need to come [i.e. to make the hat lawful].'[47]

Mutahhari's reasoning for abandoning the turban – a tradition which has several hundreds of years background as well as Islamic legitimation – because of changing customs, appears somewhat inconsistent when compared with his intransigent stance on the hijab, the donning of which he believed was mandatory according to Islamic law. Perhaps Mutahhari was influenced in his writings by the more secular intellectuals who had addressed similar questions about changing sartorial fashions in Iran, such as Ahmad Kasravi, who had initiated a discussion in the 1930s with the readers of his newspaper about the benefits and detriments of wearing the necktie.[48] Rather than present a 'backward-looking' image of Islam, Mutahhari desired to offer a vision of Islam that was capable of responding to new situations – at least for men.

But how did Mutahhari respond to similar issues, the 'modernising/Westernising' challenges that were imposed upon women? Covering for women is linked with modesty, and Riza Shah's sartorial policy for women did not necessarily leave women bareheaded, as wearing Western style hats was a possibility. However, the custom of using a face veil appears relatively common in Iran during the 1930s, and in addition, the practice of using a *chādur* to drape around the head offered women a traditional form of social distancing from men. The removal of the head-covering and *chādur* was therefore a threat to Islamic notions of female modesty. The prophetic utterances on the turban are not connected with modesty or chastity, but more with distinctions from non-believers, and so comparisons with the hijab are problematic if these criteria are used to value the rationale for their use.

---

47 Mutahhari, *Islām va Muqtażiyāt-i Zamān*, 241.
48 Lloyd Ridgeon, 'Ahmad Kasravi and "pick-axe" politics', *Iran* 56.1, 2016, 59–72.

*

In September 1966, Mutahhari commenced a series of seven lectures, concluding in January 1967, on the subject of the hijab. These lectures have been translated and published by Laleh Bakhtiar as *The Islamic Modest Dress*.[49] The English translation is structured into seven lessons. Mutahhari admitted, however, that he added more material to his Persian book since delivering the lectures, and this new material does not seem to appear in Bakhtiar's translation.[50] Of particular interest in this respect are Mutahhari's dealing with the *jilbāb* (my translation of which is included at the end of Part Two).[51]

This work on the hijab was one of the most substantial considerations of the topic in the respect that not only did it focus on specific Qur'anic verses and sacred sayings about the hijab, albeit in a rather condensed fashion, but it also reflected on the criticisms and arguments related to the topic that had emerged from non-seminarian critics. The work was a 'wake-up call' to the established seminarians in Iran. They disliked the work, as they believed Mutahhari's writing on the subject was deviant. One contemporary Iranian mulla observed, 'The only crime of Martyr Mutahhari, who was seen as an outcast, was that he addressed the issue of women.'[52] It seems seminarians realised that issues related to women were problematic, but they desired to address the problem 'behind closed doors'. Mutahhari's main aim was to include women in society, and the traditional forms of thinking and sartorial custom prevented this. For Mutahhari, women had a full role to play in society, which would have been difficult if they were obliged to cover their hands and face. Indeed, such an understanding of how women should be concealed had generated a false understanding of Islam, and this, combined with the onslaught from secularising intellectuals, had caused women to reject the religious tradition outright. Mutahhari said:

> We all know that today a large section of society which incorrectly calls itself

---

49 Mutahhari, *The Islamic Modest Dress*, trans. Laleh Bakhtiar, USA 1988.

50 See Mutahhari's comments in his introduction to the second print-run.

51 The two works are structured differently. Whereas Mutahhari's Persian original has five chapters, Bakhtiyar divides her translation into seven chapters. She largely follows the same contours, although on occasions a paragraph or topic of discussion appears missing, only to appear several paragraphs later.

52 Cited in Mir-Hosseini, *Islam and Gender*, 107–8. Ja'fariyan mentions a Dr. Baqer Hojjati as one among the critics of Mutahhari. See R. Jaʿfariyān, *Dāstān-i Ḥijāb dar Irān Pīsh az Inqalāb* [*The Case of the Hijab in Iran Before the Revolution*], Tehran 1383/2004–5, 156,

> 'intellectual' looks at Islam in a negative fashion on issues related to women. They do not know what Islam has said, and they are unaware of Islam's social philosophy, and so their negative views are absolutely groundless. Following its sensual desires, this group in practice is not bound to the hijab or modesty, rather, since they are unaware of the Islamic hijab and its logic, they believe that this is a superstition. It is a command that is the cause of human misfortune, and this way of thinking causes distance, indeed, their estrangement and exit from Islam.[53]

Mutahhari's *Mas'ala-yi Ḥijāb* is an attempt to present the Islamic 'truth' about the commands on women's covering, while trying to convince two audiences. The first (and primary audience) was the conservative seminarian who believed women should cover completely (including their hands and face). The Iranian scholar Davari considers the work in the context of the wives of Iranian mullas who not only wore a hijab to cover their head hair, but also a face-veil, and thereby placed even those women who had adopted the scarf and manteaux under intense pressure.[54] The second audience was the modern, educated secular individuals who viewed such sartorial traditions as anachronistic.

At the beginning of the work, Mutahhari proceeded to refute philosophical, social, economic, ethical and psychological explanations for the introduction of the hijab in Islamic society. He rejected the philosophical argument that it had been instituted following a turn to ascetic practices which attempted to subdue the ego, because in his idealist understanding of Islam, asceticism was not prescribed as an activity to be followed. Mutahhari then rejected the social argument, which was based on the supposed insecurity people felt in society. He excluded this argument too, claiming that insecurity was social or group based, and indeed, tribal conflict meant that not only were women taken, but so too were men and children. Covering was not a solution for this form of insecurity according to Mutahhari. Unfortunately he did not really address the way traditional Islamic histories of the early period of the Islamic community connect the harassment of uncovered women with non-Muslim Arabs.[55] The third reason relates to economic modes of production, presumably in response to perceptions of communism and socialism in Iran which were popular among the student population. Here Mutahhari

53 Mutahhari, *Mas'ala-yi Ḥijāb*, 161.
54 Davari, *The Political Thought*, 51.
55 The insecurity faced by women in pre-Islamic Arabia and also within the period of Muhammad's prophetic career is discussed in Fatima Mernissi, *The Veil and the Male Elite: A Feminist Interpretation of Women's Rights in Islam*, Reading 1997, 148–60.

contested the classification of four historical periods, the second and longest of which was supposedly an era during which men ruled women and put them to work in the house and considered it an advantage to 'put women behind a curtain and prevent them coming and going'.[56] Again, relying upon an idealist vision of the Islamic message, Mutahhari rebutted such economic reductionism. And he said that there was no such justification for this binary division of labour inside and outside the home in Islam. Here Mutahhari's arguments appear to be more solid, as there are examples in early Islamic history of active female involvement in various spheres, such as the economic role played by Khadija, Muhammad's first wife. The ethical reason, or the fourth, discusses how the inherent nature of man desires to enjoy woman exclusively for himself. Mutahhari condemned this view, since he held that the natural instinct to guard women should not come from jealousy but zeal (*ghayrat*), and thus it should be orientated to society and not the individual. The last reason explaining the adoption of Islamic modest dress is the psychological one. Mutahhari understood this reason as being based on the belief that some women think they lack something organic in their body in comparison to men, which is exemplified by their menstrual cycle. The argument is less than clear, but Mutahhari seems to imply that people believed that covering was a means to protect symbolically against this deficiency. He repudiated the psychological view with reference to scriptural evidence that menstruation is not as deplorable an event as it was, for example, believed to be among the Jews.

Regardless of the relative strengths or otherwise of Mutahhari's criticisms of these five reasons for the adoption of Islamic modest dress, the significance of his text is the argumentation of his writing, his confidence in tackling 'modern' theories and his citation of Western thinkers. While his citations do not reach the standards of contemporary critical analysis (there are no specific references), Mutahhari peppered his arguments with testimonials from the likes of Will Durant,[57] Bertrand Russell,[58] and Sigmund Freud,[59] and in this manner he gave his arguments the semblance of academic learning. This may be understandable in the light of increasing numbers of Iranian students attending universities who might

56 Mutahhari, *The Islamic Modest Dress*, 31. (All references to the Islamic Dress in this chapter of the book are to Bakhtiar's translation, unless otherwise stated.)
57 Mutahhari, *The Islamic Modest Dress*, 10.
58 Mutahhari, *The Islamic Modest Dress*, 33. See the Persian original, *Mas'ala-yi Ḥijāb*, 112–15.
59 Mutahhari, *The Islamic Modest Dress*, 38.

have appreciated references to 'masters' of 'Western' knowledge, even though Mutahhari's use of such arguments was selective and very general.[60]

Having dismissed five of the contemporary reasons for the command to wear the hijab in Islamic society, Mutahhari proceeded to explain the 'real' cause. He defended the hijab from the criticism that it 'imprisons a woman and makes her a slave',[61] and instead he countered by claiming that the Islamic modest dress bestowed dignity, honour and respect. Wearing the hijab did not mean that women had to stay in the house; if they left the house correctly attired, 'it prevents the interference from men who lack ethics and morality'. This argument was augmented with references to sacred scripture which alluded to the private nature of one's home, and the need to show respect to its inhabitants (females), and not simply for those who wished to enter a house to barge in uninvited, which would have caused embarrassment to the female occupants if they were unsuitably dressed. In addition, Mutahhari referred to Q. 24.30 which commands men and women to 'cast down their glances', and 'to guard their private parts'. This verse is not specific to clothing, but it concerns correct morality and demeanour.

One of Mutahhari's main concerns in the text was exploring the concept of whether the face and hands should be covered, which reflected the disquiet of the seminarians in the 1960s, and the associated debate about the participation of women in society. As such, the contemporary controversy about hair and covering head hair was peripheral to Mutahhari's book, and he seldom mentioned the need to cover hair. But there are a couple of passages which suggest hair-covering is mandatory, such as: 'Covering [places] other than the face and hands is necessary (*vājib*) for a woman, and from the perspective of jurisprudence there exists no doubt about this.'[62] This passage, however, may simply refer to covering the breasts and the private parts.

He also comments on the narration from Imam Sadiq that it is permissible to look at the hair of women from Tahama (on the outskirts of Mecca), female Arab bedouin, women who lived on the outskirts of cities, and women with no religion among the non-Arabs, because they had not accepted Islam even after they were warned.[63] Mutahhari noted that some jurists, such as Ayatollah Aqa Sayyid ʿAbd

60 Ziba Mir-Hosseini, 'Rethinking gender: Discussions with Ulama in Iran', *Critique: Critical Middle Eastern Studies* 7.13, 1998, 52.

61 Bakhtiar, 41.

62 Mutahhari, *Masʾala-yi Ḥijāb*, 196. See also Mutahhari, *Masʾala-yi Ḥijāb*, 221.

63 Mutahhari, *Masʾala-yi Ḥijāb*, 215. Kadivar cites the very same narration that runs to this effect. See Part Four. Kadivar references *Al-Kāfī*, vol. 5, 524, hadith no. 1; *al-Faqīh*, vol. 3,

al-Hadi Shirazi,[64] had related that reproaching city-dwelling women – who were compared to village women – and urging them to cover had no effect on their behaviour of appearing bareheaded, and so the gaze of men upon the hair of such women was not prohibited. Mutahhari extended that command to urban women who refused to listen to pietistic admonitions. While he admitted that other great *marjaʿ taqlīd*s had issued opinions and given fatwa similar to that of the aforementioned Ayatollah, he was careful to note that most of the jurists did not share this opinion, even in relation to rural women. Mutahhari did not give his own opinion, yet at the very least, the narration may easily be understood as endorsing a policy that does not imply compulsion, which assumes greater significance in the more recent situation in Iran in the twenty-first century.

That Mutahhari did approve of the necessity of head-hair covering is supported by his referral to a hadith in which Muhammad responded to seeing Asma, the daughter of Abu Bakr, who entered the Prophet's house in a thin form of clothing which showed her bodily shape, by saying that women over the age of puberty should only show their faces and hands, the inference being that the head hair should be concealed.[65]

Mutahhari's belief in the necessity of covering head hair is also implicit in his discussion of the *khimār* (pl. *khumur*), a word used in the Qurʾan 24.31 ('let them draw their *khumur* over their breasts').[66] The Qurʾan does not specify what the *khimār* was like, and since it only occurs in the text once, its exact form is open to speculation. Mutahhari simply glossed the *khimār* as *rū-sarī* (scarf, head-covering), which he supposed was used to conceal the head and the breasts. One of his chief concerns was to refute the idea that the *khimār* was like a face-veil that hung below the eyes and covered the nose and mouth, also concealing the breasts and chest. He argued that leaving the face free and visible, the *khimār* was a like a small scarf and covered the head and hair (*mū-hā*), and it was the *jilbāb* (a large scarf – *rū-sarī-yi buzurg*) that covered the breasts and other regions.[67] Mutahhari's analysis here is weak because he fails to show that these garments were used to cover the head.

300, hadith no. 1438; *ʿIlal al-Sharāʾyi*, 565, hadith 1; *Dhikr ahl al-Dhimma badl al-ʿUlūj, Wasāʾil, abwāb Muqaddamat al-Nikah*, vol. 113, hadith no. 1, vol. 20, 206.

64 Ayatollah Aqa Sayyid ʿAbd al-Hadi Shirazi was a mulla based in Iraq and who was famous for his anti-communist and anti-socialist stance at a time when pro-communist forces were strong. He died in 1962.

65 Mutahhari, *Masʾala-yi Ḥijāb*, 159.

66 Mutahhari, *Masʾala-yi Ḥijāb*, 206–7.

67 Mutahhari, *Masʾala-yi Ḥijāb*, 207.

The word *jilbāb*, mentioned above, occurs in Q. 33.59–60: 'O Prophet! Say to your wives and daughters and the believing women that they draw their outer garments (*jilbāb*) close to them.' Mutahhari recognised that the word *jilbāb* offers its own challenges, simply because it is unclear what this garment was like at the time of the Prophet. He referred to the *Munjid* (presumably the *Munjid al-Muqriīin wa-Murshid al- Ṭālibīn* of Ibn al-Jaziri (d. 1350)), and reported that in this work a *jilbāb* is described as a 'loose dress' (*pīrāhan yā libās-i gushād*).[68] Mutahhari did not like this description of the *jilbāb*, probably because a loose dress might not be able to cover the hair. He then referred to the *Mufradā* (*al-Mufradā fī Gharib al-Qur'an*) by Raghib Isfahani (d. 1108), who defined the *jilbāb* as a dress and a scarf (*pīrāhan va rū-sarī*).[69] Mutahhari also cited a report attributed to Imam Riza, who said that old women may put aside the *jilbāb* and it is not a problem if one looks at the hair of old women. Mutahhari then stated, 'here it is not clear if the *jilbāb* covered the hair and the head'. In effect, Mutahhari's discussion of the *jilbāb* does not convince the reader that this garment was meant to cover the hair. It certainly leaves a chink in the argument about hair covering which later scholars were to probe further.

The importance of Mutahhari's text is that at the time of the Islamic Revolution, and subsequent to this, it has been recognised as the standard and authoritative statement on the hijab and the religious value that it holds. Although written in a context of the late 1960s when Iran was still in the process of being 'modernised' by the Shah, and when female voices were not as audible as they are in the contemporary period, the text remains crucial and has been cited approvingly even by thc likes of Ayatollah Montazeri. Aside from issues relating to covering, with which the more recent New Religious Thinkers take issue (to be explored in Parts Three and Four), Mutahhari's text also contains vestiges of a worldview that is not consonant with Western notions of gender as a social construct. Consider the following: 'That which exists within a woman is the desire to show herself off, it is part of her nature. That which exists within man is an inclination towards looking, not just looking but flirting and receiving pleasure from it.'[70]

68 Mutahhari, *Mas'ala-yi Ḥijāb*, 186.
69 Mutahhari, *Mas'ala-yi Ḥijāb*, 186.
70 Mutahhari, *Mas'ala-yi Ḥijāb*, 278. Mutahhari, *The Islamic Modest Dress*, 64.

4

Translation of Mutahhari's 'The Philosophy of Covering in Islam'[1]

As stated earlier, Mutahhari's lectures of 1966–67 were translated by Laleh Bakhtiar into English and published as *The Islamic Modest Dress* in 1988. The Persian publication of these lectures has been through several editions since Mutahhari himself refined and edited the lectures for publication, which appeared in print form in 1969. Bakhtiar's English version of the lectures does not vary significantly from Mutahhari's sanitised version. However, the order of sub-sections is sometimes changed, and occasionally Mutahhari has cut some subsections from his text. One example is the discussion of 'Muslim Custom' in which he argues that customs may be abandoned if they are found not to have existed within the Prophet's community. Covering the face, according to Mutahhari, is something that Islam does not prescribe, and thus reflects a custom from pre-Islamic times.

The discussion in the previous section focused on, among other things, Mutahhari's rejection of the five reasons that the critics of the hijab gave for its appearance in society. As a rejoinder, Mutahhari provided the Islamic perspective, and it is this section of his work that is translated here. It features the third chapter, or discussion, in the Persian text. (The text used for this translation is Mutahhari, *Mas'ala-yi Ḥijāb*, second edition, Tehran 1969–70. The Persian text is between pages 71–94). Subsequently his discussion about the *jilbāb* is translated.

The page numbers of the original Persian are given in the text in bold font, inside square brackets. Mutahhari provides limited footnoting. I have supplemented this by adding a few explanatory footnotes which appear in square brackets.

1 *Falsafa-yi Pūshish dar Islām.*

THE PHILOSOPHY OF COVERING IN ISLAM

[71] The philosophies that we mentioned previously for covering are often justifications that the opponents of covering have created and used. They have called [the hijab] something illogical and irrational. It is a method whereby if a person supposes the issue is based on superstition to begin with, its explication will also conform with superstition. If the discussants investigate the subject impartially, they will discover that the philosophy of covering and the Islamic hijab are not [included] in their empty and baseless discourses.

We believe in a particular philosophy for the covering of women from an Islamic perspective, which accords with reason. And from an analytical viewpoint one can consider it as the basis of the hijab in Islam.

The Word 'Hijab'

[72] Before we begin our arguments on this topic, it is necessary that we remember one point. This concerns the lexical meaning of hijab which in our time has become a word for covering women. The word hijab means both covering (*pūshīdan*) and also veil (*parda*) and screen (*ḥājib*). Mostly, its usage bears the meaning of a veil. This word conveys the meaning of covering because a veil is a way of covering. Perhaps one might even say that in the origin of the word every covering is not a hijab; that covering is called a hijab when it takes place through a veil. In the glorious Qur᾿an, in the story of Solomon, the setting of the sun is described in this way: 'until the sun was covered' [38.32]. The diaphragm separating the heart from the stomach is called a 'hijab'.

In a command that the Commander of the Faithful wrote to Malik Ashtar, he states: **[73]** 'Mingle with the people. Spend less time inside your home, hidden from the people. Do not separate your chamberlain (*ḥājib*) and doorkeeper (*darbān*) from the people, rather present yourself and be in contact with them so that the weak and helpless can tell you of their needs and complaints, and you will be aware of the way things are going.' In [his] *Muqadamma*, Ibn Khaldun has a chapter bearing the title 'Chapter explaining how governments do not consider a separation to exist between themselves and the people, but gradually a separation and a veil between the ruler and the people gets larger until finally it produces disagreeable consequences'. Ibn Khaldun used the word hijab in the sense of veil and distance, not covering.

The use of the word hijab on the topic of covering women is a relatively new form of expression. In the old times and, in particular, in the expressions of the jurists, the word *sitr*, meaning covering, was used. The jurists used the word *sitr*, not hijab, whether in books on prayer or in books on marriage, where this issue has been referred to.

It would have been better if this word [*sitr*] had not been replaced, and if we still used **[74]** it for covering (*pūshish*). But just as I said, the common meaning of the word hijab is a veil, and it has been used for covering and conveys the meaning of a women behind a curtain, and it is this very fact that has caused a great number [of people] to suppose that Islam has wanted women to be imprisoned in the house behind a curtain, and not to go outside.

The duty of covering, which Islam has established for women, does not mean that they [can] not go outside the home. Women's imprisonment and captivity has not been propounded in Islam. In some of the countries of old, like ancient Persia and India, such things existed, but it does not exist in Islam.

Covering women in Islam [means] that a woman covers her body during her association with men, and she does not exhibit and expose [her finery]. The relevant verses allude to this very meaning and the fatwas of the jurists also confirm this very case, and we will discuss the extent of this covering by using the Qurʾan and the sources of the Sunna. The relevant [Qurʾanic] verses have not used the word 'hijab'. The verses on this topic, whether in Chapter 24 (*al-Nūr* – 'Light'), whether in Chapter 33 (*al-Aḥzāb* – 'The Parties'), have discussed the extent of a women's covering and her contacts with men without using the word 'hijab'. The verse which has used 'hijab' is related to the wives of the Prophet of Islam.

We know that specific commands were recorded in the glorious Qurʾan about the **[75]** Prophet's wives. The first verse addressed the Prophet's wives and began with this sentence: 'O Prophet's wives! You are different from other women' [Q. 33.32]. Islam gave [them] this particular favour. The Prophet's wives stayed in their homes during his lifetime, and after his death for mostly social and political considerations.

The glorious Qurʾan says quite clearly to the Prophet's wives, 'Stay in your houses!' [Q. 33.33]. Islam desired that the 'mothers of the believers' would not misuse the respect given to them by the Muslims, and that they would not become an instrument to be used by the selfish and the self-seeking in political and social affairs. The 'Mother of the Believers' (ʿAʾisha), who violated this command, brought deplorable political circumstances into the world of Islam. She always expressed regret and used to say, 'I wanted many children from the Prophet, [but] **[76]** he died. However, I did not stop making a nuisance.'

So, in my opinion, this is the reason that the Prophet's wives were forbidden **[76]** from marrying someone else after his death. In other words, a wife might misuse her husband's fame and respect, and sow discord among the people.

Therefore, if there is a command about the Prophet's wives, it is more emphatic and stricter for this reason.

In any case, the verse in which the word 'hijab' is used is Q. 33.54, which says: 'If you ask them for any object that you need, ask them from behind a curtain [hijab].' In the expressions of history and in the hadith, wherever the name 'hijab verse' appears, for example, such and such was the case before the descent of the hijab verse, and [such and such was the case] after the descent of the hijab verse, the implication is this verse, which is related to the Prophet's wives, not the verses in Q. 24.30–1, which say: 'Say to the believing men that they cast down their glances – to the end – Say to the believing women that they cast down their glances.' Or the verse of the Chapter of Light, which says: 'Draw their outer garments around them – to the end.'

So how was it, in recent times, the words hijab and curtain (*parda*) and covering (*pardagī*) have become common, in place of the expression popular among the jurists, in other words, covering (*sitr va pūshish*)? It is unclear for me. Perhaps they mistook the Islamic hijab for those that have been traditional in other nations. **[77]** We will explain this more, later.

*

The philosophy of Islamic covering, in our opinion, [consists] of several things. Some of them have a psychological dimension, and others a dimension related to the house and the family. Yet others a sociological dimension, and some are related to raising the dignity of women and preventing prostitution.

Hijab in Islam is rooted in a general and fundamental problem. [The problem] is that Islam desires to regulate all kinds of sexual pleasure, whether it is looking or touching, or whether it is of a different kind within the family environment and the framework of a legal marriage [so that] society is limited to the work-place and its functions. [This is] in contrast to the Western system of the present age which mixes work and activity with sexual pleasure-seeking. Islam desires these two environments to be completely separate from one another.[2]

The Real Meaning of the Hijab

[78] The reality of the issue is that on the question of covering, and using a contemporary expression, [i.e.] hijab, it is not a discussion of whether a good woman

2 [Up until this point, the text reflects the discussion in Bakhtiar, 8–11.]

appears covered or naked in society. The crux of the discussion is whether a man's [sexual] use of a woman should be gratuitous. Does a man have the right to have much [sexual] pleasure from any woman, in any way, even if it is adulterous?

It is true that the outer reality of the question is this: what should a woman do? Should she go outside covered up or [should she go outside] exposed (*'uryān*)? In other words, the person about whom this question is posed is a woman, and frequently the question is asked in a polite manner, whether it is better for a woman to be free or to be condemned and a prisoner in a hijab. But the truth of the question, and the inner reality of the subject is something else. It is whether a man should have absolute freedom or not in taking sexual advantage of a woman, even in adultery?

In other words, on this question, the beneficiary is the man, not the woman. And at the **[79]** very least the man is more the beneficiary than the woman. In the words of Will Durant: 'The mini-skirt is a blessing for the whole world but not the tailor.'

When looking at the essence of the question, Islam replies: 'OK, men can only enjoy [themselves] with women who are their legal wives within the confines of the family and legal marriage [which] establish a series of heavy responsibilities, but it is forbidden to enjoy women [sexually] who are unknown to them. And it is forbidden for women too, in any shape or form, to enjoy men outside of the family situation.'

So, the crux of the question of [sexual] enjoyment is [whether it is] limited to the family environment and [one's] legal spouse, or [to] freedom of enjoyment and extending it to [wider] society. Islam supports the first supposition.

From the perspective of Islam, from a psychological dimension, limiting sexual enjoyment to the family environment and [with one's] legal spouse helps the psychological well-being of society; and from a family dimension, it assists in strengthening the relations between the members of the family and establishes complete intimacy between the husband and wife; and from a societal dimension it is the cause of protecting and strengthening work **[80]** and activity in society; and from the perspective of establishing a woman on a par with man, it raises the worth of women to that of men. Now we shall [examine] these four elements.

Tranquillity of the psyche

The absence of boundaries between men and women, and the freedom of uninhibited association increase sexual arousal and excitement, resulting in a sexual need in the form of unquenchable craving and desire. The sexual instinct is powerful, as deep as an ocean. However much it is obeyed, one becomes more subservient [to it]. It is like a fire, the flames of which grow bigger when fuel is added to it. In order to comprehend this issue, it is necessary to pay attention to two things.

(1). History has recorded those who craved wealth and who with bewildering greed and covetousness continually sought to acquire money and wealth, and they became greedier as they [tried to] acquire more. It also mentions the covetous for sexual pleasure, who did not stop in any way from seizing and possessing beautiful [women]. This was the case of those who **[81]** owned harems, and in truth, all those who had power to use.

Christensen, the author of *L'Iran sous les Sassanides*,[3] writes in chapter nine of his book: 'We see only a few of the 3,000 women that Khusraw [Parviz] had in his harem in the carving of Taq-i Bustan. This king was never satisfied in this inclination. Whenever they presented maidens, widows and women with children [to him], he admitted them into his harem. Whenever he desired to replenish his harem, he sent letters to [his] governors, and he would describe the qualities of a woman of perfect quality. So, his agents sent him any woman they saw whenever she matched the qualities described in the letter.'

One can find many of these kinds of stories in ancient history, but today these stories do not take the form of harems, but appear in other ways, the difference being that today it is not necessity for someone to have the same amount of possibilities as Khusraw Parviz or Harun al-Rashid. Today, with the blessings of contemporary culture, it is possible for a man who has only a thousandth of the possibilities of [Khusraw Parviz] and Harun al-Rashid to enjoy women sexually.

(2). Have you never wondered what lies behind the human desire to compose love poems? A segment of world literature is about love in which man praises his beloved, makes supplications **[82]** in her presence, glorifies her and belittles himself. He considers himself worthy [only] of her smallest blessing. It is claimed that, 'A hundred valuable souls can be purchased with a little attention, so why is there a shortfall in this transaction?'[4]

What does this mean? Why don't humans behave in the same way about their other needs? Have you ever seen a man who worships money and another who worships fame and position, write love poems? Have you ever seen a man hungry for bread compose love poems? Why does everyone derive pleasure from the

3 [Arthur Christensen, *L'Iran sous les Sassanides*, Copenhagen 1936.]

4 [This is a line in a ghazal by Hafiz. See Khanlari's edition of the *Dīvān-i Ḥāfiẓ*, ghazal no. 195, line 6, 390. Mutahhari's version has slightly different wording, but the meaning remains the same.]

poems and sonnets of someone else? Why is it that everyone enjoys the collection of Hafiz's poems so much? Is it not because it conforms to the deep instinct that has taken root in them, from head to toe? How mistaken are those who say that the fundamental cause of human acts is an economic one!

Humans have a special kind of music for their sexual loves, just as they also have a special music for [their] spirituality, whereas there is no music for their material needs, such as bread and water.

I don't want to claim that all loves are sexual, and I have never said that Hafiz, Saʿdi, and other composers of love poetry wrote only as a result of a deep-seated sexual instinct. This **[83]** subject is one that must be discussed separately [from this book].

But what is clear is that many love poems have been written by men for women. It is sufficient to recognise that a man's need for a woman is not like his need for the bread and water that fills his stomach. Rather, it comes either in the form of greed and worship of variety, or it comes in the form of love and love poetry. Later on, we shall discuss under which condition the state of greed and sexual desire is strengthened, and under which condition the shape of love and love poetry appears and takes a spiritual colouring.

In any case, Islam has paid much attention to the amazing power of burning instinct. And there are many narrations about the danger of a 'look', the danger of being alone together with a woman, and finally the danger of the instinct that unites men and women together.

Islam has established a plan for regulating and domesticating this instinct, and it has **[84]** also fixed responsibilities on this subject for both women and men. One common duty prescribed for both women and men is related to looking: 'Say to the believing men to cast down their glances and guard their private parts … Say to the believing women to cast down their glances and guard their private parts' [24.30]. A summary of this command is that women and men must not stare at one another, they must not flirt with one another, they must not gaze at one another with lust, and they must not look at one another with the purpose of having sexual pleasure. One particular command has also been prescribed for women, which is that they must cover up their bodies from strange men, and they must not flaunt themselves or act coquettishly in society. In no shape or form should [women] do anything to attract the attention of strange men.

Humans are extremely vulnerable to temptation. It is a mistake if we suppose that human temptation is limited and has a particular extent, and will be satisfied once it has reached that limit.

Just as human beings in general, [both] men and women, are never satisfied or satiated with the wealth [they have] and the fame [they achieve], they are never content in the sexual dimension either. No man is satisfied in possessing beautiful women, and no woman is satisfied in attracting men and possessing their hearts, and ultimately no heart is satisfied in [attaining its] desire.

In one respect, unlimited desire is never fulfilled, and it is always connected to a kind **[85]** of feeling of deficiency. Not attaining [one's] wishes leads to psychological disorders and illnesses.

Why have all of these psychological sicknesses increased in the Western world? Its cause is the freedom of sexual standards and excessive sexual stimulation which [appears] in newspapers, magazines, cinemas, theatres, and formal and informal parties, and even in the streets and alleys.

But the reason that the command for covering is specific for woman is that the inclination for showing off and flaunting is particular in woman. Woman is the hunter from the perspective of capturing hearts, and man is the prey, and in the same way man is the hunter from the perspective of possessing bodies, and woman is the prey. A woman's inclination to show off results from this kind of hunting instinct of hers. In not a single location in the world is there a precedent for men to wear body-revealing and stimulating clothes. It is the woman who at the command of her particular nature desires to enchain [men's] hearts and make men slaves, caught in the trap of devotion to her. Therefore, the corruption of flaunting oneself and nakedness are specific to women, and the command to cover, too, has been prescribed for them.

We will discuss [later] the rebellious sexual instinct, and (contrary to the arguments of **[86]** people like Russell) [that] the sexual instinct is never satisfied and satiated, despite having complete freedom and, in particular, in having the means to excitement, like the corrupting lustful eye in men and the corruption of flaunting in women.

Strengthening family relations

There is no doubt that whatever causes family relations to be stronger and results in intimate relations between the spouses is beneficial for the family unit, and no effort must be spared in establishing this. And whatever causes spouses' relations to weaken and results in coldness between them damages family life, and it is necessary to fight against this.

Discovering sexual fulfilment and pleasure in the family context and within the legal boundaries of marriage fortifies the relationship between a woman and her husband, and it results in stronger attachment between the spouses.

The philosophy of covering and preventing sexual profligacy with someone other than one's legal partner from the family perspective is so that one's legal partner is considered the **[87]** source of the other's happiness from a psychological point of view. In a system of sexual profligacy, a legal wife is considered a rival, a nuisance and a prison guard from a psychological point of view [and,] consequently, enmity and hate will be the basis of the family unit.

The youth of today flee from marriage and say, 'It is too soon, we are still children,' or they give some other excuse whenever marriage is suggested. In the days gone by, one of the most cherished hopes of young people was to get married. Before [the present age], young people did not think about cheap and abundant women as goods which were a blessing from the world of Europe.

In the past, marriages were made after a period of expectation and hope, and for this reason, the spouses considered each other as the cause of their fortune and happiness. But today, sexual satisfaction outside of marriage is common, and it is a cause [for the youth] to become animated.

Open relationships and unlimited [contact] between boys and girls have resulted in marriage taking the form of a duty, an imposition and a confinement that must be imposed upon the young with moral advice, and frequently – just as some magazines suggest – with **[88]** force.

The difference between a society that restricts sexual relations to the family and legal marriage with a society that allows open relations is that marriage in the first society is the end of expectation and privation, and in the second society it is the beginning of privation and limitation. In the system of open sexual relations, the marriage contract concludes the period of freedom for the girl and boy, and it compels them to be faithful to one another. In the Islamic system, it ends their privation and expectation.

The system of open relations, firstly, is the reason that boys, as far as possible, avoid marriage and having a family, and only when their youthful energy, excitement and vivacity have weakened do they get married. In such circumstances, they only want a woman to give birth to children and often to perform domestic chores. Secondly, [the system of open relations] weakens the existing marriage relations, and it is the reason that the wife and husband look at each other as rivals, as opponents of freedom, and as bringing limitations or, in idiomatic terms, they become guards of each other. [This is] instead of the family being set firmly upon pure love and deep affection, with both wife and husband recognising each other as the source of **[89]** their happiness.

When a boy or a girl says, 'I am married,' she or he says to herself or himself, 'I have taken on a prison guard.' What is the meaning of this interpretation? It is because he or she was free before marriage to go wherever he or she wanted, and to dance with whomever he or she pleased, and there was nobody to say, 'Are you not ashamed?' But after marriage this freedom is restricted. If he or she returns home late one night, he or she is chastised by his or her spouse. And his spouse complains to him if he dances excitedly with a girl at a party. It is clear how cold, weak and insecure the family relations are in such a system.

Some, like Bertrand Russell, have thought that the prevention of free interaction is only for the sake of a man's certainty in relation to [his] offspring. In order to solve [these] problems, they have suggested the use of birth control, but the issue is not only the clarity [of fatherhood] of the offspring. Another important problem is establishing the purest and most intimate emotions between the spouses, and creating complete oneness and unity within the family. The confirmation of this aim is possible when the spouses cover their eyes to relationships of any other kind (the husband does not look at other women, and the wife, too, **[90]** does not provoke or attract the attention of anyone except her husband), and [this is possible when] the principle of forbidding any kind of sexual satisfaction outside of the family, even before marriage, is observed.

In addition, in the case of a woman who follows the likes of Russell, and imitates those in the school of 'the new sexual ethics' by having a legal husband [and] seeks her love elsewhere, and also becomes pregnant from another man to whom she is attached, what certainty is there that she will not take pregnancy preventative action with regards to her husband whom she does not like, become pregnant from the man whom she loves, and then place the child at the feet of her husband? Surely such a woman will be inclined to place the child she has had before her lover, and not before the man who is her husband by law, and according to law she should not become pregnant by anyone other than her husband. Statistics in Europe clearly show the numbers of illegitimate children have risen remarkably despite the existence of preventive pregnancy measures.

Strengthening society

Taking sexual enjoyment out of the [family] framework and into society weakens the work ethic and activity in society. Contrarywise, when the opponents of the hijab have made criticisms and said, 'Hijab paralyses the strength of half of the people in society,' [we reply **[91]** that] not having a hijab and encouraging open sexual relations paralyses the strength of society.

That which has caused paralysis in a woman's strength and imprisoned her talents is the kind of hijab that imprisons and precludes her from cultural, social and economic activity. In Islam such a thing does not exist. Islam does not say that woman should not leave the house, and it does not say that she has no right to study, rather [acquiring] wisdom and knowledge have been recognised as a common obligation for men and women. [Islam] has not designated a particular form of economic activity for women. Islam never desired women to remain idle and lazy, and have a worthless and futile existence. Covering the body, other than the face and hands does not prevent [the woman from participating in] any kind of cultural, social or economic activity. The cause of paralysis in a society's strength is the pollution of the workplace by pleasure-seeking passion.

Suppose boys and girls study separately, and suppose the girls study and cover their bodies and have no adornment on them. Wouldn't they study, think and listen to what the teacher says in a better manner than [in a situation] when next to each boy sits a made-up girl with a short skirt reaching above her knee? Will the work and activity of a man be better in a street, a bazaar, an office or a factory or somewhere else where he always pays attention to the provocative and stimulating forms of made-up women, or will [the work and activity be better] in an environment where he is not faced with such an image? If you don't believe [me] then ask the people who work in these kinds of environments. Any institution or factory or office that really wants to undertake good work must prevent this kind of mixing [between men and women]. If you do not believe me, go and carry out research [yourself].

The truth is that this situation of the lack of hijab [among Iranian women] is a disgrace that exists among us, and we were even ahead of Europe and America. It is among the characteristics of filthy, capitalist Western societies, and one of the results of the worship of money and of the covetous capitalists of the West, indeed, it is one of ways and means that they use to stupefy and desensitise humane societies and compel them to consume their products.

Mutahhari on the *Jilbāb*[5]

[182] The main verses related to the duty of covering are those verses of the sura 24 which were discussed, and several verses too in the sura 33 that can be mentioned on the margins of this discussion, and we will engage in an explication of them as an appendix.

O wives of the Prophet! You are not like other women. If you are God-fearing,

5 [This section occurs between pages 182–95 of the Persian text (ed).]

> be not overly soft in speech in case one in whose heart is a disease be moved to desire, and speak in an honourable way. [Q. 33.32]
>
> And remain in your houses and flaunt not your finery as they did flaunt them in the age of ignorance. [Q. 33.33]

The addressees are the wives of the Prophet in these two verses: o wives of the Prophet! You are not like other women. If you are cautious – [then] take care that you do not speak in a gentle, feminine and flirtatious (*shahvat ālūd*) manner which incites desire in the sick-hearted. Speak well and in a worthy manner. Keep yourselves in your homes, and do not show off outside of the home like in the time of ignorance. **[183]** The purpose of this command is not to keep the Prophet's wives in the house, because the history of Islam shows clearly that the Prophet took his wives with him on journeys, and he did not give the command to prevent them coming out of the house. The purpose of this command is that a woman [must] not come out of the house with the intention to show off, and this duty is stricter and stronger especially for the Prophet's wives.

Q. 33.53 states:

> O you who believe! Do not enter the Prophet's houses unless you have been given leave, to a meal, without waiting for the proper time. Rather, when you are invited, enter at the proper time; and when you have eaten, leave. Do not linger for mere talk. That causes trouble for the Prophet, and he is shy of telling you. But God does not shy away from the truth. When you ask something of them (his wives), ask them from behind a veil (hijab). That is purer for your hearts and for their hearts. It is not for you to cause hurt to God's messenger, as it is unlawful for you to marry his widows after him. That would be an enormity in God's sight.

The Muslim Arabs entered the Prophet's rooms without a thought. The Prophet's wives were also in the house. The verse first revealed that you are not allowed to enter the Prophet's house suddenly and without permission, and you should come on time if you have been invited to eat food, and then you should get up and not take time in chit-chat and conversation because this **[184]** upsets the Prophet and he is too shy to make you leave his house. But God is not shy of you. And second, when you want to ask something from the Prophet's wives, ask [them] from behind a curtain (*pusht-i parda*) without having to enter [their] room. These actions are [to keep] your hearts pure, and [make] their hearts tranquil. You must not annoy the Prophet, and you must not marry his wives after the death of the

Prophet, for this is a great [crime] before God.

In this verse, the word 'hijab' has been mentioned. Just as we said previously, whenever the ancients spoke about the verse of the hijab, [their] intention was this very verse. The command of the hijab which is in this verse is unlike the command for covering (*pūshish*) which is the topic of our discussion. The command which has been mentioned in this verse refers to family customs and behaviour that people must observe in other people's houses. According to this command a man must not enter the space [occupied by] a woman, rather, if he wants something or if he needs something he must call out over the wall. This topic is not related to the discussion of covering (*pūshish*) which in juristic terminology has been called '*sitr*' and has not been called 'hijab'.

The sentence 'that is purer for your hearts and for their hearts' [Q 33.53], just like 'it is better if they abstain' which is included in Q. 24.61, indicates that **[185]** if a man or woman observes *sitr* and covering and rejects the compulsion to look [then this] is nearer to fearing God and purity. Just as we said: [in spite of] the dispensations for ease and moderation which have been made a requirement in the command (*ḥukm*), one must not forget the excellence in the morality of *sitr* and covering, and giving up looking.

Q. 33.59–60 say:

> O Prophet! Tell your wives and daughters, and the women of believers to draw their cloaks (*jalābīb*) over them. Thus, is it likelier that they will be known and not be disturbed. And God is Forgiving, Merciful. [Q. 33.59]

> If the hypocrites do not desist, and likewise those in whose hearts is a disease, as well as those who spread false rumours in the city, We shall surely spur you against them, then they will not be your neighbours, save for a short while. [Q. 33.60]

[186] In this verse there are two topics to which attention must be paid. One concerns the *jilbāb* and what is meant by drawing it closer. The other is: what is the meaning of 'is it likelier that they will be known and not be disturbed'?

On the first topic, what kind of clothes do they say the *jilbāb* was? The explanations of the interpreters and philologists differ, and it is difficult to render a correct meaning of the word.

In *al-Munjid*, it is written: the *jilbāb* is a shirt (*pīrāhan*), or loose clothing (*libās-i gushād*).[6]

---

6 [This refers to the *Munjid al-Muqri'īn wa Murshid al-Ṭālibīn* by Ibn al-Jazari (d. 1350).]

In the *Mufradāt* of Raghib, which is a precise and reliable book and which specialises in explaining Qur'anic words, it is written about the *jalābīb*, in other words, shirts and scarves (*pīrāhan va rūsarī*): 'The *jilbāb* is an expression for a shirt or a loose and large garment, smaller than a *milḥafa* or itself a *milḥafa* (like a *chādur*) which women use to cover the whole of their body or a shawl (*chārqid*).'[7]

[187] In the *Lisān al-'Arab*, it says: 'The *jilbāb* is a garment larger than a shawl (*chārqid*) and smaller than a cloak ('*abā*) which a woman uses to cover her chest and head.'[8]

The expression in the *Kashshāf* is close to this.[9] And in the Qur'anic interpretation (*tafsīr*) called *Majma' al-Bayān*,[10] it is written on the meaning of the word: '*Jilbāb* is an expression for a head-scarf (*khimār*) which is put on when leaving the house, and it covers the head and face.' But when interpreting the verse, it says: 'In other words, the purpose is that a woman covers her upper chest and neck (*garībān*) with the garment that she draws to herself.' Then it says that the *jilbāb* is the same as the *chārqid*, and the purpose of this is that the free women cover their fronts and heads when they go outside.

[188] You will notice that the meaning of *jilbāb* is not so clear in the interpretations of the commentators. What appears to be more correct is that in origin the word *jilbāb* included any garments that were loose, but were often used as head-coverings (*rū-sarī-hā*) larger than shawls (*chārqid*) and smaller than a cloak (*ridā*). At the same time, it is clear that two kinds of head-covering were common for women. One was a small head-covering that they called a *khimār* or *miqna'a*, and they usually used it inside the house. The other kind was a large head-covering which was specific for use outside the house. These meanings are compatible with narrations in which the word *jilbāb* has been mentioned, like the narration of 'Ubayd Allah Halabi which we related in the interpretation of Q. 24.61.[11] The contents of it was concerned with elderly women who were permitted to take off

7 [*Al-Mufradāt al-Gharīb al-Qur'ān* by Raghib Isfahani (d. 1108), a dictionary of Qur'anic terms.]

8 [*Lisān al-'Arab* is regarded as one of the most authoritative and comprehensive Arabic dictionaries. It was completed by Ibn Manzur in 1873. It is usually published in multi-volume sets (the most commonly cited has 20 volumes).]

9 [*Kashshāf 'an Ḥaqā'iq al-Tanzīl* (*The Unveiler of the Realities of Revelation*) is a Qur'anic commentary by the rationalist Persian/Arab theologian Zamakhshari (d. 1144).]

10 [This was a Qur'anic commentary by Shaykh al-Tabarsi (d. 1153).]

11 [On page 180, Mutahhari cites the narration: ''Ubayd Allah Halabi said that Imam Sadiq said that the meaning of a head-covering is the *chahārqid*.' He cites his source as *Kāfī*, vol. 5, 522; *Wasā'il* vol 3, 25–6.]

the *khimār* and *jilbāb*, and that there was no obstacle to looking at their hair. From all of this, it is understood that the *jilbāb* was a means to cover the head hair.

In the same way, in other narrations in *Kāfī*,[12] in the interpretation of the same verse it is said that His Excellency Sadiq said: when a woman is elderly it is permissible [for her] to let the *chārqid* and head-covering fall to the floor. **[189]** Therefore the meaning of drawing the *jilbāb* around [themselves] is wearing it; in other words, when they wish to leave the house, they put on their large head-covering. Certainly, the philological meaning of drawing something around [oneself] is not wearing that [thing]. It is used in this way. When they say to a woman 'draw your clothes around you', the meaning is: do not take it off, but arrange it properly, and put it on yourself.

Women's use of large head-coverings which they tied around their heads was of two kinds. One kind was merely a formality and in name, just as in the present age we see some women in *chādur*s that are merely formal, and they do not cover any part of their body with the *chādur*, and they let [the *chādur*] loose. The way they wear the *chādur* shows that they do not refrain from interacting with unknown men and they do not mind being looked at with interest. The second kind has stood and stands in the opposite fashion; a woman who arranges her clothes properly and does not let her body show is among the modest and chaste. She spontaneously stands alone, and she makes the impure at heart despondent.

[190] On the second topic,[13] that is, the discussion about the reason for this command [of Q. 33.59], the interpreters have said: a group among the hypocrites bothered slave women (*kanīz-ān*) in the alleys and streets in the early evening when it became dark. Covering the head was not compulsory for slave women. Just as we have said previously, sometimes these annoying and corrupt youths also harassed free women, and later they claimed, 'We did not know they were free women. We thought they were slave women.' Therefore, the command has been given to free women not to leave the house without the *jilbāb*, in truth, without complete clothing, so that they could be distinguished from slave women and thereby avoid being bothered and harassed.

The above explanation is not above criticism, because it makes one think that [the command] does not cover the harassment of slave women, and the hypocrites have raised [this argument] as an acceptable excuse for their behaviour, whereas this is not the case. Although covering the head hair was not compulsory for slave women, perhaps the reason of this was that slave women were not usually

12 [*Kāfī*, vol. 5, 522.]
13 [A reference back to the beginning of page 186.]

attractive or appealing or did not arouse the desire **[191]** in others. And in addition, their work was to serve others, just as we have pointed out. In any case, this harassment, even among slave women, has been considered a sin, and the hypocrites were not able to use targeting a slave woman as an excuse for their behaviour.

Another probability for all of this is that when a covered and pious woman came out of the house and observed [the etiquette] of modesty and chastity, the hypocrites were not brave enough to harass them.

Based on the first probability, the meaning of the sentence, 'Thus, is it likelier that they will be known and not be disturbed,' is that they would be recognised as free and not as slave women because [of the *jilbāb*], and so they would not be harassed and pursued by the young [hypocrites]. But based on the second probability, the meaning of the sentence is that they will be known because they are chaste and modest and the sick-at-heart who desired them would lower their eyes because it would be known that here are the boundaries of modesty, and desiring eyes are blinded, and treacherous hands are cut off.

In this verse, the extent of covering is not described. It is not possible to understand from this verse whether it is necessary to cover the face or not. The verse that presents the extent of covering is Q. 24.31, which was discussed previously.

The subject that is used in this verse, and is an eternal truth, is that a Muslim woman must **[192]** be aware of modesty, dignity, sobriety and purity when in society, and she must be recognised as [possessing] these attributes. It is in such a situation that the sick-at-heart (who go around hunting) start to despair of [such] women, and the thought of snaring one of them departs from their imaginations. We see that wild youths always harass immodest, wanton and barely clothed (*lukht*) women. When it is asked of them, 'Why are you bothering [them]?' They reply, 'If she had not wanted these things then she would not have come out of the house like this.'

The command which has been revealed in this verse is similar to the command twenty-five verses previously, in an address to the wives of the Prophet: 'be not overly soft in speech, lest one in whose heart is a disease be moved to desire' [Q. 33.32]. In other words, do not speak with female tenderness and flirtatiousness which instigates desire in the sick-at-heart. In this command, dignity and modesty are explained in speaking, and in the verse that is the subject of discussion the command of dignity in coming and going is discussed.

Previously, we said that people's movements and silences sometimes speak volumes. Sometimes, the manner of the clothes, the way of walking, and a woman's style of speaking is meaningful and says in a non-verbal fashion, 'Give me your heart, be my desire, follow me!' Sometimes, contrariwise it says non-verbally, 'Go away.' **[193]** In any case, what may be applied from this verse is this: [there is] no special manner for covering. It is only Q. 24.31, on the manner of covering, that explains this matter ['guard their private parts and they should not display their finery except that which is visible. And let them draw their *khumūr* over their breasts']. And since this verse [Q. 33.59] was revealed after the verse in the Light chapter, one can understand the purpose of [Q. 33.59] 'draw their cloaks over them', which is that [the women] completely observe the previous command in sura 24 so that they are not bothered by the evils of harassment.

The previous verse says: 'As for those who affront believing men and believing women for other than what they may have committed, they bear the burden of calumny and manifest sin.' [Q. 33.58] This verse formally chastises people who harass Muslim men and women. Without any break, it commands women to observe complete modesty and dignity in their behaviour so that they [may] find security from the harassment of troublesome people. Paying attention to this verse helps for a better understanding of the meaning of the verse in question.

Commentators frequently have understood that the intention (*hadaf*) of the sentence 'draw their cloaks over them' is covering the face. In other words, they have understood this sentence as an allusion (*kināya*) to covering the face. They have accepted that the original purpose (*mafhūm-i aṣlī*) of 'draw' is not covering, but they have often thought that [the purpose of] this command has been **[194]** to distinguish free women from slave women, and they have interpreted it in this fashion. But we said previously that this interpretation is incorrect. It cannot be accepted whatsoever that the glorious Qur'an is only concerned with free women, and does not care about the harassment endured by Muslim slave women. What seems very strange is that commentators like Zamakhshari and Fakhr-i Razi[14] have said that mostly there are those who in the interpretations of the sura of Light have said completely openly that covering the face and two hands is not necessary, and they have not considered it a sin.

The reality is that these commentators have not considered the difference in the purpose of Q. 24.31 and Q. 33.59. They have understood the Light verse as a general and eternal command whether there is any harassment or not. But they have understood the verse of the Parties as referring to a special case when a free woman or a woman without any condition (*muṭlaq zan*) is harassed by vagabonds.

The point about the verse in question is that people who harass women in alleys and streets deserve severe and harsh punishment according to the laws of

14 [Fakhr al-Din Razi died in 1209.]

Islam (*qanūn-i islām*) **[195]**. It is not enough when these people are arrested by the police and have their heads shaven. The punishment [should] be much more severe. The Qurʾan states, 'If the hypocrites do not desist and likewise those in whose hearts is a disease, as well as those who spread false rumours in the city, We shall surely spur you against them, and they will not be able to remain in it as your neighbours except for a little while.' [Q. 33.60] At the barest minimum, an understanding of this verse is to exile them from the pure Islamic society. A society that gives all the more respect for modesty and purity and believes in stronger punishment for offenders.

Part 3

HIJAB AS DESIRABLE (*MUSTAḤABB*): THE VIEWS OF AHMAD QABIL

5

The Islamic Republic and the Hijab Controversy (1978–2012)

Introduction

The first chapter of Part Three (chapter five) of this book provides a general contextual survey of issues relating to the hijab from the departure of Muhammad Riza Pahlavi, to the establishment of the Islamic Republic Party as one of the most authoritative organs within the political system in Iran, the legal institutionalisation of hijab as an essential element of Islamic modest dress for women, and the concomitant challenges and opportunities this has provided for women. New sartorial standards were implemented during a time when there were increasing levels of education and employment, as well as better standards of technology which contributed to a greater call among women for agency and participation in all socio-political spheres. The change in the socio-political context helps in part to explain for the development of New Religious Thinking about the mandatory veiling of women, and for women themselves to adopt informed positions on either side of the debate.

The last two chapters of Part Three (chapters six and seven) of this book present the views of Ahmad Qabil, who composed his major works from 2000 onwards. His jurisprudential fame lies with a fatwa he issued in 2004, rejecting the compulsory status of the hijab, and instead declaring the wearing of the hijab to be preferable, or desirable. This must be considered in the context of the Muslim classification of actions into five categories: obligatory (*vājib*), desirable (*mustaḥabb*), permissible (*mubāḥ*), discouraged (*makrūh*), and forbidden (*ḥarām*). Chapter six explores Qabil's life and thought, which has not been examined by Western scholarship, save for a few scattered remarks, offered almost as an afterthought in many works that look at the New Thinking among the ulama.[1] But aside from being important as a fierce critic of ʿAli Khamenei, Qabil's contribution to New Religious Thinking is of great significance as his worldview rests upon a belief in the rationality of sharia and making it more acceptable to the general populace without compelling believers to behave in stringently prescribed fashions.

Chapter seven provides a translation of Qabil's essay on the hijab, taken from the larger work, *Commands Pertaining to Women*, which illustrates his effort to hand agency over to women. Ahmad Qabil's influence extends beyond the borders of Iran to wherever Iranians have established communities. The following anecdote about the hijab, reported by Soroush, is indicative of this:

> I paid careful attention to the late [Ahmad] Qabil's writings, and I read and appreciated his opinion about marrying sharia with rationality. I [also] liked his discussion on the hijab which was juristically well-thought out and brave. He also made a reference to humble me when I said the hijab is the banner of the Prophet of Islam. Indeed, one day that fatwa [on the hijab] became of some use to me. A young lady in America came to see me. She was tired of wearing the hijab and she wanted to stop wearing it. I said, 'Don't do this because it's an act of disobedience. Say, "I am doing it because of Ahmad Qabil's fatwa so therefore I am [still] within the boundary of obedience."' In the words of Mawlana: 'Oh *ghulām*! [Don't] seek acceptance or rejection / Always consider commands and prohibitions.'[2]

The Context of the Hijab Controversy (1979–2005)

The departure of Muhammad Riza Shah from Iran on 16 January 1979 signalled the end of the Pahlavi regime. Likewise, the arrival in Tehran of Ayatollah Khomeini from exile on the 1 February foreshadowed the establishment of the Islamic Republic. It became clear that the goal of Khomeini and many of his supporters was not simply a political revolution, in the sense of establishing new executive and legislative structures in the country, rather a wholesale revision was envisaged that encompassed political, economic, social and cultural dimensions of Iranian life. The social and cultural dimensions included reforms along gender lines, and there was to be a

1 In the course of writing this book I have published an article that introduces the political and jurisprudential thought of Qabil, see Lloyd Ridgeon, 'Ahmad Qabil, a reason to believe and the New Religious Thinking in Iran', *Middle Eastern Studies* 56.1, 2020, 1–15.
2 *Yād-nāma-yi Aḥmad Qābil*, 328–9.

particular focus on how women should participate and appear in public, which predictably included guidance and eventually rules about sartorial etiquette. Khomeini's own pronouncements on the hijab resembled the positions adopted by Mutahhari, and the former's views reveal a remarkable consistency over the years. This stands in contrast to the changes in his general stance towards women's participation in the public sphere. For example, in 1963, Khomeini had opposed the Shah's White Revolution which enfranchised women, but by the time of the Islamic Revolution he fully endorsed female involvement in political and other spheres of public life. Azadeh Kian has suggested that this change 'reflected the pragmatism of a man in power who was more preoccupied by political considerations and consolidating the Islamic regime than respect for religious precepts or traditions'.[3] Such a view denies the possibility of Khomeini developing new ideas which are best understood as interpretations of sharia law over time, that is, responses to evolving circumstances, as a change in the subject demands a change in the ruling. In other words, Khomeini's perspectives were based on his jurisprudential understandings, which may of course indicate the pragmatism inherent in the system. Nevertheless, Khomeini's views remained consistent on the subject of the hijab, reflecting the deep scars that Riza Shah's unveiling laws had scratched out upon the face of Iranian society. In many speeches subsequent to the deposition of Riza Shah, Khomeini returned to the trauma and shame experienced by Iranian women and men, so that in 1978 he remarked:

> God only knows how this nation of Iran suffered when he forced the women to remove their veils. The veil of humanity was rent asunder. God knows which women he dishonoured in this way, which people he humiliated. He forced the ulama at bayonet-point to attend celebratory parties with their wives, which they did with heavy hearts and which ended with the people crying. Other people as well, different groups in turn, were invited and obliged to attend parties with their wives. This was the freedom for women, which Riza Shah enforced. He used bayonets and the police to compel the respected people, the merchants and thc ulama, to attend these parties on the excuse that he himself had organised them. At some of these celebrations – as the regime called them – the people cried so much that those agents with a sense of shame regretted having forced them to attend (9 January 1978).[4]

---

3 Azadeh Kian, 'Gendered Khomeini', *A Critical Introduction to Khomeini*, ed. Arshin Adib-Moghaddam, Cambridge 2014, 170.

4 Ruhollah Khomeini, *The Position of Women from the Viewpoint of Imam Khomeini*, Tehran 1380/2001–2, 205.

And on 18 February 1978 he rejected the freedom of unveiling:

> Could any Muslim agree with this scandalous uncovering of women? The women of Iran have themselves risen up against the Shah and given him a punch in the mouth with the cry: 'We don't want to live this way! We want to be free!' To which this good-for-nothing replies: 'But you are free! The only thing is that you cannot go to school wearing a *chādur* or head-covering!' You call this freedom?[5]

And following Mutahhari's perspective that the ideal Islamic morality did not necessitate seclusion of women in their homes, but that the hijab was a part of the modest Islamic dress, Ayatollah Khomeini announced on 6 March 1979 that women should don the hijab at the workplace. Khomeini made a speech at the Fayziya Seminary in Qum, during which he said, 'Sin cannot be committed in Islamic ministries. Naked women must not enter Islamic ministries. Women must wear the hijab in the ministries.'[6] The reaction to this proclamation was immediate. The 8th of March 1979 was International Women's Day, and according to Paidar 'a celebration had been planned by a consortium of Marxist-Leninist women's groups'.[7] The celebration in Tehran, however, turned into a demonstration against the measures that had been taken by the Provisional Government that impacted on women's rights and privileges, including the dismissal of female judges, the suspension of the Family Protection Law and, of course, the pronouncements about the hijab. The scale of the demonstrations was captured by Hengameh Golestan, a young photographer, whose shots captured 'the day 100,000 Iranian women protested the head-scarf'.[8] They came from all sectors of society, and included the young and old (**Figures 9** and **10**).[9] The demonstrations that were to last for six days did not have a lasting impact. Some mullas expressed a degree of accommodation, such as Ayatollah Taliqani, who said that

5 Khomeini, *The Position of Women from the Viewpoint of Imam Khomeini*, 205.
6 The words of Nasser Mohajer, as reported by Eskandar Sadeghi-Boroujerdi, 'The Post-Revolutionary Women's Uprising of March 1979: An Interview with Nasser Mohajer and Mahnaz Matin', *Iranwire.com*, 2013, https://iranwire.com/en/features/24.
7 Parvin Paidar, *Women and the Political Process in Twentieth century Iran*, Cambridge 1997, 234.
8 Pip Cummins, 'The day 100,000 Iranian women protested the head-scarf', *The New York Times* 15 September 2015, http://nytlive.nytimes.com/womenintheworld/2015/09/15/the-day-100000-iranian-women-protested-the-head-scarf.
9 Paidar, *Women and the Political Process*, 234.

the hijab should not be enforced, rather it should be taken voluntarily,[10] and he argued that the protesters 'had not correctly understood the complete meaning of Ayatollah Khomeini's announcements about the Islamic hijab, and they have interpreted it as a prohibition to work in various offices, departments and social activities'.[11]

As the demonstrations ended after six days, and after sufficient time had passed during which the Islamic Republic had consolidated its position in Iran, the implementation of compulsory veiling commenced in the summer of 1980, when it was declared that public sector workers were obliged to wear the hijab. In practice, what this meant was the adoption of a headscarf that did not allow a single hair to be visible, a long and loose manteaux that concealed the bodily contours, and trousers. By 1983, the Islamic regime felt sufficiently comfortable to make the hijab compulsory, not just in public spaces, and non-compliance was punishable by seventy-four lashes under the Islamic Punishment Law.[12] Subsequently, the compulsion to wear proper Islamic clothing was strictly imposed by groups of moral law enforcers. A part of the duties of these groups, comprised of both male and female members, was to chastise and punish women who did not conform to the new standards. Any 'loose' manner of wearing the hijab became known as *bad-ḥijāb*. This 'can include letting the hair show from under the veil, wearing clothes that cling to the body or are otherwise ostentatious, and using makeup, lipstick, nail polish, or perfume'.[13] The activities of this moral police force have been graphically portrayed by Kaveh Basmenji.

> 'Moral police' had stormed Vali Asr [one of the major boulevards in Tehran] aided and abetted by Ansar-e Hezbollah thugs. Under the watchful gaze of officers in olive-coloured uniforms, female police agents clad in black chadors stopped young women, barking at them, questioning them and dragging the more defiant ones towards buses waiting in line. Members of Ansar-e Hezbollah were busy chanting 'Marg bar Badhejab' (death to those with improper hijab), breaking with stones the windows of shops displaying

10 Paidar, *Women and the Political Process*, 232–3.

11 Mahnaz Matin and Nasser Mohajer, 'Guftagū ba Ayatollah Taliqani' [Conversation with Ayatollah Taliqani], *Zanān-i Irānī dar Inqilāb* [*Iranian Women in the Revolution*]; Mahnaz Matin and Nasser Mohajer, *Khīzish-i Zanān-i Irān dar Esfand 1357* [*The Uprising of Iranian Women in Esfand 1357*], vol. 2, Paris 2010, 44.

12 Paidar, *Women and the Political Process*, 342.

13 Faegheh Shirazi, *The Veil Unveiled: The Hijab in Modern Culture*, Gainesville 2001, 94.

> lingerie or short robes, and beating up whomever happened to be in their way. Pedestrians were looking on in desperation.[14]

The importance that the Islamic Republic gave to proper covering for women is in no small way related to the hijab being the symbol of the revolution; it was (and remains) a hyper visible symbol that on the one hand rejected the Pahlavi monarchy and, by extension, the corruption and imperialistic policies associated with the West, and on the other advanced an idealist and morally chaste form of Islam. Whilst promoting a purist form of Islam, such a message was entwined with nativist sentiments. Modesty in the period leading up to the revolution and in the immediate aftermath was not the sole preserve of the Islamic Republic Party and its supporters; leftist guerrilla organisations such as the Mujahidin-i Khalq and the Fidaʾyan-i Khalq also recruited 'women clad in black *chādur* and holding rifles'.[15] However, the hijab and the values pertaining to modesty became associated with the ruling regime in Iran, and its agenda became that much easier to implement in Iranian society at large following the invasion of southern Iran by Saddam Hussein's Iraqi forces in September 1980. A sense of crisis galvanised the population behind the defence of Iran (whether for Islamic or nationalist reasons), and the 'cumbersome' nature of the mandatory sartorial culture for women of the new Islamic Republic paled in significance with the new urgent wartime conditions that Iran faced. The war situation enabled the Islamic Republic to further its ideological understanding of gender, whereby females were segregated, and greater emphasis was placed on family relations (women as daughters, wives and mothers) rather than women as individuals in their own right.

This segregation cannot be divorced from veiling, for the veil was one of the instruments by which women were rendered 'safe' from the male gaze. The word hijab is, of course, derived from the Arabic trilateral root *ḥajaba*. Fatima Mernissi has highlighted the three dimensions of *ḥajaba*: the first is to hide, the second is to separate, and the third dimension is ethical and belongs to the realm of the forbidden. The hijab supposedly hides and separates women from unwanted advances from males, and it signifies that such women are forbidden to men.[16] Yet for many, the hijab was an extension of a wider *ḥijābī* culture in Iran, which transcended sartorial concerns. Hamid Naficy has observed how the 'instances of veiling abound

14 Kaveh Basmanji, *Tehran Blues: Youth Culture in Iran*, London 2005, 300–1.
15 Firoozeh Kashani-Sabet, *Conceiving Citizens: Women and the Politics of Motherhood in Iran*, Oxford 2011, 212.
16 Mernissi, *The Veil and the Male Elite*, 93.

in Iranian culture: the inner rooms of a house protect/hide the family; the veil hides women; decorum and status hide men; high walls separate and conceal private space from public space; the exoteric meanings of religious texts hide the esoteric meanings; and the perspective-less miniature paintings convey their messages in layers instead of organising a unified vision for a centred viewer'.[17]

The veiling of women in Iran, therefore, not only had the backing of leading mullas, and some secular political groups as mentioned above, but a significant proportion of the Iranian cultural tradition tended to endorse the practices associated with hiding. However, the compulsory nature of the separation of the sexes and laws on the hijab met with opposition, and such policies were not easy to implement. The Islamic Republic also encountered anomalous situations in attempting to promote the *ḥijābi*/separation culture. For instance, riding in shared taxis was a regular occurrence in urban areas where it was common that unrelated males and females squeezed into the passenger seat in the front of the car, rendering the segregation and separation of the sexes in busses absolutely meaningless. The following section focuses upon both such anomalies and difficulties related to enforcing this culture facing the regime since the inception of the revolution until 2005.

Anomalies and Difficulties in Implementing Compulsory Hijab

Anomalous depictions of women in hijabs in posters

The symbolism inherent in the hijab in modern Iran reflects the Islamic Republic's aim of promoting modesty, whether among schoolgirls, mothers or grandmothers. After the revolution, traditional functions for women were promoted that endorsed binary gender roles, and women were encouraged to adopt the more 'conventional' tasks of housekeeping, rearing the young, and providing a comfortable and secure environment for husbands, although there was a conspicuous female presence in the public sphere. The roles that were advanced for women by the Islamic Republic were reflected in various artworks of the time. Posters from the 1980s reveal the increasing importance of women in the public sphere. Whereas at the beginning of the war the faces of women were frequently obscured by their veils, or there was little detail in their faces (**Figures 11** and **12**), later images clearly reflected a change in attitudes. The lack of detail in the faces of

17 Hamid Naficy, 'Veiled vision/powerful presences', *In the Eye of the Storm: Women in Post-revolutionary Iran*, ed. Mahnaz Afkhami and Erika Friedl, London 1994, 136.

women in some posters may be related to the ideal of identifying women with Fatima, the daughter of Muhammad and mother of Imam Husayn who was killed at the battle of Karbala. Traditionally, Fatima, like the Prophet and the imams, was frequently depicted with a veiled face (**Figure 13**).

The increasing visual presence of women in both the public sphere and in art is related to the greater active participation of women in society, which was due to several factors, including the growing numbers of women in the work force (since men had been conscripted to the warfronts), and the inclusion of women in religious rituals, such as mourning for the dead soldiers.[18] Posters from this era depict women in hijab as active participants in the war effort (**Figure 14**); although they do not fight, they are engaged in encouraging their male relatives and other soldiers to face the enemy, even pushing young children forward to engage in acts to undermine Iraq (**Figure 15**). The very young are included as well, as one poster shows a pre-pubescent girl who can be no more than about five years of age, depicted in full 'Islamic clothing' with only her face and hands showing, holding a rifle with soldiers in the background (**Figure 16**). During the period of the war, women were encouraged to avoid strong colours and decorative appearances, as these would not be conducive to the solidarity sought for families experiencing war grief and sorrow.[19] And yet the depiction of women as mothers produced some rather anomalous images, such as that of a woman helping a young boy to read in a poster, dated 1981. The woman is shown with a hijab wrapped around her head so that not a strand of hair is visible. In this domestic scene, the viewer would assume that this is an image that depicts a mother and son. However, in the home setting, it is highly unlikely that an Iranian mother would cover herself so rigorously in front of close family members (**Figure 17**). (Interestingly the boy is shown reading a copy of Mutahhari's *Dāstān-i Rāstān*.)

Anomalous depictions of women in hijabs in films and the challenge of cinema and social media

The social and political transformations resulted in scrupulous attention being paid to the activities and outputs of all cultural institutions, so that, for example, the early 1980s witnessed the production of Persian films that were made with

18 Kamran Scott Aghaie, *The Women of Karbala: Ritual Performance and Symbolic Discourses in Modern Shi'i Islam*, Austin 2009, 46.
19 Zahra Kamalkhani, *Women's Islam: Religious Practice Among Women in Today's Iran*, London 1998, 138.

a particular emphasis away from the *film-fārsī* genre that depicted women in either frivolous, glamourous or highly sexualised roles. With the onset of the revolution and the adoption of the hijab, one of the pressing questions that faced Iranian directors was how to portray females. For example, in scenes that included women the revolutionary Iranian cinema laws enforced strict veiling, since as witnesses to an unveiled woman a male audience would violate her privacy and loosen public morality.[20] Naficy has identified three phases during which women emerged out of the shadows and became powerful presences in the film industry. In the early 1980s, images of unveiled women were cut out of existing Iranian films, and in local productions 'women were excised from the screens through self-censorship'.[21] Following this first phase, during the mid-1980s, the second phase, women 'appeared on screens as ghostly presences in the background or "domesticated" in the home environment'.[22] As Mottahedeh has observed, 'during the years that immediately followed the Iranian Revolution and the Iran-Iraq war (1980–88), close-ups of women were strictly forbidden as well. 'A close-up of a woman's face on screen would put a nonfamilial or unrelated male in the audience in close proximity to her in representational form.'[23] During the third phase, from the late 1980s and into the 1990s, a very different presentation of women emerged. Although still fully veiled, women now enjoyed major roles, and films explored a number of issues that were pertinent to women at the time.[24] Typifying this trend is *Bāshū, Gharība-yi Kūchik* (1989), a film by Bahram Bayzaʾi, in which Susan Taslimi featured in the lead role, and included a memorable camera shot where she stares directly at the audience, thus challenging the private, pious standards sought by the more conservative ulama (**Figure 18**).

Despite the emergence of women in the public sphere, mandatory veiling remained a cornerstone of the Islamic Republic. After the death of Khomeini, the subsequent Leader of the Islamic Republic, ʿAli Khamenei continued to endorse the hijab. Resistance to the mandatory veil was sporadic over the years. In the period shortly after Khomeini's death there were events that symbolised antipathy to the veil. Typifying an extreme response is the 1994 case of Huma Darabi who refused to wear the hijab, claiming that it interfered with her work as a medical

---

20 Negar Mottahedeh, *Displaced Allegories: Post-revolutionary Iranian Cinema*, Durham 2008, 9–10.
21 Naficy, 'Veiled vision/powerful presences', 132.
22 Naficy, 'Veiled vision/powerful presences', 132.
23 Negar Mottahedeh, *Representing the Unpresentable: Historical Images of National Reform from the Qajar to the Islamic Republic of Iran*, New York 2008, 191.
24 Naficy, 'Veiled vision/powerful presences', 132–3.

doctor. As a result, she was fired and then killed herself by self-immolation in a busy square of north Tehran. She tore off her headscarf, and shouted chants for freedom before setting herself on fire.[25] Other responses to mandatory veiling represent a degree of compromise or accommodation; Islamic clothing was adopted by women who devised ways to express a full range of symbolic meanings to their sartorial choices. As Kamalkhani, writing in 1998, observed, 'A decade after the Islamic revolution, the discourse of veiling is not a question of "to veil or not to veil"; nor is it a question of being secular or religious … rather it is a question of how and where to veil and which veil to adopt.'[26] She mentions that after Khomeini, President Rafsanjani's moderate public agencies recognised different forms of veiling and covering.[27] One understanding of a motive for veiling was expressed by the film director Samira Makhmalbaf who remarked: 'You get used to it … the headscarf is a law. Even when I am outside the country. I obey Islamic law because I want to come back to Iran. There's another thing. It's sort of like my national dress.'[28] Moreover, as Kamalkhani states, 'Women have become more creative and fashion-conscious, constantly attempting to subvert the blandness of the conventional veil. They have adopted various Islamic covering garments that play with colours, fabrics and design.'[29] Increasing levels of liberalisation and globalisation no doubt contributed to this phenomenon, for example, in 1989, it was reported that one young Iranian woman had answered on a radio programme that she regarded Oshin (an unveiled non-Iranian, non-Muslim woman), the leading character in a Japanese drama, as a more appropriate role model for young women than Fatima.[30] Different forms of veiling and covering became increasingly apparent in the 1990s. This is also reflected in the cinema, as Mohsen Makhmalbaf's hit of 1996, *Gabbeh*, depicted a female nomad whose electric blue attire was a direct contrast (and challenge?) to the conservative black so favoured by state

25 'Iranian Activist Wins International Human Rights Award for Hijab Campaign', *Feminist Newswire* 2 March 2015, https://feminist.org/blog/index.php/2015/03/02/iranian-activist-wins-international-human-rights-award-for-hijab-campaign/. See also Parvin Darabi and Romin P. Thomson, *Rage Against the Veil: The Courageous Life and Death of an Islamic Dissident*, New York 1999.
26 Kamalkhani, *Women's Islam*, 134.
27 Kamalkhani, *Women's Islam*, 142.
28 Cited in Basmenji, *Tehran Blues*, 42.
29 Kamalkhani, *Women's Islam*, 147.
30 Majid Tehranian, 'Islamic fundamentalism in Iran', *Fundamentalisms in Society: Reclaiming the Sciences, the Family and Education*, ed. Martin E. Marty and R. Scott Appleby, Chicago 1993, 359. Tehranian adds, 'The "Oshin" fad was further manifested through clothing, personal effects, and toys displaying Oshin's picture.'

institutions that enforce public morality[31] (**Figure 19**). Makhmalbaf was at the forefront of a movement to push back the boundaries of the Iranian censors, so much so that in 1998 he released a film called *Sokout* (*Silence*), in which the protagonist, a young girl who appears to be about eleven or twelve years of age, appears throughout the film unveiled when many of the 'good' girls would have their hair covered, with close-up shots of parts of her face, and she even dances to traditional Iranian music (**Figure 20**). The film was banned in Iran between 1997 and 2000, and perhaps it was the election of Muhammad Khatami as President of Iran in 1997 that finally resulted in the release of the film.[32]

Another famous Iranian film director who courted controversy was Abbas Kiarostami, who in 1997 was awarded the Palme D'Or at the Cannes Film Festival for his film *The Taste of Cherry*. This film about suicide was rendered even more problematic for the socially 'conservative' elements in Tehran when Kiarostami kissed Catherine Deneuve on the cheek as he collected his award.[33] A film that was even more challenging to the hijab regulations was Kiarostami's 2002 film *10*. Shot inside of a car that is driven by a young woman, *10* records the conversations that she has with her passengers.[34] One of these is a young woman who tells the driver how the man she loves refuses to marry her. She has fastened her hijab tightly around her head, and her female driver notices this and asks why. The passenger gradually lets the scarf slip from her head, revealing that she has shaved away all of her hair. Unsurprisingly, the film was banned by the Islamic Republic, and it resulted in Kiarostami's first open criticism of censorship within the film industry. As a proponent of the depiction of 'real' life, Kiarostami said, 'I can assure you that it is all very true to life … In other Iranian films there is

31 The literature on Mohsen Makhmalbaf's work is considerable. For an analysis of *Gabbeh*, see Eric Egan, *The Films of Makhmalbaf: Cinema, Politics and Culture in Iran*, Washington 2005, 155–61. Kamalkhani noted the presence of local tribeswomen in Shiraz, in their colourful clothing which 'strongly contrast with the dark colours and veils worn by the *ḥezbullāhi* women'.

32 For a discussion of *Sokout*, see Lloyd Ridgeon, 'Listening for an "Authentic" Iran: Mohsen Makhmalbaf's Film "The Silence" (Sokut)', *Iranian Intellectuals, 1997–2007*, ed. Lloyd Ridgeon, London 2008, 139–53. Makhmalbaf subsequently left Iran and settled for a time in France, although at present he lives in London. He has produced several controversial films. Perhaps one of the most significant is *Scream of the Ants* (2006) that includes a scene in which the bare breasts of an unveiled actress (Luna Shad) take central position in the camera shot.

33 Stewart Jeffreys, 'Landscapes of the Mind', *The Guardian* 16 April 2005, https://www.theguardian.com/film/2005/apr/16/art.

34 Blake Atwood, *Reform Cinema in Iran: Film and Political Change in the Islamic Republic*, New York 2016, 115–23.

always someone who goes around adjusting the women's headscarves just before they start filming, but that is frankly the death of cinema.'[35]

The ruling on the hijab on screen is only applied to domestically produced shows and films, and given the strength of the black market for videos, CDs, DVDs, and now streaming, Iranians have access to films coming from the West. That is not to say that the regime and certain conservative media outlets approve of the dissemination of Western shows which may include images of 'inappropriately' dressed females. There have been instances when the bodies of such women have been 'blacked out'.[36] Advances in social media and the internet have also created difficulties for the Islamic Republic in policing and enforcing public morality. One of most relevant and well-known cases involves Zahra Amir Ibrahimi, who was a famous actress in the TV soap show called *Nargis*. It is claimed that Ibrahimi appeared in a sex-tape that was made in 2004 and was widely disseminated thereafter on DVD and on the internet. The interest in the case came to the attention of the state authorities, and the Iranian Chief Prosecutor, Saʿid Murtazavi, ordered a special investigation. According to one source, Ibrahimi was convicted and sentenced to prison, but she left for France before being imprisoned;[37] however, other sources claim she was neither accused nor convicted.[38] But the significance of the case lies in the easy availability of material (pirated or otherwise) via social media. The younger generations of Iranians, who are well-known as IT literate, have easy access to photos, paintings, and all kinds of images to which the 'traditionally' minded ulama object.

Hijab and initiation rituals

Very soon after the revolution and the establishment of the mandatory hijab, a

35 Cited in Atwood, *Reform Cinema in Iran*, 117.
36 Of interest in this regard is the case of Charlize Theron, the American actress who in February 2016 presented the Oscar award of Best Foreign Film to the Iranian director Asghar Farhadi for his movie *The Salesman*. Theron was dressed in a Dior dress without sleeves and a low-cut front, which resulted in the Iranian Labour News Agency photoshopping the coverage by blacking out the offending skin. See Catherine Shoard, 'Iran news agency gives Charlize Theron a polo neck in altered Oscars footage', *The Guardian* 01 March 2016,
https://www.theguardian.com/film/2017/mar/01/
iran-news-agency-charlize-theron-polo-neck-oscars-asghar-farhadi-salesman.
37 Fatemeh Shams Esmaeili, 'The Iranian actress's sex tape scandal', *Free Speech Debate* 12 June 2012, http://freespeechdebate.com/case/the-iranian-actress-and-sex-tape-scandal/.
38 Robert Tait, 'Iranian actor in sex video scandal says ex-fiancé faked footage', *The Guardian* 22 November 2006.

brand-new ritual emerged known as *jashn-i taklīf* (the celebration of responsibility). This ritual marks the ninth birthday of young girls, the age when they become adults, and responsible for their actions. As young adults they have to wear the hijab in public and in front of all non-*maḥram* individuals. The ritual became mandatory in all schools, but in many cases the ceremony is also performed privately at home with family and friends, and involves the performance of prayers, competence in answering religious questions, and the ritual donning of the hijab. The *jashn-i taklīf* is 'a rite of legitimacy for a state that sees itself as the prime representative of the "common good". It can be seen as a propaganda coup, publicising people's purported loyalty to the new order'.[39] And yet the *jashn-i taklīf* may be regarded not only as an Islamic and spiritual rite of passage, but it may also be considered a ritual that includes more material, class-based and commercial trappings, especially among the rich and those who hold private parties. Azam Torab, who has studied the ritual, mentions presents, the celebratory cake and white dress that the young girl wears. Moreover, Torab points out that during her fieldwork, the main pre-occupation of the mothers of the girls was their daughters' marriage in the distant future. In addition, perhaps conscious of the accusations that their celebrations manifested a set of values at variance with those of the state, one mother exclaimed that it was possible to be modern and Islamic at the same time. Thus, the creation of this ritual, while intending to hoist the banner of both individual purity and chastity and also the larger moral high-ground of the Islamic Republic, has been performed by Iranians with a wide range of meanings and purposes, and manifests sentiments among girls and families oscillating between support and collaboration, acquiescence and toleration, and sedition and rejection.[40]

The Berlin Conference

Following the death of Khomeini in 1989, and after Rafsanjani's two terms as president, Iranians elected Muhammad Khatami as president. Khatami was regarded as a reformist who was popular among women and the young, and his two terms of office (1997–2005) witnessed a number of milestones in the advancement of women's rights in Iran. He selected a woman as one of his six vice-presidents, and appointed a woman as his advisor on women's affairs. Significantly, he also chose

39 Azam Torab, *Performing Islam: Gender and Ritual in Iran*, Leiden 2007, 182.
40 The whole of Azam Torab's chapter on the *jashn-i taklīf* is worth close inspection. See her *Performing Islam*, 169–93.

Jamila Kadivar (the sister of Muhsin Kadivar) as his special advisor on press affairs during his second term of office. Women's participation in society was assisted by huge educational achievements; it is claimed that at the advent of the revolution 35% of women were literate, but this increased to 74% by the end of the 20th century.[41] Moreover, by 2002, women accounted for 62% of successful candidates for national college examinations.[42] The increasing levels of globalisation and an IT literate population meant that it was difficult to restrict the flow of Westernisation and various forms of modernisation. Access to social media, films and music served to whet the appetite of those desiring to mimic or support Western fashion. It would not have gone unnoticed by women and the younger generation of Iranians that when the Iranian lawyer (and former judge) Shirin Ebadi was awarded the Nobel Peace Prize in 2003, she attended the ceremony in Oslo without a hijab. The social context of Iranian women had changed dramatically since the 1978–9 revolution, which was won by a wide coalition of groups that shared the primary aim of overthrowing the Shah. The discourse of the Islamic Republic after Khomeini's death in 1989, reflecting the ideology of Murtaza Mutahhari, had empowered women to the extent that there were demands for female participation in all dimensions of society.[43] Increasing demands revealed the realities of Iran in the modern age, which had experienced a devastating war with Iraq that gave new opportunities for women to engage in the jobs that had once been performed by their husbands, fathers and brothers, who were now enlisted at the warfronts. It is no surprise that from the end of the war, questions pertaining to gender roles were frequently being articulated, as women became increasingly visible in the media and public sphere. Eventually, the compulsory nature of the hijab became the subject of inquiry, to the extent that some members of the ulama even started to ask whether it was a necessary command within Islam. Matters came to a head at the infamous Berlin conference of April 2000.

The difficulties experienced by the Islamic regime in enforcing a strict

---

41 Mahmood Monshipouri and Mehdi Zakerian, 'The State of Human Rights in Iran', *Inside the Islamic Republic: Social Change in Post-Khomeini Iran*, ed. Mahmood Monshipouri, London 2016, 161.

42 Mitra K. Shavarini, 'The Feminisation of Higher Education', *International Review of Education / Internationale Zeitschrift für Erziehungswissenschaft / Revue Internationale de l'Education* 51.4, 2005, 329–47.

43 The general demand for greater female rights in society are typified in an article by Sachedina, 'Woman, Half-the-man? The Crisis of Male Epistemology in Islamic Jurisprudence', 169–78. In Persian, the writings of Mihrangiz Kar became increasingly popular; see, for example, her *Khushūnat 'Alayh-i Zan dar Irān* [*Violence Against Women in Iran*], Tehran 1380/2001.

interpretation of the hijab arguably resulted in a shift among some ulama that reflected a more flexible attitude towards hijab. Such a position shifted the responsibility for wearing the hijab on to the woman as a matter of private belief, and supported a policy of encouraging women to dress modestly, using education rather than force. The change was dramatically witnessed in the events and presentations that took place in a conference in Berlin in 2000. The conference was held in the wake of the power struggle between 'reformists' and 'conservatives' among the ulama, which was played out in the trial in 1999 at the Special Clerical Court (*dādgāh-i vīzha-yi rūḥānīyat*)[44] of ʿAbdollah Nuri, a mulla who had been Khatami's Minister of the Interior, and had launched the reformist newspaper, *Khurdād*.[45] The trial was most likely an attempt by the more conservative ulama to stem the reformist tide and to take a stand against Nuri, who had published articles by the leading dissident Akbar Ganji and other reformists including Muhammad Majid Muhammadi. It is here that the reformist ulama and the more secular (though by no means irreligious) thinkers joined forces. Muhammad Majid Muhammadi's articles were representative of much of the thinking of the late 1990s and early 2000s which argued that ideological understandings of religion reified the lifestyle and values of a certain group at the expense of those that were held by other individuals and groups. In effect, Muhammadi called for greater tolerance and pluralism in society, allowing people to choose their own lifestyle within the general parameters of Islamic ethics. It was this kind of perspective that the conservative Special Clerical Court denied, accusing Nuri of upholding such a worldview. The Court condemned him for advocating this in the form of material published in his newspaper, and argued that allowing people greater freedom to choose their lifestyles endangered Islamic purity and promoted corruption and immorality. This contravened the principle of 'promoting the good and forbidding the evil', a collective duty which is enshrined in Article 8 of the Constitution of the Islamic Republic. At the heart of the argument lay the issue of the hijab.[46]

Nuri's arrest gave him the opportunity to argue that Islam permits different lifestyles, typified in the fivefold classification of acts according to the laws of *fiqh* (mentioned earlier). Moreover, by pointing to the non-compulsion for the hijab on

44 For this court see Mirjam Künkler, 'The Special Court of the Clergy (*Dādgāh-Ye Vizheh-Ye Ruhāniyat*) and the Repression of Dissident Clergy in Iran', *The Rule of Law, Islam, and Constitutional Politics in Egypt and Iran*, ed. Said Amir Arjomand and Nathan J. Brown, Albany 2013, 57–100.

45 Mir-Hosseini and Tapper, *Islam and Democracy in Iran*, 136–48.

46 Mir-Hosseini and Tapper, *Islam and Democracy in Iran*, 143–5.

non-believing women and non-Muslims, Nuri suggested that the requirement to cover the head was not as straightforward as some have asserted. He subsequently pointed to the temporal and contingent nature of some laws as they pertained to women, such as female enfranchisement. Although Nuri did not produce a systematic argument that argued for or against the hijab, his defence of the general principle to allow different lifestyles indicated where his sympathies lay.

In the wake of this show case trial, participants at the Berlin conference of 2000 refused to let the matter drop. More significantly, the arguments presented in Germany by Eshkevari offered more depth and sophistication. Although his speeches at the Berlin conference were not specific to the hijab, his arguments were based on general jurisprudential principles, the logical conclusion of which challenged the kinds of presumptions held by conservative ulama on a range of issues including the head-covering for women. Religious scholars such as Eshkevari were able to justify adopting a more flexible position because of Khomeini's comments about paying due regard to 'time and place' (discussed in Part One). The correlation between time and place is related to the jurisprudential principle that the ruling follows the subject matter (*ḥukm tābiʿ mawżūʿ ast*).[47] This means that when a subject matter changes, the ruling too will change. The implication is that Qurʾanic rulings pertaining to the covering of females were revealed as specific verses that were time-bound or contextual, and they were not necessarily meant as universal and applicable to all women at all times. Eshkevari made it explicit that 'the Prophet did not legislate the laws relating to women, nor the penal laws, nor many others'.[48] He explained that 99% of the laws that the Prophet implemented in Medina had already been practised by the Arabs, and thus these laws were merely 'approved' (or validated) rather than legislated. He added, 'This is a matter of custom and has nothing to do with religion and the basis of the sharia.'[49] Eshkevari stated that the hijab was a matter that pertained to the ruling (i.e. modesty) and the subject matter (women), and that women should be able to choose whether they want to wear it or not. He also pointed out that at the start of the Islamic Revolution the hijab was not supposed to be compulsory, and all issues pertaining to women (not just the hijab) need to be reconstructed from the foundations.[50] Eshkevari was arrested on 6 August 2000 on his return to Iran. He was accused of apostasy because of his denial of the immutability of Islamic

47 Mir-Hosseini and Tapper, *Islam and Democracy in Iran*, 165.
48 Mir-Hosseini and Tapper, *Islam and Democracy in Iran*, 168.
49 Mir-Hosseini and Tapper, *Islam and Democracy in Iran*, 168.
50 Mir-Hosseini and Tapper, *Islam and Democracy in Iran*, 169–70.

laws, and because of his opposition to mandatory veiling.[51] His arrest resulted in a number of respected authorities rushing to his defence, including Ayatollah ʿAli Akbar Muhtashami, Ayatollah ʿAli Garami and Mihdi Karubi (speaker of the parliament).[52] The treatment meted out to Eshkevari was reflected in the clamp-down on the newspapers and press around the same time. It is of interest that Fatima Mernissi's book, *The Veil and the Male Elite*, was translated and published in Iran,[53] but within months (18 May 2002) it was banned, and unsold copies were gathered and destroyed.[54] Mernissi's work argued that the covering of women in Muhammad's community was specific to the Prophet's wives, and resulted from the pressure that his companion, ʿUmar, exercised over him. As such, her work argued the point, similar to Eshkevari's, that the covering laws were contextual, and were not meant to be applicable to all women and at all times.

51 Although these charges were overturned, Eshkevari was subsequently sentenced to prison in 2002 for 'propaganda against the Islamic Republic' and 'insulting top-rank officials', https://www.englishpen.org/campaigns/hojjatoleslam-hasan-yousefi-eshkevari.
52 Charles Kurzman, 'Critics within: Islamic scholars' protests against the Islamic state in Iran', *An Islamic Reformation*, ed. Michelle Browers and Charles Kurzman, Lanham, MD 2003, 92–3.
53 *Zanān-i Parda-nishīn va Nukhbigān-i Jawshan Pūsh*, trans. Maliheh Maghazeʾi, Tehran 1380/2001. I am grateful to Ziba Mir-Hosseini for pointing me to this translation and also to the subsequent discussion about the banning of the book.
54 'Jamʿ-āvurī-yi *Zanān-i Parda-nishīn va Nukhbigān-i Jawshan Push*' ['The Gathering of *The Veil and the Male Elite*'], http://www.bbc.com/persian/news/020518_h-book.shtml.

6

Mullas without Turbans and Women without Veils: The Life and Thought of Ahmad Qabil

Introduction

Ahmad Qabil was a mid-ranking jurist who achieved prominence in Iran for his radical approach of foregrounding reason in establishing a sound basis for discovering sharia law. His call to re-thinking the sharia, which he termed *sharīʿat-i ʿaqlānī* (rational sharia), is among the most significant developments in jurisprudential thought that has emerged from the Iranian seminaries in recent years. His steadfast support for reason did not result in a loss of faith; rather, he viewed rational thinking and belief in Islam as perfectly harmonious and congruent to life in the modern world. Although similar views had been expressed by seminarians in modern times (e.g. by Mutahhari), without a doubt Qabil's worldview reflects a more steadfast and dedicated attachment to reason. His commitment to rational sharia was intricately bound up with a political idealism that was pluralist, and any belief or idea that was a cause of controversy or which did not correlate with the findings of science or with reason needed to be discussed and debated to prove its worth. Such a preparedness to examine ideas, terms and scripture also necessitated a rigorous scrutiny of the social and political institutions of Iran, and Qabil was not hesitant in highlighting several serious obstacles that he believed had restricted the progress of Iranian society, politics and culture, especially after the death of Ayatollah Khomeini. It is perhaps for his stinging criticisms of ʿAli Khamenei, as the foremost representative of an undemocratic clique, that Qabil is best remembered among Iranians. The image of Qabil shuffling in to the Special Clerical Court in May 2010, accused of having carried out subversive activities against the Islamic Republic, only served to re-enforce the perception of him as a champion of the Green Movement that emerged in Iran after the 'rigged' presidential election of 2009. It also reflected the same intransigent opposition to Khamenei that his spiritual mentor Ayatollah Montazeri had expressed during the last ten years of his life.

Qabil's own untimely death in 2012 of a brain tumour meant that *sharīʿat-i ʿaqlānī* could not be developed and expanded beyond the ten works that have been published and made available online by his friend and fellow jurist and theologian, Muhsin Kadivar.[1] These works have not been seriously analysed by researchers on Islamic or Iranian studies. Indeed, Qabil is mentioned only very rarely in the English literature on Iran, usually in a list of reformists that includes the usual figures of Soroush, Eshkevari, and Shabistari. The absence of studies on Qabil's thought is attributable to both the relative short space of time since his works were made available, and also the complexity of his Persian writing which is laced with juristic and Islamic terminology. The following is an attempt to familiarise a Western audience with the main ideas of *sharīʿat-i ʿaqlānī* and its real-life implications.

The first part of this section on Qabil, however, presents the main contours of his life and his political dispute with Khamenei. Subsequently, the main features of *sharīʿat-i ʿaqlānī* are presented and analysed by investigating his work of the same name. This is followed by a translation of his writing on the hijab, which appears in his book *Aḥkām-i Bānūvān dar Sharīʿat-i Muḥammadī* (*Commands Pertaining to Women in the Muhammadan Sharia*). A translation of the section that deals with the hijab contained herein reveals his difference of opinion with Mutahhari; thereby, further attesting to the vibrancy of interpretive techniques of *fiqh*, and demonstrating both Qabil's firm attachment to what he called 'reliable scripture' and reason, and the radical nature of his message.

Qabil's Political Life

As stated previously, little has been written on Ahmad Qabil in the West. Researchers must rely on Persian sources to trace the outlines of his life, and fortunately a website has been constructed where his writings, interviews and speeches may

1 Kadivar has also written a critical article that examines Qabil's jurisprudential thinking. See *Mujāhidat-hā-yi ʿIlmī-yi Marḥūm Ahmad Qabil* [*The Scientific Struggles of the Late Ahmad Qabil*], which is on Kadivar's website: https://kadivar.com/9795. For the Youtube version see: https://www.youtube.com/watch?v=K1g1CezEhe8.

be read. One of the most useful sources on this website is an ebook titled *Yād-nāma-yi Ahmad Qabil* (*Remembrance of Ahmad Qabil*), which offers a reflection on his life. The present section of this chapter utilises this ebook (supplemented with other sources) to reconstruct the main political events in Qabil's life.

Ahmad Qabil was born in 1957, in a rural town near Turbat-i Jam in North-East Iran, close to the border with Afghanistan. His father had come to this region from Najaf to educate the local people, but the family soon relocated to the neighbouring city of Mashhad, famous for the shrine of the eighth Shiʿi imam, and also the location of Iran's most prestigious seminary (with the exception, perhaps, of Qum). Qabil was sent to a state school in Mashhad, but he was to pursue a religious education and began elementary studies at the seminary in Mashhad in 1350/1971 under the guidance of Ayatollah Milani. He then went to Qum to continue his religious education in 1357/1978, and once there he supported the opposition to the regime of Muhammed Riza Pahlavi. He was a keen reader of the works of pre-revolutionary thinkers,[2] including lay religious thinkers such as ʿAli Shariʿati,[3] and the leader of the Freedom Movement, Mihdi Bazargan,[4] but also thinkers among the ulama such as Ayatollah Taliqani.[5] Following the revolution, Qabil worked for a while in Mashhad with the Revolutionary Guards (Sipah-i Pasdaran), set up specifically to guard the Islamic nature of the Revolution, and he also spent some time at the warfront, fighting against the Iraqi forces. After the war, Qabil was able to return to his studies in Qum, where he also served as an interrogator (*bāz-pursī*) in the Special Clerical Court, before leaving after two years of service. He returned to North-East Iran to help his father in the running and teaching of a seminary in Fariman.[6]

In Qum, Qabil had commenced an association with Ayatollah Montazeri who was considered one of the greatest teachers at the level of advanced jurisprudential studies (*dars-i khārij-i fiqh*). In fact the relationship was not merely one of teacher-student, rather it resembled a father-son bond which lasted for more than

2 *Yād-nāma-yi Ahmad Qabil*, 71.

3 For an overview of ʿAli Shariʿati's life and thought, see Ali Rahnema, *An Islamic Utopian: A Political Biography of ʿAli Shariʿati*, London 2014. It is interesting to compare Qabil's clearly positive response to Shariʿati and his works with that of Mutahhari. The latter's distaste for Shariʿati reached an extent that he referred to Shariʿati's death prior to the Revolution as a 'divine blessing'. See Ghamari-Tabrizi, *Islam and Dissent*, 173.

4 For an overview of Bazargan, see Forough Jahanbakhsh, *Islam, Democracy and Religious Modernism in Iran, 1953–2000*, Leiden 2001, 80–98.

5 The life and thought of Ayatollah Taliqani have not been adequately researched in English. The most extensive treatment is in Dabashi, *Theology of Discontent*, 216–72.

6 *Yād-nāma-yi Ahmad Qabil*, 64.

Figure 1. Painting of Shaykh Safi al-Din (d. 1334), Shiraz, Iran, dated Shaʿban 990 AH / August–September 1582, opaque watercolour, ink and gold on paper @ The Aga Khan Museum, AKM264.

Figure 2. Illustration from Chardin's work showing the different forms of female fashion during the Safavid era. His two-volume book was originally published in 1720.

Figure 3. Studio Portrait: Man, Woman and Infant by Antoin Sevruguin. Myron Bement Smith Collection: Antoin Sevruguin Photographs. Freer Gallery of Art and Arthur M. Sackler Gallery Archives. Smithsonian Institute, Washington D.C. Gift of Katherine Dennis Smith, 1973-1985, FSA_A.4_2.12.GN.26.07.

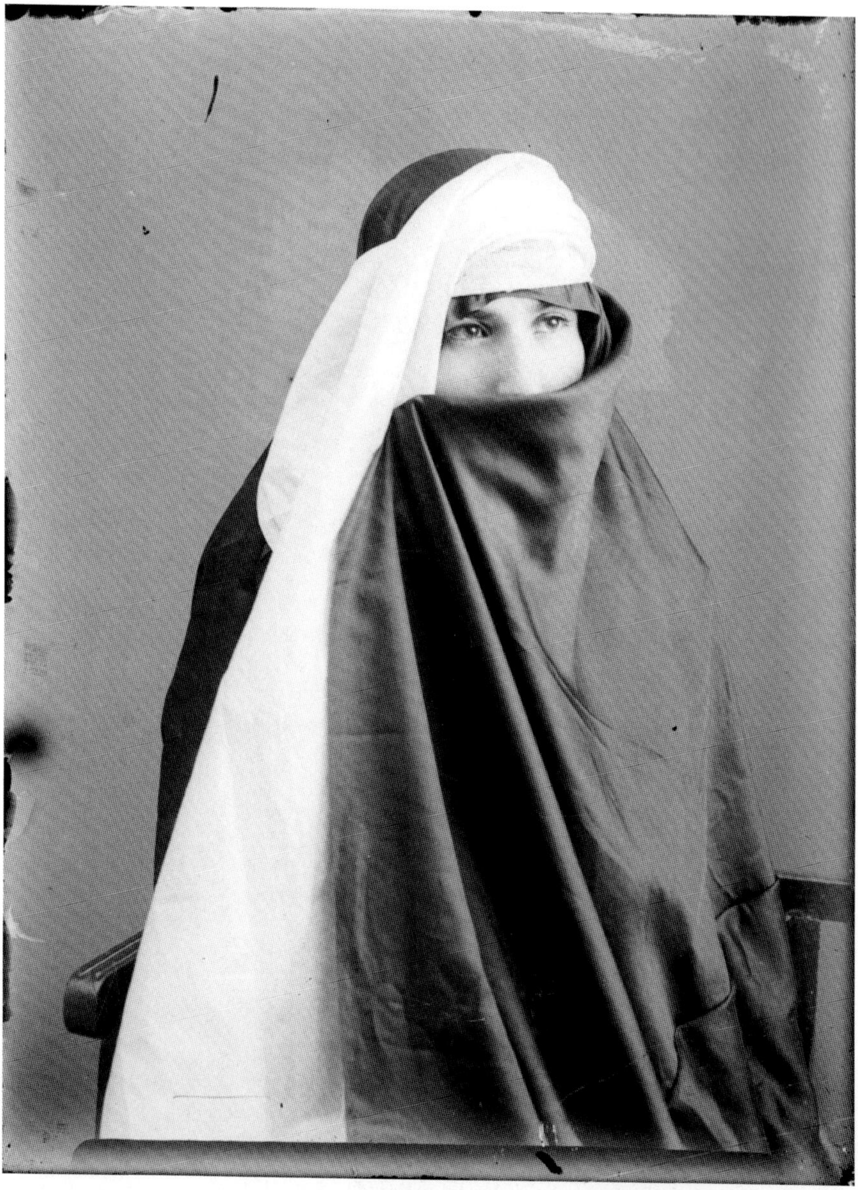

Figure 4. Studio Portrait: Veiled Woman by Antoin Sevruguin. Myron Bement Smith Collection: Antoin Sevruguin Photographs. Freer Gallery of Art and Arthur M. Sackler Gallery Archives. Smithsonian Institute, Washington D.C. Gift of Katherine Dennis Smith, 1973-1985, FSA_A.4_2.12.GN.02.05.

Figure 5. Veiled Women Boarding a Train, One of 274 Vintage Photographs, probably Antoin Sevruguin, late 19th century. Brooklyn Museum, Purchase gift of Leona Soudavar in memory of Ahmad Soudavar, 1997.3.12.

Figure 6. Studio Portrait: Seated Veiled Woman with Pearl by Antoin Sevruguin. Myron Bement Smith Collection: Antoin Sevruguin Photographs. Freer Gallery of Art and Arthur M. Sackler Gallery Archives. Smithsonian Institute, Washington D.C. Gift of Katherine Dennis Smith, 1973-1985, FSA_A.4_2.12.GN.02.07.

Figure 7. Shahla Vahabzada, the winner of the 1967 '*Dukhtar-i Shāyista*' (worthy lady). Image taken from the front cover of *Zan-i Rūz*.

Figure 8. Poster for the film *Haft Shahr-i ʿIshq* (from Hamid Naficy's collection of Iranian film posters, held at North Western University. Courtesy of Northwestern University Archives.

Figure 9. The 8th March 1979 march on International Women's Day. Hengameh Golestan, *Untitled* (Witness '79 series), photograph, March 1979, Anatole France (Neuphle le-Chateau) Street, opposite the USSR (Russian) Embassy, Tehran; © Hengameh Golestan, Courtesy of Archaeology of the Final Decade.

Figure 10. Berating the seminarians on International Woman's Day. Hengameh Golestan, *Untitled* (Witness '79 series), photograph, March 1979, Anatole France (Neuphle le-Chateau) Street, opposite the USSR (Russian) Embassy, Tehran; © Hengameh Golestan, Courtesy of Archaeology of the Final Decade.

Figure 11. Caption reads, ‘Fatima Rising, Celebrate the True Leader’ (1979). Middle Eastern Posters Collection at University of Chicago, box 2, no. 30. Special Collections Research Center, University of Chicago Library.

Figure 12. Caption reads, 'We created you from men and women' (Qur ʾan 49.13). Middle Eastern Posters Collection at University of Chicago., box 2, no. 45. Special Collections Research Center, University of Chicago Library.

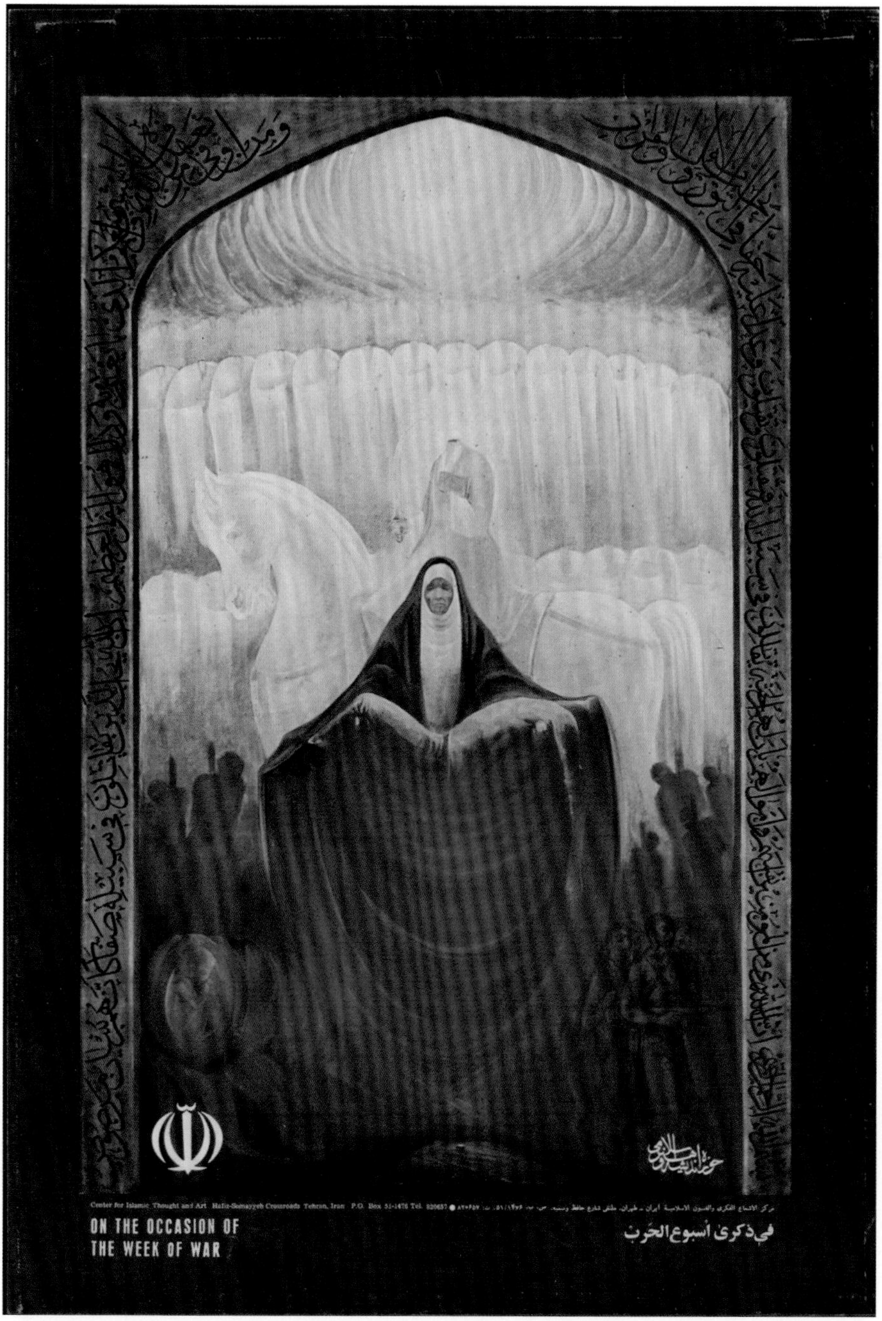

Figure 13. Fatima on the occasion of the Week of War. Middle Eastern Posters Collection at University of Chicago, box 3, no. 67. Special Collections Research Center, University of Chicago Library.

Figure 14. Women off to war. Middle Eastern Posters Collection at University of Chicago, box 3, no. 60. Special Collections Research Center, University of Chicago Library.

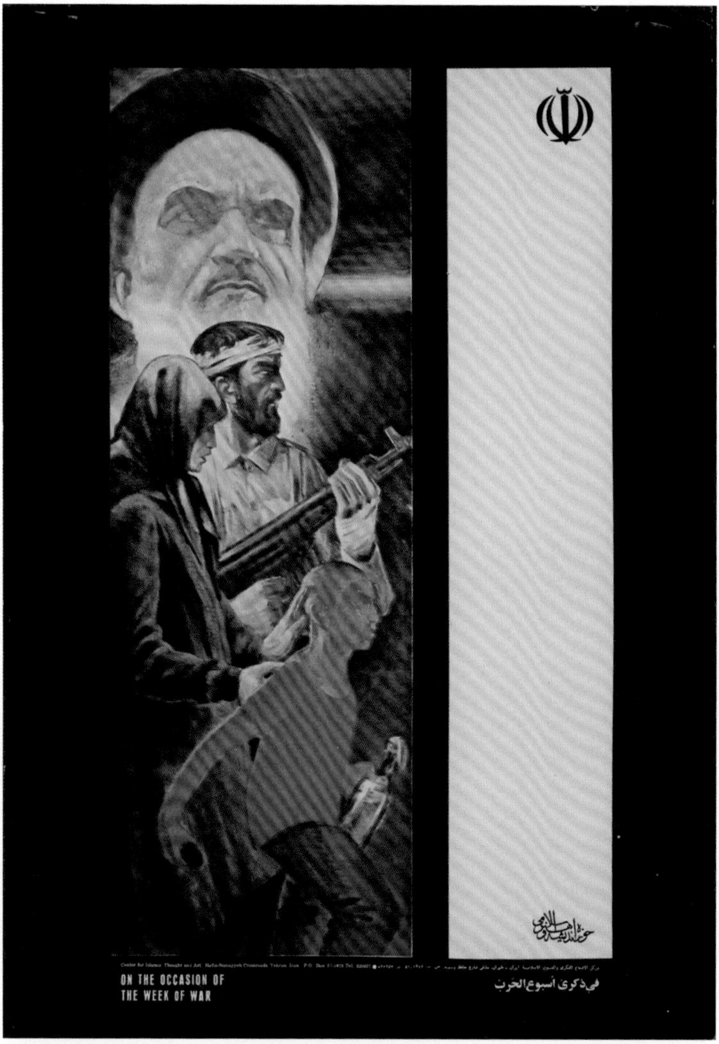

Figure 15. Encouraging sons to join the war effort. Middle Eastern Posters Collection at University of Chicago, box 3, no. 71. Special Collections Research Center, University of Chicago Library.

Figure 16. 'Our army does not only belong to our brothers in the armed forces'. Middle Eastern Posters Collection at University of Chicago, box 3, no. 77. Special Collections Research Center, University of Chicago Library.

Figure 17. 'Reading *Dāstān-i Rāstān*'.

Figure 18. Poster advertising the movie *Bāshū*, showing the scene when Susan Taslimi looks directly at the camera.

Figure 19. Poster advertising Makhmalbaf's film *Gabbeh* (1996). The actor is Shaghayeh Djodat, the nomad dressed in electric blue. Photography by Mohammad Ahmadi. Source: Makhmalbaf Film House.

Figure 20. Nadereh Abdelahyeva in Mohsen Makhmalbaf's 1998 film *Sokout*. Photography by Maysam Makhmalbaf. The copyright is held by the Makhmalbaf Film House.

Figure 21. Ahmad Qabil (left) in non-traditional garments. In the middle with the black turban and a mulla's gown is Muhammad Khatami. In the white turban is Hadi Qabil. The fourth person (far right) is a religious student, Mihdi Maliki, who was an assistant of Qabil, and who also helped Muhsin Kadivar assemble Qabil's works on the website *Sharīʿat-i ʿAqlānī*.

Figure 22. Ahmad Qabil with Ayatollah Montazeri.

twenty years.[7] Qabil's thesis was a critique of the practice of stoning to death as a punishment for adultery.[8] It was Montazeri who declared publicly in 1998 that Qabil was sufficiently qualified to issue his own opinions (*ijtihād*), not only on matters of jurisprudence, but also on hadith and theology. Indeed, in 2002, Montazeri appointed Qabil (along with Muhammad ʿAli Ayazi and Muhsin Kadivar) as deputies responsible for answering questions sent to his website.

Montazeri was not the only leading mulla from whose guidance Qabil benefitted. He enjoyed the company of the reformist Ayatollah Saniʿi, as well as and other well-known ulama such as Ayatollah Fazil Lankarani.[9] The long association with Montazeri coincided with the period in which the Ayatollah had commenced his critique of certain policies being pursued by the Islamic Republic of Iran. In particular, Montazeri had been worried at the numbers of prisoners held in custody and summarily executed in the summer and autumn of 1988, and so he had sent a letter of concern to Khomeini in July 1988.[10] This may well have contributed to his 'fall from grace' – after having been appointed in 1985 as the deputy leader of the regime, second only to Khomeini – for in 1989 he was dismissed from office and placed under house arrest. It is in this light that Qabil's continued support and connection to Montazeri should be considered. It might have been all too easy for Qabil to extricate himself from his spiritual guide, had he desired to further his education and career within the ranks of the ulama. However, Qabil's commitment to truth and the same kind of values espoused by

---

7 Ibid., 66. Qabil's relationship with Montazeri deserves further study. He refers to his master constantly and occasionally quotes him. For example, Qabil quoted Montazeri's approval of the use of reason:

> We recognise reason as the mother of proofs, in other words as the basis of proofs and evidence, and we do not recognise commands and laws that contradict reason. *Shar*ʿ commands never contradict reason, and the *shar*ʿ and the Qur'an direct us to reason. On many topics the Qur'an has set forth the discussion on rationality, understanding and thinking, and ordered people to consider existential and non-existential affairs. We recognise in Islam ('there is no compulsion in religion') that its meaning is that force is unacceptable. We say, 'Every command of the sharia is a command of reason, and every command of reason is a command of the sharia.' The command of reason and the *shar*ʿ are harmonious, and there is no contradiction between them. If a contradiction is witnessed, then whatever reason says takes precedence (*muqaddam*) because it is the mother of proofs (*Mabāni-ye Sharīʿat*, 234).

8 On this topic see Qabil's *Aḥkām-i Jazāʾī dar Sharīʿat-i Muhammadi* [*The Commands for Punishment in the Muhammadan Law*]. See: http://www.ghabel.net/shariat/books.

9 *Yād-nāma-yi Ahmad Qabil*, 66.

10 See Ulrich von Schwerin, *The Dissident Mullah: Ayatollah Montazeri and the Struggle for Reform in Revolutionary Iran*, London 2015, 109, which comes in a chapter devoted to Montazeri's 'fall' within the religious establishment of the Islamic Republic (90–131).

Montazeri ensured that he remained faithful to the cause that eventually segued into the Green Movement.[11]

Qabil's independent mind and support for Montazeri resulted in him becoming somewhat distant from certain aspects of the traditional religious establishment. This was typified by his refusal to wear the robes and turban so often associated with Iran's Shiʿi ulama (**Figure 21**). Sartorial preferences have long been an element of controversy in Iran, especially where the ulama have been concerned. In the early 20th century, the iconoclastic rational thinker Ahmad Kasravi, who was trained as a mulla, refused to follow certain of the sartorial traditions observed by his fellow mullas, which gave an indication of his eventual disillusionment with the religious establishment.[12] The controversy over forms of clothing came to the fore in Iranian society with the dress reforms of Riza Shah, implemented in the late 1920s and early 1930s, although the ulama were exempt from the new regulations.[13] Qabil claimed that he had cast off the mulla's gown and turban in the summer of 1991,[14] having worn them since 1975 when he first went to Qum.

---

11 For the Green Movement see Hamid Dabashi, *The Green Movement in Iran*, New Jersey 2011. Qabil summarised the views and demands of the Green Movement with which he clearly sympathised. See 'Mushtārakāt-i junbish-i sabz' [The Common-points with the Green Movement], *Vaṣiyat bi Millat-i Irān*, 115–20:

1. The common demand of the people in the current uprising is nothing other than the rejection of tyranny and the verification of the authority of the nation based on democracy.
2. The basis of all the laws of the country must be established on human rights.
3. The right to freedom of expression.
4. All the socio-political efforts of the Green Movement of the nation of Iran [must] be in the framework of 'national unity, and the oneness of the land of Iran'.
5. The rejection of violence.

That he was identified with the Green Movement is typified in the following remark by Eshkevari made on 22 October 2012:

> In recent years, Qabil has also been among the well-known opposition leaders of the Green Movement. On this topic too, he was successful and dignified. In following Ayatollah Montazeri (his master and leader in jurisprudence, politics, piety and morality) with his particular [form of] bravery, he clearly and firmly criticised and battled the political power and tyranny of the ruler in relation to religion and the sharia from basically a jurisprudential and religious perspective (*Yād-nāma-yi Ahmad Qabil*, 324)

12 See Lloyd Ridgeon, *Sufi Castigator: Ahmad Kasravi and the Iranian Mystical Tradition*, London 2006, 7.

13 The reforms of Riza Shah are detailed by Chehabi, 'Staging the emperor's new clothes', 209–29. See also the discussion related to male sartorial reforms in Iran under Riza Shah in Ridgeon, 'Ahmad Kasravi and "pick-axe" politics', 59–72.

14 'Chirā libās-i rūḥāniyat-rā kinār guzashtam' [Why I put aside the clothes of the men of religion], *Naqd-i Khud-kāmagī*, 95.

He offered several reasons for his actions. First, he pointed to the practical consideration that these clothes are cumbersome, especially in the heat of the Iranian summer when many individuals mill around, travel, drive, and engage in all kinds of energetic activities. Second, Qabil claimed that the false pride among most people dressed in a mulla's garment had led to the non-observance of human and Islamic morals in many social interactions. Third, Qabil argued that Muhammad and the imams had not adorned themselves in any particular garment, but had worn the same clothes as ordinary people. Fourth, Qabil reflected upon a reliable narration from Imam Sadiq that 'the best clothes in any time are the ordinary clothes of the people of that time'.[15] The above reasons are repeated by Hadi Qabil, Ahmad Qabil's brother, who elaborated on how his brother argued with the religious courts over sartorial issues:

> Being a seminarian (*ṭalabagī*) does not mean that we should wear these clothes. Once when the Special Clerical Court sent their file to the Revolutionary Court, they said, 'We do not recognise him [Ahmad Qabil] as a seminarian (*ṭalaba*).' Ahmad Aqa [...] said, 'The Special Clerical Court has told a lie and is mistaken. This is because several years ago they arrested me and compiled a file about me. Some of my documents are even in there. [But] let's leave aside all of this. Right now, I receive a stipend (*shahriya*) from the seminary and I have seminary insurance. Therefore, being a seminarian has nothing to do with clothes. Many of your judges are seminarians, and they do not wear [a mulla's] clothes.' The judge also agreed and said, 'He has spoken the truth.' Ahmad Aqa insisted he was a seminarian, and wherever he went he said, 'I am an ordinary seminarian, not one who believes there is a certain distinction from it.'[16]

Qabil's claim that it is not necessary to wear a mulla's garment or turban to be a seminarian is justified too with reference to the practice of eminent mullas of bygone generations. In particular, two of the most famous mullas of recent generations who refused to wear seminarian garments are Jahangir Qashqa'i (1827–1910) and Ayatollah Rahim Arbab (1875–1975). The former came from a non-urban background and was more familiar and comfortable in the nomadic garments of the Qashqa'i tribe around Isfahan where he was born.[17] The latter

15 'Chirā libās-i rūḥāniyat-rā kinār guzashtam', 95–6.
16 *Yād-nāma-yi Ahmad Qabil*, 68.
17 Abbas Qumi, *Fawā'id al-Razwiya*, Tehran 1327/1948–49, vol. 1, 88.

believed that the turban was for the prophets alone, and so he never donned one.[18] Nevertheless, not sporting a gown and turban is very unconventional, and marks out an individual in the seminary from the rest of the crowd.[19]

Despite Qabil's refusal to wear the gown and turban, his attachment to the religious establishment and its learning should not be overlooked. Perhaps Qabil was inspired by the example set by Ayatollah Montazeri, who under house arrest, remained steadfast in his religious duties in as much as he was allowed to perform them (**Figure 22**). Nevertheless, Qabil must have been concerned with the religious institutions in Iran and their connections with the state. It is to be wondered, for example, if the conflict between Montazeri and Khomeini produced an inner turmoil in him. This conflict was an issue with which many Iranians have struggled. Montazeri was critical of those who claimed Khomeini's legacy, such as Khamenei, and the dispute between two of the most senior figures associated with the Islamic Revolution provoked the kinds of questions about how it was possible to support and endorse the reformist ideas of Montazeri on the one hand, while remaining loyal not only to the legacy of Khomeini, but even to the figure of Khomeini who had dismissed the former.[20] Hadi Qabil's account of his brother's solution to this conundrum may have a lot of resonance among Iranians, for he claimed that Ahmad Qabil accepted Khomeini as the leader of the country and regarded him with great respect. However, he insisted that Khomeini was not infallible (*maʿsūm*) and could fall into error.

> Despite the attachment that Imam [Khomeini] had for Ayatollah Montazeri, considering him the fruit of his life, Ahmad Aqa used to say that [… some] steps were taken by some people that were inappropriate (*ṣaḥīḥ na-būdan*) and they persuaded the Imam [to take] such a decision. But with the passing of time, many [people] understood that this conflict was a mistake, and the conflict with Ayatollah Montazeri did both damage to the regime and also to those people who had arranged those first steps … Until the very end of his

18 Gulshan Abrar, *Jamīʿi az Pazhuhishgarān-i Hawza-yi ʿAmaliya Qum*, Qum 1385/2006–7, vol. 3, 354.
19 I am grateful to Muhsin Kadivar for pointing me to the examples of Jahangir Qashqaʾi and Rahim Arbab.
20 Central to this point is the discussion of Khomeini's *vilāyat*. Qabil's fullest consideration of this concept is an article titled 'Vilāyat-i faqīh', *Fiqh, Kārkard-hā va Qābiliyat-ha*, 75–96. No analysis of Qabil's view on the topic has been written yet, but it is a subject worthy of further investigation.

life, Ahmad Aqa held to that very belief, but his respect for the Imam never decreased. He believed in the Imam, but not [as an] infallible [person ...][21]

Qabil's support of Montazeri may have contributed to the regime's attempt to silence the former. Montazeri had warned Khamenei in early 1995 about mixing politics and religion, which was clearly a rejection of the latter's attempt to assume the position of *marja'iyat*.[22] Soon after the election of President Muhammad Khatami, the 'reformists' believed the time was ripe for change. However, Khamenei and his supporters hit back in what was being perceived as a challenge to their authority. Qabil was distributing some advice that Montazeri had written for the new president, when he was arrested by the security forces and taken to Mashhad, and kept for a while in prison. And then in 2001 he was arrested once more in Tehran and taken to the Special Clerical Courts. According to his brother, he spent more than 70 days in solitary confinement, having been accused of acting against national security, insulting the Leader (Khamenei), and spreading propaganda against the political system.[23] Qabil was eventually released after posting bail.[24] Other sources maintain he spent up to 125 days in solitary confinement.[25]

On release, Qabil moved to Tajikistan, and still undaunted he composed a virulent criticism of Khamenei, dated 31 May 2005, in which he lambasted the Leader for many of Iran's political and social ills. His long letter contained seven points in which he criticised Khamenei's leadership of the country. The candour and the direct nature of the criticisms are astonishing, and it is to be speculated that it was these harsh words, more than the message of a reformed sharia, that tainted Qabil in the eyes of the regime. It is worth summarising these seven criticisms and providing examples of the language used, if only to give an indication of the nature of the letter.[26]

---

21 *Yād-nāma-yi Ahmad Qabil*, 73.

22 von Schwerin, *The Dissident Mullah*, 161. The position of *marja' taqlīd* (source of emulation) has traditionally been the highest spiritual rank among Shi'i practitioners. A *marja'* controls a seminary, its administration, its curriculum and its finances. As such a *marja'* is independent from the state. Khamenei, according to many sources, did not hold the requisite educational background to become a *marja'*. His attempts to secure this position reflected, perhaps, his desire to assume greater spiritual standing in Iran and among Shi'i communities outside of Iran.

23 *Yād-nāma-yi Ahmad Qabil*, 77.

24 Muhammad Sahimi, 'Progressive Muslim Scholar and Political Dissident Ahmad Ghabel: 1954–2012', http://www.payvand.com/news/12/oct/1157.html.

25 Sahimi, 'Progressive Muslim Scholar'.

26 This letter simply titled 'Nāma bi rahbar-i jumhūrī-yi Islāmī-yi Irān' [Letter to the Leader of the Islamic Republic] is available in full on the following site: http://www.bbc.com/persian/iran/story/2005/06/050601_ahmad-Qabil-letter.shtml.

The first criticism refered to the 'great mistake of our religiosity' (*rūḥāniyat-i mā*) which claims the right to government without having the requisite knowledge for it, believing that jurisprudence is a sufficient qualification to appoint mullas to leadership and positions of power and demanding the authority of absolute guardianship (*vilāyat-i muṭlaqa*). Qabil claimed that such a view had in fact been questioned by Khomeini himself in the last year of his life, in his remark that 'contemporary jurisprudence was insufficient'.

The second criticism concerned the internal politics of the Islamic Republic, which, Qabil claimed, had become a trap of the cruel (*khushūnat-ṭalabān*), who eliminated and dishonoured political opposition (including the National Front, the Freedom Movement, the Mujahidin-i Khalq and Marxists). Moreover, they 'drove the country down a deep and terrifying gorge of revenge, murder, war-mongering and utter insecurity'. He continued by linking this culture with Khamenei's silence while his old friend and intellectual companion Habibollah ʿAshuri was accused of apostasy and killed.[27] Qabil asked, 'Didn't this unlawful bloodshed, and the blood of hundreds of other sinless people … [spilt by] the revolutionary courts in the years between [13]60–68/1981–1988 point to today's serious situation?'

The third criticism continued in a similar vein: 'During your (twelve-year) leadership [i.e. Khamenei] the tyranny of the courts of justice and the apparatus of justice, information and security has increased more than ever … the opponents of your politics have been crushed severely and have faced various privations of [their] individual and public rights.' Qabil offered several examples, including the 'Harsh, illegal and ill-mannered treatment meted out to Ayatollah Montazeri … perpetrated by officials from the official judiciary and security services, and those who are connected to you [Khamenei]'. Qabil continued by pointing out that the use of terror against political opponents had led to the habitual practice of terror by governors to solve their problems. He also reminded Khamenei that he had accused the reformist press of being 'the enemy's den' in 2000–1, which

27 Habibollah ʿAshuri was active in the uprisings leading to the removal of the Shah. He was within Khamenei's circle of young mullas in Mashhad, and published a book called *Tawḥīd* (Unity). Khamenei did not approve of the book, claiming that it consisted of notes that ʿAshuri took from Khamenei's own lectures. This was the cause of the breakdown in their friendship. After the victory of the revolution, ʿAshuri was arrested and accused of propagating heretical ideas in his book, as he advocated a classless society, similar to that advanced by Marx and the leftist groups in Iran. He was executed in 1981. See Mehdi Khalaji, 'Becoming anti-American', *Gulf Magazine* 24 August 2015, http://www.washingtoninstitute.org/policy-analysis/view/becoming-anti-american. James A. Bill calls ʿAshuri a 'moderate cleric'. See his 'Power and Religion in Modern Iran', *Middle East Journal* 36.1, 1982, 40.

was instrumental in their closure. Qabil mentioned well-known mullas, journalists and politicians who had been jailed, including ʿAbdollah Nuri, Akbar Ganji, and ʿAbbas ʿAbdi, which all reflected the lack of confidence in the structures associated with the Leadership. His list of accusations against Khamenei on this point implicated the Leader in almost all of the controversial issues that occurred in Iran during the first decade of the 21st century.

The fourth, fifth and sixth criticisms were much shorter, and they all concerned foreign relations. The fourth asked about the 'incorrect assumptions made by the great leaders of the Islamic Republic' concerning its ability in foreign affairs which led to insecurity in the region and internationally, such as the eight-year war with Iraq, and the breaking of relations with other nations (including the US). He also mentioned both the assistance that had been given to silence various opposition groups located outside of Iran, which amounted to aiding and abetting terrorist operations, and the interference in Afghanistan, Lebanon, and Saudi Arabia. This short criticism is worthy of further consideration because it calls into question not just Khamenei, but also the revolutionaries during the early years of the revolution, including Khomeini. Perhaps it was for this reason that Qabil did not offer more than three brief paragraphs to expand on his initial criticism. The fifth criticism continued the theme of foreign relations. Qabil stated that the consequences of the past 25 years of foreign policy were beginning to show, and he accused Khamenei of not revealing the reality of Iran's weakness vis-à-vis European powers by promoting propaganda and by belittling international powers. In the sixth criticism, Qabil asked Khamenei what role he played in the American policy of advocating regime change in Iran which had kept Iran in a weak position. Connected with regime change, he pointed out that there was a movement within Iran calling for a referendum on the political order, or for changing the structure of power in the fundamental laws.

The final point contained Qabil's recommendations to reform the system. This included a general pardon for all political prisoners, the freedom for all kinds of publications, and a guarantee for the security of those who wished to return to Iran from abroad. Subsequently, he requested a written statement to guarantee that the programme of the president would be carried out, a clear nod to the problems encountered by President Khatami during his two terms in office, when his attempts at creating a civil society were blocked by the more 'conservative' individuals within the regime. Finally, he called for invitations to international organisations to supervise elections.

Despite these cutting criticisms, Qabil's other writings reveal that he chose his words with care. Indeed, there is some evidence that at times he was extremely cautious in what he said or wrote in public. Aside from Khamenei, Qabil was reluctant to identify any particular individual for criticism. He attempted to preserve common decency and respect for free expression of opinion. An enlightening example of his commitment to this principal is contained in his responses to readers' questions on his weblog, included on the *Sharīʿat-i ʿAqlānī* website. It is worth quoting the passage:

> Although they say 'weblogs are a private space', I see them as a way for readers, also, to have rights. Therefore, I have refrained from deleting, controlling and censoring other [peoples'] views […] From 2005 and the beginning of both my own weblogs until now [15 Adhar 1387/ 5 December 2008], I have deleted a sum of three views. One of them, in its own words, was 'an opinion holder', and another abused Mr Khamenei very strongly, and another had insults and was impertinent about my mother. During all of this time I did not even delete curses and insults that were directed at me, for I believe the price of freedom is enduring both vexations of this kind and misuses [of this technology] by some people.[28]

Despite his respect for the views of others, Qabil was aware that his own opinions were highly controversial and dangerous. And it is perhaps because of this that he composed his letter in criticism of Khamenei from the safe haven of Tajikistan, and it would not have been surprising if he had intended to use his sojourn there as a stepping stone to a more permanent move to Europe or North America. According to Hadi Qabil, his brother's aim in going to Tajikistan was to pursue his study and research in Europe and North America, and eventually to live there. Ahmad Qabil appeared to be speaking of his aims in establishing some sort of research institute outside of Iran when he composed what was to become his seminal work titled *Sharīʿat-i ʿAqlānī*:

> The solution to this great obstacle [to promote rational sharia] is investment in a believable religion, where people live in free, non-Islamic societies (*ghayr-i islāmī*) [and where the people] can develop the necessary opportunities and facilitate emigration for some wise people and opinion-holders believing in this perspective [of rational sharia] […]
>
> […] perhaps without the need of renewed investment one may take advantage of existing facilities in the aforementioned societies and in

28 *Sharīʿat ʿAqlānī*, 248.

> establishments such as mosques, Islamic centres, Islamic establishments [...], and in [these] new places fulfil the hopes of great thinkers like Burujirdi, Taliqani, Sahabi, Bazargan, Montazeri and Shariʿati. And one must present [the rational sharia] in a humane society to lovers of wisdom, good morals and faith. The lovers [of wisdom who are] settled in those regions must pursue this mission, and if they themselves are not able to prosper from the required finances, they must enter discussions with the wealthy (and those who have a believable religion), and prepare the groundwork for making this project systematic, as far as their ability allows.[29]

On returning to Iran for medical reasons,[30] Qabil had his passport confiscated which prevented him from leaving his country of birth.[31] Despite his previous experiences, he persisted in his criticism of Khamenei, reflected in another public letter following the arrest of his brother who was a supporter of the reform movement. Qabil's letter of April 2008 accused Khamenei of absolute dictatorship, saying, 'That Mr. Khamenei insists that nobody's view is important but his, and that, for example, no one should express any opinion about Iran's nuclear programme, indicates nothing but absolute dictatorship,' and, 'I am waiting for the day when he [Khamenei] is put on trial.'[32] Hadi Qabil was eventually sentenced to 40 months of incarceration, defrocking, and a fine of 5,000,000 rials.

In June 2009, Qabil issued his 'testament' (*Vaṣiyat bi Millat-i Irān*) a thirty page essay in which he continued to castigate Khamenei for his damaging leadership of Iran.[33] He persisted to irritate the conservatives in the regime when he published an article in November 2009 titled 'A brief critique of the occupation of the American Embassy in Iran',[34] in which he claimed Montazeri had also pointed out that it had been an improper act.[35] In December 2009, Montazeri died, and on his way to the funeral Qabil was arrested again. He was brought to

---

29 *Sharīʿat ʿAqlānī*, 55–6.
30 *Yād-nāma-yi Ahmad Qabil*, 80.
31 Sahimi, 'Progressive Muslim Scholar'. See also Ahmad Qabil, *Naqd-i Khudkāmagī*, 139–150.
32 See http://zamaaneh.com/news/2008/04/post_4531.html.
33 The whole document is produced in *Vaṣiyat bi Millat-i Irān*, 33–63.
34 A reference to the capture and taking hostage of 52 American citizens and diplomats in the American Embassy in Tehran. Hostages were held for 444 days, from 4 November 1979 – 20 January 1981.
35 'Naqd-i ijmālī-yi ashghāl-i sifārat-i Āmrīkā dar Irān' [A brief criticism of the occupation of the American embassy in Iran], *Fiqh, kārkard-hā va Qābiliyat-ha*, 1388/2009, 129–42.

the court in May 2010, this time in chains.[36] Having spent 170 days in prison, Qabil was released on 1 July 2010 after posting bail.[37] He continued to antagonise the regime, and in September 2010 he claimed that groups of prisoners had been executed in Mashhad's Vakilabad prison.[38] Unsurprisingly, Qabil was re-arrested a short time later and, on 10 December 2010, he was sentenced to 20 months in prison.[39] Towards the end of his life, he reflected that state tyranny had been exercised over him for a considerable time. Speaking in February 2011, he said, 'It is more than five years now that I have been prohibited from leaving the country, and more than twenty years that I have been forbidden from teaching in the official centres of the seminary and universities, and about six years that they have not given a licence for the printing and publication of my books.' He also claimed that the authorities targeted his family and friends by bugging their telephone, intimidating his wife, threatening her with arrest, and continually pestering and asking his relations and friends questions about him.[40] Whilst in prison, Qabil complained of severe headaches and he said that his eyesight was impaired. His health began to fail to the extent that the left side of his body was paralysed, and he was unable to dress himself properly.[41] Eventually the authorities let him receive medical treatment in hospitals outside of Tehran where scans revealed he had a brain tumour. Several operations failed to improve his condition, and he passed away on 22 October 2012.[42] It is worth pointing out Qabil believed that the main reason for his incarcerations was political, for his criticisms of the Leader and the state, and his jurisprudential and theological writings were a secondary consideration.[43]

The Jurisprudential Worldview of Qabil

> Qabil's rationalism, which appears extreme at times, is a big step, and if it is considered positively by the jurists and those who study the sharia, it can

36 *Yād-nāma-yi Ahmad Qabil*, 46.
37 Sahimi, 'Progressive Muslim Scholar'.
38 *Yād-nāma-yi Ahmad Qabil*, 46.
39 Sahimi, 'Progressive Muslim Scholar'; *Yād-nāma-yi Ahmad Qabil*, 79.
40 Qabil, 'Durānī nīst ki mānnand Gālīleh az harfam bar gardam' [This is not the time for me to recant like Galileo], *Vaṣiyat bi Millat-i Irān*, 286.
41 *Yād-nāma-yi Ahmad Qabil*, 48–9.
42 *Yād-nāma-yi Ahmad Qabil*, 49–50, 78–9.
43 See Qabil's views in 'Durānī nīst ki mānnand Gālīleh az harfam bar gardam', 291–2, 295.

> really open the jurisprudential and interpretive path of change, and make the road and the winding path clearer and gentler.[44]

The significance of Qabil's contribution to jurisprudential thinking should not be underestimated; the extent of his adherence to, or foregrounding of, reason is unprecedented in Shiʿi circles, and has led Sussan Siavoshi to observe that it was 'a clean break with the traditional jurisprudence'.[45] Given this, it is all the more surprising that Qabil's thought has not attracted more scholarly attention in the West. The reluctance of Western scholars to engage with Qabil's ideas may be attributable to the number of other important ulama such as Ayatollah Montazeri, Ayatollah Saniʿi, and Shabistari, who have had very interesting things to say about Islam, or who had alternative views about the Islamic revolution. And it may also be attributed (as already suggested) to the style and nature of Qabil's writings, which are often difficult to fathom, for his works are juristic and composed in a fashion that demands multiple readings for the non-Persian. Qabil was not an author in the conventional sense; he was not permitted to publish books, which might have provided him with a greater literary audience. Indeed, typifying the new IT literate generation of Iranians, his ideas were disseminated on a website, and many of his shorter compositions were assembled in 'book' form. At present the Persian website devoted to him lists ten works:

1. *A Critique of the Culture of Violence* (Political Notes, 1375–79 [1996–2000])[46]
2. *Criticism of Autocracy* (Political Notes, Reflections and Poetry, 1380–88 [2001–2009])[47]
3. *Testament to the Iranian Nation* (Political Notes and Interviews, 1388–91 [2009–2012])[48]
4. *Islam and Social Security*[49]

44 From a text written by Eshkevari, 1 Aban 1391/ 22 October 2012. In *Yād-nāma-yi Ahmad Qabil*, 322.

45 Sussan Siavoshi composed an abstract for a conference paper, titled, 'Human reason in contemporary reformist Shii jurisprudence: From Montazeri to Kadivar, to Qabel'. The abstract may be read in the website for the Association of Iranian Studies: https://associationforiranianstudies.org/content/human-reason-contemporary-reformist-shii-jurisprudence-montazeri-Kadivar-Qabil.

46 *Naqd-i Farhang-i Khushūnat*, 1381/2002–3, 376.

47 *Naqd-i Khūdkāmagī*, 1391/2012–13, 456.

48 *Vaṣiyat bi Millat-i Irān*, 1391/2012–13, 420.

49 *Islām va Tāʾmīn-i Ijtimāʿī*, 1383/2004–5, 486.

5. *Foundations of the Sharia* (Discussion on the Basis and Principles of Jurisprudence)[50]
6. *Religious Fear and Hopes* (Speeches 1383–88 [2004–2009])[51]
7. *Rational Sharia* (Articles on the Relation between Reason and the Law)[52]
8. *Jurisprudence, Applications and Potentials* (Jurisprudential Articles and Answers to Religious Questions, 1382–89 [2003–2010])[53]
9. *Commands Pertaining to Women in the Muhammadan Law* (The Non-Superiority of Men, Inheritance, the Veil, Temporary Marriage, Divorce …)[54]
10. *The Commands of Punishment in the Muhammadan Sharia* (Apostasy, Stoning, Death Penalty, Temporary Detention, Capital Punishment, Unlawful Taking of Confession and Judgement)[55]

In addition to these ten volumes, the website also contains a memorial to Ahmad Qabil of 498 pages, as mentioned earlier, and contains interviews with family members, friends and supporters, along with their own reflections on his life and significance. The aforementioned work also includes copies of letters of condolence from eminent Iranians to Hadi Qabil and his family. The names of those who sent condolences give an indication of the esteem in which Ahmad Qabil was held; they include mostly persons who have been associated with the Green Movement including the family of Ayatollah Montazeri, Ayatollah Saniʿi, Muhammad Khatami, ʿAbdollah Nuri, Aʿzam Taliqani, Muhsin Kadivar, and the wife and children of Mihdi Karubi.[56]

Sharīʿat-i ʿAqlānī

It is difficult to divorce Qabil's political activities from his belief that a jurist's duty is to search for the truth and express his or her opinions forthrightly, even if they conflict with the prevailing political or spiritual views of those in authority. Certainly, his political stance is a necessary corollary of his jurisprudential

50 *Mabānī-yi Sharīʿat*, 1391/2012–13, 356.
51 *Bīm va Umīd-hā-yi Dīndārī*, 1391/2012–13, 283.
52 *Sharīʿat ʿAqlānī*, 1391/2012–13, 328.
53 *Fiqh, Kārkard-hā va Qabiliyat*, 1392/2013–14, 290.
54 *Aḥkām-i Bānuvān dar Sharīʿat-i Muhammadi*, 1392/2013–14, 228.
55 *Aḥkām-i Jazāʾī dar Sharīʿat-i Muhammadi*, 1390/2011–12, 342.
56 There are many more letters of condolence, which are all included in *Yād-nāma-yi Ahmad Qabil*, 89–135.

approach as set out in his compositions. The writing for which he is best known is called *Sharī'at-i 'Aqlānī* (*Rational Sharia*), and it is analysed herein. Qabil's scholarly endeavour in the realm of jurisprudence stretched over more than twenty years, which demonstrates that he was, indeed, primarily a man of *fiqh*, even if his perspective held significant political implications. It is worth noting too that Qabil considered himself a seminarian and wished to distance his views from those of secular thinkers. He said, 'I do not agree with being labelled an expert in [both] religious knowledge and in Muhammadan sharia with [the same] understanding of that group of enlightened secular thinkers. I consider their claim incorrect because it is derived from their limited information of Islam and its foundations.'[57] The significance of his seminarian background was highlighted by Eshkevari:

> Ahmad Qabil got his knowledge from the seminary in Qum, and he was a product of the traditional seminary of jurisprudence and jurisprudential knowledge (*fiqāhat*) [...] Whilst maintaining fundamental loyalty to the traditional way of thinking and to the traditional seminarian structures, he bravely took giant strides in [promoting] open-minded thinking within this hard-headed tradition.[58]

This background meant that Qabil was less familiar with Western philosophy, which has often inspired other Iranian reformists in attempts to 'modernise' Iranian and Islamic thought, whether these are secular intellectuals, such as Soroush,[59] or mullas who spent periods in the West, such as Shabistari,[60] or others trained in the seminary but who gradually drifted to alternative intellectual vistas, such as Mustafa Malikiyan.[61] That Qabil spent his life primarily in Iran – save

57 Qabil, 'Junbish-i sabz, iṣlāhāt, rūhāniyat va vilāyat-i faqīh' [The Green Movement, Reforms, the Clergy and the Guardianship of the Jurist], *Vaṣiyat bi Millat-i Irān*, 2011, 328.
58 *Yād-nāma-yi Ahmad Qabil*, 320.
59 Soroush spent periods in the West prior to the Islamic Revolution. In 1972, he went to England and received a master's degree in analytical chemistry from the University of London and then he studied history and philosophy of science at the Chelsea College. He returned to Iran just before the Islamic Revolution.
60 It is interesting to note that a number of high-ranking and respected mullas served as directors of the Islamic Centre in Hamburg, including Muhammad Bihishti (1965–70), Muhammad Mujtahid-Shabistari (1970–78) and Muhammad Khatami. Shabistari's inclination for German philosophy has been discussed by Amirpur, *New Thinking in Islam*, 170–4. Khatami's attitude to Western philosophy is less clear.
61 It is of interest that Qabil named his worldview 'Rational Sharia' which bears a certain resemblance to Mustafa Malikiyan's 'Rationality and Spirituality'. But the content of the two and the attention paid to specifically Islamic and jurisprudential approaches are completely

for trips to Uzbekistan, the United Arab Emirates, Turkmenistan, Saudi Arabia and Tajikistan[62] – may have contributed to the perception that his thinking was uncontaminated by Western philosophies and 'isms'.[63] Qabil's following words are instructive on this point: 'I have never taken my ideas from non-Islamic books. For the majority of my studies, and in truth perhaps I can say that the only source and reference books that I use are Islamic books. Now I am opposed to the tyranny of governance – which I see as my duty. Have I picked up foreign books demonstrating [opposition]? Or [have I acted] according to religious teachings, according to the value that has been emphasised in the Qurʾan and our narrations to stand up to tyranny and not to give in to it?'[64] Again, Eshkevari explains: 'The most important point is this, that Qabil was a follower of the traditionalists, a follower of Aristotelian reason, and paid virtually no attention to modern logic, cognition, or new fields of study [...] and most probably he was unaware of them.'[65] Certainly Qabil's attention to traditional means of investigating concrete issues, such as the hijab, is clear. Nevertheless, an education in the seminary would not necessarily have made a young religious scholar inherently antagonistic to rational enquiry. There is a long history within the Islamic tradition for studies based primarily on the use of reason, although some scholars seem reluctant to admit this, such as Eshkevari:

> We know that in Shiʿi jurisprudence from the 5th/11th century onwards reason was one of the four proofs for *ijtihād*. But there have been and are

different. For Malikiyan's thought, see Sadeghi-Boroujerdi, 'Mostafa Malekian', 279–311. In the course of studying this project, several Iranian students have asked me why I do not investigate Malikiyan's thought, which is an indication of his popularity among the current generation. However, as mentioned previously, his ideas do not specifically address the hijab, or for that matter Islam. As Sadeghi-Boroujerdi has observed 'his project of *maʾnaviyat va ʿaqlaniyat* ... is an eclectic melting pot of disparate ideas encompassing *inter alia*, Buddha, Kierkegaard, and Kant ...', 307.

62 'Karūbī va Mūsāwī bi jurm-i mukhālifat bā istibdād habs shuda-and' [Karubi and Musavi have been imprisoned for the crime of opposing tyranny], *Vaṣiyat bi Millat-i Iran*, 369.

63 Qabil, 'Ṭarḥ-i mawrid-i adʿā-yi "Islāmī kardan dānishgāh-hā" rāhī juz-i shikast na-khwāhad dāsht' [The plan to 'Islamicise the universities' will be a path to failure], *Vaṣiyat bi Millat-i Iran*, 341.

64 Qabil, 'Ṭarḥ-i mawrid-i adʿā-yi "Islāmī kardan dānishgāh-hā" rāhī juz-i shikast na-khwāhad dāsht', 341.

65 *Yād-nāma-yi Ahmad Qabil*, 467. Qabil's work does not betray explicit influences of 'Western' Muslim academic thinking. In a private email dated 6 May 2018, Kadivar expressed a belief that Qabil was unaware of the influential ideas of the Pakistani scholar Fazlur Rahman, who ended his career as a professor at the University of Chicago.

> various thoughts and opinions on the definition and limits of reasoning within jurisprudence and *ijtihād* – the kind of connection between reason and related texts (*ʿaql va naql*) […] In our *fiqh* and in traditional Usuli *ijtihād*, other than in limited cases, there is almost no use of human rationality.[66]

Eshkevari's views may be questionable, but it is his perception of the limitations on reason that is important and helps to illustrate that Qabil's foregrounding of reason is rare in the modern Iranian context. Of those with a seminary education it would be possible to point to Ahmad Kasravi and Shariʿat-Sangalaji from the Pahlavi era who foregrounded the role of reason to any comparable degree. In any case, Kasravi withdrew from the seminary and seems to have had little esteem for Twelver Shiʿi Islam. Shariʿat-Sangalaji remained a mulla until the day he died, and the propagation of his works may have been restricted by the pressure of his fellow mullas and the need to pay due respect to the Pahlavi line.

'*Sharīʿat-i ʿAqlānī*' is also the name Qabil chose for the main section of his website, where his writings and speeches are currently located,[67] and as such it epitomises the methodology in all of his works that have been uploaded there. Aside from being the name of his website, *Sharīʿat-i ʿAqlānī* is also the term used for a collection of essays that has been assembled in book form. It is very much a distillation of his main ideas, and it is therefore instructive for researchers to consider this work of his before exploring any of the others. The composition consists of six articles which were written during his sojourn in Tajikistan and shortly after his return to Iran – covering the period 2005–7, a time frame which coincides with writing his letter of criticism to Khamenei.[68] It seems unlikely that Qabil thought that *Sharīʿat-i ʿAqlānī* would catch the public imagination as much as it did. He claimed that he distributed the six chapters among his friends and sent it to one website that focused on news (*Irān-i Imrūz*). However, unbeknown to Qabil, one of his friends sent the book to the BBC Persian service, and from then on the work enjoyed greater circulation and popularity.[69] One of the reasons that Qabil may

66 *Yād-nāma-yi Ahmad Qabil*, 466.
67 Muhsin Kadivar, 'Introduction', *Sharīʿat ʿAqlānī*, 20.
68 The first four chapters were written in Tajikistan in 1383/2004–5, chapter five was finished in Mashhad on 24 February 2006, and the last chapter was completed on 20 February 2007 in Fariman.
69 *Sharīʿat ʿAqlānī*, 117. Aside from its six 'chapters', the work *Sharīʿat ʿAqlānī*, as it now appears on online, includes responses from readers, who include Mihdi Jami from the BBC, dated 13 January 2005. Jami mentioned that Qabil lives in Tajikistan, suggesting that he was writing before the final chapters of *Sharīʿat ʿAqlānī* had been completed. The first five chapters must have been uploaded onto the website before the completion of the work.

have been surprised at the reception of his work because he did not think it was ground-breaking or original. He remarked, 'I have admitted repeatedly that my understanding is not original, and one can discover its footprints in the depths of human history and the history of the Muhammadan sharia.'[70] These humble comments reflect the desire to present such ideas as normative, although it is clear to some observers how radical they are in the context of the Islamic Republic of Iran.

The titles of each chapter of *Sharīʿat-i ʿAqlānī* are:

1. Reason and Emotion (*ʿaql va iḥsās*)
2. Reason and Divine Law (*ʿaql va sharʿ*)
3. On Reason and Divine Law I (*dar mawrid-i ʿaql va sharʿ*)
4. On Reason and Divine Law II (*dar mawrid-i ʿaql va sharʿ*)
5. Reviewing Narrations with the Criterion of Reason *(bāzbīnī-yi naql bā maʿyār-i ʿaql)*
6. The Relationship between Reason and Narration (*nisbat-i ʿaql va naql*)

The titles of the chapters do not lend themselves to clarity in the signposting of the details and differences between each chapter. Moreover, the work defies simple summarisation, as the flow and progression of the text is often interrupted by Qabil's penchant for repeating key themes. While a summarisation is difficult, it is possible to identify the most salient of these themes.

The first and most important and dominant theme is the congruence that Qabil saw between reason and revelation, and he justified this view with recourse to both Qurʾanic discourses that advise humans to think and use their reason,[71] and

---

Another response, dated 14 February 2005, and written by the same author appeared on the Malackut weblog: http://sibestaan.malackut.org/archives/۰۱/۲۰۰۵/post_۲٤٦.shtml. The online version of *Sharīʿat ʿAqlānī* has other responses from authors that appeared on the *Malackut* weblog, as well as *Wiblāg-i Pūyān* and *Irān-i Imrūz*.

70 *Sharīʿat ʿAqlānī*, 118.

71 Ibid., 49. See also Qurʾan 9.12. In addition to advancing reason beyond these traditional jurisprudential parameters, it is interesting to speculate that his attachment to reason was probably the main cause of Qabil's unease with gnosticism (*ʿirfān*), which has enjoyed considerable intellectual popularity in Iran. 'I condemn the gnostics (*ʿurafā*) for running away from reality and from giving answers because, just as you know, one of the valleys that the *ʿurafā* count is the valley of perplexity (*taḥayyur*) and the station of bewilderment (*ḥayrat*), and they say a gnostic must reach the station of bewilderment. I do not accept these beliefs (*iʿtiqādāt*). He is like someone who is being chased. When he reaches a lake-edge, he dives into escape from his pursuer. Therefore, these [actions] are a kind of escape from giving answers' ('Ākharīn Muṣāḥiba-yi Ahmad Qabil' [Last interview with Ahmad Qabil], dated 7 June 2012, *Vaṣiyat bi Millat-i Irān*, 408).

to sayings of eminent Shiʿi figures (both imams and more recent scholars). Qabil cited the well-known narration from Imam Kazim to illustrate the equivalence of reason and revelation, that God has an internal proof which is reason and an external proof who are the prophets.[72] He also referred to past masters to demonstrate how rational thought must be employed to smooth away any apparent discrepancies between reason and revelation.[73] He quoted al-Tusi (d. 1067), who is regarded by some as the founder of Shiʿi jurisprudence, who said, 'If a verse of the Qurʾan opposes the guidance of the sciences, it is necessary to read [the verse] in the interest of the guidance [found in] the sciences, and interpret [the Qurʾan] in harmony with that.'[74] With such authoritative backing, Qabil had sufficient confidence to suggest that reason tips the scale of revelation:

> All of these studies show that in the relationship between reason and revelation, not only is the benefit of narration not greater, rather, there is not even equality between the two. So, reason enjoys the main and superior position, and narration must be a follower of reason and support it.[75]

Nevertheless, Qabil was aware how the above kinds of comments might be misconstrued, and so he frequently reminded his readers that, in reality, reason and revelation support each other. One of the ways that Qabil raised reason to such elevated heights was by insisting that the discoveries of human rationality were constantly developing and improving. Thus, there could be no fixed understanding of revelation, as he remarked, 'What I have understood [...] is this: that on all principles and secondary aspects of the law, the basis and proof of reason is in progress.'[76] And this ongoing process meant a continual re-appraisal of revelation (both the Qurʾan and narrations): 'The responsibility for reviewing the commands

72 Narration found in the *al-Kāfī* of Kulayni, vol. 1, '*Uṣūl*. The Book of Reason and Ignorance', Tehran 1379/2000–1, vol. 2, 71. Qabil, *Sharīʿat ʿAqlānī*, 49.

73 It is noteworthy too that Qabil claimed his use of reason and his overall message was nothing new. He mentioned that he was shocked to find major Shiʿi scholars had said exactly the same thing: 'Great [scholars] like Shaykh Ansari, Sayyid Murtaza and Muqaddas Ardabili were among those who had spoken on this topic [...] and who according to some, had not been caught up in modern thought, but they advanced the discussion in a scientific way and not even the New Religious Thinkers employed the words they spoke!' (*Vaṣiyat bi Millat-i Iran*, 399).

74 *Sharīʿat ʿAqlānī*, 108. Qabil commented that the source of the quote is al-Tusi's *al-Rasāʾil al-ʿAshara*.

75 *Sharīʿat ʿAqlānī*, 109.

76 *Sharīʿat ʿAqlānī*, 49.

of the sharia [...] is an undertaking for a number of wise people who of necessity possess refined thinking, based on scientific and logical methods.'[77] Qabil claimed that the profundity of revelation (and so its contemporary congruence with reason) had not been fully realised throughout history, and that some things had remained hidden and only gradually would those secrets be understood. In other words, peoples of previous generations were simply not ready to accept certain ideas since their reason or scientific understanding had not developed sufficiently for a full comprehension of these matters. He justified this with reference to the Qur'an 2.33: 'No soul is charged beyond its capacity [to understand].'[78] And he added,

> Rising scientific levels, knowledge and general human experience in the present age in comparison [with the levels of comprehension] in the first two or three centuries of the Muhammadan sharia is an example of the 'readiness of the people of this age for comprehending more truths and accepting more advanced subjects'.
>
> In other words, if the peoples' lack of readiness in the age of God's Prophet and the guiding imams has been the reason for an absence in explaining some commands or has been the cause for the lack of opposition to some current and unpopular methods or for the confirmation of other methods, then today the necessary readiness exists to explain [both] those hidden commands and the opposition of the sharia with unpopular methods.[79]

This secret or hidden knowledge, or rationality, contained within revelation, helps to explain for the traditional Shiʿi practice of dissimulation (*taqiyya*). He even cited a narration from Imam Riza that, 'The Prophet of God died performing dissimulation.'[80] Qabil's explanation stands in contrast to the usual understandings of *taqiyya* as a pragmatic, political response to persecution of Shiʿi beliefs. Nevertheless, he associated *taqiyya* with the Prophet and also the Qur'an 5.101: 'Do not ask about the things which, were they disclosed to you, would displease you.'

This kind of *taqiyya*, along with an unceasing search for meaning makes the sharia, or human understandings of Islamic Law, infinitely flexible and responsive to the challenges of the modern day. Indeed, his argument is made with reference

77 *Sharīʿat ʿAqlānī*, 77.
78 *Sharīʿat ʿAqlānī*, 75–6.
79 *Sharīʿat ʿAqlānī*, 77.
80 *Sharīʿat ʿAqlānī*, 76. Qabil clearly thought this was an important point as he expanded on his understanding of *taqiyya* in other works, such as in *Fiqh, Kārkard-hā va Qābiliyat-hā*, 34–43.

to the prophets sent by God, as Qabil pointed to the traditional understanding of the 'seal of the prophets' – i.e. Muhammad – which has been taken to mean the end of the line of prophets whom God had entrusted with a message for humans. He observed that the age of prophethood had resulted in the sending of 'large numbers of divine prophets […] the great majority of whom were active in their task without themselves knowing they were prophets, and there have been sages, wise people, and normal rational individuals in different human societies'.[81] Having highlighted the role of reason in the prophetic age, Qabil then advanced his argument on the continuation of reason, 'With the death of the seal of the prophets, the sending of prophets came to an end, and so began the era [when humans had to] rely on common reason and knowledge.'[82]

The second major theme that Qabil weaved throughout his text is the critique of the contemporary doctrinal (*madhhabī*) culture which belittled reason. The term *madhhabī* in many contexts is a derogatory word that denotes strict and literal allegiance to a belief system. In the following paragraph, Qabil may well have been referring to the regime headed by Khamenei:

> But now and in the current *madhhabī* culture [… it] is this jurisprudence that determines morality and beliefs. If the linear arrangement of primary ordinances and secondary ordinances are observed, one should not prefer a proof that has erased human morality, such as giving permission to insult, steal, kill, and other [actions] such as this in relation to any 'non-believer'. Indeed, if the aim of the assigner of jurisprudential inclinations is moral, it is preferable that he refers to narrations that say, 'God does not place the smallest tyranny before humans, even if they are unbelievers.'[83]

This kind of *madhhabī* culture, aside from its cruel and oppressive nature, was also linked to excessive emotionalism, which is contrasted with the more reasoned approach. Qabil castigated those who manifested their emotional attachment to Shi'i Islam in an extreme fashion, and directed his antipathy to people who had a disproportionate attachment to Imam 'Ali, beyond the limits of reason and rational discourse. Qabil lambasted Shi'i ulama who irrationally praised 'Ali even beyond the normal devotion paid to God, and endowed the imam with the

81 *Sharī'at 'Aqlānī*, 64.
82 *Sharī'at 'Aqlānī*, 64.
83 *Sharī'at 'Aqlānī*, 91–2.

same degree of divine wisdom, power and authority.[84] In a rhetorical flourish targeted at extreme Shiʿi practices, Qabil denied that ʿAli was martyred just so that some may benefit through the acquisition of sustenance through praising or ritualised commemoration (*rawża-khwānī*), or by making the people cry with elegies for him; nor was he martyred for the 'wearers of black' and for warning people of this or that; neither was he martyred for the sake of creating borders with Sunnis, and nor for intercession for Shiʿi sinners on the Day of Resurrection.[85] Qabil did not wish to belittle ʿAli or Shiʿi Islam. Rather, he wanted them to be accorded their proper historical value. For example, he pointed to the view of ʿAli as an individual who demonstrated rationally the existence of God, spoke of the Muhammadan sharia, enforced legal commands, and fought with a sword against the enemies of the believers, even killing many Jews among Banu Qurayza – a controversial topic.[86] Qabil also indicated that, from the perspective of universal rationality, ʿAli also paid attention to the compassionate dimension of life, which included deep love for God's creatures. Another feature of the *madhhabī* culture that Qabil criticised was its tendency to deny people agency in the decision-making process. He argued that since the vast majority of humans were rational beings it follows that they should be allowed the freedom to determine and work out the commands that are not based upon worship. He used juristic terminology to define this method: *iṣālat al-ibāḥat al-ʿaqlīyat* (the principle for the permission [to exercise] rationality), claiming that a corollary of this principle is the authorisation to do all things that bring benefit to humans, except those things which with reliable proof have been deemed harmful. Qabil subsequently claimed that the opposite of the appropriateness for the permission [to use] rationality had become dominant in Iran. This opposite, termed *iṣālat al-ḥizr*, denies the permissibility for the performance of anything except in cases where there are reliable proofs to the contrary.[87] Although it is not explicitly stated, the connection with the situation of Iran under the leadership of Khamenei springs to mind, with censorship over political regulations on who may stand as

84 *Sharīʿat ʿAqlānī*, 43–4
85 *Sharīʿat ʿAqlānī*, 44–5.
86 See for example, M. J. Kister, 'The massacre of the Banu Qurayza: a re-examination of a tradition', *Jerusalem Studies in Arabic and Islam* 8, 1986, 61–96.
87 The juristic discussion about permission and denial of permission has a long history in Imami thought. For example, it was discussed by al-Sayyid al-Murtaza (d. 1044). See Robert Gleave, 'Imami Shiʿi Legal Theory', *Oxford Handbooks Online*, 2018, 8, http://www.oxfordhandbooks.com/view/10.1093/oxfordhb/9780199679010.001.0001/oxfordhb-9780199679010-e-31.

a candidate in elections and strict social parameters relating to sartorial issues, including the hijab. Qabil said:

> With deep regret, the reaction of the majority of jurists on a great many juristic issues is that they have given an opinion [that is] influenced by 'the principle of prohibition'. According to the theory, [these jurists] uphold the 'principle for permission [to use rationality]', but [in practice] they side with the 'principle of prohibition' [...] We see at our side a number of realistic wise people of the law who in private or in public have expressed sympathy with us. But when it is time to explain [the law's] meanings, [the numbers of] these companions decrease, or they become silent and prefer to withhold their companionship.[88]

Qabil argued that with regards to these two positions, the appropriateness for permission [to use] rationality and the appropriateness of prohibition, there are many issues that yield contrary conclusions. And it is at this point that the breadth of the general question that he asked becomes apparent. He produced a list of thirty-one issues that required debate, ranging from questions relating to marriage, divorce, inheritance, times and conditions for prayer, Islamic punishments (*ḥudūd*), and a host of problems concerning freedom. Qabil aspired to initiate debate among the ulama, and to investigate the rational and scriptural foundations on questions that many have regarded as conclusive and incontestable. He was not the first Muslim thinker to do this, as other 'radical' and 'liberal' Muslims had raised similar questions; indeed, his endeavour to reaffirm that these are issues upon which there are differences of opinion (*ikhtilāf*) simply confirmed Khomeini's insistence about the need to recognise and act on this juristic principle (as discussed in Part One). However, the sheer scope of the enterprise and the bravery in raising these issues places Qabil among the few Iranian mullas who have demanded such a wholesale re-assessment of religious thinking.

The third major theme of *Sharīʿat-i ʿAqlānī* concerns the role of the *mujtahid*. The establishment of the Islamic Republic and the creation of political institutions in which legislation has been prepared and discussed might be considered to have impinged somewhat on the role of *mujtahid*s, as, of course, all laws in modern Iran are deliberated within the framework of Islam. And members of the Parliament (*majlis*) are not all *mujtahid*s or have an Islamic background or education – which was one of reasons for the creation of the Council of Guardians,

88 *Sharīʿat ʿAqlānī*, 51.

one of the functions of which is to ensure that all legislation from the *majlis* is in conformity with Islam.[89] While it might be argued that governmental structures offered assistance from experts with specialised knowledge to decision-makers, Qabil's call to discuss the aforementioned thirty-one issues should be seen in the context of the government restricting access to governmental posts, and curtailing public discussions, hence inevitably influencing the scope with which the *mujtahid*s engaged in said discussions.

Qabil recognised that the advancement of science and specialised fields of knowledge in all disciplines has meant that it has been impossible for a *mujtahid* to be an expert in all aspects of learning. Moreover, the disparate nature of academia, and the lack of a cohesive interdisciplinary culture, caused him to advocate the creation of a 'thinktank':

> From one perspective, I believe that the fundamental problem of religious thought is excessive individualism and not having the willingness to work together [as a team]. From another perspective it is not valuing the role of the wise [who work in] the humanities (in all of its disciplines) to discover the purpose of God, the Glorious, and the Master of the sharia.
>
> To put it another way, the absence of a collective approach for [both] the production of religious thought and unity of thinking among the wise religious people are two basic misfortunes in religious and legal thinking. To allay these misfortunes, I attempted to establish an organisation that assembled various disciplines within the humanities and position it alongside theologians, interpreters [of sacred scripts] and jurists in order to produce [new] thinking in the name of sharia and religion so that it could take steps to publish [their findings] after professional consultation and research among all the groups interested in the topic.[90]

Qabil also commented that such an organisation required sufficient investment, and it needed to be located 'where people live in free, non-Islamic societies (*ghayr-i islāmī*)'. This statement might reflect his belief that free intellectual exchange was not yet possible in Iran, and that the Council of Guardians had not facilitated such an endeavour – perhaps due to the overriding influence of Khamenei. The

89 The Council of Guardians is composed of six senior scholars chosen by the Leader and six judges to be chosen by the *majlis* but who are nominated by the Head of the Judiciary (who is chosen by the Leader).
90 *Sharī'at 'Aqlānī*, 65.

statement was made whilst Qabil was in Tajikistan, where he experienced conditions more amenable to a frank and free exchange of ideas. He added,

> I supposed that if the organisation was established in a freer environment and with more security and possibilities (which of necessity must be outside of the sham *dār al-Islām*) than in Iran, perhaps it would be possible to conquer these historical problems by transferring some of the *mujtahid*s of the seminary who believe in the rational sharia, and show the truthful face of the sharia with the establishment of an academic staff [...] outside of Iran according to [their] understanding and ability. It is a task still at the level of wishful thinking, but certainly I am hopeful of God's bounty on this path.[91]

Qabil did not explain what the role of the *mujtahid* would be, and he did not advance the idea espoused by Kadivar that the role of jurisprudence would shrink with the emphasis placed on ethics and individual faith – the strength of which would deepen, as discussed in Part One. In short, Qabil's commitment to a free exchange of knowledge opened wide the doors of debate, and he envisaged a path forward to investigating Islamic ethics, spirituality and jurisprudence which was not the preserve of the *mujtahid* alone; it necessitated collaboration with experts in academic fields in which the *mujtahid*s were not specialists. As we have seen, this has been a call among 'reformist' seminarians that pre-dated Qabil, typified in the efforts of Mutahhari.

The fourth major theme of *Sharīʿat-i ʿAqlānī* concerns the hermeneutics of scripture, more specifically the historicity of scripture. Since this element of Qabil's thought was dealt with in Part One, it is not necessary to repeat the same material here, suffice it to say that he considered Qurʾanic verses that are *thābit* as fixed commands, and the *mutaghayyar* as those which may be abrogated. It is the second kind of verses that were of interest to Qabil, because he claimed that the commands of the sharia that have been changed reflect the development of discoveries brought about through the exercise of human reason. 'Replacing contradictory commands with the collective reason of humans in the present age [...] is nothing other than "asserting the changeability of these commands".'[92] Moreover, the desire to promote a version of Islam that was compassionate, humane

91 *Sharīʿat ʿAqlānī*, 66.

92 Ibid., 70. Qabil did not expand on this point, perhaps because he assumed his audience was aware of the history underlying the issue. More extensive treatment of these kinds of verses is found in *Mabānī-yi Sharīʿat*, 218–30.

and tolerant set Qabil's Qurʾanic hermeneutics at odds with those who desired a 'literalist' and strict interpretation of specific *aḥkām* – this is not to say that Qabil was unique, as in the long trajectory of Islamic history it is relatively easy to find scholars who argued along very similar lines. In interviews, he gave specific examples: when asked if he believed it was right to amputate the hand of a thief (as suggested in Q. 5.38), Qabil answered that it was not right to amputate the hand of someone who stole from the public wealth, because the thief too had a share in it. He added that the law of amputation was a 'validating command', and one of the 'changeable commands'. He also observed that the private property of people should be kept out of reach of thieves, and this may be considered a kind of metaphorical amputation of a thief's hand.[93] Qabil must have been aware that his position was tantamount to rejecting so much of the traditional Islamic heritage of Iran that had been embraced by the Islamic Republic.[94]

A fifth major element relates to a modern understanding of sharia, different from that of previous centuries where there seemed to be a zero-sum competition of religion. Qabil clearly did not accept this, and stressed the plurality of religions and sharias by emphasising the need to determine the right kind of attitude or the appropriate understanding for studying legal approaches. Qabil argued that religion (or *islām*) was more than just jurisprudence; it also encompassed theology and morality. The point here is that he understood *islām* in the sense of submission,

93 Qabil, *Vaṣiyat bi Millat-i Irān*, 385. The common perception in the West about the *ḥudūd* fails to recognise that there are numerous mitigating factors, such as poverty and repentance. This is not to say, however, that these punishments have not been carried out in the Islamic Republic. See 'Iran's Prosecutor Says Amputations Reduced To Avoid International Condemnation', *Radio Farda* 16 January 2019, https://en.radiofarda.com/a/iran-prosecutir-says-amputations-reduced-to-avoid-condemnation/29714019.html.

94 Qabil discussed the fixed and changing verses in more detail in *Mabānī-yi Sharīʿat*. The historicising and unfolding of the Qurʾan to advance rational interpretation is discussed by Qabil in a section titled 'the criteria for distinguishing the fixed and changeable [verses] from the perspective of the master'. The master in question is of course Ayatollah Montazeri who pointed to the changing meaning of some verses because of alterations in the subject (*mawżūʿ*) of the Qurʾanic command. Qabil listed examples: (i) the abrogation (*naskh*) of commands; (ii) when there has been a change in the subject matter of the command (i.e. just as when animal waste transforms into compost); and (iii) when the subject of a command is changed by governmental order due to its benefit or corruption. The key factors are the benefit or the corruption for all of the changeable commands, and this, of course, involves judgement and reason. Qabil attempted to preserve the 'unchanging and eternal word' of God by claiming that it is not so much the command that changes, but it is the subject that has changed and necessitated a new command. In this way, no damage is done to the narration that 'the *ḥalāl* of Muhammad is *ḥalāl* until the day of resurrection, and the *ḥarām* of Muhammad is *ḥarām* until the resurrection' (*Mabāni-yi Sharīʿat*, 228).

rather than the reified version of Islam, with all of the rituals and laws that have been established by tradition. In other words, it is necessary to consider the 'plurality of sharias' (Jewish and Christian), which all demand the need to perform 'righteous deeds'. Qabil even claimed that the practice of righteous deeds had been 'the subject of attention in the [various] sharias, *but it is not exclusive to them*'.[95] While recognition of Abrahamic traditions has long been a feature in the worldview of many seminarians, it is the final clause in Qabil's quote that demands attention, as it is clearly suggestive of the acceptance of an expanding range of different worldviews, which logically could include secular and even atheist perspectives. The implications were not carried to any conclusion, however, and Qabil simply continued by foregrounding good deeds, which he understood as a reference to morality. In other words, doing good deeds is more of a general nature rather than the specificities of jurisprudence. Morality also accorded with human reason, and it was given some clarity by referring to the aim of the sharia, which is justice. This does not mean that Qabil endorsed a form of justice that demanded 'an eye for an eye'; rather he emphasised divine mercy, as discussed previously. Qabil was keen to foreground divine compassion, for instance: 'The wise Law-giver, the Omniscient, the Kind, the All-Aware and Compassionate and Merciful is not a God who does nothing but mete out anger, fury, wrath and painful punishment to His creation.'[96] He cited the Q. 57.25: 'We have sent forth Our prophets with clear proof and sent down with them the book and the balance, so that people might act justly.' His aim was to foreground the requirement for humans to act rationally and agree upon a consensual approach. In this way, Qabil called for more space in Iran for increasing open and free discussions on a whole range of religious and political issues. And he endorsed an equivalence between equality and justice, which he considered a 'solution for removing the problems between some rational and customary approaches of the present age'.[97] In his call for justice, the weight of compassion, mercy and non-compulsion tipped the scales. He held that rational believers had a choice in performing legal commands; that is to say, there is absolutely no compulsion to perform acts that cause loathing. He cited a narration from Imam Baqir to support his point:

> In the text of a reliable narration, Imam Baqir has reported from the Prophet of Islam [...] If a narration was reported from the Prophet of God, [the

95 *Sharīʿat ʿAqlānī*, 79, my emphasis.
96 *Sharīʿat ʿAqlānī*, 69.
97 *Sharīʿat ʿAqlānī*, 81.

> believer] must accept [it] if [their] heart responds positively and [they must] carry out [the commands] of the narration. If [their] heart has a negative reaction to the contents of the narration [… the believer] must abandon it and not carry out [the command]. But if the heart does not accept [the command] it is incorrect to reject the origin of the command because it is possible that it reported a reality beyond our intelligence and perception. Its meaning and the understanding of it will become clear in the future and people will benefit from it.[98]

Conclusion

The five themes of *Sharīʿat-i ʿAqlānī* open the sharia to a wider range of interpretations than has traditionally been the case. *Sharīʿat-i ʿAqlānī* provides the possibility for a flexible and compassionate understanding that may easily respond to the necessities and challenges of the age, and the criteria of justice and rationality ensure compatibility with sacred scripture. Underpinning this is the historicising of the Qurʾan and sacred scripture (discussed in Part One of this book), and the need to re-investigate the hadith and narrations. Such a move may be seen as a threat to the more 'entrenched' scholars within the religious establishment who prefer the safety and security offered by tradition. Herein lies the radical nature of Qabil's message, which conforms to the general thrust of the New Religious Thinkers. Likewise, Qabil's willingness to engage with scholars outside of the seminary is not a complete innovation, but it does further the process of returning Islam to the people.

Qabil's worldview dovetails with the 'religious secularity' discussed in Part One. An element of this concerns his rejection of *vilāyat-i faqīh*, which is best laid out in his essay on *vilāyat*, where he argued for the democratisation of the political system.[99] Although such a perspective does not necessarily entail the removal of

98 *Sharīʿat ʿAqlānī*, 86.

99 Qabil's political ideas, in particular his view of the *vilāyat-i faqīh*, requires further investigation. He appeared to excuse Montazeri for any failing in the political doctrine of *vilāyat-i faqīh*, but at the same time was ready to acknowledge jurisprudential differences with his master. On the topic of Montazeri's understanding of the *vilāyat-i faqīh*, Qabil said, 'First, he believed in "its religious legality" (*mashrūʿiyat*) through election by the people (not divine appointment), and second [based on] the difference between [the position] being jurisprudential and [the occupant of the position] being more of a politician (*siyāsatmadār-tar*), officially he believed in its political nature rather than its jurisprudential nature. In the year 1990 or 1991, I said to him that this preference was an indicator of "lack of permanency of the *vilāyat-i faqīh*"' ('Junbish-i sabz, iṣlāhāt, rūhāniyat va vilāyat-i faqīh', 323). When

seminarians from political structures, it does require a meritocracy with the checks and balances that are typical in Western nation states. His inclusive views may also be tied to discussions about the 'way of reasonable people' (*sīra-yi ʿuqalā*), a term that occurs with regularity in his writings, and which reflects the collective rationality of the reasonable people of the time. In fact, in other places Qabil used the term 'common' or 'collective rationality' (*ʿaqlāniyat-i mushtarak*). The significance of this discussion assumes importance in the light of Qabil's clear distaste for individualism, so, for example, in *Sharīʿat-i ʿAqlānī*, he remarked that 'excessive individualism' (*fardgarāʾī-yi afrāṭī*) and the unwillingness to work as a team was one of the basic religious problems in modern Iran. In other words, Qabil was unwilling to trust the reasoning of single individuals who asserted a monopoly over wisdom. Interestingly, he also claimed that another major problem was the unwillingness to value the role of the wise who work in the humanities, a clear jibe at those who sought to limit understandings of the sharia to the ulama.[100] Given Qabil's struggles with Khamenei and the discussion among the Iranian New Religious Thinkers about the 'excessive' power enjoyed by the Leader within the structure of the ruling system of *vilāyat-i faqīh*, it is easy to read a political message into the promotion of collective rationality. It is to be wondered whether Qabil was influenced by his mentor, Ayatollah Montazeri, who discussed the difference between classical/traditional reason and modern reason in a work published in 2006 (sometime shortly before Qabil's own writing). Classical reason is viewed with other faculties such as lust and anger, whereas modern reason is collective and 'realised by means of discussion and dialogue'.[101] Montazeri's own

asked whether the doctrine of *vilāyat-i faqīh* was practical for running society, Qabil answered, 'From those days when he [Montazeri] propounded this doctrine, notwithstanding all of the proofs that he and Ayatollah Khomeini, his teacher, had propounded, I have not been content that God has given a special right to the jurists' ('Dastgīrī-hā bā imżā-yi Ayatollah Khamenei sūrat girifta ast' [The arrests have taken place with the authorisation of Ayatollah Khamenei], dated 31 July 2010, *Vaṣiyat bi Millat-i Iran*, 274. The scope of this chapter does not permit a full investigation of his views on *vilāyat*. Qabil's fullest and most systematic treatment of the topic appears in 'Vilāyat-i faqīh', *Fiqh, Kārkard-hā va Qābiliyat*, 2006, 75–96. His politics, theology and jurisprudence cannot be separated from one another, as it is argued herein. In short, Qabil was of the opinion that the divisions of the power structure in Iran had been strangled by Khamenei. See 'Tashkil-i shūrā az sū-yi rahbarī, iqrār bi ikhtalāf-i shadīd bayn-i qavast' [The creation of a council by the leadership acknowledges the serious split among the powers of government], dated 27 August 2011, *Vaṣiyat bi Millat-i Irān*, 364.

100 *Sharīʿat ʿAqlānī*, 65.

101 Siavoshi, *Montazeri*, 215. Montazeri's work is *Islām va Dīn-i Fiṭrat* (*Islam and the Religion of [Original] Nature*). This is available at: https://amontazeri.com/static/books/

conflict with the political authorities may have led him to prefer the collective nature of reason. Qabil's attachment to collective rationality persuaded him of the need to find common answers to society's problems.[102] To this end he attempted to create a think tank, composed of jurists and also specialists in the humanities, that would critically, rationally and scientifically focus on relevant issues. He noted, too, that unfortunately similar attempts in the past had not achieved such goals, but had merely turned into centres for those who sang in praise of the imams (*madāḥān*) or reciters of the sufferings of the imams (*rawża-khānān*).[103]

Another issue which emerges form *Sharīʿat-i ʿAqlānī*, although not in an explicit fashion, is the intrinsic compatibility of the sharia with Western ideas as they are expressed through the reasonable people, such as equality for women, abolition of slavery, and the abolition of cruel and violent punishments. Of course, the paramount role allocated to reason in Qabil's worldview caused him to accept the universal validity of rationality, and to this end in the rights for all humans, not just Muslims. He did not consider one culture or region as intrinsically better than another, and so he cited approvingly Muhammad's dictum that, 'There is no pride for the Arab over the non-Arab, or for the non-Arab over the Arab, or for the white person over the black or red, or for the black and red over the white.'[104] What is at stake here is Qabil's view of what might be called very general and universal standards of human rights. He did not engage with counter-arguments that the rights enshrined, for example in the Universal Declaration of Human Rights, might not reflect a compatibility between revelation and reason, or that there are still debates, for instance, about 'natural rights', leading to more particular discussions, such as the 'naturalness' of binary sexualities – i.e. a person is either male or female and must adopt the appropriate social role, which warrants different rights and duties.[105] Interestingly, he justified his argument with reference to the logic of

Eslam_Dine_Fetrat.pdf. Montazeri's distinction between classical and modern reason appears on page 51.

102 Qabil said, 'If collective human reason affirms or negates the rationality of a situation, then it must be followed. And approaches contrary to it (even if it has been stated in the Qurʾan, to say nothing of the narrations of the consensus of the jurists) will not be religiously legal (*nā-mashrūʿ*) because they are irrational.' See *Sharīʿat ʿAqlānī*, 175.

103 Qabil specifically mentioned the Islamic Centre of Hamburg, established by Ayatollah Burujirdi, as well as the efforts of Ayatollah Montazeri in creating similar centres in Europe, Africa, Canada and Lebanon, the attempts of Ayatollah Taliqani, Bazargan, Sahabi and Shariʿati in Europe (London [Society of] Unity), and the Centre for Belief in Los Angeles in America. *Sharīʿat-i ʿAqlānī*, 162.

104 Qabil, *Fiqh, Kārkard-hā va Qābiliyat-hā*, 148.

105 Such arguments have implications for males and females, and for those whose gender does not fit these neat binary divisions.

signing a pact based on human reasoning (*istidlāl*), but he was at pains to remind his readers that a violation of it is also a repudiation of the sharia:

> But the opponents of this reasoning (including all the countries that are members of the United Nations and also Islamic countries) will be obliged and duty-bound to carry out [the declaration] after signing (*imżā*) or verbally accepting [the Universal Declaration of Human Rights], to remain loyal to its contents, and to accept permanent membership of the United Nations as an international promise and covenant. They know that any steps taken in violation of this international agreement are considered big sins (*gunāh-i kabīra*), because violating a pact is prohibited by the sharia, even if on one side of the pact and agreement is the Prophet of God and on the opposite side are infidels and unbelievers (*kuffār va mushrikān*).[106]

Of course, he considered the human rights that are endorsed by the United Nations as completely compatible with Islam. The following rhetorical passage typifies the kind of perspective he adopted, and at the very least it provokes some interesting questions:

> If the Prophet were sent on a mission in the contemporary age to France, Spain, Canada, Australia, Japan, India, South Africa, China, Russia or Scandinavian countries, what would he do? Which of the existing human relations would he validate (*imżā*)? From which cultures do his validating commands arise? How would he set the sentences for punishing criminals? Wouldn't he set the criteria for perceiving and understanding, and the acceptance of the people and the wise (*ʿuqalā*) of this time as the foundation for legislating his social commands?[107]

And in a stunning assessment of the state of Islam in the contemporary world, he made the following observation:

> Citizens of non-Islamic countries today are closer in rank to the manners and aims of religion and sharia, whereas citizens of Islamic countries are further in rank from the aims and manners of the sharia. Sayyid Jamal al-Din Asadabadi spoke the truth more than one hundred years ago when he said: 'I went to

---

106 'Ḥuqūq-i bashr', *Fiqh, Kārkard-hā va Qābiliyat-hā*, 242.
107 Qabil, *Fiqh, Kārkard-hā va Qābiliyat-hā*, 149.

> the West. I saw Islam but I did not see Muslims. I came to the East. I saw Muslims but I did not see Islam.'[108]

He despaired of the kind of Islam found in Iran itself, and he cited the following saying that reflects the strength of his feeling:

> A day will come for the Muslims when nothing of Islam will remain but the name, nothing will remain of the Qur'an but the script. Its people will be called Muslims, but they will be far from Islam. From the perspective of decoration, their mosques will be flourishing, but from the perspective of guidance they will be empty. The jurists of these times will be the worst people under heaven. They will cause strife and it will fall upon them.[109]

108 Qabil, *Fiqh, Kārkard-hā va Qābiliyat-hā*, 150. The origin of this quote is disputed. An internet search reveals only several sites which attribute it to Afghani's friend and collaborator for Islamic reform, Muhammad ʿAbduh, who was at some point the rector of Al-Azhar University in Cairo. Both Professors Mark Sedgwick and Oliver Scharbrodt who have published on ʿAbduh have said that they have not come across this sentence in ʿAbduh's works (both private emails received on 1 May 2019). One online source that attributes the quote to ʿAbduh is Ahmed Hasan, *Foreign Policy Journal*, 2 July 2011.
109 Qabil, *Fiqh, Kārkard-hā va Qābiliyat-hā*, 150. This is a well-known hadith. See, for example, Bayhaqi, *Shu'ab al-Imān* [*Branches of Faith*], no. 2/788.

7

Translation of Qabil's 'The Desirability for Covering the Head and Neck'

Introduction: Qabil and the Hijab

The most detailed treatment of the hijab penned by Qabil appears in his book *Commands Pertaining to Women in the Muhammadan Sharia*. This is a work that is composed of sections devoted to women's rights in the Qur'an, the hijab, temporary marriage, a woman's right to separation from her husband, and there is also a section in which Qabil gave answers to seven legal questions related to commands for women. The section of the book on the hijab is composed of four elements: Qabil's fatwa, an essay called 'On the Hijab', and two short sections in which he answered criticisms pertaining to his writings on the subject. The most important section is 'On the Hijab', which is twenty-four pages in length in the Persian original, and clearly a very different kind of work from Mutahhari's offering of 286 pages. As argued in Part Two, Mutahhari attempted to address not only the newly educated Iranian youth, many of whom were influenced by Western studies in philosophy, history, politics and psychology, but also the traditional seminarian who clung on to the image of women covered from head (and face) to foot. Qabil's chapter on the hijab, in contrast, was arguably addressed primarily to the ranks of the ulama with a deep knowledge of the Shiʿi tradition. He utilised and cited the works of slightly under forty of the most well-respected religious scholars; some from the very early period of Shiʿi history. Whilst many of these scholars would need no introduction to seminarians or students of Shiʿi theology, it is highly unlikely that the 'average Iranian' would have been familiar with such figures and they would have been unaware of their significance. This indicates that Qabil was targeting a very specialised audience. Nevertheless, his two-page fatwa, which precedes his essay 'On the Hijab' in the book, is a distillation of the main essay, and as such, it was very much designed for wide dissemination among the public. The essay, then, is a piece of highly specialised juristic research. An attempt is made here at clarity by numbering the points (paragraphs) in the text, and also by dividing the text into two main sections. Nevertheless, the text is heavy, and is not an easy read. The next couple of paragraphs summarise his arguments.

In the first half of the essay, Qabil's aims to disprove the necessity for wearing the hijab based on the idea of *ikhtilāf* (discussed in Part One). Qabil demonstrates differences of opinion among the jurists and scholars on several vital issues. He includes attempts to define *ʿawrat*, the lack of necessity for covering the head and neck of the free Muslim woman, the lack of harmony between covering for prayer and covering in other situations, and a discussion of juristic opinions on how it is not necessary to cover the area of hair that extends beyond the neck and the lack of necessity for covering the hair.

In the second half of the essay, Qabil analyses Qurʾanic verses related to the hijab – 24.30–1 or the modesty verse, and 33.59 – and concludes that these verses have produced differences of opinion about the necessity, desirability and refraining of wearing the hijab. He produces several arguments to demonstrate that head-covering is not advocated in the Qurʾan. First, he stresses the moral nature of the verses, eliding over the more traditional ways that they have been perceived as commands. Qabil's understanding of the relevant Qurʾanic passages places not compulsion upon the believer, but rather choice, as he considers the verses as guidance. Second, he claims the verses indicate that the Qurʾan adopts the practices that were customary at the time of revelation.

In conclusion, Qabil claims there is a 'lack of certainty for a consensus for the need to cover the head and neck', resulting in his own preference (not compulsion) for women to wear the hijab. His methods of utilising past Shiʿi masters to argue his case demonstrates that his views were not 'new or contrived'. And his conclusion reflects the observation made repeatedly in *Sharīʿat-i ʿAqlānī* about the principle for the permission to exercise rationality, and in so doing he delivers agency back to women, the wearers of the hijab. After his analysis of the narrations and Qurʾanic verses, Qabil adds a few stinging words about contemporary practice in the Islamic Republic, and he points to the hypocrisy that he sees in emphasising head-covering when the rest of the body may be left more or less visible. His exasperation is not difficult to identify in the following memorable passage:

> Even if a woman [wears] non-see-through, tight leggings (*jūrāb-i shalvārī-yi astrīj*) which reveal the shape of the *ʿawrat*, and a blouse from which the

> shape of body is visible, she can be present on the streets, on television, in cinema and theatre, so long as she wears a veil (*miqna'a*) that does not permit even a single hair to be seen.

Qabil's opinion on the hijab did not change; indeed, in his last interview before he passed away he repeated the same kinds of sentiments, containing the barely disguised incredulity at the hypocrisy of the views of some of the jurists:

> The issue of the hijab is [about] covering the body, not covering the head and neck. I don't understand all this sensitivity about a single strand of hair! Where have they got it from?
>
> In fact, these discussions reflect demagoguery more than a scientific discussion. What does it mean when according to a jurist a single strand of hair causes God's throne to tremble, and then the very same jurist says that it is not necessary to cover the shape of a woman's body? [...] the respected jurists who have advocated for the absence of the necessity to cover the shape of a woman's body, imagine a female manakin, next to a hijab-covered model that they have brought along, and they place her hijab on the manakin, and then they stare at this model. Aren't they ashamed that they have made this an example of the covering of Muslim women![1]

*

The footnotes placed in square brackets are mine. Qabil's own numbering, which is represented by figures in rounded brackets, has been preserved in the text. The only additions to the work are the page numbers of the original essay, which are in squared brackets with bold font. The text is dense, and readers are expected to be familiar with the names of the great scholars of Shi'i Islam, suggesting that Qabil's intended readership were those within the seminary. In order to help the reader, a list of those scholars that he mentions is provided at the end of the text, to prevent cluttering the translation with footnotes. The list is based on the order in which the individual scholar appears in the text.

1 'Ākhirīn muṣāḥaba[yi] Ahmad Qabil: ḥijāb va islām-i siyāsī az manżar-i sharī'at-i 'aqlānī' [The last interview [with] Ahmad Qabil: hijab and political Islam from the perspective of *sharī'at-i 'aqlānī*], *Vaṣiyat bi Millat-i Iran*, 7 June 2012, 406–7.

THE DESIRABILITY OF COVERING THE HEAD AND NECK[2]

1. The principle of covering the *ʿawrat* for male and female Muslims is necessary.[3]
2. Jurists have different opinions about what is included in the *ʿawrat* (especially in relation to women).
3. The majority of jurists have considered covering the head necessary for free (non-slave) Muslim women, and they hold the head and neck too among parts included in the *ʿawrat*.
4. Ibn Junayd Iskafi, who is one of the famous Shiʿi jurists and who lived in the same generation as the masters of Shaykh Mufid, considered the parts comprising the *ʿawrat* in men and women as the same and equal.
5. All the Shiʿi jurists (indeed, all the Islamic jurists) considered covering the head and neck unnecessary for Muslim women who were slaves; rather, much like Shaykh Saduq and a group of clerics from Qum (in the time of Shaykh Saduq), they considered it illegal (*ḥarām*) for slave women to cover the head; whereas covering the *ʿawrat* was necessary for them.
6. Sahib-i Javahir considered covering parts of the body (with the exception of the face, hands and feet as far as the ankle, the neck and head hair) as consensual (*ijmāʾī*). In other words, regarding [those] exceptions, the opinions of the jurists varied, and no agreement existed.
7. He cites the words of ʿAllama Tabatabaʾi, the master of Sahib-i Javahir, and 'Sahib-i Madarik' [and] says that covering the 'head and neck' is unnecessary in their opinion, and he writes, 'Judge **[56]** Ibn Baraj has attributed to some of the Shiʿi clerics [the belief] that covering the head and neck is unnecessary.'

---

2 [Qabil adds a footnote which says: 'This subject is an answer to a question by Husayn Khudadad (a pseudonym) which has been published in Bahman 1382 (January/February 2004), together with the command on the permissibility of [eating/buying/selling?] slaughtered [animals] of the People of the Book, and marriage with the [People of the Book].']

3 [Qabil does not discuss the meaning of *ʿawrat*, which is a word that does not need explanation within the context of the seminary. It is a Qurʾanic term, often being rendered as 'exposed' or 'vulnerable'; Q 33.13 says: 'Truly our houses are exposed, though they were not exposed.' In the twelfth century the Shiʿi scholar al-Tabarsi remarked that: '*ʿAwrah* refers to anything which can be easily harmed just like a bare or exposed place. Therefore, it becomes clear that the body of a woman is referred to as vulnerable because it is like a house which contains no walls and can be easily harmed and must be covered with the appropriate clothing' (*Majmaʿ al-Bayān*, vol. 8, 2312, Tehran 1338/1959–60).]

8. Sahib-i Javahir has expressed his opinion in this manner: 'Covering head hair is based upon [observing] caution.' Indeed, [he gave] a stronger (*qavītar*) [opinion for caution]; therefore, he has not issued a clear fatwa for the need [to cover] it; rather based on caution and probability, firstly he has [expressed] caution and then he preferred (*tarjīḥ*) [covering] it.
9. From all of these studies it is clear that the issue is controversial, and the consensus of Muslims on this act (covering the head and neck) has not been reached.
10. Some [Qur'anic] verses and reliable narrations appear [to support] its non-compulsory nature (like 33.59 ['O Prophet! Tell your wives and daughters, and the women of the believers to draw their cloaks over themselves']), although there are also some verses and reliable narrations that mention the necessity to cover the head. Certainly, the requirement to harmonise (*jam'i 'urfī*) necessary proofs and non-necessary proofs depends on the contexts. If [the harmonisation] is practised according to this rule, the conclusion of the verses and narrations support the non-necessity of covering the head and neck, and only affirm preference (*isthiḥāb*).

Regarding the aforementioned topic, I consider it necessary to cover the body based on scientific proofs, but covering the head and neck is legally desirable (*mustaḥabb-i shar'ī*).

(Tehran, 20 Bahman 1382/ 9 February 2004)

[57] ON THE HIJAB

(1). Based on narrations coming from the Prophet of God and the imams on the subject of 'a woman is *'awrat*', many Islamic jurists (both Shi'i and Sunni) have made mistakes and have imagined that 'the whole of the woman's body (other than the face, hands and feet as far as the ankles) is *'awrat*'. And they have understood [the whole body] as the real *'awrat*. They have claimed consensus for this incorrect supposition.

As an example, we turn to the words of Sahib-i Javahir, which he has related from his master:

> There is no doubt that whole of the woman's existence is *'awrat*. It is clear that they used the word *'awrat* in the Arabic language for understanding

woman, and according to common usage also it was customary and usual that they used the word *ʿawrat* in place of the word 'woman', and calling women *ʿawrat* was common and prevalent to the extent that it was not possible to say 'woman is not *ʿawrat*'. From this perspective the sharia has also affirmed that 'woman is *ʿawrat*'. The context of some narrations and the consensus of jurists also has held to this [view] that 'all of the existence of the woman is *ʿawrat*', but they [considered] some things (like hands and the face) as exceptions.[4]

[58] In order to prove the correctness of this claim (the tendency of the majority of jurists to understand the *ʿawrat* as the whole body of the woman), one can refer to books [including] *Nihāyat al-Aḥkām* (1/365) of ʿAllama Hilli, [who says], 'As for the free mature woman, her whole body (*badan-hā*) is *ʿawrat*', and *al-Muʿtabar* (153–4) of Muhaqqiq Hilli, [who says], 'As for the free women, her whole body (*jasad-hā*) is *ʿawrat*', and *al-Kāfī* (139) of Abu'l-Salah Halabi, and *al-Fiqh ʿala al-Madhāhib al-Arbaʿa* (1/192) in the text and margins, etc.

Certainly, a group among the great masters of jurisprudence, like Sahib-i Riyaz and Sahib-i Javahir have criticised this view and they say, 'From the perspective of the necessity of covering, [women] come under the ruling of *ʿawrat*, although the word *ʿawrat* does not mean "woman" and such a concurrence [in meaning between woman and *ʿawrat*] has not been verified in legal terminology'. The learned opposition of these two great masters (and other greats agreeing with them) neither denies the reality of the well-known tendency in relation to 'understanding *ʿawrat* as pertaining to the whole of the woman's body', nor does it deny that such a perspective continues to exist. Rather, there is no doubt that this tendency has been the well-known approach of Shiʿi and Sunni jurists.

The interpretation of 'the woman's body being *ʿawrat*' has been emphasised by many jurists, such as Shahid-i Avval, Miqdad al-Suyuri, Shaykh Tusi, Judge Ibn Baraj, Shahid-i Thani, Muhaqqiq Karaki, etc.

Fazil Abi, in *Kashf al-Rumūz* (1/141) has said:

> The origin of the difference is this. Either the feet are part of the *ʿawrat* or not. The person who says 'yes' considers covering them necessary. And the person who says 'no' does not consider covering them necessary, rather he considers it desirable.

4 *Javāhir al-Kalām*, 8/164.

Therefore, people who do not make an exception for the feet have a difference of opinion with those who do on what is included in the *ʿawrat*. In other words, people who have considered woman's feet until the ankles as part of the *ʿawrat* **[59]** have considered covering them necessary, and people who do not consider them part of the *ʿawrat* do not consider covering them necessary.

Just as Fazil Abi emphasised in detailed juristic books, there are other cases too where there are differences of opinion on the issue of 'being *ʿawrat* or not'. It shows the lack of agreed consensus among the jurists, and it demonstrates differences on *ʿawrat* as a term in the section [of books] on covering (*sitr*) and 'the claim of consensus' on these particulars is incorrect.

(2). The lack of necessity for covering the head and neck (*gardan*) of a slave Muslim woman (which requires reliable narrated proofs and a desire for consensus) is an indication of this very important point, since: 'It is not forbidden for the head and neck of each Muslim woman to be visible and open.'

In other words, 'neither being a woman, nor being a Muslim woman' is a reason for the necessity to cover the head and neck. Because 'slave Muslim women' were both 'women' and 'Muslim', covering the head and neck and even some other parts of the body was not necessary for them, based upon the clear declarations of some jurists. Some have even believed in the repugnance or shame of covering the head for slave Muslim women.

Certainly, covering the head and neck was the condition for a woman's social respect. Female slaves (Muslim and non-Muslim) did not cover their bodies, including [their] head and neck, because they were not paid much respect from a social perspective which considered them with contempt. In the same way that in Iran too, prior to the advent of Islam (the Sassanian period), high-class women were protected in public gatherings, far from the eyes of men (even from male relations other than their husbands), and they concealed women beneath austere and burdensome coverings. But destitute women who were connected to the lower classes were present in public gatherings with [their] head, face, neck, forearms and legs showing. **[60]**

(3). Although many of the aforementioned differences among the jurists appeared within discussions of 'prayer covering', attention must be paid to the great jurists such as Muhaqqiq Hilli in the book *al-Muʿtabar* (153 and 154), ʿAllama Hilli in his last jurisprudential book, *Nihāyat al-Aḥkām* (1/366), and many others who in their books on jurisprudence used proofs related to covering at non-prayer times in [their] discussion about prayer covering,[5] and they used proofs related to prayer covering [in the discussion for] non-prayer covering. A great many of them have brought both discussions in *The Book of Prayer* side by side and without separating [them from each other] which in their opinion indicated 'the unity of the foundation of each of the two discussions'.

Therefore, the soundness of [both] the general approach of the subjects and proofs presented for both discussions has been vouchsafed in the jurists' popular opinion, although a smaller group of jurists have opposed 'the unity of proof and harmony of these two discussions'.

For the peace of mind of some readers, I call everyone's attention to the clear statement of the great martyr, Ayatollah Mutahhari, in the book *The Issue of the Hijab* (224) where he says:

> Just as it is seen on the topic of covering during prayer, Islamic jurists rely on the Q. 24 in a verse which is unrelated to prayer, because [these Islamic jurists hold that] whatever must be covered during prayers is the same thing that must be covered [outside of prayer times] from non-*maḥram* [men]. If perchance there is a discussion, it is this: during prayers, is it necessary to cover or not [anything] in addition to what must be covered [outside of prayer time] in front of the non-*maḥram*? However, there is no discussion about whether whatever does not need to be covered during prayer, does not need to be covered in front of the non-*maḥram* also.[6]

On the next page, on this very topic he relates the words of Ayatollah Muhammad Javad Mughniya in the book *al-Fiqh ʿala al-Madhāhib al-Khamsa.* **[61]**

Shaykh Yusuf Bahrani too in his detailed book of jurisprudence, *al-Ḥadāʾiq al-Nāżara*, has pointed to 'the unity of proof and harmony of covering for prayer and for [times] other than prayer', and he has considered [the unity] a result of 'clear narrations and explanations of the Shiʿi jurists'.

Therefore, differences among the jurists on the subject of 'how much covering for prayers' extends to the discussion of 'covering in general'.

---

5 [The usual reference is to Q. 7.31: 'O Children of Adam! Put on your finery (*zinatakum*) at every place of worship.' Here finery probably means some form of covering. At other places in the Qur'an it seems to have other meanings.]

6 [It is unclear which version of Mutahhari's text Qabil used. The quote in question appears on page 273 of the version used for part two of this book (the second printing (*chāp-i duwwum*), 1348/1969–70).]

(4). ʿAllama Hilli, one of the great Shiʿi jurists, was one of many Shiʿi jurists nearer to the time of Ibn Junayd Iskafi (the master of Shaykh Mufid), and one of his jurisprudential books is extant. He reported an expression from [Ibn Junayd] on the subject of 'covering': 'The two *ʿawrat* is the amount of the body that must be covered, and they say that it is the front and behind of the man and woman,' and his own understanding has been set out in his own words:

> These words of Ibn Junayd, on the equivalence of men and women, according to him, point to this: 'The amount necessary for a woman is her front and behind, and it is not necessary to cover [anything] except for these [two places].'[7]

He reports these words after relating the discourse of Shaykh Tusi ('It is necessary for her to cover her head and her body from her head to her feet'). The expression 'except for these' is clear about the lack of necessity for covering the rest of the woman's body (except the necessity of covering the two *ʿawrat*). **[62]**

I think that ʿAllama Hilli's understanding of Ibn Junayd (which has been [recorded] in his book *al-Mukhtaṣar al-Aḥmadī fī Fiqh al-Muḥammadi*) gives more assurance than the various understandings of wise men (*ʿalim-ān*) who live in these times and do not have access to his missing books.

In other words, a researcher is not following a wrong path if he prefers to rely on the understanding of ʿAllama Hilli and other great masters of Shiʿi jurisprudence about the explanations of Ibn Junayd, and based on their reports he follows the issue of covering within the commands of the Muhammadan sharia.

In addition to these understandings of Ibn Junayd's words, jurists such as Shahid-i Avval (*Dhikr*, 139), the author of *Miftāḥ al-Karāma* (2/168), ʿAllama Majlisi (*Biḥār al-Anwār*, 83/180), Muhaqqiq Tabatabaʾi (*Riyāż al-Masāʾil*, 2/378), Muhaqqiq Naraqi (*Mustanad al-Shīʿa*, 4/242) and a number of others among the ancient and more recent [jurists] have attributed [sayings] to him, and one should consider unrealistic and false the understanding of all of these jurists on Ibn Junayd's sayings (especially people who have seen his book).

(5). Judge Ibn Baraj (d. 481) has said in the book *Sharḥ Jumil al-ʿIlm wa al-ʿAmal* (73):

> There is no difference of opinion that it is necessary for a woman who is

7 *Mukhtalif al-Shīʿa*, 83.

> not a slave to cover her head during prayer. This covering of the head is not necessary for a female slave. On the topic of a free Muslim woman who covers her head but [some] hair has not been covered, a group of jurists have differences on opinion about whether **[63]** it is necessary to cover all the hair. Whatever the case, they have agreed about the necessity of covering the head.

i. Ibn Baraj establishes that 'a group of jurists believe it is not necessary to cover hair which is longer than the head and neck'.
ii. He says, 'On the topic of the necessity of covering the head, there probably exists agreement, but apparently there has been differences of opinion on the quantity and quality of it.' This explanation too confirms the lack of consensus for covering hair. Because reporting an opposite [view], derived from a group of Shiʿi jurists, convinces someone about the lack of verification for consensus about 'the absolute necessity of covering the head of free women'.

(6). ʿAllama Najafi, famous as 'Sahib-i Javahir' has said on this subject:

> Probability for the exemption of long hair has been given from the command that requires the covering of head hair [...] although [the principle of] caution is closer [to the truth] (*nazdīk-tar*), the proof for covering it is stronger (*qavītar*).[8]

In confirming the lack of certainty of proofs for the absolute necessity of covering the head of free Muslim women in relation to 'hair that is longer than the head and neck', Sahib-i Javahir uses the expression 'more caution and more strong'. Even if the expression 'more strong' comes after 'more cautionary', it indicates preference for 'the command for the necessity of covering' on the part of the believer, **[64]** but he makes it completely clear that 'reliable, related proofs' for definitive commands on the 'necessity of absolute covering of the head hair of free Muslim women do not exist in primary sharia texts'.

(7). Muhammad Baqir Sabzavari has said in the book *Kifāyat al-Aḥkām* (16):

> A better opinion is this: the whole of the free Muslim woman's body is *ʿawrat*, aside from the face, hands as far as the wrists, and feet as far as the ankles. There are problems on the topic of proving the command for 'the need to

8 *Javāhir al-Kalām*, 8/169.

cover a woman's neck' and in most declarations and expressions of the jurists there has been no mention of 'the need to cover the hair'. Although Shahid-i Avval considered it necessary, one should hesitate in agreeing with his perspective on this topic.

i. He has considered that the 'need to cover the neck' [is] difficult, and in the end, he considers it problematic to give a fatwa for it.
ii. On the topic of 'the need to cover the hair' too he deliberates and says, the expressions of many of the Shiʿi jurists have not mentioned it, even though Shahid-i Avval (d. 786) believed it was necessary.

(8). Sayyid Muhammad ʿAmili, the author of *Madārik al-Aḥkām*, in this book (3/188) has said:

[65] Know that in this passage, just as [in the] declarations of other Shiʿi jurists, there has been no engagement with 'the need to cover the hair'. Rather, from this passage it is clear that 'covering the hair is not necessary' [...] and Shahid-i Avval has considered it closer [to the truth] (*nazdīktar bi vāqiʿa*) and his support is a report of 'Ibn Babuya from Fuzayl' which has been reported from Imam Baqir [...] and this narration, if its chain of transmission (*sanad*) is trustworthy, does not include any proof for the need to cover the hair.[9] Yes, one can reason the lack of need to cover from this narration, and the narration of 'Zarara' (which appeared before [in the text *Madārik al-Aḥkām*]) too points to the lack of necessity for covering.[10]

i. He admits that there is no discussion about the need to cover the hair in most of the expressions of Shiʿi jurists.
ii. He considers that the words of most jurists are clear in relation to 'the lack of need to cover the hair', and he believes that [covering] has been understood as 'the application of an action whilst in prayer'. [In other words] it is specific to prayer,

9 [The narration in question runs: 'Abu Jaʿfar [Imam Baqir] says, "Fatima – greetings upon her – would pray while wearing a cloth and a *khimār* and it was not more than what would cover her hair and ears."' The implication seems to be that the covering might not be sufficient to cover long hair or the neck.]

10 [The narration reads: 'Zarara says I asked Abu Jaʿfar (Imam Sadiq) about the least (clothing) that a woman is allowed to have in prayers. He said a cloth and sheet that she would spread along her head and cover with it.' The point is that there is no necessity to cover the neck.]

[and] there is no need to cover the hair [in general]. And other narrations, too, are silent in affirming [the need] to cover the hair.
iii. He does not think the reasoning of Fuzayl's narrative from Imam Baqir about the need to cover the hair as sufficient. Rather, the logical possibility of reasoning with this narration is permissible for the lack of a requirement to cover the neck.
iv. He says that the narration of Zarara b. A'yan[11] also points to the lack of the need to cover the neck.
v. Although in his text, he relies upon the argument of 'doing [it] at prayers' and 'the lack of emphasis of it in narrations' but 'proving something does not prove things other than that thing', and proving the lack of necessity during prayer is not the same as the necessity for it at non-prayer time.**[66]**
vi. His reliance upon the expressions of many authors can be an indication that in none of the discussions related to the juristic subjects (either on veiling or on covering by a person praying) there are any explicit words from most of the scholars before him for covering hair. If this is not the case, he would have referred to it (even in the form of a separate topic). Therefore, the conclusion he makes relates to the principle of the necessity or the lack of necessity of covering the hair.

(9). Muhammad Baqir Majlisi writes in a discussion about the need to cover the *'awrat* and after reporting the words of some wise men like Abi'l-Salah Halabi and Ibn Junayd on the topic of the origin of covering the *'awrat*:

> So, know that in the discussions of many Shi'i jurists there is no talk of 'the need to cover the hair'. Shahid-i Avval considered the need to cover the hair as closer [to the truth] (*nazdīktar bi vāqī'a*), and this approach of his corresponds more with [the principle of] caution.[12]

i. When 'Allama Majlisi speaks of the origin of the need to cover the *'awrat* and discusses the areas to be covered during prayer or non-prayer [situations], he says, 'In the words of most of the Shi'i jurists, the topic does not allude to "the need to cover the hair".'[13]
ii. He himself too, after giving attention to all the reasons and discourses of the jurists, does not give a definitive fatwa for 'the need to cover the hair', rather, he is cautious, based upon the general method of the Akhbaris.
iii. With respect to the Shi'i Akhbaris ([who] basically referred to narrations,

11 [Died in 150 AH.]
12 *Bihār al-Anwār*, 83/180.
13 *Bihār al-Anwār*, 83/177.

and reflected upon them based on legal commands, and on this path too usually trusted unreliable narrations), it must be asked: how has it come to pass that one of the most famous Akhbari Shiʿi jurists, **[67]** who has assembled the most comprehensive collection of Shiʿi hadith (*Biḥār al-Anwār*, 110 volumes) – and there is no other person more famous among the Shiʿi Akhbaris – ultimately resorted to [the principle of] caution and could not find the support for a 'fatwa' and 'clear command specific to covering hair'?

(10). Mulla Ahmad Naraqi writes in his book *Mustanad al-Shīʿa* (4/246):

> From this study, the command [of the sharia] related to 'hair' is clear, and 'covering the hair is not necessary', just as some Shiʿi jurists have argued. But the [sharia] command also makes clear 'the lack of a need to cover the neck', just as some jurists have related. And the command for 'the lack of a need to cover the ears' is also clear. Certainly [there must be] 'caution in covering the ears' and perhaps 'caution in covering the neck'.

i. He has given a fatwa with complete decisiveness for 'the lack of a need to cover hair' that hangs over the face and shoulder. And this fatwa has also been attributed to some [other] jurists.
ii. He has also explained 'the lack of a need to cover the neck and ears', although he is cautious on both points. Certainly [these] words about the lack of necessity for covering the neck are also attributed to some Shiʿi jurists.
iii. No clear discourse exists in his work for earmarking this fatwa for covering at prayer. In other words, the attribution of his words includes both discussions.

[*]

(11). The most important Qurʾanic reason on the topic of covering the body and its application to men and women is in 24.30–1. Now, let us turn to these verses: **[68]**

> Tell the believers to cast down their eyes and guard their private parts. That is purer for them. God knows what they do. And tell believing women to cast down their eyes and guard their private parts and not show their finery (*zinatahunna*), except the outward part of it. And let them drape their bosoms (*juyūb*) with their veils (*khumur*) and not show their finery except to their husbands, their fathers, their husbands' fathers, their sons, the sons of their

> husbands, their brothers, the sons of their brothers, the sons of their sisters, their women, their maid-servants, the men followers who have no sexual desire or infants who have no knowledge of women's *ʿawrat*. Let them also not stamp their feet so that what they have concealed of their finery might be known. Repent to God, all of you, o believers, that perchance you may prosper.

In these two verses, the commands on the subject of covering the body have been discussed. The significant points on this topic are:

i. For a man or woman not to look at unrelated people. ('Tell the male believers to cast down their eyes and tell believing women to cast down their eyes.')
ii. For women not to reveal natural and non-natural finery in front of strangers and unrelated people ('and not show their finery').
iii. Permission to display the finery that [women] usually and naturally show, like the hands, face and the usual finery. The tradition among them [was] that women usually displayed themselves with that [finery] within various groups ('not show their finery, except the outward part of it').
iv. Permission to show hidden finery, in front of some members of their family (related) [to] the woman, like the husband, the father of the husband, her grandfather, her son and the male and female offspring, the son of [her] husband (who had been born from another wife of her husband), brother, nephew and his male offspring, niece and her male offspring, unknown women, male slaves who were in her possession, **[69]** and a man or boy slave who does not understand sexual matters ('and not show their finery except to their husbands...').
v. Putting on veils (*rū-sarī*) in such a way that it covers their breasts (*garībān*) ('let them drape their breasts with their veils (*khumur*)').
vi. Not stamping, with the intention of showing unrelated males their hidden finery ('Let them also not stamp their feet').

Certainly, there are different opinions among jurists of the sharia about the proofs of some of these cases regarding the necessity, observation, desirability or refraining, just as there are various perspectives about some of the aforementioned cases.

On this point, one should remember that on the issue of the woman's family, subjects like 'father and grandfathers, sons-in-law, paternal uncles, paternal grand-uncles, maternal uncles and maternal grand-uncles' have been added to the male subjects in the verse (on the topic of the permissibility of revealing [a woman's] hidden finery). This topic is proved in other verses and narrations, and there does not exist many differences of opinion about it.

i. These two verses (upon which the jurists rely) are positioned among a group of verses in sura 24 [that are] related to each other. Paying attention to all [the verses] illuminates the basic purpose and aim.

The subject starts from verse 27 on the topic of 'the need for asking permission and greeting'[14] when entering the dwelling of other [people], and ends at verse 33 [which is] on the topic of choosing chastity for those who do not have the opportunity to marry, and not forcing female slaves to fornicate.[15] In between [are verses about] the veiling of women (*rū-sarī-yi zanān*) ([with a] cloak (*khimār*) in such a way that it covers the beasts (*garībān* (*jayb*)), and it also mentions [the need] to refrain from showing hidden finery in front of mature, wise and unrelated people. **[70]**

One can even say that all the verses of the chapter (which are on the subject of adultery, cursing, accusations of dishonour, indecency and the joining of evil with evil, and good with good (verses 1–21)) are related to issues about dishonour and sex, and the relationship between good and bad people on this topic, in moral and legal (*fiqhī*) terminology.

Certainly, the verses at the end of the chapter (verses 58–60) once more return to the discussion of permission and you may say the basis of this chapter is related to matters of sex and honour.

ii. The introductory verses until verse 21, which is about fornication, indecency, accusing chaste women and slander, uses the strongest words at the end of the aforementioned verses. Sentences like: 'let no pity move you regarding them'; 'let a group of believers witness their punishment' [2]; or 'that has been forbidden for the believers' [3]; or 'for those are the wicked sinners' [4]; or 'and he who bore the brunt of it all shall have a terrible punishment' [11]; or 'This is a manifest slander' [12]; or 'those are, in God's sight, the real liars' [13]; or '[you would have been visited], due to your chatter, by a terrible punishment' [14]; or 'in God's sight it was very grave' [15]; or 'for them is a terrible punishment in this world and the next' [19]; or 'they are accursed in this world and the next and they shall have a terrible punishment' [23].

14 ['O believers! Do not enter houses other than your own before you ask leave and greet their occupants.']

15 ['Let those who do not find the means to marry be abstinent, until God enriches them from His bounty. Those whom your right hands own and who wish to pay for their emancipation, conclude a contract with them, if you know that there is some good in them, and give them of God's wealth which He gave you. Do not force your slave-girls into prostitution, if they wish to be chaste, in order to seek the fleeting goods of this life. Whoever forces them, surely God, after their being forced, is Forgiving, Merciful.']

At the same time, [the following] are introduced: the particulars of permission, lowering the gaze, guarding the *ʿawrat*, not showing hidden finery (verses 27–33), all [expressed] in a warning tone, the threat (of punishment), and the obligation to leave those set free, and it uses a moral language, such as, 'this is better for the believers' [27], or 'more chaste' [30], or 'chastity for old-women is better', 'Verily to refrain is better for them' [60].

Therefore, if someone claims that in themselves these verses do not prove necessity, then he has not spoken nonsense, for his words simply conform to the literal meaning of the Qur'an. **[71]**

On the topic of 'permission for looking at the *ʿawrat* of non-Muslims', [Mulla Ahmad] Naraqi writes in his book *Mustanad al-Shīʿa* 16/42 and 43: 'In contrast Ibn Idris Hilli, and ʿAllama Hilli in [his] book *Mukhtalif al-Shīʿa* which relies upon Q. 24.30, believe [in the "non-permission for looking at the *ʿawrat* of non-Muslims"]. In answering the perspective of these two jurists, it is said: "the meaning of the verse is short and vague" but even if one accepts that "there is no brevity or vagueness in its meaning", still this verse does not indicate the necessity of lowering the glance.' He makes it clear that 'the verse does not prove the necessity'.

iii. According to this understanding, all of the commands and prohibitions present in the above verses (in particular 30–1), prove the lack of necessity with regard to the teaching in them ('that is purer for them'). In other words, they have considered the commands desirable and its prohibitions purifying.

iv. Nearly all of that group of jurists who have expressed their opinion on the topic of the verses of sura 24 and its proof for covering the body, have emphasised the use of 'obligation' (*ilzām*), and they have considered the instruction of these two verses as obligatory and prohibitive. But, there is not a clear command in these verses to cover the head and neck (*sar va gardan*), and only by relying upon proofs by implication or expediency (*dalālat-i tażmanī yā iltizāmī*) do they say: 'The command to cover the bosoms with the *khimār* is a command for the necessity to put the *khimār* over the head too.' It is possible [that] this approach arises from an interpretation (*tafsīr*) of the verses with some narrations, the proofs of which are also unconvincing about the need to cover the head and neck. Basically, in these verses, particular cases for covering have been clearly indicated: **[72]**

First, covering the *ʿawrah*, for women and men.

Second, covering the bosoms for women because the breast (or collar) of the clothes of the season at that time were wide and open, and the other parts of a woman's body were visible within their collars when [they were] busy or [had some] activity outside the house or [when they were] receiving guests.

Since undergarments were not common, the possibility of provoking corruption increased because of this. Therefore, by using clothes in fashion at that time (*khimār*: a piece of material that they put on the head and tied behind the ears, and showed the neck, shoulders and ears in front of other people), in Q 24.31, the glorious Qur'an has only explained the covering of shoulders by using possibilities that were fashionable [at the time] and one cannot attribute any other definitive recommendation to the word of God, the Glorious.

Third, covering the hidden finery of a woman's body.

Fourth, according to custom, [there were] cases when covering was unusual, it was excluded from the recommendation to cover. In other words, the lack of covering of bodily parts was considered permissible where covering them was unfashionable.

Muqaddas Ardabili gave his opinion about the particulars of the [bodily] parts that were not usually covered: **[73]** If one looks at the apparent custom and tradition of the time [when] the verse was revealed, in particular, [the custom of] poor women, usually the neck, the upper chest, the forearms, the shins, and some other places too were uncovered, and in short, the command on the issue is problematic.[16] So, there are no clear words on the subject of 'the need to cover the head and neck' in the verses of sura 24. Rather, it confirms the permissibility of not covering parts of the body (that according to the custom of the time when the revelation came) as it was fashionable not to cover them. Historical research too confirms the unfashionable [nature] of covering the head and shoulders (in all circumstances and in all public places).

(12).[17] With regard to Q. 33.59,[18] and the lack of its proof for the need to cover the head and shoulders, I direct readers to the opinion of Ayatollah Muhaqqiq Damad, which was reported by Ayatollah Javadi Amuli in *Kitāb al-Ṣalāt*, 2/51–2:

> Discovering the secret of the descent of this verse and the confusion of its beginning and the end renders a conclusion contrary to proving the need of cover. It convinces the jurist that the command in this verse explains non-obligatory [but] preferential customs … and it is clear that these words and the language that

16 *Zubdat al-Bayān*, 2/687.

17 [The numbering of the text in Persian is faulty from this point onwards. The Persian text has this as point number 11, which we have already come across.]

18 ['O Prophet, tell your wives and daughters and the wives of the believers to draw their outer garments closer. That is more conducive to their being known, and not being injured. God is all-Forgiving, Merciful.']

> is used is not in principle an expression of requirement or necessity … So, the glorious verse, in relation to conveying necessity is incomplete …

By paying attention to expressions like 'non-obligatory' and 'incomplete in relation to conveying necessity' and 'is not in principle an expression for necessity', there is no doubt **[74]** in Muhaqqiq Damad's opinion that there is no proof for the need to cover parts of a woman's body in Q. 33.59.

In addition, Ayatollah Shaykh Muhammad Mahdi Shams al-Din foregrounded this understanding too: 'The language of this verse does not [indicate] compulsion or necessity; perhaps it expresses desirability and distaste more than anything' (*Masaʾil Ḥurja fī Fiqh al-Marāt*, 1/195).

If we combine these understandings with the causes [of revelation] in the glorious verse ('That is more conducive to their being known, and not being injured'), we reach the conclusion to which Tabarsi pointed in his commentary [called] *Majmaʿ al-Bayān* [in his discussion] of the occasion of the revelation of the verse. [This] is the very same thing that Muhaqqiq Damad also argued.

Now, if we consider permissible the various understandings of the commentators and jurists, we conclude nothing except [that there have been] differences of opinion among the commentators and jurists on the interpretation of this verse. Therefore, one cannot use this verse as a categorical proof for 'the need to cover a woman's head and neck'.

(13). I have never claimed 'consensus in denial for the need to cover the head and neck'. Rather, my effort about the existence or non-existence of consensus on this issue has been to prove the 'lack of certainty in consensus for the need to cover the head and neck'. Articles which have been written about jurists' differences of opinion on the particulars of [covering] the head and neck are among the sources that prove the existence of [this] difference of opinion. [In order] to demonstrate the existence of contrary opinions, one should not rely on the claim of a well-known consensus of the jurists.

If one refers to the well-known explanations of the Shiʿi jurists and 'their claims to the certainty of consensus', one can understand why I insist on 'the lack of certainty for consensus' and there being disagreement about covering the head and neck. **[75]** When it is claimed that the issue is consensual and that no disagreement exists, [then] the path of investigation on the origins of the issue and research on the proofs is virtually closed. Even some of the great jurists, like Muhaqqiq Naraqi (*Mustanad al-Shīʿa*, 4/242–3) and the Master of Laws, Mirza Abu'l-Qasim Qummi (*Ghanāʾim al-Ayyām* 2/255–256) have pointed out 'the main and basic proof on this issue is consensus'. The claim of consensus has been repeated in most books which until now I have made reference to, and in some other juristic books, and most of them are certainly related to the principle of the 'need to cover the *ʿawrat* or to cover the body'.

Even if the proof of certainty of consensus is applied here, it still does not provide an independent value for consensus because the claimed consensus could have been based on documentation. And it is clear that a consensus based on documentation is not a satisfactory reason.

In my opinion, the outcome of harmonising consensus (*jamʿ dalalī*) and the need to apply it on this subject does not lead to anything but accepting the reality that covering the head and neck is preferable (*istiḥāb*). This is not a baseless claim of a person unaware of Shiʿi jurisprudence. In fact, great people among the jurists and in *Uṣūl* and who are virtuous, pious and holy have paid attention to this.

Muqaddas Ardabili wrote on these particulars:

> If there is no fear that there is a claimed consensus, there has been and is a logical possibility of exceptions for [parts] other than the face and hands, in other words, the head and other things that have been visible most of the time.
>
> **[76]** So, hesitate at this point … 'the harmonisation of proofs' in a way which points to desirability is a clear and accepted method, so hesitate.[19]

A summary of the argument is that these narrations confirm the aforementioned exceptions (in particular, the face and hands up to the wrists) because showing them is [like] 'the lack of the need to cover the head', so what should one do about the feet?

I think the words of this Usuli Shiʿi jurist about 'the harmonisation of proofs', 'points to desirability (*istiḥab*)', and because this is the method of a clear and recognised path, are sufficient enough to support the point that we have been trying to make. Likewise, the expression 'lack of need to cover the head' is sufficiently clear and unambiguous.

(14). Hajj Aqa Riza Hamadani also has said on the reliable narration of Ibn Bakir from Imam Sadiq that 'the free Muslim woman can pray without covering the body':

> If it had not been for the well-known approaches of the jurists, there would

19 *Majmaʿ al-Fāʾida waʾl-Burhān*, 2/105.

> have existed a logical possibility for gathering proofs of these narrations and most of the narrations mentioned previously which indicates the desirability [of the practice].[20]

Therefore, the 'indication of desirability' is not something new or contrived: rather, it is based on [the views] of a number of great Shiʿi jurists who lived centuries ago and who also researched this topic, in particular 'covering the head' [and] they left it as a legacy. Paying attention **[77]** to accepted basic facts, to the legacy of the pious ancestors and to scientific choice on controversial problems, [these] are not innovations or a departure from the method and foundation of current jurisprudence.

The late Ayatollah Khuʾi does not consider 'the ulama's complete opposition to act on a reliable tradition' an obstruction to its value or worth, especially if it is a non-weak proof that has been reported (*Kitāb al-Ṭahāra* 3/359, and *Kitāb al-Ṣawm*, 2/103–4). So, what happens in cases which are opposed only by popular [understandings] of the ulama? (In other words, some of the ulama have put [the narration] into practice or they have considered it reliable.) Therefore, the logical and scientific possibility exists for indicating desirability in the same way.

(15). On the subject of the possible misuse of these kinds of discussions, I also agree with the people who hold this to be a concern. But one must ask them: 'What must one do?' Is the need to explain viewpoints which are yielded through accepted scientific methods and (which are completely clear) and the need to set out opposing views which is the only path for the survival of the Muhammadan sharia and its jurisprudence less than the need to guard the popular sharia (*ḥifz-i ʿurf-i mutasharia*)? Doesn't the scarcity of clear thinking in theological, moral and jurisprudential circles in the face of the unceasing needs of the present generation (even in scientific and lawful societies outside of the Islamic world) arise from excessive caution which always wants to defend the sharia?

With regard to some of his fatwas, wasn't the founder of the Islamic Republic the target of criticism from some of his friends and students? (My intention is not to compare myself with him.) And didn't he say in response, 'May God [wish it that] humans do not deny the commands of God for the sake of ...' Didn't he say in another place, 'Some caution is contrary to caution'?

Observing customs in all societies is a necessary task according to reason, and praise be to God my family situation too did not and does not need a strategy for

20 *Miṣbāḥ al-Faqīh*, 10/3854.

such thinking, but what should be done in the face of the conclusions of scientific study? **[78]**

A red line has been drawn for the controversy of covering the head and neck, and a sanctuary has been made for it. It is as if no duty existed but regurgitating repetitions and confirming populist understandings for researchers and jurists of the current age. Establishing the limits for [the hijab] has reached the extent that it has been called 'the Islamic flag', an invented name, and all the efforts of our great [scholars] in *fiqh* have been and are spent to protect it. There has been so much sensitivity on this topic, but in contrast, they have not and do not show any sensitivity in relation to the judgements (*fatawī*) and declarations of clear opinions on the topic of 'the lack of necessity of covering the *ʿawrat* of men and women' (which incites much more corruption than 'the lack of cover for the head and neck').

How can one accept that covering 'a woman's and man's *ʿawrat*' (which is more of a great instigator than 'the hair, head and neck') is unnecessary? Some of the great jurists understand it as 'a requirement of Muslim behaviour' (ʿAbd al-ʿAla Sabzavari, *Muhadhdhab al-Aḥkām*, 5/244) and even in some Persian books (the publisher of which receives support from official governmental and seminary centres) the commands are clearly stated. From another perspective, attention is not paid to the possibility of its misuse, but the declarations of opinions on the hair or the necks of women are looked at with all the more sensitivity.

Ayatollah Mutahhari writes on the particulars of covering the breast (*ḥajm*):

> *Chādur*s (not the face veil (*rū-band*) and the wide trousers *chāqchūr*) do not reveal humps or bumps. [This garment] is good for two reasons. First, it completely covers the shape of a woman's body; it does not show [bodily parts that] protrude or which are flat and slim (covering the shape is not necessary but undoubtedly it is a cause of discord). Second, at the present, [this garment] is a cypher for keeping distant.[21] **[79]**

He clearly says that 'covering the shape is not necessary' and it is a method that is related to covering in times other than prayer. Of course, his words [indicate] the 'desirability' of covering the shape.

The required approach of nearly all of the jurists on the subject of the necessity to cover a man's and a woman's body is this: even if a woman [wears] non-see through, tight leggings (*jūrāb-i shalvārī-yi astrij*) which shows the shape of the

21 *Yād-dāsht-hā*, 3/168.

ʿ*awrat*,[22] and a blouse from which the shape of body is visible, she can be present on the streets, on television, in cinema and theatre, so long as she wears a *miqnaʿa* that does not permit even a single hair to be seen. And this agrees completely with the law. With regard to hair and the head and the neck there is all of this attention lest it be the subject of misuse.

My claim is not that: 'One must not consider covering the shape of the body and ʿ*awrat* as legally necessary without a rational or narrated proof.' Rather I make the claim that 'if the criterion for the rational requirement or narrated necessity for covering parts of the body' is [its] ability to incite corruption, one can have no doubt about the success of inciting corruption due to not covering the shape of the ʿ*awrat* and the body compared to not covering the head and neck. Therefore, how can one consider 'the greater possibility for stimulation and inciting corruption as appropriate, and understand the possibility of lesser levels as forbidden?'

One can also see this well-known method in the words of great, contemporary jurists. Jurists like Ayatollah Burujirdi (*Taqrīr al-Baḥth* 1/75), the writings of Ayatollah Ishtihardi from the discussions of [Ayatollah] Burujirdi and Ayatollah Khomeini (*Taḥrīr al-Wasīla* 1/143) also adopt this approach. **[80]**

In any case, there are these topics and questions such as 'what difference exists between slave Muslim women and non-slaves in terms of incitement [to corruption] when covering the head and neck is not necessary for them but is necessary for the free?' (At the time of the imams some of the female slaves were from Iran and Europe, and they were more beautiful and attractive due to the variety in hair colour than many of the Arab women in Mecca, Medina and Yemen); [So] it is necessary to find a suitable response to defend the rationality of the Muhammadan sharia in today's world, just as in the past.

Since the source of beauty in the head and neck lies in the beauty of the 'eyes, eyebrow, nose, teeth, chin, and their arrangement', and Islam has considered it unnecessary to cover these, what particular attraction is there in a woman's hair and neck that the necessity of covering them has made this kind of topic so prominent among Muslims?

These questions, and issues like this for a scholar of jurisprudence and sharia, must produce a scientific and satisfying explanation, and if not, a researcher's reliance on imitation is not permissible.

Certainly, [there are] some criticisms, such as: 'If there was a difference of opinion on this issue, Riza Shah was aware of it. He used the court clerics to confirm "unveiling", and he took advantage [of them]. Since this was not the case,

22 [Literally 'the texture [of the leggings] does not show the colour [of the ʿ*awra*].']

it is clear that a difference of opinion did not exist!' [Even] after recalling differences of opinion (including documents and sources worthy of reference for the dear reader) and the report of [different] perspectives, there is not much [material] worth attention, and it is unscientific. In the same way, it was written on one of the internet sites connected to the authorities in Iran, 'This perspective is for defending Riza Shah's removal of the veil.'

The preferred approach of [this] writer is that 'more and complete covering is desirable'. So, from where comes the idea that 'an ignorant and oppressive person gives himself the permission **[81]** to remove by force the clothes that a woman likes, without her consent? What would happen to half of the population of a nation that approved of the sharia?'

Conclusion to the Discussion

In my opinion, all of the arguments presented [herein] provide the necessary resources to make a brief judgement on the subject of 'the suitability of paying attention, or not paying attention, to the claim of a scholar such as Ahmad Qabil', although [the arguments] may not provide sufficient resources [to yield] harmonious and shared views.

It is better for me to leave this part of the discussion to researchers and critics, so that they may reach a conclusion and assess this claim. They will have bestowed a favour upon him if they consider the author's view on this particular topic as worthy of attention, and they will have offered him their complementary views or scientific criticisms.

I wish for health, happiness, comfort, justice, safety and felicity in this world and the next for all readers from the merciful God. With these explanations I hope I have covered a little of a large [topic] and removed some of the ambiguity of my approach.

22 Tir 1384, Tajikistan (13 July 2006)

Part 4

HIJAB DEPENDING ON TIME AND PLACE: THE VIEWS OF MUHSIN KADIVAR

8

The Hijab Controversy Continues (2005–)

The discussions about the hijab by Nuri and Eshkevari unfolded during the Presidency of Muhammad Khatami, whose attempts at promoting dialogue among civilisations and social and institutional reform in Iran by encouraging rule by law and civil rights were thwarted by those whose understanding of Islam was not so 'liberal' and 'pluralistic'.[1] The complexity of categorising and defining Iranian politics and individual jurists and theologians and their views with such terms as 'liberal' and 'pluralistic' is evident in the example of Ayatollah Montazeri. As noted in Part Three, Montazeri was the spiritual guide of Ahmad Qabil; both were highly critical of ʿAli Khamenei and both were popularly regarded as upholders of the Green Movement. Although they shared much politically, there is no reason to assume a corresponding similarity in jurisprudential matters, as Qabil noted,

> Several times I asked my late teacher in written form about issues such as the problem of the hijab. Some friends outside of the country, some Arab and some Persian-speaking students asked him, 'to what extent is Ahmad Qabil's view related to yours[?]' He explained that merely being a student of someone does not mean that their jurisprudential views must be the same. At any rate, the difference of my opinion on the problem of the hijab with that of my master was not the [only] one, as on other jurisprudential issues it was clear that although I was his student, his opinion, with all its parts, was not the same as mine.[2]

1 See Arshin Adib-Moghaddam, 'The pluralist Momentum in Iran and the Future of the Reform Movement', *Third World Quarterly* 27.4, 2006, 665–74.
2 Ahmad Qabil, 'Amr ghayr-i ʿaqlānī dar sharīʿat pazīrufta na-mī-shavad' [Non-rational acts in the sharia are not acceptable], *Vaṣiyat bi Millat-i Irān*, 401.

Montazeri had been at the vanguard of the Islamic Revolution and was designated as Khomeini's successor. He played a major role in the institutionalisation of the Supreme jurist, or the *valī-yi faqīh*, in the late 1970s, but by the mid-1980s he had become disillusioned at the course that the revolution was taking. In particular, he was concerned by the mass-killings carried out in the prisons.[3] By 1985, Montazeri had even changed his mind about the nature of *vilāyat-i faqih*, and he was dismissed from his position as Khomeini's deputy. Nevertheless, Montazeri attracted a very different support base during the 1990s as his antipathy towards Khamenei became evident, and his support for Khatami became known. He won even more support for his criticisms of the regime in June 2009, in a fatwa that 'established him as the spiritual guide of the Green Movement'.[4] He also insisted that violence should not be used in the political disputes that engulfed Iran, and his fatwas stated the Qur'an did not endorse execution for apostates and that even Bahais had the same civil rights as other citizens.[5] And yet, despite this apparent 'liberalism', Montazeri's views on the hijab were very traditional, and very similar to those advocated by Ayatollah Mutahhari.

Montazeri's views on the hijab appear in a volume published in 1389/2010–11, a year after his death, titled *Pāsukh bi Pursish-hā-yi Dīnī* (*Answers to Religious Questions*).[6] The ninth chapter is titled 'Masā'il-i pūshish va ḥijāb' (Issues of covering and hijab) and contains fifteen questions relating to the hijab, to which he provides short but very interesting answers. Unfortunately, there are no dates given for either questions or answers, but Montazeri's answers which repeatedly prohibit the use of violence to enforce the hijab suggest that these date from after 1985, or at least from the period of Khatami's presidency when he increasingly enjoyed something of a dissident status.

Throughout, Montazeri is unequivocal that the hijab is compulsory (*vājib*), and he states that it is one of the orders of God (*az dastūrāt-i khudā*)[7] and one of the necessary commands of Islam (*az aḥkām-i żarūri-yi islām*).[8] He argues that a woman's hair is part of her *zinat* (finery), referring to the Qur'an (24.31). He

3 See Siavoshi, *Montazeri*, 129–34.
4 Ulrich von Schwerin, *The Dissident Mullah: Ayatollah Montazeri and the Struggle for Reform in Revolutionary Iran*, London 2015, 227.
5 Anja Pistor Hatami, 'Nonunderstanding and Minority Formation in Iran', *Iran* LV, 2017, 92–3.
6 *Pāsukh bi Pursish-hā-yi Dīnī* [*Answers to Religious Questions*], Tehran 1389/2010–11, also available on https://amontazeri.com/book/posesh/356.
7 *Pāsukh bi Pursish-hā-yi Dīnī*, 361.
8 *Pāsukh bi Pursish-hā-yi Dīnī*, 364.

states, '[*Zinat*] is something personal for a woman, and it is the cause of pleasure among men and attracts their attention … this meaning [of *zinat*] is a reality which has been created in the nature and make-up of women and men.'[9] In one answer, he essentialises gender in the following manner:

> The nature of women and men and their physical and spiritual make-up is different. Women have been created in such a way that [their] spiritual dimension is more delicate and more sensitive than that of men. Their nature is in such a way that in the course of history they have always been ill-treated and abused by men. For this reason, Islam has wanted to protect them and it pays more attention to them.[10]

One of the questions asked why men were not required to cover their hair, and the petitioner enquired 'is the nature (*jins*) of my hair different from that of men?' Unfortunately, Montazeri did not dwell too long on the question; he responded quite simply that, 'Women are precious jewels which other [people] desire. Every rational person wants to hide valuable things from the eyes of other people.'[11] Interestingly, one question put to Montazeri asked if it was hair that was inherently the problem, and if head hair were to be shaven, would it still be necessary for women to wear the hijab? (Such a question calls to mind Kiarostami's film *10*, discussed in Part Three.) Montazeri replied, 'A woman's finery is not limited to her hair, rather, her complexion (*bashara*) and skin of her head, like other parts of her body, are enticing for men.'[12]

Montazeri also responded to the question of whether people should accept out-of-date, validating commands (*aḥkām-i imżāʾī az rūz khārij shuda*),[13] which as mentioned before played such a significant part in ʿAbdollah Nuri's reformulation of Islam, and as espoused by Eshkevari. As Nuri explained, many commands merely validated existing practices, and so such commands were time-bound and thus flexible. Montazeri did not specifically address the question, but rather than viewing the *aḥkām-i imżāʾī* as validating existing cultural practice, he argued that the rules pertaining to the hijab were part of the religion of Islam that could not be negated. He appealed to the majority of believers in society, for he claimed that the incorrectly observed hijab weakened the rights of those who wore the hijab

9 *Pāsukh bi Pursish-hā-yi Dīnī*, 362.
10 *Pāsukh bi Pursish-hā-yi Dīnī*, 368.
11 *Pāsukh bi Pursish-hā-yi Dīnī*, 358.
12 *Pāsukh bi Pursish-hā-yi Dīnī*, 363.
13 *Pāsukh bi Pursish-hā-yi Dīnī*, 364.

properly. Linked to the discussion of the hijab being a pre-Islamic Arab custom, Montazeri observed in one of his answers that the head-covering current at the time covered the hair, and so it did not need to be explicitly stated in the Qurʾan. This reflection was a response to a point made in a letter that verse 24.31 of the Qurʾan only commands women to pull their garments over themselves.[14] Montazeri was uncompromising in the requirement for women to wear the hijab, even if her profession required her to remove it: 'If a women has a job or she desires to do something that makes it impossible for her to observe [the necessity] of the hijab, she must abandon that job or that task and choose another so that she is able to observe the legal [requirements] of the hijab.'[15] He offered only a very slight compromise by stating, 'In that condition it may be argued that to the extent that is necessary and is needed to avoid extreme difficulty, she can take off that part of hijab that has to be removed. This is with the condition that taking off Islamic cover in these situations does not make her forget and forego the hijab, which is the symbol of religion.'[16] In spite of this concession, Montazeri's perspective resembles that of Ayatollah Mutahhari, and he even advised his readers to refer to the latter's work on the hijab.[17]

However, Montazeri was at pains to remove himself from the culture that permitted squads of para-military police to enforce the 'proper' hijab. The following is a typical example of this attitude:

> Of course, legal commands must not be executed with force and in an irrational fashion for certainly this will bring about the opposite effect. Rather, [the legal commands] must be enforced with reason, philosophical explanation and its rational necessity, and with wise and compassionate council. And the levels of 'enjoining the good and forbidding the evil' with its conditions [must be] considered and observed. It seems that when understandings are rational and logical, and the philosophy of the social commands of the holy law, including the hijab, are explained clearly, then reason will not deny them, but

14 *Pāsukh bi Pursish-hā-yi Dīnī*, 363.
15 *Pāsukh bi Pursish-hā-yi Dīnī*, 361.
16 *Pāsukh bi Pursish-hā-yi Dīnī*, 361. Montazeri's answer to this question is of interest, in light of the comments that were recorded by Haleh Esfandiari, *Reconstructed Lives: Women and Iran's Islamic Revolution*, Baltimore 1997. Esfandiari reports one Iranian woman who commented, 'They just don't understand that you cannot perform surgery on a patient wearing a loose robe with wide long sleeves and with a *maghnae* strangling your throat,' 137.
17 *Pāsukh bi Pursish-hā-yi Dīnī*, 358. See also page 367 where Montazeri answered a question that raises the distinction made by Mutahhari that made the hijab a privilege (*masūniyat*) and not a restriction (*maḥdūdiyat*).

> it will rather accept them and support that command, or at least remain silent before it. It will not, as it is claimed, attempt to overturn it.[18]
>
> In cases where there is an infringement, it is incumbent upon people, without [committing] violence or irrational acts, to adopt methods that make people obliged to wear the hijab.[19]
>
> With regard to people who do not observe [the regulations to wear] the hijab, the Islamic state must encourage them to observe the Islamic hijab with correct explanations and cultural steps. Policing and violent acts in these cases usually have the opposite effect.[20]

Although Montazeri held 'reformist' views on political matters, such as the need to ameliorate the system of government, namely the *vilāyat-i faqīh*, his views on the hijab as indicated above fell in line with those of Khamenei, the Supreme Leader and representative of the *vilāyat-i faqīh*. Khamenei has demonstrated unflinching rigidity in his categorical endorsement of the hijab, which is revealed in his numerous speeches over the years, and which have been uploaded onto his website.[21] While Khamenei has not composed a single, lengthy work on the topic, he has consistently returned to the issue and given his support to the necessity of observing the hijab to uphold Islamic morality. His position reflects the views of Ayatollah Mutahhari,[22] and he has been unswerving in his vociferous opposition to *bad-ḥijābī*. His commitment to obstruct cultural erosion, in addition to the belief that the hijab is sanctioned by sacred scripture, has resulted in his consistent opposition to *bad-ḥijābī*, typified in his statement in response to the movement of 'Girls of Inqalab Street' outlined in the introduction to this work. Khamenei most likely feels that he does not need to justify his position with an extended piece of writing, as there are many others among the ulama who endorse his position. A good example is Grand Ayatollah Makarim-Shirazi whose perspective may be found in an essay called 'Guidelines to the true realisation of hijab and modesty in the Islamic society from the viewpoint of Grand Ayatollah Makarim-Shirazi',[23] and which has been uploaded onto his website. However, of

18 *Pāsukh bi Pursish-hā-yi Dīnī*, 365.
19 *Pāsukh bi Pursish-hā-yi Dīnī*, 360.
20 *Pāsukh bi Pursish-hā-yi Dīnī*, 364.
21 The website is called The Office of the Supreme Leader. See: http://www.leader.ir/en.
22 There is no indication in Mutahhari's writings that he envisaged the use of force to implement the policy on hijab.
23 See: https://makarem.ir/main.aspx?lid=1&typeinfo=1&catid=44908&pageindex=0&mid=400479.

interest is Makarim-Shirazi's fatwa of 2016, which may be seen to offer a degree of flexibility in light of the 'onslaught' of Islamophobic sentiment in Europe and North America. His fatwa states:

> If committed Muslim females are deprived of higher education, this will prepare the ground for irresponsible and non-religious people to occupy top posts; therefore, the pious believers will be authorised under such special circumstances to unveil, but in other cases they are to abide by and maintain the hijab.[24]

Despite the pressures from the state to conform to the Islamic Republic's 'decent' sartorial standards, there has been a consistent degree of opposition during the timeframe in question. Many women have felt sufficiently empowered to initiate a campaign to advance their rights in a movement known as the 'one million signatures for the repeal of discriminatory laws', which was launched on 28 August 2006. It was led by a number of activists, the most well-known of whom was Shirin Ebadi, and the campaign soon won the support of leading film directors, including Tahmina Milani and Rakhshan Bani-Itemad, as well as the poet Simin Bihbihani.[25] The campaign was not specifically targeted at the hijab, which received little attention in its literature compared to other issues, such as the lack of equality in marriage and divorce, child custody, and family relations. Also figuring prominently were the right to pass on citizenship to one's children; equality in blood money, inheritance, and giving testimony; access to leadership positions; changing the age of criminal responsibility; and banning of honour killing and stoning. The issue of the hijab had to share the bill with a number of other pressing issues facing women. Many of the leaders and activists of the campaign suffered harassment and some were even arrested and imprisoned.[26] Although the campaign did not secure the one million signatures, it did 'create a discourse on women's rights at the highest levels of government and in the public'.[27]

24 Islamic Republic News Agency, 'Senior cleric's new fatwa authorizes Muslim female students overseas to unveil', 6 July 2016, http://www.irna.ir/en/News/82139546.
25 'One million signatures battle gender equality', https://tavaana.org/en/content/one-million-signatures-battle-gender-equality-iran#_ednref16.
26 'The Campaign from a Different Perspective: A Series of Articles to Commemorate the Campaign's 4th Anniversary', http://www.learningpartnership.org/lib/oms-4years.
27 Sussan Tahmasebi, 'The One Million Signatures Campaign: An Effort Born on the Streets', Amnesty International Middle East North Africa Regional Office, http://amnestymena.org/en/Magazine/Issue20/TheOneMillionSignatureCampaigninIran.aspx?media=print.

The themes of this campaign reflect the 'larger' issues pertaining to women in Iran at this time. And this is also shown in the writings of Sadiqa Vasmaqi,[28] who was a professor at the Faculty of Theology at the University of Tehran. With a deep knowledge of theology and jurisprudence, Vasmaqi became a champion of woman's rights, which are articulated in a scholarly fashion in her 2008 publication *Zan, Fiqh, Islām.*[29] In this book, Vasmaqi did not concern herself with the hijab (which was referred to in passing), but there is a pronounced emphasis on weightier issues such as polygamy, marriage and divorce, custody of children, women's testimony in law, and female judges.[30] Vasmaqi's book, just like the 'one million signatures' campaign, came in the wake of Khatami's two terms in the presidential office, and despite its relatively unsuccessful attempts to establish a society based on the execution of law, at the very least, issues related to gender became the subject of discussion. In other words, it was not just senior mullas in the political structures, such as Khamenei, who controlled the agenda on issues such as the hijab. Khatami had refused to be drawn into the hijab argument. The range of issues articulated by the reformists fed into the defensive responses by those in authority that the hijab was a minor issue and that Iran faced more serious difficulties that needed to be addressed. However, Khatami's successor as president, Mahmud Ahmadinejad, was soon to be drawn into the issue.

While the dispute between Khamenei and Khatami was clearly concerned with the rule of law and the openness of the Islamic regime, the dispute between Khamenei and the subsequent president, Mahmud Ahmadinejad (who served two terms as president between 2005–2013) represented a different kind of conflict, but which involved argumentation over the hijab. The disagreement between Khamenei and Ahmadinejad centred on the nature of power in Iran, that is to say, seminary versus non-seminary. While Khamenei's seminary background is long and well established, Ahmadinejad had no such credentials. Nevertheless, it has been argued that he attempted to derive some kudos by appealing over the heads of senior mullas, thus freeing his hand as President of the Islamic Republic to

28 Sadiqa Vasmaqi spells her name somewhat idiosyncratically Sedigheh Vasmaghi.
29 This has been translated into English as *Women, Jurisprudence, Islam*, trans. M. Ashna and Philip G. Kreyenbroeck, Wiesbaden 2014.
30 Following the 2009 Presidential election, Vasmaqi participated in the protest movement and was 'forced' to leave Iran in 2012. She went to Sweden and taught some courses in Uppsala University. On retuning to Iran in 2017, she was arrested and held for several weeks before being released. See 'Iran: writer and poet Dr Sedigheh Vasmaghi arrested upon return from Sweden', English Pen Freedom to Write Freedom to Read, 3 November 2017, https://www.englishpen.org/campaigns/iran-writer-and-poet-dr-sedigheh-vasmaghi-arrested-upon-return-from-sweden/.

implement policies that seminarian figures in the political establishment might potentially reject (such as the issue of the hijab). Ahmadinejad commenced a programme which he attempted to legitimise with reference to messianic support. This involved making claims that he had witnessed the Mahdi whilst delivering a speech to the United Nations in New York,[31] and he also advanced the development of the Jamkaran construction programme, a site near Qum which had associations of a messianic nature connected to the Twelfth Imam.[32] Related to this stand-off between Khamenei and Ahmadinejad was the latter's stance on the hijab. In a televised interview, Ahmadinejad remarked that the government had no role in the fight against *bad-ḥijāb*: 'The government has nothing to do with it and doesn't interfere in it. We consider it insulting when a man and a woman are walking in the streets and they're asked about their relationship. No one has the right to ask about it.'[33] These remarks, made in 2010, need to be considered in the context of the growing debate on the hijab, and the remark made by the temporary prayer leader of Tehran, Kazim Siddiqi, that 'many women who do not dress modestly [i.e. do not have appropriate hijab] lead young men astray, corrupt their chastity and spread adultery in society, which increases earthquakes'.[34] Some observers have claimed that Ahmadinejad advocated a cultural approach to earthquake control that would persuade women to adopt the hijab rather than a forceful policy using the patrols to roam the streets and impound people's cars or fine or whip offenders.[35] Others have been more critical and argue that he was 'quick to send *gasht-i irshād* patrol units into the streets of large cities; their task was to watch whether women in the streets, shopping centres or on public transport

31 Abbas Amanat, *Apocalyptic Islam and Iranian Shiʿism*, London 2009.
32 See the discussion in Amanat, *Apocalyptic Islam and Iranian Shiʿism*, 227–32.
33 'Ahmadinejad, the hijab and women in his car', Radio Free Europe, 16 June 2010, https://www.rferl.org/a/Ahmadinejad_The_Hijab_And_Women_In_His_Car/2073879.html.
34 'Women to blame for earthquakes, says Iran cleric', *The Guardian* 19 April 2010, https://www.theguardian.com/world/2010/apr/19/women-blame-earthquakes-iran-cleric. An interesting twist to this episode came when Jennifer McCreight of Purdue University started 'Boobquake day' on her Facebook page for 26 April, and she encouraged women to wear low cut or very tight tops. It is claimed that hundreds of thousands participated via Facebook and Twitter. See Pat Pilcher, 'Islamic cleric causes Boobquake', *NZ Herald* 27 April 2010, https://www.nzherald.co.nz/technology/news/article.cfm?c_id=5&objectid=10641150. Of interest is that this campaign foreshadowed the 'My Stealthy Freedom' campaign against the compulsory hijab, initiated by Masih ʿAlinejad several years later.
35 Thomas Erdbrink, 'Ahmadinejad and clerics fight over scarves', *The Washington Post* 22 July 2011, https://www.washingtonpost.com/world/middle-east/ahmadinejad-and-clerics-fight-over-scarves/2011/07/12/gIQAhoqJPI_story.html?utm_term=.7ed77022d3c5.

complied with the principles of hijab'.[36] Whatever the case, the conflict between Ahmadinejad and Khamenei spilled out into the public in 2011, when the controversy intensified over a 259-page supplement on the hijab, published by a newspaper that was regarded as Ahmadinejad's mouthpiece.[37] Although the supplement endorsed the hijab, the problem lay in the attempt to place the hijab in a historical context, which potentially opened the door to divorcing rulings on the hijab from connections with sacred scripture. One article even argued that black *chādur*s were not necessarily based on the Persian culture, but rather were 'imported from the West'.[38] The accusation that the rationale behind Ahmadinejad's statements and position on the hijab reflected a concern to increase his standing 'among the middle classes who despise him'[39] may not be too far from the truth.

And support for a less rigid approach came from within the seminarian establishment. For example, Muhammad Mujtahid-Shabistari, who had been 'persuaded' to resign from his university post in Tehran in 2006, acknowledged in 2008 that the Prophet did not criticise women who did not wear a veil. He added that such a 'distortion' occurred much later, during the Abbasid period.[40] A few years later, another member of the ulama, in a much more indirect fashion, presented an interpretation of how women wore the hijab during the Prophet's lifetime, which seemed to indicate a more relaxed approach. Amir Turkashvand composed a large work (of over one thousand pages) titled *Ḥijāb-i Sharʿī dar ʿAṣr-i Payghambar* (*Legal Hijab in the Age of the Prophet*) in 2010–11. While he did not seek to prescribe how the hijab should be worn in contemporary Iran, some have considered his caution and refusal to make explicit statements about the contemporary situation a smokescreen for a more malleable policy on the hijab.[41] It is perhaps for this reason that Turkashvand did not receive permission

36 Magdalena Rodziewicz, 'From Compulsory Unveiling (*kashf-e hijāb*) to Compulsory Veiling (*hijāb-e ejbari*): Hijab in the Iranian Perspective', *Politics and Society in the Islamic World*, ed. Izabela Kończak, Magdalena Lewicka and Marta Widy-Behiesse, Warsaw 2016, 235.

37 Ramin Mostaghim, 'Iran: Ahmiadinejad's newspaper in fight with hardliners over hijab', 16 August 2011, http://latimesblogs.latimes.com/babylonbeyond/2011/08/ahmadinejad-newspaper-hijab.html.

38 'Iran's Judiciary Jails Ahmadinejad Press Allies', *Iranwire* 20 June 2016, http://www.journalismisnotacrime.com/en/features/1325/.

39 Ramin Mostaghim, 'Iran: Ahmadinejad's newspaper in fight with hardliners over hijab', *Los Angeles Times* 16 Auguest 2011.

40 Fatma Segir, 'Interview with Muhammad Mujtahid Shabistari (Part 1): "Islam Is a Religion, Not a Political Agenda"', https://en.qantara.de/content/interview-with-mohammad-mojtahed-shabestari-part-1-islam-is-a-religion-not-a-political.

41 See Zahra Jalaeipour, *Hijab in Transition Dress Code Changes amongst Iranian Diaspora*

from the state to publish his book. Nevertheless, the work has circulated online, and it has received much attention from both the ulama and secular scholars.[42] (Kadivar makes a reference to the work as we shall see.)

Expectations of a more moderate approach to the hijab among the seminarians, along with the support of the reformists, may have been one of the reasons for the electoral success of Hassan Rouhani who was elected President of Iran in 2013. That being said, Rouhani's evolving perspectives on the hijab reflect the political maneuverings and developments within the Islamic Republic. At some points in his career, Rouhani has advanced a strict policy of veiling. In his memoirs he has observed that 'in March 1979, it was not easy to talk about a dress code or hijab. A lot of women did not have head scarves at schools and offices immediately after the February 1979 revolution. Women in hijab were a minority'. He added, 'I was tasked to make hijab compulsory in the offices that were part of the army. First, I told the women at the office of the Joint Chief of Staff to come to work with hijab. Some of them objected to the idea, but I stood firm. Then I made the hijab mandatory across the armed forces gradually, although I told them they did not necessarily need the head to toe black cover (*chādur*).'[43] However, Rouhani's view on the subject seems to have mellowed somewhat. Perhaps his experience of study in Scotland contributed to a less strict understanding, or maybe it was his realisation of the difficulty in satisfying different interests as president. Rouhani has been cautious in his pronouncements about the hijab, and has had to use allusion and hints which require deciphering between the lines. Thus, his comment in 2014 that 'you can't send people to heaven by the whip'[44] has been understood as a critique of the *bad-ḥijābī* vigilante squads. However, his ambivalence on the specific issue of the hijab is all too apparent, as, for example, when challenged by a French journalist with pictures of unveiled Iranian women, he responded by saying, 'What an issue! We have so many issues, so we don't have time for these things. Everyone in Iran is free in their own private lives to do as they please. But when someone lives in Iran, they should abide by the laws of the country.'[45] In

in London, Submitted for MPhil University of Sussex, May 2016, 109, http://sro.sussex.ac.uk/72698/1/Jalaeipour%2C%20Zahra.pdf.

42 Amir Turkashvand, *Ḥijāb-i Sharʿī dar ʿAṣr-i Payghambar* [*Legal Hijab in the Age of the Prophet*], https://www.academia.edu/1228672/.

43 Majid Muhammadi, 'How Iran's Ruling Clerics Distort Facts About Hijab', Radio Farda, 4 February 2018, https://en.radiofarda.com/a/iran-hijab-khamenei-facts/29017675.html.

44 'Rouhani clashes with Iranian police over undercover hijab agents', Reuters, 2 June 2016, https://www.reuters.com/article/us-iran-rights-rouhani-idUSKCN0XH0WH.

45 Heather Saul, 'French journalist confronts President Rouhani with picture of an Iranian woman without a hijab', *The Independent* 12 November 2015, https://www.independent.

this particular instance, Rouhani's response echoes the defensive perspectives of those who staunchly uphold institutionalised values of the Islamic Republic and complain of the Western cultural onslaught that minimises the significance of the hijab. But the opponents of mandatory hijab point out that it is not just a simple issue of covering the hair, as it is in fact symbolic of something much greater. Masih ʿAlinejad, the founder of the White Wednesdays campaign, is all too familiar with such views and counters by claiming that 'fighting compulsory hijab is about much more than hair and dressing modestly, just as Rosa Parks refusing to give her seat to a white man on a bus in Montgomery, Alabama, in 1955 was about more than an unjust seating policy. It's about fighting for what is right'.[46]

Rouhani is in a difficult position because he has had to satisfy different constituencies. On the one hand, he has to pacify the 'reformist' elements of society, but he cannot afford to be too 'liberal' which would completely alienate the more 'conservative' factions in Iran and deliver them with an opportunity to further erode his already tenuous grip on power. Typifying the continued attempts to promote the hijab was the establishment of the 'International Week of Hijab and Chastity', the dates of which were 8–14 July 2016.[47] Minu Aslani, the director of Iran's Women's Basij Society, said that 'the week will be celebrated simultaneously in 70 cities across the world … Brochures in different languages will be distributed and interviews will be conducted'.[48] And there has also been a continual stream of publications that promote the virtues of wearing the hijab, such as the three-volume collection of articles published under the title *Ḥijāb*.[49]

Nevertheless, Rouhani's attempt to limit the force used to 'persuade' women to wear the hijab is not the only one emanating from senior mullas, as was suggested in the introduction to this book. A good example is the article published in 2013 by Ayatollah Muhammad ʿAli Ayazi,[50] who at one point was one of the

---

co.uk/news/people/french-journalist-confronts-president-rouhani-with-picture-of-an-iranian-woman-without-a-hijab-from-a6732001.html.

46 Masih Alinejad, *The Wind in My Hair: My Fight for Freedom in Modern Iran*, London 2018, 189.

47 The dates were chosen to commemorate the events of the Gawharshad Mosque incident in Mashhad of 12 July 1935 (discussed in Part Two).

48 Hessam Emami, 'Inside Iran, a Diversity of Opinions Emerging over Hijab', *Iranian Diplomacy* 17 July 2016, http://www.irdiplomacy.ir/en/news/1961173/inside-iran-a-diversity-of-opinions-emerging-over-hijab.

49 *Ḥijāb: Masʾūliyat-hā va Ikhtiyārāt-i Dawlat-i Islāmī* [*Hijab: The Responsibilities and Rights of an Islamic State*], ed. Ibrahim Shafiʾi Sarvastani, Qum 1387/2008–9.

50 Muhammad ʿAli Ayazi, 'Naqd va barrasī-yi adilla-yi fiqhī-yi ilzām-i ḥukumat-i ḥijāb' [A critique and study of jurisprudential reasons of the governmental requirement [to wear] the hijab], *Fiqh*, 31 Tir 1392/ 22 June 2013.

deputies of Montazeri. Ayazi's views on the hijab are close to those of Montazeri, as he regards it necessary according to the sharia. He considers the hijab a private matter, like praying, paying religious tax, and just like people's use of their own property not a social concern that is punishable.[51] Here Ayazi involves himself in an intricate matter to which others have alluded.[52] It may be a relatively easy matter to determine whether or not the Qur'an or sayings of the imams have a particular stance on whether a woman's head should be covered, and if so, when. It is another matter to decide on whether head-covering is a public or private matter. It is an issue described well by Muhsin Kadivar (to be discussed later), for it is like the wall of a house, which from one side pertains to the private sphere and the home, but at the same time the wall may be seen by others, and in this sense it is public.

Nevertheless, in his article, Ayazi begins by claiming that all Islamic schools agree on confirming the necessity to cover the body, as it is a command enshrined in the Qur'an, and so is eternal and for all times. Although Ayazi appears to include the head within the general term for body (*badan*), he asks whether there is juristic precedent to punishing *bad-ḥijābī*. There are some, he says, that believe it is necessary according to the sharia to wear the hijab, and that it is illegal (*ḥarām*) to do otherwise. In addition, these people believe such behaviour is punishable, and hold that it is a governmental right to enforce the hijab. He gives seven reasons that such advocates of the hijab offer, and methodically proceeds to rebut their rationale, one by one. This is not the place to summarise these arguments, but Ayazi concludes his article by saying: 'If the Islamic government wants the culture of hijab to dominate society, and change [the culture so that it becomes] a general custom, it must use cultural paths and indirect methods together with programming, and along with expertise and observing psychological subtleties.'

The views of Ayazi and Montazeri represent one dimension of changing attitudes within the Islamic Republic, and another shift is represented by the alternative opinion of Ahmad Qabil. The full range of seminarian views has been completed in the compositions of Muhsin Kadivar. All of these views reflect the responses, largely from Iranian women, who have expressed dissatisfaction with mandatory

51 See Introduction, note 33.

52 For instance, Kadivar points out that even if the hijab is considered necessary according to the sharia, there are other devotional rites, such as fasting, which are necessary before the sharia, but non-observance of which is not punishable. See Kadivar, 'Ḥijāb: hadd-i sharīʿ, hadd-i qanūnī' [The hijab: the religious limit and the legal limit], https://kadivar.com/?p=2116.

veiling. The Iranian state authorities have tended to react harshly to those who do not comply with its policy on hijab, typified by campaigns to crack down on '*bad-ḥijābī*'. The hijab, or rather the non-observance of the 'correct' hijab, has become something of a litmus test to reflect the purity and morality of society and the extent of cultural erosion in Iran.

9

The Worldview of Muhsin Kadivar

The Life of Muhsin Kadivar[1]

Born in 1959, Muhsin Kadivar was seventeen when he entered the University of Shiraz to study chemistry in 1977. He was soon caught up in the pre-revolutionary disturbances which resulted in his arrest by SAVAK. After the Islamic Revolution, he became interested in humanities, and in 1981 began to study theology in Qum under several eminent theologians and jurists. In 1988, Kadivar was given permission to exercise *ijtihād* by Ayatollah Montazeri, and was later appointed as one of the deputies who answered questions sent to his website.[2] Kadivar continued to study, earning a PhD in Islamic Philosophy from Tarbiyat Mudarris University (TMU) in Tehran in 1999. At the same time, he was active in expressing his dissatisfaction with the trajectory of policies in the Islamic Republic. Typifying this was his refusal to support the revisions to the constitution of the Islamic Republic in 1989 which gave more power to the Supreme Leader. His activities in Qum were restricted from 1995 onwards, following certain publications which were critical of the regime. Considering him a threat to the Islamic regime, on 17 February 1999 the Special Clerical Court brought charges against him and sentenced him to 18 months in prison, for both a public speech in Isfahan (which was titled 'The *Shar*ʿ Prohibition against Terror'), and an interview with the reformist newspaper *Khurdād* in which he gave a damning twenty-year 'report card' of the Islamic Republic.[3] Kadivar was released from prison in July 2000.

1 For a biography see the homepage of Kadivar's website: https://enkadivar.com/sample-page-2/.

2 See Introduction, note 39.

3 The proceedings of Kadivar's trial at the Special Clerical Court are recorded in Zahra Rudi-Kadivar, ed., *Bahāʾī-yi Āzādī: Dafāʿiyat-i Muhsin Kadivar dar Dādgāh-i Vizha-i*

Between 1998 and 2005, Kadivar occupied senior academic positions, perhaps the most prestigious being the Elected Chair of the Department of Philosophy at Tarbiyat Mudarris University. From 2001, he spent considerable time outside of Iran, lecturing and researching at various institutions in the US, Japan and Europe. His tortured relationship with the Iranian regime continued, however, as in 2007 his passport was confiscated at Imam Khomeini Airport in Tehran, and he was told that he could not leave the country. The Special Clerical Court and the Ministry of Intelligence filed a complaint, interrogated and accused him of 'propagating against the regime and publishing untruths with an intent to disturb public minds'. Despite the confiscation of his passport in 2007, Kadivar was able to go to the United States in 2008 at the invitation of the University of Virginia, and he subsequently accepted a post at Duke University in North Carolina, where he has remained since.

Kadivar's opposition to, and criticism of, certain policies within the Islamic Republic roughly coincided with the activities of Ahmad Qabil. Indeed, the similarities between the two are striking; aside from a five-year age difference, they were both students and loyal supporters of Ayatollah Montazeri, both were firm advocates of New Religious Thinking among those with a seminarian background, both became associated with the Green Movement, both were forced to defend themselves before the Special Clerical Court in Tehran, and both endured subsequent periods in prison for their convictions.

Kadivar's Compositions

The books, articles, chapters, speeches and other outputs by Kadivar are all available online on his website.[4] A limited number of the articles on his website are in English (translated from the Persian) and they demonstrate his commitment to an overhaul of the jurisprudential system by stressing the importance of justice and reason in the *maqāṣid al-sharīʿa*, which needs to be prioritised at the expense of traditional jurisprudential foregrounding of specific Qurʾanic commands. These English articles focus on human rights, gender and jurisprudence. Perhaps the most significant is his composition titled, 'From Historical Islam to Spiritual Islam' ('Az islām-i tārīkhī bi islām-i maʿnawī'), where the implication of taking justice and reason to their logical conclusions are fully articulated. This

Rūḥaniyyat [*The Price of Freedom: In Defence of Mohsen Kadivar at the Special Clerical Court*], Tehran 1378/1999–2000.

4 See: https://en.kadivar.com.

work represents 'a departure from his previous published works … [for] Kadivar went on to present an unequivocal alternative after critiquing two approaches in Islamic jurisprudence'.[5] Kadivar himself claimed that 'this article is a turning point in my intellectual life'.[6] He has continued this line of rethinking Islam for the contemporary period with articles such as 'Ḥuqūq-i bashar va rawshanfikrī-yi dīnī' ('Human Rights and Enlightened Religious Thought').[7] His works have also been the subject of a number of academic studies, which have either focused in a general way on his jurisprudential ideas, or else foregrounded the political implications of his ideas. None have focused on his views of the hijab.[8]

The English translations of Kadivar's articles represent a fraction of his Persian academic activity. These Persian publications form a coherent whole that emphasises the political nature of jurisprudence. One block of work focuses on the deficiencies of the Iranian political system, and these books include *Naẓariya-hā-yi Dawlat dar Fiqh-i Shīʿa* (*Theories of the State in Shiʿi Jurisprudence*),[9] *Daqdaqa-hā-yī Ḥukūmat-i Dīnī* (*The Concerns of a Religious Government*),[10] *Ḥukūmat-i Intiṣābī* (*Government by Appointment*),[11] and *Ḥukūmat-i Vilāyī*

5 Yasuyuki Matsunaga, 'Mohsen Kadivar, an advocate of postrevivalist Islam', *British Journal of Middle East Studies* 34.3, 2007, 324.

6 Kadviar's article appeared in English as 'From Traditional Islam to Islam as an End in Itself', *Die Welt des Islams* 51, 2011, 459–84. For his claim about the significance of the article see the first footnote.

7 Originally published in *Aftāb* 27, 1382/2003, 54–9; 28, 1382/2003, 106–15. Translated as 'Human Rights and Intellectual Islam', *New Directions in Islamic Thought: Exploring Reform and Muslim Tradition*, ed. Kari Vogt, Lena Larsen and Christian, London 2009, 47–74. One work not mentioned in Part One is 'Freedom of thought and religion in Islam', *The New Voices of Islam: Reforming Politics and Modernity – A Reader*, ed. Mehran Kamrava, London 2006, 119–42.

8 These include the following: Farzin Vahdat, 'Post-revolutionary discourses of Mohammad Mojtahed Shabestari and Mohsen Kadivar: Reconciling the terms of mediated subjectivity', *Critique: Journal for Critical Studies of the Middle East* 17, 2000, 135–57; Mahmoud Sadri, 'Sacred defence of secularism: The political theologies of Soroush, Shabestari and Kadivar', *International Journal of Politics, Culture and Society* 15.2, 2001, 257–70; Yasayuki Matsunaga, 'Mohsen Kadivar, an advocate of postrevivalist Islam in Iran', *British Journal of Middle Eastern Studies*, 2008, 317–29; Yasuyuki Matsunaga, 'Human Rights and Jurisprudence in Mohsen Kadivar's Advocacy of "New-Thinker" Islam', *Die Welt des Islams* 51.3/4, 2011, 359–81; Ali Akbar and Abdullah Saeed, 'Interpretation and mutability: socio-legal texts of the Qur'an; three accounts from contemporary Iran', *Middle Eastern Studies* 54/3, 2018, 442–58;

9 *Naẓariya-hā-yi Dawlat* [*Theories of the State*], Tehran 1998.

10 *Daghdagha-hā-yi Ḥukūmat-i Dīnī* [Apprehension about Religious Government], Tehran 2000.

11 Ḥukūmat-i Intiṣābī [Government by Appointment], https://kadivar.com/category/1-books/b-10/0-b-10/.

(*Theocratic Government*).[12] A second block of publications include four volumes in a series called 'The Dissident Ayatollahs of the Islamic Republic of Iran', and this includes collections on Ayatollah Shariʿatmadari (d. 1986),[13] Ayatollah Azari-Qumi (d. 1999),[14] Ayatollah Sayyid Muhammad Ruhani (d. 1997),[15] and Ayatollah Mahallati (d. 1981).[16] In addition to highlighting the 'dissident' nature of some of the seminarians during the time of the Islamic Republic, a similar selection of publications highlight the activities of mullas who have endorsed reform. These include publications on Mulla Muhammad Kazim Khurasani (1839–1911),[17] Aqa ʿAli Mudarris Tihrani (1307/1929),[18] and Ayatollah Montazeri.[19] A third block is specifically political and includes works on the Green Movement,[20] and a criticism of ʿAli Khamenei.[21]A fourth block is comprised of less politically oriented works but deals with more easily identifiable 'Islamic' topics. Nevertheless, the political substrate is indeed inherent in these works too, coming under the general rubric of 'Islam and Human Rights Series'. Two books in this series include works on human rights,[22] and on apostasy and freedom of religion.[23]

---

12 *Ḥukūmat-i Vilāyī* [*Government of Authority*], Tehran: 1378/1999–2000, https://kadivar.com/category/1-books/03-b/1-b-03/.

13 *Asnādī az Mazlūmiyyāt-i Ayatollah Shariʿatmadari* [*Documents of the Oppression of Ayatollah Shariʿatmadari*], May 2015, https://kadivar.com/category/1-books/17-b/b-17-0/.

14 *Farāz va Furūd-i Azari-Qumi* [*The Rise and fall of Azari-Qumi*], February 2014, https://kadivar.com/category/1-books/b-18/b-18-0/.

15 *Inqilāb va Niẓām dar Būta-yi Naqd-i Akhlāqī* [*Testing the Revolution and the Regime with Ethical Criticisms*], December 2015, https://kadivar.com/category/1-books/b-19/b-19-0/.

16 *Bi-Nām-i Islām: Harcha Mī-khāhad Mi-kunad* [given the English title by Kadivar of *Arbitrary Rule in the Name of Islam*], January 2018, https://en.kadivar.com/wp-content/uploads/2018/05/English-Preface-1.pdf.

17 *Siyāsat-nāma-yi Khurasani* [Khurasani's Political Philosophy], Tehran 2006, https://kadivar.com/1253/.

18 *Majmuʾa-yi Musanafāta-yi Ḥākima Muʾassiss Aqa ʿAli Muddaris Tihrani* [The Compilation of the Works of the Sage and Originator Aqa ʿAli Moddaris Tehrani], Tehran 1999, https://kadivar.com/1302/.

19 *Sūg-Nāma-yi Faqīh-i Pāk-Bāz Ustād Muntaziri* [*A Tribute to the Virtuous Theologian*], https://kadivar.com/category/1-books/15-b/0-b-15/.

20 *Nidā-yi Sabz: Rawāyātī az Junbish-i Sabz-i Mardum-i Iran* [*The Green Call: A Narrative of the Iranian Green Movement*], https://kadivar.com/category/1-books/b-22/b-22-0/.

21 *Ibtizāl-i Marjiʿyat-i Shiʿa: Istizār Marjiʿat-i Maqām-i Rahbarī, Ḥujjat al-Islām wa'l-Muminīn, Sayyid ʿAlī Khamenei* [translated by Kadivar as *The Trivialization of Shiʿi Marjaʿiyyat: Impeaching Iran's Supreme Leader on his Marjaʾiyyat*], May 2014, https://kadivar.com/category/1-books/b-20/b-20-0/.

22 *Ḥaqq al-Nās* [which Kadivar translates as *Islam and Human Rights*], Tehran 2007, https://kadivar.com/category/1-books/b-12/b-12-0/.

23 *Majāzat-i Murtad va Āzādī-yī Mazhhab* [which Kadivar translates as *Apostasy, Blasphemy, & Religious Freedom in Islam*], July 2014, https://kadivar.com/category/1-books/b-21/b-21-0/.

Kadivar, Sharia and Politics

While the breadth of Kadivar's scholarly efforts do not permit a complete survey, it is necessary to highlight the salient features of his jurisprudential theories to appreciate the full significance of his contribution to modern *fiqh*. His understanding has profound political implications, as we shall see, and it is not difficult to comprehend why the more 'entrenched' positions within the Islamic Republic of Iran have considered him a threat to their continued existence. As a product of the seminary, Kadivar has always had a keen interest in *fiqh* and his attention has gravitated to the role of reason in jurisprudential and theological questions. Of interest is Kadivar's observation that ' …[the] rational approach has not found much reflection in *fiqh*', and he proceeds to summarise the observations of Sayyid Muhammad Baqir al-Sadr (d. 1980), the leading Shiʿi Ayatollah in Iraq, who remarked that it is possible to avoid the use of reason because it cannot discover the essential harms and benefits of matters including human rights, and that the only recourse is to scripture and sharia.[24] Kadivar's commitment to reason is evident in his works such as his *Daftar-i ʿAql* (*Book of Reason*),[25] which looks at the role of reason in the worldviews of well-known Islamic theologians and jurists. These included the likes of al-Farabi (d. 951), Ibn Sina (d. 980), Fayz-i Kashani (d. 1680) and Shaykh Mufid (d. 1022). Such works demonstrate Kadivar's deep attachment and mastery of Islamic history, theology and the various Islamic sciences, which he put to use in his re-evaluation of Islamic jurisprudence once the reform movement in Iran found its voice in 1997.

Kadivar shares much in common with other New Religious Thinkers, in particular, the commitment to justice and reason. He foregrounds the *maqāṣid al-sharīʿa*, which he believes are based on the aforementioned twin pillars of justice and reason, and this is contrasted with the traditional juristic tendency to focus on specific Qurʾanic commands. He says: 'People who have elevated secondary precepts and practical forms above the aims and objectives of religion, and who have lent sanctity to the customs of the age of revelation, while disregarding the sacred aims of religion and the exalted objectives of the sharia, are at some distance from the correct way of formulating opinions.'[26] Kadivar considers that there is a great threat to Islam from outdated regulations that were specific to seventh-century Arabia, and which are inappropriate to the conditions of Iran in the

24 Kadivar paraphrases Sayyid Muhammad Baqir al-Sadr's *Al-Fatāwi al-Waziha* in his 'Human Rights and Intellectual Islam', 50.

25 *Daftar-i ʿAql* [*Book of Reason*], Tehran 1377/1998–9, https://kadivar.com/category/1-books/02-b/1-b-02/.

26 Kadivar, 'Human Rights and Intellectual Islam', 72.

twenty-first century. One of his methods to 'modernise' sharia is to demonstrate this time-bound nature of the impermanent Qurʾanic commands. He does this by paying particular attention to Qurʾanic commands that have been understood as legitimising practices such as slavery and discrimination based on different religious traditions and gender, and which fall outside contemporary standards of reasonableness and justice. But Kadivar remains firmly attached to specific juristic methods to determine appropriate responses to the challenges of the modern age. Reason, corroborated with those Qurʾanic verses that have not transcended any time limitation (i.e. those that are permanently just and reasonable, and retain their beneficent quality), can annul verses the applicability of which was appropriate to a certain age, but which now appear outdated. When discussing reason, it is important to note that he also utilises the concept of the way of reasonable people (*sīra-yi ʿuqalāʾ*), which was discussed in Part One. What distinguishes Kadivar in this argument is his readiness to employ this juristic method in a nonconventional fashion. Traditionally, following the way of reasonable people meant permitting a custom or a way of doing things unless there was a specific command in sacred scripture. However, according to Kadivar, the way of reasonable people (which of necessity is just and rational) abrogates practices that are considered irrational and unjust, and promote corruption, and which are based on specific Qurʾanic commands that endorse outdated customs such as wife-beating, polygamy, slavery, etc., which 'traditional Islam' holds to be eternal and unchanging.[27] Contrary to the position of the traditional Islamic perspective, Kadivar holds that if a commandment (precept or *aḥkām*) opposes the way of reasonable people or negates the criteria of justice, or increases corruption over benefit, it is 'expose[d] … as fleeting and not permanent'.[28] As time-bound and impermanent commandments are abrogated, 'reasonable laws are posited by the public opinion', and these laws 'should in no wise be attributed to religion'. In other words, even though the aims and goals of reasonable people may accord with those of religion, they are still human, and this is one of the reasons that the domain of jurisprudence will decrease.

The implications of Kadivar's commitment to reason and justice are far-reaching and are best illustrated with reference to his article 'Traditional Islam to Islam as an End in Itself'. In this article, he examines the notion that commands may be classified into two groups: constant and variable. He summarises three different perspectives on this classification. The first was advanced by ʿAllama Muhammad

27 The term 'traditional Islam' is Kadivar's own.

28 Kadivar, 'From Traditional Islam to Islam as an end in Itself', 480.

Husayn Tabataba'i (d. 1981), who believed that variable commands were the responsibility of the ruler. (These commands are not to be considered as divine commandments and are 'not called religion in religious terminology'.[29]) The second perspective was offered by Mirza Muhammad Husayn Gharavi Na'ini (d. 1936), who held that the people's representatives (the parliament) should decide on the variable commandments. These commandments are non-explicit (*ghayr al-manṣūṣ*); although Kadivar does not indicate how Na'ini distinguished between explicit and non-explicit commandments.[30] Also espousing the second perspective is Sayyid Muhammad Baqir Sadr, who likewise called for the people's representative to decide on variable commandments, although he argued that these must be limited to the sphere of permissible activities.[31] The third perspective is advocated by Kadivar himself: those commandments related to belief – God and the afterlife, and so on – and also to devotional activity and rituals, and to ethical and moral values, are the 'major parts of religion which all transcend time and place and are eternal'.[32] The variable commands are connected in most modern states to criminal law, the penal code and civil law, which in the pre-modern period were based on the reason and justice of the time, but which are now outdated. Thus, based on the criteria of reason and justice, 'if we are certain in the belief that a commandment does not achieve the ultimate goal (and not supposing it), that commandment loses its legitimacy and a new commandment to reach that lofty [goal] should be considered'.[33] Kadivar concludes that this third perspective on the variable commands will result in the reduction of the number of commands: 'The scope of religion relative to the two previous models is smaller, but is deeper.'[34] A few pages later, Kadivar repeats the same point: 'In this perspective, the sphere of jurisprudence (*fiqh*) and the sharia is gradually reduced, while the scope and depth of religion is increased.'[35] Of significance is how he does not consider there to be a role for a jurist in the third model, in the same way that there is in the previous two models.

Kadivar's conclusion about the variable commands, and who has the authority to decide on such matters, represents a huge challenge to the Islamic Republic, because it questions the very basis of the *vilāyat-i faqīh*. Indeed, he appraises

---

29 Kadivar, 'From Traditional Islam to Islam as an end in Itself', 463.
30 Kadivar, 'From Traditional Islam to Islam as an end in Itself', 465–9.
31 Kadivar, 'From Traditional Islam to Islam as an end in Itself', 469.
32 Kadivar, 'From Traditional Islam to Islam as an end in Itself', 478
33 Kadivar, 'From Traditional Islam to Islam as an end in Itself', 480.
34 Kadivar, 'From Traditional Islam to Islam as an end in Itself', 478.
35 Kadivar, 'From Traditional Islam to Islam as an end in Itself', 483.

Ayatollah Khomeini's jurisprudential views on the 'Absolute Appointed Mandate of the Jurisconsult' (*vilāyat-i intiṣābī-yi muṭlaqa-yi faqīhān*) as one of the weakest among the nine extant Shiʿi political philosophies, because of its feeble rational, Qurʾanic, and legal foundations. He concludes that Khomeini's theory '... is not intuitively obvious, rationally necessary, or required by the principles or auxiliary axioms of Shiʿa Islam'.[36] Subsequently, Iran's Special Clerical Court found him guilty of 'weakening the regime' in such articles as 'Illegality of Islamic Terrorism' and 'The Progress Report of the Islamic Government', and sentenced him to imprisonment. This decision was not surprising given Kadivar's tone: 'The revolution destroyed only the form, not the essence, of the Iranian empire. It reproduced the royal system by bestowing absolute, extra-legal and permanent power on a divinely ordained and sacred leader.'[37] Kadivar treated his eighteen-month imprisonment (1998–1999) with equanimity and defiance, and continued to compose works that contained similar criticisms.

There is no denying Kadivar's own deep belief in Islam; however, the implications of foregrounding the *maqāṣid al-sharīʿa* on justice and reason in such a radical fashion draws parallels with more secular thinkers. Kadivar's writings indicate that there will be some major consequences should such a worldview be adopted wholesale. As mentioned earlier, one of the most significant is that the dimension of *fiqh* decreases as the depth of faith increases. And this brings forth the associated issue of what happens to the numbers of *mujtahid*s as the dimension of jurisprudence is reduced. While it is unclear whether there would be a concomitant shrinkage in numbers, the need for the *mujtahid* remains vital. This is because the ability to discern whether a ruling or command in the Qurʾan, or in the hadith and sayings of the imams, is a permanent ruling or whether it can be abrogated is a specialist task. Kadivar confirms that it must be performed by a *mujtahid*, because of his/her expertise in jurisprudence and due to his/her awareness of time and place.[38] But he seems to extend the duty of rethinking Islam beyond traditional parameters, as he observes: 'It is the responsibility of the mainstream of scholars of religion and Islamologists to distinguish whether or not commandments of the sharia are in agreement with the criteria of justice and the way of reasonable people (*sīra-yi ʿuqalāʾ*) and not just the jurists.'[39] Attention should be paid to the non-exclusivity of Islam in this effort, as he mentions scholars of religion and

36 Kadivar, *Ḥukūmat-i Vilāyī*, 234
37 Kadivar, *Daghdaghā-yi Ḥukūmat-i Dīnī*, 610–22
38 Kadivar, 'Revisiting Women's Rights in Islam', 231.
39 Kadivar, 'From Traditional Islam to Islam as an End in Itself', 482.

reasonable people, who are not necessarily Muslims. Kadivar believes that if the Islamic classes – 'insightful religious authorities (*mujtahid*s), informed *fuqahā* and Islamologists' – fail to rise to the challenges of modernity, 'serious religious and cultural problems and crisis will eclipse religion and the sharia'.[40] He also sets out ways to determine the conclusions of reasonable people: 'The mainstream of scholars and specialists in various fields of the humanities and determining their majority is the loftiest way of finding the way of reasonable people (*sīra-yi ʿuqalā*), and learning of the exigencies of time and place.'[41]

Kadivar's rationalising tendencies should be seen within the larger Usuli tradition of Shiʿi Islam. The break with the 'literalist' scripturalism of the Akbaris became increasingly apparent in the 19th century that rationalism asserted itself at the vanguard of change. Kadivar's writings are peppered with references to 'traditional Islam' or 'historical Islam' to foreground the difference with New Religious Thinking. For example, he offers the following list of Ghazali (d. 1111), Ibn Abi al-Hadid (d. 1258), Yusuf al-Bahrani and Sahib-i Javahir as illustrations of 'how small a part was played by reason in the derivation of sharia precepts'.[42] (The latter, Sahib-i Javahir, is of note because he is known as one of the major Usuli scholars of the 19th century.) In addition, Kadivar considers that one of the problems that Muslims have inherited is the over-emphasis on jurisprudence within Islam. He desires to see a balance between faith, ethics, worship and commandments; jurisprudence is concerned with the last two of these. This balance does not mean an eradication of jurisprudence, rather a re-alignment away from the tendency of traditional Islam to 'fatten' it, as it is certainly not the most important component of Islam.[43] In short, in might be argued with some justification that Kadivar has taken the Usuli school to its logical conclusion with such a pronounced emphasis on the role of reason.[44] His theological positions, such as his opposition to *vilāyat-i faqīh*,

40 Kadivar, 'Human Rights and Intellectual Islam', 73.

41 Kadivar, 'From Traditional Islam to Islam as an End in Itself', 482.

42 Kadivar, 'Human Rights and Intellectual Islam', 70.

43 Kadivar, 'Pursish va pāsukh', https://kadivar.com/1066.

44 The movement that foregrounds the *sīra-yi ʿuqalā* is indicative of this late Usuli trend. Robert Gleave identifies it with al-Shaykh Murtaza Ansari in the 19th century. See Robert Gleave, 'Imami Shiʿi Legal Theory', *Oxford Handbooks Online*, 19: http://www.oxfordhandbooks.com/view/10.1093/oxfordhb/9780199679010.001.0001/oxfordhb-9780199679010-e-31. The concept was developed further in the twentieth century by Muhammad Husayn Gharavi Isfahani in *Nahāyat al-Dirāya fī Sharḥ al-Kifāya* and by his student Muhammad Riza al-Muzaffar (I am grateful to Muhsin Kadivar for supplying this information). And of course, it has been taken a stage further by the New Religious Thinkers.

lead him into territories that sit comfortably with many of the positions advocated by the religious secularists such as Saʿid Hajjariyan,[45] Akbar Ganji and Soroush – although this does not mean he accepts everything that the latter has advocated, such as regarding revelation as Muhammad's dream experience.[46]

Kadivar and the Hijab

Muhsin Kadivar's understanding of the hijab is of particular interest in this study because it reveals substantial change and development in his thought.[47] Indeed, the shifts in his ideas on the hijab is not the only issue on which there is substantial development. Kadivar's idea about homosexuality, for instance, reflects a similar movement in the direction of what might be termed 'liberal' or 'tolerant'.[48] He started from a traditional perspective on the hijab, similar to that of Mutahhari, but has most recently advocated positions on several issues that bear more similarity with interpretations that settle more comfortably within the norms of Western society than those traditional understandings that have been endorsed by the Islamic Republic. Moreover, he goes beyond the views of Ahmad Qabil, whom he regards as a good friend despite jurisprudential differences of opinion.

(i). Kadivar's initial acceptance of the traditional perspective of the hijab is best reflected in an Arabic work dated to April 2004. In private communication, Kadivar noted that this is his 'oldest viewpoint'.[49] He concludes this work with a summary of his position:

> It is a sharia obligation upon the women who are believing and free (*harāʾir*) [from slavery], after the revelation of the covering (*sitr*) verse, that they cover

45 For Hajjariyan's thought, see Eskandar Sadeghi-Boroujerdi, 'From Etelāʿāti to Eslāhtalabi: Saʿid Hajjariyan, Political Theology and the Politics of Reform in Post-Revoultiuonary Iran', *Iranian Studies* 47.6, 987–1009.
46 Abdolkarim Soroush, 'Muhammad ravi-ye al-ru'ya-ha-yi rasulani', http://www.rahesabz.net/story/71738.
47 I am exceedingly grateful to Kadivar who pointed out his intellectual development on the issue of hijab in an email dated 25 August 2018. He also brought my attention to the texts cited in this section, which are all available on his website.
48 M. Alipour, 'Shiʿa neo-traditionalist scholars and theology of homosexuality: review reflections on Mohsen Kadivar's shifting approach', *Theology and Sexuality* 24.3, 2018, 200–18. Alipour refuses to acknowledge Kadivar's intellectual development on this point and continues to regard him as a neo-traditionalist, a point on which Kadivar has expressed some surprise (private email, dated 17 October 2018).
49 Private email from Kadivar, dated 25 August 2018.

> all their bodies except for their face and the two hands, even the head, the hair, the chest and the neck, from [all] except the husband and *al-maḥārim* [who are those men whom it is naturally forbidden for her to marry] for which there are considered examples in the Book and in the Sunna and by the consensus that has no opposers amongst the jurists of the two groups [the Shiʿa and the Sunni?]; and the claim of the permissibility of her uncovering the head and the hair, or that it is only desirable for them to be covered, is not based on any legitimate *sharʿī* evidence that is creditworthy (*muʿtabar*), and cannot be used to argue for them.[50]

Kadivar also directed me to a work dated at around a similar time, a little earlier, in December 2003, which is a commentary on a fatwa issued by Montazeri about the permissibility of men shaking hands with women. Kadivar concluded that on the basis of Montazeri's fatwa, it is permissible for men to shake hands with Muslim women who do not cover their heads and do not regard their bareheadedness as dishonourable.[51] He notes that the new fatwa removed many of the difficulties faced by Muslims and Shiʿis in non-Islamic societies.

(ii). Between 2002 and 2007, Kadivar and Qabil discussed the issue of the hijab. Kadivar has stated that Qabil's revision of the hijab was prior to his own, and there existed differences of opinion between the two. For example, Kadivar was critical of Qabil's understanding of the fatwas of the early jurists about the hijab worn by women at prayer and when outside of the house.[52] In 2005, Qabil and Kadivar debated the issue of the hijab publicly in Tehran in front of an audience of about 50 people. Subsequently, they presented their arguments and differences (related to the fatwas of the early jurists, as mentioned above) in private before Ayatollah Montazeri. Kadivar claims that Montazeri listened carefully, and admired both presentations, but he 'did not confirm Qabil's generalisation and fatwa' and advised the two scholars not to discuss the meeting in public.[53]

---

50 Kadivar, 'Kalām ijmālī fī sitr al-murāh' ['A brief discussion about covering women'], 2004, https://kadivar.com/?p=267.

51 Kadivar, 'Musāfaha bā ajnabiya' ['Shaking hands with foreigners'], December 2003, https://kadivar.com/?p=8429. This is based on a discussion of the narrative that says, 'There is no problem in looking at the heads of people of Tahamah, Arabs, the Bedouins and the those who live away from cities. This is because when they are forbidden [from revealing their heads] they do not accept it.' The same narration is cited by Mutahhari, and he notes that some apply this narration to city-dwellers (discussed in Part Two).

52 Private email from Kadivar, 25 August 2018.

53 Private email from Kadivar, 25 August 2018.

In any case, Kadivar claims that the first major shift in his thought occurred while he was still in Iran, and is focused on the distinction between the legal hijab and the *sharīʿ* hijab in an interview with Daryush Darvishi and Mustafa Mukhtari.[54] (The text, called 'Hijab: Religious Limits and Legal Limits', is dated to November 2007.) He begins his discussion with reference to Q. 33.59, which he believes is specific only to the Prophet's wives, and so is not obligatory for other women. However, he alludes to the private and public nature of the hijab by comparing it to the wall of a house, which is both private and inward looking, but at the same time it is visible and outward looking. In other words, the question is complex and defies simplistic solutions. He states that most societies have basic limits of clothing, but that problem surfaces in countries which are undemocratic, do not reflect public opinion, and which impose their views on the citizens. It is all too easy to guess that between the lines Kadivar is speaking about Iran.

Nevertheless, he holds to a vision in which the ideal form of covering for believing women includes covering the body, head and neck. Indeed, he has subsequently made it clear that at this point he still believed the hijab was obligatory (*vājib*).[55] Despite believing in the necessity for believing women to cover, his attitude is far softer than that adopted by the state authorities. He legitimises his perspective by locating practice within a private domain. So, for example, there are several religious duties, such as praying and fasting, and no-one is compelled in performing these religious devotions, nor are there state punishments for non-observance. Kadivar reflects on the lack of success in the implementation of the hijab laws in Iran since the revolution, and observes that 'the element of free-choice, the most important of which was faith, was reduced to the element of legal coercion and legal requirement'. He adds, 'Force and legal compulsion produce neither faith nor modesty and chastity … although the religious hijab is a command of God, should one live with God's laws [that are implemented] with force and punishments? The Prophet influenced people through their hearts, but not with the force of the sword or military might.' Kadivar expresses the view that the hijab must be based on faith, which is a matter of choice. Therefore, the command or religious ruling of the hijab must take precedence over the legal ruling, and he admits that the '*bad-ḥijābī*' look has become the social norm and it is no longer considered ugly or bad. From the religious perspective, covering is

54 'Hijāb: ḥadd-i sharīʿ, ḥadd-i qanūnī' ['The hijab: the religious limit and the legal limit'], 2007, https://kadivar.com/?p=2116.
55 Private email from Muhsin Kadivar, 9 November 2018.

then a matter of choice, but if it remains a legal obligation and people still do not observe it, it would be impractical to punish all who abuse the law.

Kadivar introduces the interesting example of how the Islamic Republic shows foreign films on television which feature women without hijabs. These women on film are not believers in Islam. Whilst Kadivar holds that true believers are those who have chosen to believe, there are also those who have chosen not to believe, and Kadivar refers to the narration from Imam Sadiq about those women far from civilisation who refuse to accept the commands even when they are admonished. The linkage, not explicitly made, is of such women with contemporary Iranian women who do not wear the hijab, and also foreign women on Iranian TV who do not wear hijab. Kadivar states that there are no verses, or narrations, that legitimise force to compel such women to cover. Although their example is a sin, they will taste the recompense in the next world.

The policy of exercising force adopted by the Islamic Republic has failed according to Kadivar. He offers the examples of Turkey and Malaysia which permit freedom to wear the hijab or 'Western' clothing to illustrate the success in educating women to wear the hijab in non-compulsory systems. Kadivar concludes that wearing the hijab is defensible for the believing woman, but it must be optional. And he castigates the regime in its policy of strict enforcement of the hijab, and its inability to raise the level of religious faith, to say nothing of cultural, political and economic improvements. In short, he states that legal commands (or state rules) must be less than religious commands.

(iii). The second major shift in Kadivar's thought came in the second decade of the 21st century and may be read in many articles, long and short, published since 2011. He has pointed me in particular to a very short piece titled '*Sharīʿat*: a legal order or moral values?' which is dated 19 October 2013, and which seems to have been the basis for a lecture given in California.[56] The piece repeats the idea that the Qurʾan is a divine book of guidance, rather than a series of eternal laws: 'There is not one reason that these few verses [of the Qurʾan] are eternal, in particular outside of the Hijaz. The Qurʾan has never called itself a book of the *sharīʿat* or law and rights, rather it has called itself a book of guidance. The Qurʾan can certainly be the source of inspiration for law and the basis of moral values, but certainly it is not a book of law.' In this piece, Kadivar sees 'Islamic rights' (*ḥuqūq-i Islāmī*) as having their basis in Islamic commands rather than

56 Kadivar, 'Sharīʿat: niẓām-i ḥuqūqī yā arzish-hā-yi akhlāqī?' ['*Sharīʿat*: A legal order or moral values?'], 19 October 2013, https://kadivar.com/?p=12859.

Islamic law (*qānūn-i Islāmī*). He suggests that laws (*qawānīn*) for punishment, trade, civil, international and political laws have all been made by rulers and political powers, and therefore suggests that they have nothing to do with Islam. He then makes the claim that in fact 'Islamic law' has never existed. Whilst the hijab is not mentioned, it is clear what the implications are. As guidance, the Qur'an does not compel women to cover. Moreover, Kadivar comments that time and place offer flexibility and commands can be put into place with inspiration from these fixed [moral] values in various conditions [depending on] time and place.

Kadivar has subsequently addressed the inconsistencies in the policy of the Islamic Republic concerning the hijab. He points to the policy of punishing women who do not wear the hijab,[57] which is based on Ayatollah Khomeini's fatwa where he called it a major sin.[58] In Khomeini's subsequent list of forty-five major sins there is no mention of the hijab. But Kadivar observes that the Qur'an does not offer a punishment for the woman who does not cover her head, and likewise in the prophetic Sunna and in the reliable narrations of the imams there is no discussion of compulsion or punishment.

This second major shift is also reflected in an article called 'Aḥkām-i Ḥijāb' ('Commands of the Hijab').[59] This article is not structured in the same way as his 'Hijab, Religious Limits and Legal Limits'. Rather, 'Commands of the Hijab' is based on questions and answers posted on Kadivar's website, and these are now appearing again in a 'drip fashion' without the questions, which can be inferred from the answers in any case. Nevertheless, these thoughts are worthy of consideration as they demonstrate the degree of sympathy Kadivar has with those Iranians who are demanding a less strict implementation of laws on the hijab. The dates of entry are not chronologically arranged; they range from 2012 to 2016. What is interesting about this 'article' – all in Persian without English translation – is that it reveals an ongoing and intimate knowledge of the immediate issues of Iranian society and politics, and the fatwas issued by leading Iranian mullas. It would appear that Kadivar is still writing for an Iranian audience – whether this is in Iran or else for the Iranian diaspora.

The first entry responds to the fatwa issued by Nasir Makarim-Shirazi in 2016. Kadivar states that 'the respected *marja*ʿ has said that covering a woman's hair,

57 Kadivar, 'Ḥijāb-i ijbārī fāqid-i dalīl-i muʿtabar-i sharʿī ast' ['There is no reliable sharīʿ proof for compulsory hijab'], 1 July 2012, https://kadivar.com/?p=9381.

58 Kadivar cited his source as Khomeini, *Taḥrīr al-Wāsila*, vol. 3, 477 (*Kitāb al-Ḥudud al-Khums*).

59 Kadivar, 'Aḥkām-i ḥijāb' ['The Commands of the Hijab'], July 2016, https://kadivar.com/?p=10194.

head and neck is not as important as covering the rest of her body, because it is possible to ignore [the command] in necessary circumstances', i.e. when studying abroad. Kadivar suggests that it is somewhat strange that 'a woman's face is considered more beautiful and attractive than her hair, but this beautiful face is not [included or categorised as] inner finery'. He adds that covering the inner finery (the private parts) is based on a primary source (the Qur'an), whereas concealing the hair is simply a matter of custom: 'Covering a woman's head hair is based on the local culture, regional conditions and time and place more than legal [requirements]. This has been my juristic opinion since 1391/2012.'

In his second entry, called 'Covering Women's Hair, Head and Neck from Three Juristic Perspectives', and dated 11 Aban 1392 / 2 November 2013, Kadivar contrasts his ideas with those of Ayatollah Montazeri – whose views as argued above reflect the perspective of Mutahhari – and Ahmad Qabil. He succinctly states his own view that 'there is no necessity to cover the hair head and neck in essence according to any primary command. However, Kadivar also adds some conditions to this view, as this lack of necessity depends on 'the conditions and custom of time and place'. These conditions include first, local customs of modesty and chastity (based on secondary, rather than primary commands); second, the hijab must be worn for prayer and during the hajj;[60] third, when local custom indicates that non-covering in front of non-*maḥram* does not reflect a lack of modesty (the inference being that there may some cases where the opposite is the norm); and fourth, it is expedient for cautious women to have more covering than the norm (but crucially there is no mention of head-covering). Kadivar concludes that Qabil disagreed with him on all of these points.

The third and fourth entries are very brief. The first of these, titled 'Hijab and Compulsion', dated June/July 2012, is very short, and simply rejects compulsory hijab on the basis of the famous Qur'anic verse that states 'there is no compulsion in religion' (Q. 2.256). The fourth entry which is on 'Family Compulsion', dated November/December 2012, is a good illustration of Kadivar's commitment to individual responsibility. Donning the hijab is an act that must be voluntarily chosen by the daughter of a family.

The subsequent entry implicitly criticises the Islamic Republic's policy of chastising *bad-ḥijābī*. Kadivar does this by pointing out that there is no discussion in the Qur'an about the worldly or otherworldly punishments for women who do not cover their heads, even though otherworldly punishments appear in some

60 'At the time of prayer and hajj, he [Qabil] believed in the desirability and lack of necessity for covering. I [Kadivar] believe in the necessity.'

narrations from the imams about which there is some dispute concerning their chain of transmission.

The seventh and eighth entries, dated July 2013, are related to covering during hajj and prayer. Of interest on this point is how Kadivar rejects the views of Mutahhari. Whilst other thinkers, such as Qabil, seem to be at pains to cite Mutahhari to legitimise their views, Kadivar is explicit in taking a contrary perspective to Mutahhari and claims that there is no connection between covering for prayer with covering before an onlooker.

The final entry, called 'Women's Adornment (*ārāyish*) Outside of the Home', is a collection of blogs from 2013 and 2014, in which Kadivar confirms that women may dress-up and beautify themselves, and be looked at by non-*maḥram* observers, and this is unrelated to chastity and modesty. He observes that local custom determines what is permissible, although showing-off (*tabarruj*) and garish adornment are not permitted. However, he states that women are best able to decide for themselves the limits of what is permissible in this regard, and 'moderate adornment such as modification (*iṣlāh*) of the eyebrows, face, and [the use of] henna, and other things like these are common among women who profess religion'. Kadivar stresses that the hadiths on this topic reflect the conditions of time and place of the subject matter, indicating that a change of interpretation is perfectly valid. He concludes by stating, 'There is no contradiction to the laws of the Qurʾan and Sunna by engaging in acts that accord with custom and by observing chastity and modesty, and by refraining from showing-off.'

This website demonstrates Kadivar's commitment to providing guidance to his constituencies that is realistic and contemporary. Most of the entries were written in 2013–14, some five years after his arrival in the US. It is to be wondered if and how American culture has shaped Kadivar's views, away from the stereotypes and Occidentalism that pervades much of the official state discourse about popular Western culture and the depiction of women. The general trajectory of Kadivar's thought appears to have been shifting over the course of twenty years since the turn of the century, and has not been representative of the Iranian state discourse. Since 2013–14, he has continued to oppose the mandatory hijab, and he publicly condemns the force that has been used against the 'Women of Inqalab Street'. He uses very strong language: 'The mandatory veil was born with the Islamic Republic and it will die with the Islamic Republic.'[61]

In June 2018, he published another online article titled 'The hijab: Insoluble

61 Muhsin Kadivar, 'Sanjāq kardan-i ḥijāb-i ijbārī bi ḥayāt-i niẓām' ['The linkage of the mandatory veil with the life of the regime'], 9 March 2018, http://kadivar.com/?p=16476.

cultural problems of the Islamic Republic and George Orwell's novel *1984*',[62] in which he responds to the most recent manifestations of popular culture that have been punished in the Islamic Republic, including modelling,[63] dancing,[64] and hanging the hijab on the end of a wooden pole. Pointing to the lack of respect shown to the laws on hijab in modern Iran, Kadivar quotes the words of the Iranian Attorney General, Muhammad Jaʿfar Muntazari, who seems to admit that force and violence to impose the hijab were futile: 'I swear by God, clashing with the judiciary is not the answer on cultural and hijab issues. Peaceful and calm ways should be taken, and on such a foundation we will support any plan that is effective in opposing bad-*ḥijābī*.' Kadivar also alludes to the case of Shaparak Shajarizada who received a two-year jail sentence (and an eighteen-year suspended sentence) for removing her hijab in public.[65] By giving all of these examples related to the hijab, Kadivar claims that the majority of people in Iran do not approve of the hijab laws, and he advises those responsible in the Islamic Republic to read Orwell's *1984* and *Animal Farm*: 'Read and understand; the solution to all of these cultural and social problems is nothing other than putting aside this method of ruling everything at will, tyranny and self-interest.'

Kadivar's intellectual and religious journey has been long and has resulted in him establishing a new safe base for himself thousands of miles outside of Iran. Having started with advocating the necessity of wearing the hijab according to the sharia, he now endorses a position in which there is no sharia obligation, or even desirability to wear the hijab, so long as it accords with the custom and does not

62 Kadivar, 'Ḥijāb, mushkilāt-i lāyanhall-i farhangī-yi jumhūrī-yi islāmī va rumān *1984* George Orwell' ['Hijab, insoluble cultural problems of the Islamic Republic and the novel *1984* by George Orwell'], 19 July 2019, https://kadivar.com/?p=16649.

63 See for example, Heather Saul, 'Iranian model Elnaz Golrokh leaves Iran with her boyfriend after sharing photos without hijab', *The Independent* 20 May 2016, https://www.independent.co.uk/news/people/iranian-model-elnaz-golrokh-leaves-iran-with-her-boyfriend-after-sharing-photos-without-hijab-a7037801.html. The article mentions Operation Spider II, which was 'a crackdown on women appearing in photos without their hair covered'. See also Saeed Kamali Dehghan, 'Iran arrests models in renewed crackdown on unlicensed industry', *The Guardian* 16 May 2018, https://www.theguardian.com/world/2016/may/16/iran-arrests-models-crackdown-unlicensed-industry-hijab.

64 See 'Iran women dance in support of arrested Instagram teen', BBC News, 9 July 2018, https://www.bbc.co.uk/news/world-middle-east-44760840. The specific case involved a nineteen year-old girl, Maida Hujrabi, who posted film of herself dancing (on her own). Some of the clips show her dancing without wearing a hijab.

65 See Samuel Osborne, 'Iranian woman "sentenced to 20 years in prison" for removing headscarf in protest', *The Independent* 10 July 2018, https://www.independent.co.uk/news/world/middle-east/iran-woman-hijab-protest-arrest-jailed-prison-shapark-shajarizadeh-headscarf-white-wednesdays-a8439816.html.

violate the ethical basis of the Qurʾan. Such a view is based on his analysis of the Qurʾan, which gives no explicit command to cover the head, and on the narrations. Even if some narrations, and not the majority, may suggest some form of head-covering, Kadivar believes that the changing conditions of time and place require appropriate measures for the tradition of head-covering.

*

Also reflective of this second shift are a series of lectures that Kadivar gave at Singapore University on ethical issues. The first twelve sessions are not specific to the hijab, but they are available online.[66] The second season of the Singapore lectures are those specific to the hijab, and they have been organised into nine lectures that address a certain theme. Only five of these are available for downloading, as Kadivar became involved in publishing other material which he deemed more important than publishing the lectures on the hijab. Kadivar informed me that these lectures were for graduate students of engineering in Singapore, and they were delivered online as he did not travel there. Those who attended the online sessions were of Iranian origin, many of whom are now teaching in universities in Iran or elsewhere.

The content of these lectures is listed below:

1. Hijab in the Qurʾan: a summary
2. Hijab in Shiʿi narrations
3. Hijab in Sunni narrations and fatwas
4. An investigation of the fatwas of Shiʿi jurists about the clothes of praying women
5. Looking and covering in the fatwas of the Shiʿi jurists
6. Clothing in the age of ignorance and in the age of the Prophet and imams.
7. Hijab in ancient literature (Jewish, Christian and Zoroastrian)
8. More reflection on the hijab in the Qurʾan (a summarised discussion)
9. The author's final words together with proofs and analytical documentation

The first two chapters are presented here to illustrate Kadivar's perspective on the formative periods of the hijab in Islamic and Shiʿi history.

66 Kadivar, 'Taʾamūllī dar masʾāla-yi ḥijāb' ['Reflections on the issue of the hijab'], https://kadivar.com/?p=10843.

10

Translation of Kadivar's 'Reflections on the Question of Hijab'

FIRST CHAPTER: THE HIJAB IN THE QUR'AN [– A SUMMARY]

The question of women's legal covering is an issue about which I have received the most questions. I have previously expressed my opinion in brief on this topic, but over the past five years I have reflected on this topic and reached new conclusions.

The legal hijab may be discussed in at least three categories: the hijab in the Qur'an; in the narrations; and in the fatwas. The first part of this discussion is devoted to 'the legal hijab in the glorious Qur'an'. Much has been said on this. I will get straight to the point and refrain from engaging in unnecessary argumentation. Questions on the topic of hijab in the Qur'an are:

- What is the basic concern of the Qur'an about covering and the hijab?
- What duty or duties did it establish for believing women and men on this issue?
- Which parts of a woman's body must legally be covered from public view?
- Are these duties rational ([i.e.] do the duties come with an explanation of the reason for the command), or are the cause and philosophy of the command hidden from us?
- To what extent are the commands affected by the conditions of the time and place of revelation (*'aṣr-i nuzūl*), and to what extent [are the commands] universal and for all times and places and conditions?
- What is the minimum Qur'anic covering, and what kinds of covering follow the custom of the place and the time?

Understanding the Revelation of the Verses on the Hijab

(1). Attention should be paid to the significance of the conditions of covering of the people first addressed by the Qur'an. First, at the time of the Qur'anic revelation, the Arabs of the Hijaz were very poor. This extreme poverty had many effects on their covering. Second, in comparison with [other] societies of that period, they were completely uncivilised (*ghayr-i mutamaddun*) and backward. Third, corruption, moral decline and prostitution among them was common. Each one of these three factors can be accounted for by a historical witness and Qur'anic support, and we will engage in a separate discussion of each of them.

(2). In that time, sewn clothes were uncommon. A long piece of cloth, like the *iḥrām* [worn] during the hajj or the loin cloth (*lung*) of the contemporary bath-house (*ḥamām*) were the most important body coverings. The [long piece of] cloth had [openings] cut for the head and the neck. Clothes were [made] of one piece of cloth and were singular; there was no under or over garment. Due to extreme economic poverty, unsewn clothes were not long, and parts of the arms and legs were [left] naked, to say nothing of the head, neck, and parts of the chest. Parts of the body were covered by these unsewn clothes, which could be seen easily because of the splits at the sides when [people] moved or when the wind blew, whether the person was a man or a woman.

(3). Among the Arabs of the age of ignorance (*'Arab-i jāhilī*) nakedness was not such a reprehensible matter. When they circumambulated the Ka'ba, men and women were completely naked since they could not be in the presence of God in the clothes in which they had sinned. They did not make a great effort to conceal their gaze at other people's sexual organs, and other parts of the body, to say nothing of the head and chest.

(4). Also, the dwellings of the Arabs of the Hijaz, commensurate with the economic conditions, indicated [the state of their] civilisation and morality. The elite had stone or mud houses, but most people lived in houses made of date-straw or in tents. The houses frequently did not have many rooms, and they lacked doors and even curtains. Peering inside the house and at the people inside, was [a] very common [practice].

(5). The houses were not adequate health-wise. People in the desert needed to relieve themselves far from [their] houses. A covered and sheltered space such as a toilet [simply] did not exist. In these circumstances they were seen and spoke [to each other], and often they were teased. There was no difference between men and women.

(6). Washing was infrequent due to extreme shortage of water. Private baths did not exist. Bathing took place in public, beside rivers, ponds and pools. There were no covered or sheltered places. And there were no times for separate bathing. Complete nakedness was a common phenomenon when washing [oneself].

(7). In the age of ignorance, there were no particular rules for sexual relations. [Sexual] excess, prostitution, swapping spouses and other [practices] were common. Chastity and common decency were unheard of, and open sexual relations were not condemned.

Fundamental Qura'nic Questions about the Hijab

In such an environment and backdrop, the verses of the glorious Qur'an were sent down about codes for sexual relations and covering of women and men. The Qur'an set out a complete prohibition on all kinds of sexual relations outside the family, from the beginning of the female believer's life within the family, and it [also set out] a number of restrictions pertaining to spouses and regulations for dealings with slaves. From the fifth year of the hijra onwards – in other words, less than six years before the death of the Prophet – the verses on covering were revealed. Observing the privacy (*ḥarīm-i khuṣūṣī*) of houses and the courtesies for entering other peoples' home was the next step. The biggest concerns of the Qur'an related to covering are the following:

i. Covering the private parts and sexual organs, and rejecting nakedness in countless situations is obligatory. Covering the private parts is the first step for female believers who live in a family and move in social circles.
ii. Proper and complete covering of the intimate parts of the body (*bāṭin-i badan*) with the usual clothes. Believers had to cover their bodies in the customary way. They did not wear their clothes in a manner that allowed the body parts to be seen. The customary way of those times for women was clothing from the neck to the knee and from the upper arm to the elbow. Female believers were not permitted to wear clothes in such a way that the clothed parts of the body would be seen.
iii. Remaining were three parts of the body, which in those times were not

covered with clothing: first, part of the chest (*sīna*); second, the head and neck; third, the hands from the elbow and the legs from the knees to the feet.

The verses of the glorious Qur᾽an related to the issue of covering are:

i. First group: verses on permission (*āyāt-i istīdhān*): Light (*Nūr*) 24.27–28 and 24.58–59, and The Parties (*Aḥzāb*) 33.53–55 and 33.32–33.
ii. Second group: verses on covering the private parts: The Heights (*A῾rāf*) 7.19–33 in the story of Adam and Eve.
iii. Third group: verses on the Prophet's wives, hijab and *jilbāb*: The Parties 33.33, 33.53, 33.59.
iv. Fourth group: verses on finery and the *khimār*: Light 24.30–31 and 24.60.

The command for the need to cover the private parts is clear beyond any doubt from the above verses. To find an answer to the question of what parts of the female body the Qur᾽an requires them to cover, I will concentrate on the most important verses of groups three and four, in other words, verse 59 of The Parties [Q. 33.59] and verse 31 of Light [Q. 24.31].

Verse 33.59

> O Prophet! Tell your wives and daughters, and the women of the believers to draw their cloaks (*jalābīb*) over themselves. Thus, is it likelier that they will be known and not be disturbed. God is Forgiving, Merciful (Q. 33.59).

This verse has addressed the female believer along with the Prophet's wives and daughters. There are two points of importance in [the verse]. The first point is drawing [their] cloaks over themselves, and the second point is an explanation for the reason (*῾illat*) for this command of being known and the subject of [them] being pestered.

The customary covering of the hidden parts of the body

Jalābīb (cloaks) – the plural form of *jilbāb* – has a threefold meaning. First, a sheet (*milḥafa*) (like a *chādur*) that covers the whole of the body and is put on over other clothes. Second, a wimple (*miqna῾a*) and scarf (*khimār*) (*rū-sarī*) which covers the head, or the head and face, or in addition to that [it covers] the chest and upper arms. Third, a shirt (*pīrāhan*) and baggy clothes that cover the upper body or all of the limbs of the body.

The [meaning of the word] *jilbāb* is ambiguous in two ways. The first [question] is which of the threefold meanings [should one] select? *Milḥafa*, *miqnaʿa* or *pīrāhan*? The other [question] concerns the part of the body it covers. [Is it] the head and neck, or the chest, or the whole of the body? What is for sure is that the *jilbāb* is a [form of] covering. The verse explains the manner of using the clothing so that the purpose of the verse may be understood. The emphasis of the verse is for *drawing the* jilbābs [*around themselves*] not for describing or explaining the *jilbāb*.

Drawing around [*themselves*] has two meanings. The first is bringing [something] close. The second is to make [something] fall, to lay [something] down and to bring [something] low. According to both meanings, the purpose is to enfold the loose and free clothes around oneself, to cover the limbs (*andām*) and arrange and gather clothes together. With regard to the description of clothing, which were usually unsewn and had two loose slits, the verse wants to say that the clothes, in whatever fashion they are, should cover the body and not reveal [the hidden parts] of the limbs. The slits in the clothes are guarded in whatever way possible. The verse does not introduce any new [form] of clothing. The new message of the verse is this: cover the body properly with clothes. Whether prohibiting or affirming, the verse has nothing to do with covering the head and hair.

The reason for covering

On the second point, the correct way of wearing clothes for [the purpose] of being known so that [women] would not be pestered approximates [the Qurʾanic truth]. There are two possible [interpretations] on the topic of being recognised. The first is being known for purity, chastity and nobility as opposed to debauchery, impurity and dirtiness. Without a doubt the manner of clothing is about these two manners of life. The Qurʾan has advised believing women in the first classification not to be mistaken for the women in the second group who were inclined to prostitution, and so in conclusion they would be pestered less by the immoral (*bīmār-dilān*).

The second reason is to be recognised as free-born as opposed to being [known as] a slave. The meaning of this possibility is that due to the difference in clothing for free-born women [as opposed to that of] slaves, immoral people would not molest free-born women who wore these clothes. But the result of [this] corruption is that innocent slaves remain defenceless before immoral people. The second possibility opposes Qurʾanic righteousness and Islamic standards.

On the basis of the first possible [meaning], drawing the *jilbāb*s [around themselves] does not inform [us] of anything more than [the need] to cover the chest in addition to other limbs which have been covered with clothes. Even if covering the hair and the head is one of the *jilbāb*'s meanings, due to its other implications and the definite context of the time of revelation, it is not possible to derive a reasoned command (*ḥukm-i mustafād*) from the verse, although it is not contrary to it either. [But] in order to fulfil [the requirement of] this explicit reason (*ʿillat-i manṣūṣ*), it is sufficient for a believing woman to guard her body.

Verse 24.31

> Tell the believers to lower their eyes [from sexual impurity] and to guard their private parts, that is purer for them. Surely God is aware of whatsoever they do. And tell the believing women to lower their eyes and to guard their private parts, and to not display their finery except that which is visible. And let them draw their '*khimār*' over their '*juyūb*', and not display their finery except to their husbands, or their fathers, or their husbands' fathers, or their sons, or their husbands' sons, or their brothers, or their sisters' sons, or their women, or those whom their right hands possess, or male attendants free of desire, or children who are innocent of the private areas of women. Nor let them stamp their feet such that the finery they conceal becomes known (Q. 24.31).

These verses are the most important of the verses on covering in the glorious Qurʾan. Men have been made responsible for two duties: lowering [their eyes] and refraining from impure glances, and covering the private parts. Women too have been made responsible for these two. But women have added [responsibilities] in addition to those two because of [their] bodily differences. The first is not displaying [her] unknown (*ghayr-i mutaʿārif*) finery, and the second is covering the chest and breasts and neck with the *khimār*.

Clear and hidden finery

The first point, the topic of finery, has been mentioned three times in the verse. The first is when believing women [are told] they should not reveal their finery – except their clear finery. Second, they should not show their unknown finery except to a special group of women, men and children (*maḥram*). Third, they should not walk in such a way that reveals their hidden finery. The meaning of finery in the verse is natural finery, in other words, the limbs of the woman's body, or the body and its beautiful form. Incidental and supplementary finery (make-up and jewellery) have been called *tabarruj* in the Qur'an. Finery has been classified into two groups. The first is known and clear, and the second is hidden and unknown (*'awrat*). Known and clear finery does not need to be covered. Unknown and hidden finery is only to be revealed to the individuals of that group who have been specified in that verse, and [the unknown finery] must remain covered in front of other people.

'Except that which is visible', in other words, the [parts] of the woman's body that have been visible at the time of revelation, [including] the forearms, the shin, the face, the neck and the hair. This amount of covering was a rational course of action and in most known societies this has been the amount [of covering required]. The Arabs of the Hijaz did not cover even this amount properly for the reasons [we have] given [already]. The verse is an explanation for the necessity to cover those [body parts], just as it has also been emphasised in sura 33.59.

'And not display their finery', in other words, taking care not to show the hidden finery and the limbs of the body that have been covered with clothing, from the chest to the knee, especially with clothing made from a single piece of cloth and unsewn from that era. Women of those times were not particular about guarding the principal parts of the body (*'awrat*: from the chest to the knee and upper arms). In this verse, the Qur'an emphatically prohibits believing women from showing these parts – except in front of *maḥram* persons. The principal message of the verse is the prohibition of nakedness. Taking off clothes in front of those who are not *maḥram* is not allowed.

Covering the **juyūb** *with the* **khimār**

The second point is on 'And let them draw their *khumur* over their *juyūb*'. *Khumur*, the plural of *khimār*, is a garment which has three descriptions. The first is a head-covering (*rū-sarī yā sar-andāzī*), the second is a cloak (*ridā'*) (material for covering the upper part of the body), and third a shawl (*izār*) and waist cloth (*lung*) (material for covering the bottom half of the body). With regard to the different meanings of *khimār*, it is clear that it is a garment and a covering, and the suggestion that it is a head-covering and a wimple demands [a particular] context.

Breasts (*juyūb*) are the plural of breast (*jayb*), meaning a cleft [or opening] (*shikāf*). There can be three meanings for this *shikāf*. The first: *shikāf* is the result of a parting in two sides of a garment which in those times was extremely popular. [The second] is the region around the [cleavage] of a woman's chest, and finally it indicates a [woman's] private parts. The first possibility emphasises *do not display their finery except that which is visible*, and there is nothing new to say on this. The third possibility too is another explanation for guarding the private parts which appears in the previous verse. The meaning of the expression *juyūb* is the cleavage in the region of the chest. But it is not impossible to consider any other opening or closing that excites human passion.

Drawing the *khimār* around the *juyūb* means covering the chest with the *khimār*. [The area] from the neck to the knees and upper arms – the *ʿawrat* and finery – must be covered. The cleavage at the chest (*shikāf-i sīna*) has clearly been emphasised by the glorious Qur'an because of the popularity of nakedness of that [part of the body], and [the Qur'an] has prohibited believing women from leaving it visible. Blouses (*dirʿ*) and the *khimār* were not the kind [of garment] that covered the *juyūb* (*garībān va shikāf-i sīna*). The tenor of the verse is that you use the two sides of the *khimār* in such a way that you cover completely your chest. You do not let the *khimār* (if it means a head-cover) dangle, nor do you tie it behind your head. And if it means a cloak (a shawl and cloak for the upper half of the body), you collect and gather it together so that your chest remains covered. It should not remain unsaid that if the *khimār* also means a head-covering, it is nearer to the turban of the Arabs than the legal head-covering that covers the hair.

In any case, the verse does not clearly indicate the necessity for covering the hair and head. The arguments agree with covering above the chest. With respect to the ambiguity of the word *khimār*, concerning which one of the three meanings it has – head-covering (*sar-andāzī*), cloak (*ridā'*) and shawl (*izār*) – and with regard to the possibility of the similarity of the turban, meaning a head-covering, attributing a scarf (*rū-sarī*) to cover the hair requires contexts which the [Qur'anic] verse does not contain. In addition to [the lack of] definitive contexts in the age of revelation, such as the amount of women's clothing at that time, such a possibility is quite improbable.

Conclusion

The conclusion to be understood from these verses and other verses of the glorious Qur'an is that men and believing women had the duty for upholding chastity and lowering their gazes from impure things. In addition to these two duties, believing women are legally responsible to guard their bodies, which is the 'natural finery', from non-*maḥram* individuals. And they must not allow [their bodies] from the neck to their knees and upper arms be seen by the non-*maḥram* in any circumstance. In particular, they have the responsibility to cover their chests with appropriate garments from the eyes [of the non-*maḥram*]. On the topic of covering leg-shins, the upper arms, neck, face and hair, there is no Qur'anic proof. And the expression 'except that which is visible' in the age of revelation did not [explicitly] point to these parts [of the body]. But in the fatwas of the jurists 'except that which is visible' has included [only] the face, the palms (the hands from the wrists) and the feet (from the ankle). Certainly, there is no Qur'anic support [for this], and it is based on support from the narrations. One should not expect [support] from the Qur'an too in these particulars.

It appears that this minimum of covering of the believing woman's body (neck to the knee and elbow), which is also rational, is one of the fixed religious commands and its [lawfulness] is not diminished with the changing conditions of time and place. Covering more than this certainly depends on circumstances. But God knows best.

There is no need to mention that the discussion on the legal hijab, in practice, does not finish with the Qur'an. There is a need to study the relevant narrations, the Sunna of the Prophet, and the lives of the imams. I will investigate the discussion about the emergence of the narrations and the balance of their proof and the Sunna and the lives of the friends of religion.

With regard to the importance and sensitivity of the discussion, I welcome criticisms and suggestions from those who have opinions. Praise belongs to God, the Lord of the two worlds.*

* Last week I finished studying the book [titled] *The Legal Hijab in the Age of the Prophet*, written by the respected researcher Mr Amir Turkshavand. So, I endeavour to give my own opinion about it, since the author and his readers, and many friends have also asked for it. I have greatly benefitted from this research in today's discussion of the investigation of the topic.

SECOND CHAPTER: THE HIJAB IN SHI'I NARRATIONS

This section includes one preface, eight premises, ten discussions, a summary of findings and a conclusion. The readers who do not have the patience for detailed scientific discussion can suffice with studying the preface, summary and conclusion.

Preface

A short discussion [in the previous chapter] was given about the glorious Qur'an's balance of proofs on women's legal hijab. Its conclusion was that in addition to the general duty for chastity and lowering the gaze from impurity, they are legally responsible to guard their bodies, which is the 'natural finery', from non-*maḥram* individuals. And they must not allow [their bodies] from the neck to their knees and upper arms to be seen by non-*maḥrams* in any circumstance. In particular, they have the responsibility to cover their chests with appropriate garments from the eyes [of the non-*maḥram*]. There is no Qur'anic reason for covering the shins, the forearms, neck, face and hair.

Even if one of the meanings of *jilbāb* (Q. 33.59) and *khimār* (Q. 24.31) is a head-covering (*rū-sarī*), in the Arabic language the first has been understood as meaning a sheet (*milḥafa*) and a loose shirt, and the second means a gown and shawl, and in the two verses no more than clothing per se can be understood or at least, on their own, these words do not imply a head-covering or a scarf. 'Let them draw their *jalābīb*', or in other words, gather close to you [your] untied and loose garments, cover your limbs, and arrange your clothing. Throwing the *khimār* over the *juyūb* means covering the breasts and chest with clothing. Not one of the Qur'anic verses is a proof that conforms with covering the head and hair, and the corroboration of such a command is possible only with the support of narrations.

In the second part [we] engage [in a discussion] of hijab in the narrations. Due to the lengthy discussion, the narrations are investigated in two parts: Shi'i narrations and Sunni narrations. In the first part, the hijab in the Shi'i narrations is studied, and the hijab in Sunni narrations will be presented in the subsequent part.

Some well-known questions about the narrations are [included] in this presentation. To what extent do the narrations from the Prophet and the imams corroborate women's legal hijab? In particular, what narrations support covering the hair, head and neck? Is the 'whole of the woman's body *'awrat*, and [can] only parts of it [be seen] without clothing'? Is there a reliable proof for the permission of showing and looking at it [with] the reliable support of the Prophet's and imams' [narrations]? Or, is the principle based on exemption (*bara'at*)[1] and only parts of the woman's body must be covered, and looking at them is forbidden because there is a reliable proof? Or does [the command for] men not to look at women and women not to look at men have reliable legal support? What are the words of the Prophet, or the imams, on the interpretation of the verses in sura 24 about women's external finery? Do the narrations appear successively (*mutawātir*) or are they scattered about [in hadith collections in] the chapter about the legal hijab? Are the proofs of narrations for covering the head and neck sufficient and direct, or are they indirect and necessary?

1 [This is one of the principles of application. See Murtaza Mutahhari, *Jurisprudence and its Principles*, trans. Mohammad Salman Tawhidi, New York n.d., https://wwwal-islam.org.]

Eight Premises

First premise

According to the minimum criteria of the science of hadith, narrations in collections of narratives are not attributed to the Prophet or imams without an assessment of their authenticity. The examples that are presented in this discussion are made up of reliable narrations (sound and trusted). Unreliable narrations are mentioned only to [show] the imperfection of commands that cannot be related to religion. I have selected these narrations which are discussed in four topics in the jurisprudential books on purity, prayer, hajj, and marriage, and in a way engage in a discussion about hijab and covering.

Second premise

In these reliable narrations there are very few (countable on one's fingers) commands attributed to the Prophet and the Commander of the Faithful. All the commands about the hijab have been related from four imams: Imam Baqir, Imam Sadiq, Imam Kazim, and Imam Riza. In other words, between the years 94–203 after the hijra, and in particular in the second century of the hijra. Of course, most of the narrations on other questions too come from these four imams, because in their time the possibility of explaining [matters] was greater than in the times of the other imams. But the difference on the question of the hijab with other legal questions is that the least attribution to the Prophet and the imams is evident. Among reliable narrations related to the hijab, except in the discussion about prayer, there is nothing even about Fatima Zahra. This guess (*ḥads*) is likely: that the conditions of the hijab in the second century took a stricter form, and in the first century it was closer to the Qur'anic form which has [already] been explained.

Third premise

My present discussion is limited to Shi'i narrations. With regard to the legal hijab in its current form, it is relatively the same among Shi'is and Sunnis. Investigating the Sunni narrations is a separate subject of discussion that I shall engage with when [I have] the opportunity. It seems most of these commands first took the form of narrations in the time of the caliphs in the first half of the first century. In the second half of the same century, they become more formalised, so that in the second century they are almost changed into being a part of Islamic identity. I point out briefly [that] the situation of Sunni traditions on the question of the hijab are stricter and more rigorous than the Shiʿi narrations. Comparing the narrations of the sects on the question of the hijab will cast a light on many ambiguities present in the discussion.

Fourth premise

Contrary to expectation, [the number of] reliable and direct narrations of the legal hijab are much less than expected. There are no narrations which are *tawātar lafẓī* [many narrations with exactly the same words] and there are no narrations which are *tawātar maʿānī* [many narrations with the same meaning]. The number of reliable narrations does not even reach the middle ground in terms of number (*istifāża*).[2] The majority of these reliable narrations indirectly indicate the hijab for the head and hair. Many of the answers rely upon between one to three reliable narrations. Of course, there are many narrations on the topic of covering a woman at the time of a marriage proposal (*khāstagārī*). The questions that were asked of the aforementioned four imams show that the legal hijab for their followers was not a customary issue, simply because they asked about it. These questions confirm that in the first century, and in particular in the time of the Prophet and the Commander of the Faithful, the actual customary hijab was not the prevailing custom, and even a century later questions were not asked about the clearest commands of the hijab. An example [of a question from the time of four imams] is the question asked of Imam Riza by Bazanti (d. 221 AH) about whether the sister of a husband's wife is *maḥram*. In the same manner [is the question from] the learned among the followers of Imam Sadiq about manifest finery. The [understandings] about hijab gradually became stricter, until in the time of Imam ʿAskari [people] talked of the necessity of the *niqāb* (face-covering) and the *burqa*, and this is the second half of the third century.

Fifth premise

Nearly all the commentators, narrators, hadith experts, jurists and theologians were men, and the atmosphere of patriarchy cast a shadow over religious texts. They were extremely generous with regards to the rights of men and the duties

2 [Narrations are divided into three categories. The first is *aḥad*, which is a narration from a single source. The second category is the *tawātar*, which is a narration with is cited from many sources, and the *istifāża* is a narration cited by a number between the previous two categories.]

of women, and they were extremely tight-fisted with regards to the rights of women and the duties of men. A common example of this is the obligation of the command for the non-necessity of covering a man's body with the prohibition for a woman to look at it, and the obligation of the command for the necessity to cover a woman's body and the prohibition for a man to look at it. This kind of patriarchal [thinking] on questions about the hijab clearly locates most women within the excess of 'the whole of a woman's body is *ʿawrat* unless there is a proof for it being excluded'. And the minimum covering [is recommended] for men – his front and behind, especially when it does not include his sides! In the current discussion I only interpret narrations based on traditional sources. I will save the topic about their proof and arguments to the subsequent discussion – fatwas.

Sixth premise

Legal covering (*sātir-i sharīʿ*) is divided into two kinds: a covering at ritual prayer (*sātir-i ṣalvatī*) and [a covering at the time of] non-ritual prayer. The first kind is a covering that must be observed at the time of prayer, even if there is no-one looking. The second kind is a covering that must be observed when there is someone looking in one of two situations: when the observer is non-*maḥram*, and when the observer is *maḥram*. There are varied narrations on these two kinds. The main discussion is about covering for non-ritual prayer before the non-*maḥram* observer. But the covering for ritual prayer and the covering before the *maḥram* individual will be explained in a subsequent section.

Seventh premise: covering for prayers

On the topic of covering at the time for prayer there are four groups of narrations.

First group: narrations that stipulate the necessity of covering the head at prayer time:

i. Zarara asked Imam Baqir about the least amount of clothing permissible for women when reciting prayers. He said: the shirt (*dirʿ/pīrāhan*) and coverlet (*milḥafa*) which is thrown over the head and by which she covers herself.[3]
ii. ʿAli ibn Jaʿfar asked his brother Imam Kazim about how a woman who

3 *Al-Tahdhīb*, vol. II, 217, hadith no. 853; *Al-Istibṣār*, vol. I, 217, hadith no. 1478; *Al-Wasāʾil, al-Abwāb Libās al-Muṣalā*, *bāb* 28, hadith no. 9, vol. 4, 407.

> had only a *milḥafa* could pray. He said, she should wrap it around her and cover her head [with it] and recite prayers. So, there is no problem if her feet appear from [under the *milḥafa*] and she cannot prevent it.

The instruction from these narrations is the necessity for covering the head, and the hair of the head too, like the head, must be covered. The first narration points to the complete covering of the head and the second narration deems it permissible [for women] not to cover the feet in a situation when it is not possible to do so. But these narrations do not point to the covering of long hair which passes past the neck. Regarding the covering of hair, there is a narration about the prayer of Fatima Zahra:

> Fuzayl related a narration from Imam Baqir that Fatima prayed in a long shirt with a *khimār* over [her] head. There was no more than this over her head because she had covered her hair and ears with it.[4]

Fatima Zahra's act [of covering] in itself demonstrates at most permission [to pray covered] and preference [to do so].

Second group: a narration that points to the permissibility for prayers with a bare head and without a scarf:

> Ibn Bakir related from Imam Sadiq that there is no problem for a free Muslim woman to recite prayers with a bare head.[5]

On this topic, there is this very reliable narration. There also exists another narration from the same narrator with a weak chain of transmission.[6]

Third group: narrations allowing the prayers of slaves without scarves:

i. Muhammad bin Muslim asked Imam Baqir, 'Should a female slave cover her head at prayers?' He replied, 'The *migna'a* is not [compulsory] for the female slave.'[7]

---

4 *Al-Faqīh*, vol. I, 257, hadith no. 789; *Al-Wasā'il*, *Abwāb Libās al- Muṣalā*, *bāb* 28, hadith no. 2, vol. 4, 405.

5 *Al-Tahdhīb*, vol 2, 218, hadith no. 857; *Al-Instibṣār*, vol. 1, 389, hadith no. 1481; *Al-Wasā'il*, *Abwāb Libās al-Muṣalā*, *bāb* 29, hadith no. 5, vol. 4, 410.

6 Narration of Ibn Bakir, *al-Tahdhīb*, vol. 2, 218, hadith no. 858; *al-Istibṣār*, vol. 1, 389, hadith no. 1428; al-*Wasā'il*, *Abwāb Libās al-Muṣalā*, hadith no. 6, vol. 4, 410.

7 *al-Kāfī*, vol. 3, 394, hadith no. 2; *al-Tahdhīb*, vol. 2, 217, hadith no. 855; *al-Wasā'il*,

ii. ʿAbd al-Rahman ibn Hajaj related from Imam Kazim that the *miqnaʿa* is not compulsory for the female slave during prayer.[8]

A *fourth group* should also be added, and these narrations give permission for pre-pubescent girls not to cover the head which is presented in the eighth discussion to come.

Conclusion: First, on the subject of prayer, there is only one reliable narration that clearly speaks of covering the hair, and that too pertains to the manner of prayer of Fatima Zahra, which cannot be used for the necessity of others. But other narrations are about covering the head or non-covering of it, and indirectly point to covering the hair on the head (and not hair hanging down and loose around the neck, shoulders and waist).

Second, the context of narrations in the first group is the necessity of covering [the head]. The context of the narrations in the third group is also about the necessity of covering the head and, following that, the hair of free women during prayer. The context of one narration from the second group is on the permissibility of praying without a veil or scarf.

The third point is the permission for prayers without a head-covering [only] in cases when a non-*maḥram* is not present. Ibn Bakir is definite. As for female slaves, such a condition is certainly unnecessary.

Fourth, there are reliable narrations opposed to the covering the head during prayers. What the practical duty is [for women] in light of these reliable narrations will be discussed in the next section (on fatwas).

*Eighth premise: minimum covering before non-permitted individuals (*maḥāram*)*

In accordance with Q. 24.31, it is permissible to show hidden finery in front of individuals who are *maḥram*. It is necessary to cover the *ʿawrat* for Qurʾanic reasons and based on narrations with multiple recordings (*mutawātir*). In a reliable [narration] Husayn ibn ʿAlwan [reported from] Imam Sadiq that the *ʿawrat* has been determined [as the area] from the navel to the knee;[9] in other words,

al-Abwāb Libās al-Muṣalā, *bāb* 29, hadith no.1, vol. 4, 404.

8 *al-Tahdhīb*, vol. 2, 218, hadith no. 853; *Al-Wasāʾil*, *Abwāb Libās al-Muṣalā*, *bāb* 29, hadith no. 2, vol. 4, 404.

9 Muwathiqa al-Husayn bin ʿAlwan from Jaʿfar, *Qurb al-Isnād*, 49; *al-Wasāʾil*, *Abwab Nikāh al-ʿUbayd al-Umāʾ*, *bāb* 44, hadith no. 7., vol. 21, 148.

looking at this part of the body is prohibited and not allowed for *maḥram* individuals and others.

On the specific topic of the hair of *maḥram* individuals, there is a narration: 'Sakuni relates from Imam Sadiq, from his father Imam Baqir, that it is not a problem if [a man] looks at the hair of his mother, sisters or daughter.' It appears that the limit of permissibility for *maḥram* individuals in the narrations was wider than the legal custom.

The Ten Discussions

Following these eight premises, now I will cover ten discussions studying the various dimensions of non-prayer covering in front of the non-*maḥram* individual.

First discussion: the limits of external finery

The verses of sura 24 give permission to show external finery and to look at it, but revealing and looking at the inner finery is only permitted for *maḥram* individuals. The most important narrations which explain the external and inner finery are explained below:

i. Fuzayl asked Imam Sadiq about the two forearms of a woman, whether it is a finery about which God has commanded, 'Do not reveal your finery except to your husbands'? He said, 'Yes, the finery is [the body] lower than the *khimār* and [higher than] the wrists (*much-i dast*).'

According to this narration, the [the two] forearms, above the place for bracelets, and also the body, lower than the place for the *khimār*, are considered inner finery. But the place for the *khimār*, apparently, is at the breasts (*garībān*) and it includes [anything] beneath that, from the chest down.[10]

ii. Abi Basir asked Imam Sadiq about [the meaning of] God's words, 'And do not reveal your finery except that which is clear.' [Imam Sadiq] said, '[That which is clear refers to] a ring and bangle which is a bracelet.'[11]

---

10 *al-Kāfī*, vol. 5, 530, hadith no. 1; *al-Wasā'il*, *Abwāb Muqadammāt al-Nikāḥ*, *bāb* 109, hadith no. 1; vol. 20, 200.

11 *al-Kāfī*, vol. 5, 521, hadith no. 4; *al-Wasā'il*, *Abwāb Muqadddamāt al-Nikāḥ wa Adabihi*, *bāb* 109, hadith no. 4, vol. 20, 201.

In this narration there is an allusion to a ring and bracelet, together with their locations, in other words, it includes the fingers of the hand to the wrists.

iii. Masʿada ibn Ziyad heard from Imam Sadiq that he was asked about what a woman [may] show from her finery. In answer he said, '[Her] face and two hands [up to her wrists].'[12]

This narration is a support for the famous fatwa for the lack of necessity for covering the face and the palms. According to this, it is permissible to show or look at the face and the two hands (from fingertips to the wrists) which have been included in the manifest finery.

iv. Saʿd Askaf related from Imam Baqir: 'A youth from the Ansar became aware of a woman in Medina. In that time, the women used to tie their head-coverings behind their ears. The youth looked at her as he came towards her. As she passed by, the youth glanced at her. He entered an alleyway which was called so-and-so, and just as he was looking at the back of that woman, suddenly his face scraped against a bone or some glass in a wall, and it cut his face. Once the woman had gone, he realised that blood had flowed down his clothes and chest. He said to himself, "O God! I will go to the Prophet and tell him what has happened." So, he did this. When the Prophet saw him, he asked "What happened?" So [the youth] explained what had happened. Then Gabriel descended with this verse: 'Tell the believing men to lower their glance… "'[13]

This narration which is about the occasion of the descent of sura 24.30–31, tells [us] that the women of the Hijaz used to tie their *miqnaʿa* behind their ears, and so, apparently, their necks and chests were naked. Maybe the verse indicates that women should tie their *miqnaʿa* in the front so that their necks and chests would also be covered. Certainly, hadiths are not clear on this topic.

In these hadiths, hair-covering has definitely been assumed, [but] it had not been practised. The *khimār* in the first hadith and the *miqināʿ* in the last hadith have been understood as a head-covering. In the first three hadiths, the question

12 *Qurb al-Asnād*, 40; *al-Wasāʾil, Abwāb Muqaddamāt al-Nikāḥ wa Adabhi, bāb* 109, hadith no. 5, vol. 20, 202.

13 *al-Kāfī*, vol. 5, 559, hadith no. 14; *al-Wasāʾil, Abwāb Muqaddamāt al-Nikāḥ wa Adabhi, bāb* 104, hadith no. 4, vol. 20, 192.

has been about the places of the permitted finery. These places have been fixed at the face and the two palms. All the [other] parts of the body, including the hair, are regarded as inner finery and covering it is necessary. All three narrations are from the words of Imam Sadiq.

Second discussion: permission for lightening [the command] for the hijabs of old women

Q. 24.60 has given permission to elderly women – understood as those who no longer hope to marry – to set aside their clothing (*thiyāb-ishān*) on the condition that they are not immodest (*tabarruj*) (made-up). What was the meaning of the clothes (*thiyābī*) that this group of women could set aside?

i. Halabi narrates from Imam Sadiq that [someone] recited the verse 'take off their clothes'. He said, '[It means] the *khimār* and *jilbāb*.' I said, 'In front of everyone?' He answered, 'In front of everyone [man and woman], without putting on finery. Certainly, it is better for them if they do not do such a thing' [– if they do not take off their clothes]. And the finery that they show is the thing that appears in another verse,[14] Q. 24.31 ['Except that which is visible'], and the rest of the body is in the category of inner finery.
ii. Muhammad bin Muslim [asked] Imam Sadiq about the words of God, 'As for the elderly women who have no hope of marriage', which are those clothes that it is right to take off? He said, 'The *jilbāb*'.[15]
iii. Hariz bin ʿAbdallah narrates from Imam Sadiq that he recited the verse 'they take off their clothes'. He said, 'The *jilbāb* and *khimār* when the woman is elderly.'

These three hadiths about clothing have explained the subject of the discussion of the verse as the *jilbāb* and the *khimār*. Elderly women were allowed not to wear the *jilbāb* and *khimār*. If the *jilbāb* and *khimār* mean a head-covering and scarf, these hadiths point indirectly to the permission for showing their head hair, and consequently the lack of permission for other women to show their head hair. The

14 *al-Kāfī*, vol. 5, 522, hadith no. 1; *al-Wasāʾil*, *Abwāb Muqaddamāt al-Nikāḥ wa Adabhi*, *bāb* 110, hadith no. 2, vol. 20, 202.
15 *al-Kāfī*, vol. 5, 522, hadith no. 4; *al-Wasāʾil*, *Abwāb Muqaddamāt al-Nikāḥ wa Adabhi*, *bāb* 110, hadith no. 4, vol. 20, 202.

following hadith about the hair of the sister of a man's wife – which comes in the following discussion – is clear about the permissibility for the non-covering of the hair and forearms of this kind of woman, the non-permission for other women, and the context for this, [and it shows] that the meaning of the *jilbāb* and *khimār* in these hadiths are the head-covering and scarf.

Third discussion: prohibition on looking at the hair of the sister of a man's wife

On the discussion of the hijab, a wife's sisters are not included among the *maḥram*, even if marriage at the same time with two sisters is not permitted.

> Bazanti asked Imam Sadiq, 'Is it permissible for a man to look at the hair of his wife's sisters?' He said, 'No, unless the wife's sisters are elderly.' I asked again, 'Are the wife's sisters and unknown (*gharīb*) women the same?' He said, 'Yes.' I said, 'In this case, if she is elderly, at what part of her body may I look?' He said, 'Hair and two forearms.'[16]

This hadith gives three commands. First, the prohibition of looking at the hair of the wife's sisters. Second, the prohibition of looking at the hair of non-*maḥram* women who have been mentioned in the hadith [as the same] as foreign [women]. Third, the permissibility of looking at the hair and forearms of elderly women (in this respect there is no difference between a wife's elderly sisters and an elderly unknown [woman]). This hadith is the strongest support for the necessity of covering the hair of women, and the prohibition of men looking at them. And the word 'hair' (*mū*) has been mentioned specifically in [the hadith] and it directly points to the prohibition of looking at the hair of the wife's sisters and unknown women – of course, on the condition that the need for women to cover and the prohibition for men to look is understood as inherent.

Fourth discussion: the permissibility of looking at a woman's hair (muḥasin) at the time of proposing

At the time of a marriage proposal, a woman may leave her hair uncovered, and the suitor may look at it. It is clear that such a gaze will not be without danger and pleasure. Despite this, it is permissible.

---

16 *Qurb al-Isnād*, 160; *al-Wasā'il*, *Abwāb Muqaddamāt al-Nikāḥ wa Adabhi*, *bāb* 107, hadith no. 1, vol. 20, 199.

i. ʿAbdallah Sinan asked Imam Sadiq, 'A man desires to marry a woman, so can he look at her hair (*mū-hā-yash*)?' He replied, 'Yes. He wants to buy a [spouse] at the best price.'[17]

At the time of a marriage proposal, a man may look at his future wife's hair. The previous expression is [from] a narration about the dowry.

ii. Ghiyath ibn Ibrahim related from Imam Sadiq, from his father [Imam Baqir], from Imam ʿAli, about a man who looks at the beautiful qualities (*zībā'ī-hā*) of a woman that he intends to marry. He said, 'It is not a problem. He wants to buy goods [so] that if the matter progresses [and the marriage takes place, the beautiful qualities] will be his.'

At a time of a marriage proposal, a man can look at the beautiful qualities of his wife's body. He wants to marry [her] and if her price [is good] she will be his wife. In this hadith the beautiful qualities of a woman are not specified.

iii. Bazanti relates that Yunus ibn Yaʿqub asked Imam Sadiq about a man who wanted to marry a woman, whether it is permissible or not to look at her. He said, 'Yes, and the woman is allowed to wear thin clothes, because the man wants to buy a wife at the best price.'[18]

At the time of making a proposal of marriage it is permissible to wear clothes that are thinner than ordinary clothes. The rationale of these narrations is the necessity of covering the hair and the other beautiful qualities of a woman, and the prohibition of looking at them in times other than at a marriage proposal.

Fifth discussion: the permissibility of looking at the hair and hands of dhimmī women

It is permissible to look at the hair and hands of *dhimmī* women for whom the Muslim legal hijab is unnecessary. It is clear that the command is for the permissibility for all women among the People of the Book; indeed, it unconditionally

---

17 *al-Faqīh*, vol. 3, 260, hadith no. 24; *al-Wasā'il, Abwāb Muqaddamāt al-Nikāḥ wa Ādābihi, bāb* 36, hadith no. 7, vol. 20, 89.

18 *ʿAlal al-sharāʿi.* p. 500, hadith no. 1; *al-Wasā'il, Abwāb Muqaddamāt al-Nikāḥ wa Ādābhi, bāb* 36, hadith no. 11, vol. 20, 90.

includes all non-Muslim women. Neither Islamic covering is necessary for them, nor is it prohibited to look at places that they usually do not cover. We note that the *dhimmīs* lived within the security [provided] by the Islamic government, and the Prophet did not make it compulsory for them to cover their hair. The tenor of this hadith is that it has been necessary for Muslim women to cover the hair and hands. Sakuni narrates from Imam Sadiq, [who narrates] from the Prophet, who said, 'There is no prohibition in looking at the hair and hands of *dhimmī* women.'[19]

Sixth discussion: the permissibility of looking at the head of Bedouin women

'Ubad ibn Suhayb heard from Imam Sadiq that he said, 'It is not a problem to look at the heads [of women] from Tahama [on the outskirts of Mecca], female Arab Bedouin who live on the outskirts of cities, and [women] with no religion among the non-Arabs, because they do not take heed of [advice] when they warn them.'[20]

This narration has been understood as permission [for men] to look at the heads of Bedouin women. The reason is that they do not accept [the advice to cover] when they are 'prohibited from evil' (*nahy az munkar*), and they do not take steps to cover their heads. If what has been recorded in the text is correct ('they do not accept it when they warn them'), the meaning is that it is not forbidden to look at the women whose ears are not covered by the hijab, since they have no self-respect. In any case, this narration discusses the head, and indirectly points to the hair. If looking at the hair of inattentive women is permissible, its meaning is the non-permissibility of looking at the hair of believing women and the necessity of covering for them.

Seventh discussion: the necessity of covering the heads of girls in puberty and covering women's heads from pubescent males

The [three] narrations below establish a time when it is necessary for girls to observe the legal hijab and when it is women's responsibility to observe the hijab in front of boys:

i. 'Abd al-Rahman ibn Hajaj asked Imam Kazim from which age a girl

19 *al-Kāfī*, vol. 5, 524, hadith no. 1; *al-Wasā'il*, *Abwāb Muqaddamāt al-Nikāḥ*, *bāb* 112, hadith no. 1, vol. 20, 205.

20 *Al-Kāfī*, vol. 5, 524, hadith no. 1; *al-Faqīh*, vol. 3, 300, hadith no. 1438; *'Ilal al-Sharā'yi*, 565, hadith no. 1; *Dhikr Ahl al-Dhimma badl al-'Ulūj*, *Wasā'il*, *Abwāb Muqaddamāt al-Nikāḥ*, *bāb* 113, hadith no. 1, vol. 20, 206.

who had not yet apprehended [sexual matters] must cover her head from a non-*maḥram* individual? At which age should she cover her head with a *miqnaʿa* during prayers? He said, 'She should not cover her head unless performing prayer is forbidden for her.'[21]

This hadith points to two commands. First, it is necessary for a pubescent girl to cover her head during prayer and from non-*maḥram* individuals. Second, a pre-pubescent girl can perform prayers bareheaded, without a head-covering. There is no need [for her] to cover her head in front of a non-*maḥram* individual. Once again, covering the head is explained and it indirectly points to covering the hair too.

ii. Bazanti related from Imam Riza that 'a young boy of seven years of age is compelled to pray, and a woman does not cover her hair from him so long as he does not have a wet dream'.[22]

Based on this hadith, a woman who is responsible [must] cover her hair from a pubescent boy whereas she can keep her head bare before a pre-pubescent boy.

iii. Bazanti related from Imam Riza that 'a woman does not cover her head from a young boy until he reaches puberty'.[23]

The content of this hadith is the same as the previous one, the difference being that this hadith is about covering the head and the previous one is about covering the hair.

Conclusion: Before puberty, girls and boys are not considered [sufficiently] responsible. It is neither necessary to cover the head and hair of girls, whether praying or in front of non-*maḥram* individuals, nor is it necessary for women to cover their hair in front of pre-pubescent boys. But after puberty, girls must cover their heads and hair during prayer and before non-*maḥram* individuals. Women too are duty-bound to cover their heads and hair before pubescent boys, just like [before] men.

---

21 *al-Kāfī*, vol. 5, 533, hadith no. 2; *al-Wasāʾil*, *Abwāb Muqaddamāt al-Nikāḥ wa Ādābhi.*
22 *al-Faqih*, vol. 3, 276, hadith no. 1308; *al-Wasa'il*, *Abwāb Muqaddamat al-Nikāḥ wa Ādābhi*, *bāb* 126, hadith no. 2, vol. 20, 228.
23 *Qurb al-Isnād*, 170; *al-Wasāʾil*, *Abwāb Muqaddamāt al-Nikāḥ wa Ādābhi*, *bāb* 126, hadith no. 4, vol 20, 229.

Eighth discussion: stopping the intention (dakhālat-i niyyat) of looking at women

On the discussion of looking, there is a narration that can serve as a foundation for a jurisprudential rule; repealing the command not to look at woman, depending upon a man's intention.

> ʿAli ibn Suwayd asked Imam Riza, '[My profession is such that] I am caught up with looking at women, so [sometimes] I enjoy looking at them. [Am I carrying out a prohibited profession?]' He said, 'Oh ʿAli! If God knows that your intention [in looking] is righteous, then there is no problem. But refrain from fornication because the blessing will disappear [from your work and] your religion will vanish.'[24]

Because of his job (such as a seller of cloth or a dyer) the narrator comes into contact with women, and he looks at them during business. And according to the dictates of human nature he derives pleasure from beauty, and so he enjoys the beauty [of the women] because a man derives pleasure from looking at every beautiful thing, human or non-human. The answer of the imam is conditional permission, based upon correct intention and chaste looking, free from desire. A human looking at something beautiful that is twinned with pleasure, arises from human nature. It is not a look that arises from sexual instinct, such as the look of a man upon his wife. Is it possible for a human to see a beautiful view or a beautiful face and not to derive pleasure? Yes, one must carefully distinguish the two kinds of pleasure from each other, and this is a possible task. A chaste look is permitted, and an unchaste look is an arrow from Satan's bow, and Imam [Riza] gives a warning about an unchaste look by referring to fornication, which begins with the fornication of the eye, and he points to the possibility of a chaste look and correct intention. This narration has been the topic of much [scholarly] endeavour by the great shaykh [Murtaza] Ansari.[25] For reasons of sensitivity, I related the explications of this narration as a summary and an explanation from Ayatollah Khuʾi.[26]

---

24 *al-Kāfī*, vol. 5, 542, hadith no. 6; *al-Wasāʾil, Abwāb Muqaddamāt al-Nikāḥ wa Ādabhi, bāb* 1, hadith no. 3, vol. 20, 308.
25 *Kitāb al-Nikāḥ*, vol. 1, 54.
26 *Taqrīrāt Mabānī-yi al-ʿUrwa, Kitāb al-Nikāḥ*, vol. 1, 54.

Ninth discussion: an example of some of the famous sayings, lacking reliable chains of transmission

There are a number of narrations about women which are widely repeated but they lack reliable chains of transmission. I will point to a few of these from numerous collections:

i. Shaykh Saduq related from the Prophet, 'God's anger falls upon a married woman whose glance is focused on someone who is not her husband or someone who is not her *maḥram*.'[27]

The chain of transmission is very weak because there are several unknown individuals within its narration.

ii. Tabarsi [related] from the Prophet that Fatima said to him in a hadith: 'It is better for women if they don't look at men, and men don't look at them either.'[28]

[This] narration, without a chain of transmission, is weak.

iii. Narration of Ahmad bin Abi ʿAbdallah Barqi: 'Ibn Abi Maktum [who was blind] sought permission from the Prophet to enter [his house] when ʿAʾisha and Hafsa were near them. He said to those two, "Get up and go into [another part of] the house." They said, "He is blind." He said, "Although he does not see you, you see him."'[29]

This is a *mursal* narration and its chain of transmission is weak.

iv. Tabarsi narrated about Umm Salama: 'I went to the Prophet, and Maymuna was also with him when Ibn Umm Maktum asked to enter [the house]. This was after the descent of the hijab verse. [The Prophet] said, "Cover yourselves." We said, "O Prophet of God, is he not blind?

27 *ʿAqab al-aʿmal*, 338, *al-Wasāʾil, Abwāb Muqaddāmt al-Nikāḥ wa Ādābhi, bāb* 129, hadith no. 1, vol. 20, 232.
28 *Makaram al-Akhlāq*, 233; *al-Wasāʾil, Abwāb Muqaddāmt al-Nikāḥ wa Ādābhi, bāb* 129, hadith no. 3, vol. 20, 232.
29 *al-Kāfī*, vol. 5, 534, hadith no. 2; *al-Wasāʾil, Abwāb Muqaddamāt al-Nikāḥ wa Ādābhi, bāb* 129, hadith no. 1, vol. 20, 232.

He cannot see us." He said, "Are you also not blind, and do you not see him?"'[30]

This is a *mursal* hadith and the chain of transmission is weak.

Tenth discussion: is the whole of a women's body ʿawrat?

Looking at *ʿawrat* is unpleasant (*nā-khush*) for humans. A woman's and a man's genital organs and anus [are called] the *ʿawrat*. Another way of speaking, which has gradually become current among Muslims, [is that] the whole of the woman is the agent of sedition and the means of Satan's temptation, and a woman's body, all of it, is *ʿawrat*. According to this meaning, it is necessary for [a woman] to remain covered except [in front of her] husband and *maḥram* individuals. In order to avoid the calamities that derive from a woman and her body, the best place for her is in a corner of the house. On this topic, I will point to two narrations, the chains of transmission of which are better.

i. Hisham bin Salim related from Imam Sadiq that the Prophet said, 'Women are weak. They are *ʿawrat*. Cover *ʿawrat* in the house, and you cover weakness with silence.'[31]
ii. From the Sahih [collection] of Masʿada Ibn Sadaqa, Abi ʿAbdallah said, 'The Commander of the Faithful said … and truly the Prophet said, "Women are weak and they are *ʿawrat*. Cover them with silence and cover their *ʿawrat* in the house."'[32]

These two narrations have the same content. These kinds of narrations should not be applied at all times and places. Even if some of the hadith collectors and jurists have supposed [it is possible] to extract the rule of 'a woman is *ʿawrat*' from them, the primary principle is the necessity of covering the whole of a woman's body, unless a reliable reason [for the opposite] is found within this principle, and that in only the face and hands. The lack of moderation in this reasoning in

30 *Makaram al-Akhlāq*, p. 233; *al-Wasāʾil, Abwāb Muqaddāmt al-Nikāḥ wa Ādābhi, bāb* 129, hadith no. 4, vol. 20, 232.
31 *al-Kāfī*, vol. 5, 535, hadith no. 4; *Majālis al-Ṭūsī*, vol. 2, 276; *al-Faqih*, vol. 3, 247, hadith no. 3; *al-Wasāʾil, Abwāb Muqaddamāt al-Nikāḥ wa Ādābhi, bāb* 24, hadith no. 4, vol. 20, 66.
32 *al-Kafi*, vol. 5, 534, hadith no. 1; *al-Wasāʾil, Abwāb Muqaddamāt al-Nikāḥ wa Ādābhi, bāb* 24, hadith no. 1, vol. 20, 65.

some of the fatwas will be discussed in brief, and it will be proved that this kind of foundation is baseless.

Findings

An investigation of Shiʿi narrations with reliable chains of transmission on the question of the hijab shows that:

i. Not one command about the hijab is attributed to the Prophet other than those on two subjects: one is the command giving permission to look at the hair and the hands of *dhimmī* women, and another is that women are *ʿawrat*. The second does not point directly to the issue of the hijab.
ii. Not one command on the principle questions of the hijab is attributed to the Commander of the Faithful other than permission to look at the beautiful qualities of a women at the time of a marriage proposal.
iii. Among the reliable narrations, there is not a single expression about the hijab from the first lady of Islam, Fatima Zahra. On the discussion about the hijab, there is only one reliable narration from Imam Baqir about the manner of her hijab at the time of prayer. The Mother of the Believers, Khadija, had passed away before the descent of the hijab verse.
iv. Nearly all of the commands [related to] the hijab come from the time of the four imams in the second century of the hijra; Imam Muhammad Baqir, Imam Jaʿfar Sadiq, Imam Musa Kazim and Imam ʿAli ibn Musa al-Riza.
v. There is no single narration reported by multiple reporters with the same words, or in the same meaning (*mutawātir lafẓī va maʿ ānī*)[33] about the commands on the hijab.
vi. Most commands on the hijab lack [corroboration] from well-known (*mustafayż*) narrations,[34] and many of these commands that rely on several *khabar-i vāḥid*[35]are few in number with good chains of transmission.
vii. There are conflicting narrations on the necessity of covering the hair during prayer.

33 [A *mutawātir* narration is one which is reported by a large number of reporters.]
34 [A *mustafayż* narration is one in which the *khabar* (the report or the text) has been reported by at least three narrators in every generation.]
35 [A *khabar-i wāḥid* is a hadith in which the number of narrators in all generations of transmission is not enough for it to be accepted as an authoritative saying.]

viii. In the narrations the extent of non-prayer covering in front of a *maḥram* individual is less than the usual limit.

ix. The understanding of manifest finery in the Qur'an is the face and hands, and this [understanding] is based on only a single reliable *khabar-i wāḥid* from Imam Sadiq. In two other narrations, in the first [the manifest finery is] a ring and bracelet, and in the second [the manifest finery] is lower than the *khimār* and lower than the wrists, and the forearms have been considered among the hidden finery.

x. The clothes that elderly women did not have to wear has been interpreted by Imam Sadiq as the *jilbāb* and *khimār*. One of the meanings of the *jilbāb* and *khimār* is a head-covering and scarf, and another meaning is a sheet (*milḥafa*) and long shawl which covered the upper body. [But] in the narration of Imam Riza the places [for these coverings] are understood as meaning the hair and forearms.

xi. At the end of the second century, Bazanti was unaware about the similar [requirement] of a sister of a man's wife and unknown women to cover their hair, but Imam Riza declared the necessity to cover the hair of the sister of a man's wife. The meaning of this command is the necessity of covering for other women and the prohibition of looking at their hair.

xii. At the time of a marriage proposal, a man can look at a woman's beautiful qualities, including her hair, and a woman can wear clothes that are thinner than usual. These commands were all issued by Imam Sadiq. He related from Imam ʿAli the permission to look at a woman's hair at thc time of a marriage proposal. The meaning of these commands is the requirement to cover women's hair and the prohibition of looking at them in times other than the marriage proposal.

xiii. It is permissible to look at the hair and the hands of non-Muslim women who live among Muslims; indeed, it is permissible to look at places non-Muslim women did not customarily cover. Imam Sadiq related this command from the Prophet. The meaning of it is the lack of permission to look at [those] aforementioned places of Muslim women, and in conclusion, the necessity for Muslim women to cover them.

xiv. One can look at the heads of women whose heads are not covered and who also reject the prohibition of evil. This narration, derived from Imam Sadiq, has the [following] meanings. First, in their time some of the women of the desert did not observe the [regulations of] the legal hijab. Second, the Imam did not give [any] advice other than prohibition from evil. The meaning of this narration too is the necessity for believing women to cover the head and the prohibition for men to look at women who guarded their honour.

xv. According to the principle of a narration from Imam Kazim and Imam Riza, pubescent girls must cover their hair at prayer and [when] in front of non-*maḥram* individuals. And women too are responsible for covering their hair in front of mature male youths, similar to men.

xvi. On the subject of men looking at women, Imam Riza believes that a chaste look with correct sincerity is possible. The look must be different from an impure, lewd look.

xvii. A narration containing this meaning has been attributed to Fatima Zahra: 'It is better for women not to see men and for men too not to see them [women].' [A] similar narration lacking a reliable chain of transmission points to the necessity of observing the hijab for women in front of the blind, at the order of the Prophet, and is not worthy of being attributed to the Prophet or Fatima Zahra.

xviii. It has been attributed to Imam Sadiq that he related this sentence from the Prophet: 'Women are *ʿawrat*. Cover *ʿawrat* in the house.' Supposing the [veracity] of such an expression, the discussion is whether this [saying] concerns the universality of the female sex, or [about] women [considered from the viewpoint of] the cultural particulars of that time in the Hijaz.

Conclusion

First, according to the criteria of the science of traditional hadith, it is impossible to deny that the principle commands of the legal hadith, based on the narrations of Imam Jaʿfar Sadiq, [appeared] from the middle of the first half of the second century (*hijrī*). Believing women were legally responsible for covering their body, with the exception of the face and hands, before the gaze of a non-*maḥram* individual. The head hair was included in the places that had to be covered.

Second, in the framework of traditional jurisprudence, the commands of these narrations interpret and restrict the [commands about the] Qurʾanic hijab. Fatwas based on these narrations, [using] the method of conventional *ijtihād*, will be presented in subsequent parts [of this work].

Third, the method of *ijtihād* on the sources and principles adopts a critical understanding of existing narrations, the result of which will be provided at the end of this series of articles.

The writer welcomes criticisms from those interested. Praise belongs to God.

Conclusion

The Christchurch mosque shootings in New Zealand on 15 March 2019 which resulted in 50 fatalities was commemorated by a service held at a park in front of the al-Noor Mosque where most of the victims were slain. Many of the non-Muslim women and young girls who attended the commemoration wore a headscarf in a demonstration of solidarity with the Muslim community. Thaya Ashman, a doctor in Auckland who proposed the idea of wearing the hijab for this event remarked, 'I wanted to say: "We are with you, we want you to feel at home on your own streets. We love, support and respect you."'[1] The episode reflects the reality that the hijab has become, and has been for some time, the symbol of Islam for most people in the West, even though there are voices of disquiet about essentialising Islam to the hijab.[2]

The hijab has become a political symbol, to the extent that in their attempts to disassociate themselves from orientalist and imperialist meta-narratives some 'Islamic' states have made it an obligatory element of Islamic dress. Nowhere more than in Iran has this been the case, and the recent history of the country reflects an anguished relationship with the West and understandings of modernity. As Iran painfully crawled into the twentieth century, torn between its religious traditions and modern European-based 'innovations', the relationship between Iran and the West was represented in the struggle over the hijab. Iranian tradition held that it was necessary for women to cover their hair, and discussions about the suitability of the hijab in the current nation state only commenced in Iran with the

1 Sonali Paul, 'New Zealand women don headscarves to support Muslims after shootings', *Reuters* 22 March 2019, https://www.reuters.com/article/us-newzealand-shootout-headscarves/new-zealand-women-don-headscarves-to-support-muslims-after-shootings-idUSKCN1R304O/.

2 'New Zealand women wear headscarves in solidarity with Muslims after Christchurch shootings', *Reuters/ABC* 22 March 2019, https://www.abc.net.au/news/2019-03-22/headscarves-in-solidarity-with-muslim-women-after-mosque-attack/10929734.

appearance of European powers and culture in the 19th century. Many westernised reformers and Iranian feminists adopted the meta-narrative of Western-style progress and civilisation which endorsed the presence of women in the public sphere. To this end, the discussion of 'Islamic' clothing for women was focused on the role of women in society, and the decrees of Riza Shah in the 1930s should be considered in this light, rather than a specific focus on the uncovering of head hair per se. Indeed, the major treatise by the first seminarian analysed in this book reflects a concern more with seclusion than with head-covering. Murtaza Mutahhari's work on the hijab is primarily at pains to demonstrate the compatibility of Islamic teachings with female participation in the work force, education and places within public spheres. He argued that wearing the hijab and the *chādur*, the appropriate and modest form of pious covering, should not restrict women from such active participation. The need to cover the head hair itself is not allocated much space in Mutahhari's work, although there seems to be a simple acceptance that this is indeed the correct 'Islamic' perspective. Given the context in which Mutahhari was writing, when Western fashions and trends – at their very worst typified in the *film-fārsī* incarnation – disseminated a way of life that was unthinkable for most pious seminarians, it is not surprising that *Ma'sala-yi Ḥijāb* attempted to orient the reader's attention to a more moral and philosophical end.

The Islamic Revolution of 1978–79, and the subsequent establishment of laws concerning mandatory hijab, shifted the attention to practical issues of how a modern sartorial fashion, Islamic in nature, could be implemented and promoted in society. This was not as facile an enterprise as some might have imagined, especially as a significant proportion of the female population refused to obey the law, or else attempted to 'observe' the sartorial commands in their own unique manner. Moreover, it was impossible for the Islamic state to maintain a hermetically sealed society that enforced strict and minute regulations of the hijab in a country that was becoming increasingly globalised. Within a generation of the success of the revolution, questions were raised about the nature of Islamic society and politics, typified by Ayatollah Montazeri and his circle of seminarians who queried the direction of the revolution and the openness of the state.

It is in this light that the 2004 fatwa of Ahmad Qabil should be read. His chapter on the hijab utilised the voices of traditional Shiʿi scholarship (acceptable to the state authorities) to demonstrate that state enforcement of the hijab, as reflective of a consensus of scholars, was not historically valid. In addition, his analysis of the relevant Qurʾanic verses contained three main points. First, the aim of the verses is modesty – and in this respect his argumentation accorded with that of Mutahhari – rather than the necessity to cover the head. The positioning of the verses come between passages related to matters of sex and honour, and so covering, meaning modesty, is an element of this. Second, he showed that in whatever manner covering was meant, there is no compulsion. Indeed, the Qur'an uses the language of warning. Third, he stated explicitly that there is no mention in the Qur'an of covering the head. What is mentioned is the need to cover the *ʿawrat*, and uncovering was permissible due to the custom of the times.

The third seminarian in this book, Muhsin Kadivar, understands the Qur'anic verses in a similar way to Qabil, in the respect that he concludes that not one of the commands provides a proof for covering the head. He does this with a semantic investigation into terms such as *juyūb*, *jilbāb* and *khimār*; terms with which Mutahhari had also skirted. Kadivar is unable to find satisfactory evidence for the view that the hijab is compulsory or even desirable. Through his analysis of traditions and narrations, Kadivar also claims that the hijab was not a customary item of clothing for women, and it was only in the second and third centuries of Islam when questions were asked about it, particularly in narrations of Imam Jaʿfar Sadiq, which is suggestive that the hijab had its origin outside of 7th-century Arabia.

The attempt to demonstrate that there has been no consensus on the issue of the hijab is a call more than anything for the inclusion of all opinions within the *ḥawza* on contemporary issues that affect daily life in Iran. The Islamic revolution and the establishment of state-Islam has resulted in the primacy of a single interpretation of Islam that is then sanctioned by the law. This breaks with a tradition in which there are many competing voices issuing opinions. It is perhaps ironic that the significance of the New Religious Thinkers is that they advance a worldview which has much in common with religious secularity. Kadivar accepts that the reform of Islamic thinkers will mean a reduction in the extent of traditional ways of thinking, in particular, jurisprudence, whilst other areas will deepen in scope, such as ethics and faith.

The opinions of Mutahhari, Qabil and Kadivar render meaningless and completely incoherent the simplistic view of an unchanging, essentialised sharia. The political experience of the Islamic Republic in its effort to create an Islamic state has raised questions about dissent and alternative voices, so that it is easy to understand why some express fears about a monolithic, and inflexible sharia. But the long traditions of jurisprudence among the Twelver Shiʿi communities have devised methods by which stakeholders do indeed have a voice. It remains to be seen the extent to which women themselves engage in this jurisprudential venture, which has tended to be a patriarchal domain.

Appendix

Scholars Mentioned by Ahmad Qabil in His Treatise on the Hijab

Burujirdi, Sayyid Husayn (1975–61): the leading *marja*ʿ in Iran after the departure of Riza Shah. He is largely known for his quiescent political perspective. In terms of scholarly work, he was responsible for overseeing the publication of 31 volumes of *Jāmiʿ Aḥadīth al-Shīʿa*. Burujirdi also initiated the practice of sending religious scholars to Europe and locations in the Islamic world. And he set in motion studies to reform the *ḥawza*, although the findings were not implemented.

Fazil Abi (ʿIzz al-Din Hasan ibn Abi Talib Yusufi): a scholar from the 15–16th centuries. His master was al-Muhaqqiq al-Karaki (d. 1533).

Halabi, Abu'l-Salah (Shaykh Taqi al-Din ibn Najm al-Din ibn ʿUbayd Allah ibn ʿAbd Allah ibn Muhammad) (984–85 / 1055–56):[1] most of his compositions have not survived, but it is clear that, although he was trained in the school of Baghdad and was a student of Sayyid Murtaza, he was sufficiently confident to express differences of opinion with the accepted opinions of the time and with those of his teachers.

Hamadani, Hajj Aqa Riza (Muhaqqiq Hamadani) (1834–1904): he was a

1 See Etan Kohlberg, 'Ḥalabi, Abu'l-Ṣāleḥ', *Encyclopedia Iranica*, 15 December 2003. This article is available in print: vol. XI, fasc. 6, 580–1. The text mentioned by Qabil is Halabi's *al-Kāfī fī'l-Fiqh*, ed. R. Ustadi, Isfahan 1982–83, and has been called by Kohlberg 'one of the oldest systematic codifications of Twelver Shiʿite law'.

student of Mirza Shirazi, and he assumed *marjaʿiyat* upon his death. He also studied under Shaykh Ansari.

al-Hilli, also known as ʿAllama Hilli (Jamal al-Din Abu Mansur Hasan Ibn Yusuf) (1250–1325): was an eminent Shiʿa theologian and jurist.[2] His *Nihāyat al-Aḥkām* has been edited and published.[3] He was one of the first scholars to employ the term *ijtihād* in the sense of acquiring knowledge by applying the sources of law.

Ibn Baraj (ʿAbd al-ʿAziz Ibn Baraj al-Tarablusi) (1021–88): originating from Egypt and receiving his religious education in Baghdad, he studied with two of the most famous scholars of his age: Sayyid Murtaza and Shaykh Tusi.

Ibn Idris Hilli (Muhammad ibn Mansur ibn Ahmad ibn Idris Hilli) (12th century): was a descendant through his mother of Shaykh Tusi. He earned a reputation for employing reason in his jurisprudential works, and for a penchant to not follow blindly the positions of Shaykh Tusi, which had been the custom of much of Shiʿi jurisprudence.

Ibn Junayd Iskafi (Muhammad ibn Ahmad al-Katib al-Iskafi, also known as Ibn Abi'l Junayd) (d. 991–92):[4] none of Ibn Junayd's works have survived, and scholars have to rely on quotes found in the works of other scholars.

Ishtahardi, ʿAli Panah (1917–2008): taught ethics at the *ḥawza* in Qum for many years. He was one of the editors in a group overseeing the publication of the thirty-one volumes of *Jāmiʿ Aḥadīth al-Shīʿa* (*Collection of Shiʿa Hadith*).

Javadi-Amuli (1933–present): powerful contemporary seminarian who is often regarded as a conservative and a supporter of ʿAli Khamenei. He has offices as a *marjaʿ* in several Iranian cities, and has published a multi-volume exegesis of the Qurʾan called *Tasnīm*. He has an official website: http://javadi.esra.ir/[5]

---

2 On his life, see Momen, *An Introduction to Shiʿi Islam*, 313; More detail is provided by Sabine Schmidt, 'Ḥelli, Ḥasan b. Yusof b. Moṭahhar', *Encyclopedia Iranica*, 15 December 2003, vol. XII, fasc. 2, 164–9.

3 See *Nihāyat al-Marām fī ʿIlm al-Kalām*, 3 vols., ed. Fazil al-ʿIrfan, Qum 1419/1999.

4 Wilferd Madelung, 'Ibn al-Jonayd', *Encyclopedia Iranica*, 15 December 1997, vol. VIII, fasc. 1, 31–2.

5 On his general perspective see Dahlén, *Islamic Law, Epistemology and Modernity*, 126–42.

Khuʾi, Sayyid Abu'l Qasim al-Musavi (1899–1992): leading seminarian based in Najaf, and regarded by many as the leading seminarian of the age. He was arrested several times by Saddam Hussein who persecuted members of Khuʾi's family. He was the author of many respected jurisprudential works. His official website is: https://www.alkhoei.org/

Majlisi, Muhammad Baqir (1627–99): or Majlisi al-Thani (Majlisi the Second) was an Akhbari scholar famous for his 110 volume of hadith and reports known under the title of *Biḥār al-Anwār*.

Miqdad al-Suyuri (al-Miqdad Ibn ʿAbdallah al-Suyuri) (d. 1423).

Mirza-yi Qummi, Abu'l-Qasim (1738–1815): a Qajar period *marjaʿ*, who was also influential at the royal court. He is known for encouraging a strict adherence among *muqallid*s to the decisions and declarations of the *marjaʿ*.

Mughniya, Muhammad Javad (1904–79): studied in Lebanon and Najaf and was a student of al-Khuʾi. He served as head of the judiciary in Lebanon, and also composed works on understanding the Qurʾan and Islamic jurisprudence. He wrote six volumes of *Fiqh al-Imām Jaʿfar al-Ṣādiq*. He was concerned with promoting the unity of Lebanon and had good relations with Sunni leaders.

Muhaqqiq Damad, Sayyid Muhammad (1907–69): he was the son-in-law of ʿAbd al-Karim Haʾiri Yazdi, the founder of the seminary in Qum, and so he was given the title *dāmād* (meaning 'son-in-law'). Although he did not involve himself in politics, it is noteworthy that his students included many of those who were active in the Islamic Revolution.

Muhaqqiq Hilli (Najm al-Din Abu'l-Qasim Jaʿfar Ibn Hasan, also known as Muhaqqiq-i Avval) (1205–77):[6] author of jurisprudential works, such as *al-Muʿtabar fī Sharḥ Mukhtṣar al-Nāfiʿ* and *Sharāʾiʿ al-Islām*. The latter work looks at worship, contracts, obligations, and commands (*aḥkām*). Each section mentions the status of each act: obligatory (*wājib*), desirable (*mustaḥabb*),

6 Momen, *An Introduction to Shiʿi Islam*, 313; see also Etan Kohlberg, 'Ḥelli, Najm-al-Din Abu'l-Qāsem Jaʿfar', *Encyclopedia Iranica*, 15 December 2003. This article is available in print: vol. XII, fasc. 2, 169–170.

reprehensible (*makrūh*), and forbidden (*ḥarām*). He was also a poet who wrote on ethical and mystical themes.

Muhaqqiq Karaki (Nur al-Din ʿAli ibn ʿAbd'l-ʿAli al-ʿAmili al-Karaki) (1465–1534): he was invited to Iran by the Safavid monarch Tahmasp, and he proceeded to propagate Shiʿi Islam throughout the country. His most celebrated work is a commentary on *Qawāʾid al-Aḥkām* written by ʿAllama Hilli.

Muhaqqiq Naraqi (Mulla Ahmad Naraqi) (1772–1829): influential *mujtahid* from Kashan who wrote on *fiqh*, *uṣūl-i fiqh*, mathematics and ethics. He also wrote poetry, and took an active interest in politics, helping to promote the movement to expel the Russians from Iranian territory in the early 1800s.

Muhaqqiq Tabatabaʾi (Sayyid ʿAbd al-ʿAziz Tabatabaʾi Yazdi) (1929–96): an erudite scholar who spent much energy in the academic study of Islamic history, and had a deep interest in researching manuscripts.

Muqaddas Ardabili (Ahmad ibn Muhammad Ardabili) (d. 1585): was a respected teacher and scholar of *fiqh*, *uṣūl*, theology and the history of the Shiʿi imams. He was based in both Najaf and Shiraz. His most important jurisprudential work is *Majmaʿ al-Fāʾida wa al-Burhān fī Sharḥ al-Adhhān.*

Mutahhari, Murtaza (1919–79): See Part Two of this book.

Najafi (see Sahib-i Javahir).

Sabzavari, ʿAbd al-Aʿla (1910–93): a *marjaʿ* in Najaf for only one year (between the death of grand Ayatollah Khuʾi and his own death in 1993). He was a specialist in *fiqh* and hadith.

Sabzavari, Muhammad Baqir (also known as Muhaqqiq-i Sabzavari) (1608–79): was the author of *Sufficiency of the Commands*, and he was the Shaykh al-Islam of Isfahan.

Sahib-i Javahir (ʿAllama Shaykh Muhammad Hasan Najafi) (d. 1266/1850): a famous *marjaʿ taqlid* of the 19th century.[7] The masters of Sahib-i Javahir

7 See Momen, *An Introduction to Shiʿi Islam*, 318.

included Kashif al-Ghita (d. 1812) and Sayyid ʿAli Tabatabaʾi (d. 1815–16).[8] His most important composition is the *Jawāhir al-Kalām*, and its important features are the inclusion of *ʿurf* (common sense) as a source for discovering the laws on a particular subject, and the views and opinions of past masters. The work is inspired by Muhaqqiq Hilli's *Sharāʾiʿ al-Islām*.

Sahib-i Madarik (Sayyid Muhammad ibn ʿAli al-Musavi al-ʿAmili) (1539–1600): his teachers included Muqaddas Ardabili, and he achieved fame for his text *Madārik al-Aḥkām fī Sharḥ Sharāʾiʿ al-Islām*, which was composed in three volumes and contains discussions on purity, prayer, *zakāt*, fasting, and hajj among others.

Sahib-i Riyaz (Sayyid ʿAli ibn Muhammad ʿAli Tabatabaʾi) (1749–1815): the most important work of this jurist is his *Riyāż al-Masāʾil*, which discusses the usual topics (purity, blood money, etc.) and includes the opinions of past masters.

Shams al-Din, Muhammad Mahdi (1936–2001): lived and studied in Najaf for many years, where he studied under al-Khuʾi, before attaining the rank of Ayatullah, and was also a political theoretician and the chairman of the Supreme Islamic Shiʿa Council in Lebanon.

Sayyid Muhammad ʿAmili (see Sahib-i Madarik).

Shahid-i Avval (Muhammad ibn Makki al-ʿAmali al-Jizzini) (1333–84): he was the author of *al-Lumʿa al-Dimashqīyya fī Fiqh al-Imāmīyya*, which is a typical jurisprudential work and is composed of four parts: worship, transactions, contracts, and commands. It continues to be taught in the seminaries and has had several commentaries written on it.

Shahid-i Thani (Shaykh Zayn al-Din Ibn ʿAli al-ʿAmili al-Jubaʿi) (1506–58): the author of *Al-Rawża al-Bahīyya fī Sharḥ al-Lumʿat al-Dimashqīyya*, which was a commentary on the *al-Lumʿat al-Dimashqīyya*, composed by Shahid-i Avval.

Shaykh Mufid, (Abu ʿAbdullah Muhammad ibn Muhammad ibn al-Nuʿman al-ʿAkbari al-Baghdadi) (948–1022): taught by Shaykh Saduq, he was an

8 The life of the latter is discussed briefly in Meir Litvak, *Shiʿi Scholars of Nineteenth Century Iraq*, Cambridge 1998, 49–51.

outstanding theologian and jurist. Only a handful of about 200 books of his survive, one of which is called *Aḥkām al-Niswa* (*Commands for Women*). He is regarded as a scholar who promoted the application of reason to the study of hadith in determining law.

Shaykh Saduq or Ibn Babawayh ('The Trusty Scholar') (923–91): a Shiʿa expert on hadith and eminent jurist and theologian in Qum. He was a student of Abu Jaʿfar Kulayni and master of Shaykh Mufid.[9] He was the author of *Man Lā Yahżuruhū al-Faqīh*, which is regarded as one of the four most important books on Twelver Shiʿi Islam. It is a work on narrations and their interpretation.

Shaykh Tusi (Abu Jaʿfar Muhammad ibn Hasan al-Tusi, also known as Shaykh al-Taʾifa) (996–1067): he compiled two of the four principle books used by the Shiʿa on hadith. He is considered by some the founder of Shiʿi jurisprudence, and the founder of the seminary in Najaf.

Shaykh Yusuf Bahrani (1695–1772): was an Akhbari scholar who rejected the legal reasoning of the Usulis, although his perspective has been understood as one that does not go to the extreme literalism of earlier Akhbaris. His views have been the study of a recent monograph in English.[10]

Tabarsi (Fazl ibn Hasan al-Tabarsi) (d. 1153): was the author of the *Majmāʿ al-Bayān*, considered to be one of the most important commentaries of the Qurʾan. His other works include *Makārim al-Akhlāq*.

Tabatabaʾi (Sayyid Muhammad Tabatabaʾi): was a 19th-century mulla, author of a well-known work called the *Manẓūma*. He was the son of Sayyid ʿAli Tabatabaʾi. One of his most important students was Shaykh Murtaza Ansari, the famous 19th-century *marjāʿ*.

9 See Martin McDermott, 'Ibn Bābawayh', *Encyclopedia Iranica*, 15 December 1997, vol. VIII, fasc. 1, 2–4.
10 See Robert Gleave, *Inevitable Doubt: Two Theories of Shiʿi Jurisprudence*, Leiden 2000.

Bibliography

Abdolkah, Kader, *My Father's Notebook*, trans. Susan Massotty, Edinburgh 2007.

Abdolmohammadi, Pejman, 'The influences of western ideas on Kermani's political thought', *Iran* LIV.I, 2016, 23–38.

Abdul-Raof, Hussein, 'On the dichotomy between the muḥkam and mutashabih', *Journal of Qur'anic Research and Studies* 3.5, 2008, 47–70.

Abou El Fadl, Khaled, *Reasoning with God*, London 2017.

Abrahamian, Ervand, *Iran between Two Revolutions*, New Jersey 1982.

Abrahamian, Ervand, Review of Hamid Dabashi, 'Theology of Discontent', *International Journal of Middle East Studies* 28.2, 1996, 668.

Adib-Moghaddam, Arshin, 'The pluralist Momentum in Iran and the Future of the Reform Movement', *Third World Quarterly* 27.4, 2006, 665–74.

Afary, Janet, *Sexual Politics in Modern Iran*, Cambridge 2011.

al-Afghani, Jamal al-Din, 'Answer of Jamal ad-Din to Renan', *Modernist Islam 1840–1940*, ed. Charles Kurzman, Oxford 2002, 103–10.

Aghaie, Kamran Scott, *The Women of Karbala: Ritual Performance and Symbolic Discourses in Modern Shi'i Islam*, Austin 2009.

Ahmad-Ghosh, Huma, 'A history of women in Afghanistan: Lessons learnt for the future or yesterdays and tomorrow: Women in Afghanistan', *Journal of International Women's Studies* 4.3, 2003, 1–14.

Ahmed, Leila, *A Quiet Revolution: The Veil's Resurgence, from the Middle East to North America*, New Haven 2011.

Akbar, Ali and Abdullah Saeed, 'Interpretation and mutability: socio-legal texts of the Qur'an; three accounts from contemporary Iran', *Middle Eastern Studies* 54.3, 2018, 442–58.

Akhavi, Shahrough, *Religion and Politics in Contemporary Iran: Clergy-State Relations in the Pahlavi Period*, Albany 1980.

Algar, Hamid, ''Amāma', *Encyclopaedia Iranica*, 2011.

Algar, Hamid, 'Bāfqī, Moḥammad-Taqī', *Encyclopaedia Iranica* III/4, 2011.
Algar, Hamid, 'Borūjerdī, Ḥosayn Ṭabāṭabā'ī', *Encyclopaedia Iranica* IV/4, 1989.
Algar, Hamid, 'Ha'eri, 'Abd al-Karim Yazdi', *Encyclopaedia Iranica*, 15 December 2002.
Algar, Hamid, 'Introduction', *Fundamentals of Islamic Thought: God, Man the Universe by Ayatullah Murtaza Mutahhari*, trans. R. Campbell, Berkeley 1985.
Al-i Ahmad, Jalal, *Gharbzadegi* [*Weststruckness*], trans. John Green and Ahmad Alizadeh, Costa Mesa 1980.
Alinejhad, Masih, *The Wind in My Hair: My Fight for Freedom in Modern Iran*, London 2018.
Alipour, M., 'Shi'a neo-traditionalist scholars and theology of homosexuality: review and reflections on Mohsen Kadivar's shifting approach', *Theology and Sexuality* 24.3, 2018, 200–18.
Amanat, Abbas, *Apocalyptic Islam and Iranian Shi'ism*, London 2009.
Amanat, Abbas, *Iran: A Modern History*, New Haven 2017.
Amanat, Abbas, *Resurrection and Renewal: the Making of the Babi Movement*, Ithaca 1989.
Amer, Sahar, *What is Veiling*, Edinburgh 2014.
Amin, Qasim, *The Liberation of Women & The New Women: Two Documents in the History of Egyptian Feminism*, trans. Samiha Sidhom Peterson, Cairo 2000.
Amirpur, Katajun, *New Thinking in Islam: The Jihad for Freedom, Democracy and Women's Rights*, London 2015.
Ardeshir Larijany, Sareh, 'Mutahhari and his approach to Women's Social Life: with special reference to Political Participation and Issuing Fatwas', PhD thesis submitted to the University of Birmingham, July 2020.
Arjomand, Said Amir, 'Traditionalism in Twentieth Century Iran', *From Nationalism to Revolutionary Islam*, ed. Arjomand, Oxford 1984, 195–232.
Arjomand, Said Amir, *The Turban for the Crown: The Islamic Revolution in Iran*, Oxford 1988.
Armstrong, Karen, 'My life in a habit taught me the paradox of veiling', *The Guardian* 26 October 2006.
Atwood, Blake, *Reform Cinema in Iran: Film and Political Change in the Islamic Republic*, New York 2016.

Azimi, Fakhreddin, 'Khomeini and the "White Revolution"', *A Critical Introduction to Khomeini*, ed. Arshin Adib-Moghaddam, Cambridge 2014, 19–42.

Badran, Margot, *Feminism in Islam: Secular and Religious Convergences*, Oxford 2011.

Basmanji, Kaveh, *Tehran Blues: Youth Culture in Iran*, London 2005.

Bayoumi, Moustafa, 'The Muslim Ban ruling legitimates Trump's bigotry', *The Guardian* 27 June 2018, https://www.theguardian.com/commentisfree/2018/jun/27/muslim-ban-ruling-trumps-bigotry.

Bill, James A., 'Power and Religion in Revolutionary Iran', *Middle East Journal* 36.1, 1982, 22–47.

Boroujerdi, Mehrzad, *Iranian Intellectuals and the West: The Tormented Triumph of Nativism*, New York 1996.

Brend, Barbara and Charles Melville, *Epic of the Persian Kings: The Art of Ferdowsi's* Shahnameh, London 2010.

Brown, Daniel, 'The triumph of scripturalism: The doctrine of *naskh* and its modern critics', *The Shaping of an American Islamic Discourse: A Memorial to Fazlur Rahman*, ed. Earle H. Waugh, Frederick Mathewson Denny and Fazlur Rahman, Atlanta 1998, 49–66.

Brunner, Rainer, 'Abrogation and Falsification of Scriptures', *Approaches to the Qur'an in Contemporary Iran*, ed. Alessandro Cancian, Oxford 2019, 225–42.

Bullock, Katherine, *Rethinking Muslim Women and the Veil*, Hendon, VA 2002,

Campanini, Massimo, *The Qur'an: Modern Muslim Interpretations*, London 2011.

Chardin, Sir John, *Travels in Persia*, New York 1988.

Chaudhry, Ayesha S., *Domestic Violence and the Islamic Tradition*, Oxford 2013.

Chehabi, Houchang E., 'Banning of the veil and its consequences', *The Making of Modern Iran*, ed. Stephanie Cronin, London 2003, 193–210.

Chehabi, Houchang E., 'Staging the emperor's new clothes: Dress codes and nation-building under Reza Shah', *Iranian Studies* 26.3/4, 1993, 209–29.

Cooke, Miriam, *Nazira Zeineddine: A Pioneer of Islamic Feminism*, London 2010.

Cromer, The Earl of, *Modern Egypt*, London 1908.

Cummins, Pip, 'The day 100,000 Iranian women protested the head-scarf', *The New York Times* 15 September 2015, http://nytlive.nytimes.com/

womenintheworld/2015/09/15/the-day-100000-iranian-women-protested-the-head-scarf.

Dabashi, Hamid, *The Green Movement in Iran*, New Jersey 2011

Dabashi, Hamid, *Theology of Discontent*, New York 1993.

Dahlén, Ashk P., *Islamic Law, Epistemology and Modernity*, London 2015.

Darabi, Parvin and Romin P. Thomson, *Rage Against the Veil: The Courageous Life and Death of an Islamic Dissident*, New York 1999.

Davari, Mahmood T., *The Political Thought of Ayatullah Murtaza Mutahhari*, London 2005.

Deeb, Lara, 'Thinking piety and the everyday together: A response to Fadil and Fernando', *Hau: Journal of Ethnographic Theory* 5.2, 2015, 59–88.

Derayeh, Minoo, 'The myth of creation and *hijab*: Iranian women, liberated or oppressed', *Pakistan Journal of Women's Studies: Alam-e-Niswan* 18.2, 2011, 1–21.

Egan, Eric, *The Films of Makhmalbaf: Cinema, Politics and Culture in Iran*, Washington 2005.

Emami, Hessam, 'Inside Iran, a Diversity of Opinions Emerging over Hijab', *Iranian Diplomacy* 17 July 2016, http://www.irdiplomacy.ir/en/news/1961173/inside-iran-a-diversity-of-opinions-emerging-over-hijab.

Erdbrink, Thomas, 'Compulsory Veils? Half of Iranians Say "No" to Pillar of Revolution"', *New York Times* 4 February 2018, https://www.nytimes.com/2018/02/04/world/middleeast/iran-hijab-veils.html.

Erdbrink, Thomas, 'Ahmadinejad and clerics fight over scarves', *The Washington Post* 22 July 2011, https://www.washingtonpost.com/world/middle-east/ahmadinejad-and-clerics-fight-over-scarves/2011/07/12/gIQAhoqJPI_story.html?utm_term=.7ed77022d3c5.

Esfandiari, Golnaz, 'Ahmadinejad, the hijab and women in his car', *Radio Free Europe* 16 June 2010, https://www.rferl.org/a/Ahmadinejad_The_Hijab_And_Women_In_His_Car/2073879.html.

Esfandiari, Haleh, *Reconstructed Lives: Women and Iran's Islamic Revolution*, Baltimore 1997.

Eshkevari, Hassan Yousefi, 'Rethinking men's authority over women', *Gender and Equality in Muslim Family Law*, ed. Ziba Mir-Hosseini, Kari Vogt, Lena Larsen and Christian Moe, London 2009, 191–212.

Ettehadiyeh, Mansoureh. 'Sediqeh Dowlatabadi: An Iranian feminist', *Religion and Politics in Modern Iran*, ed. Lloyd Ridgeon, London 2005, 71–98.

Faghihi, Rohollah, 'Self-proclaimed marja riles other Iranian Ayatollahs', *Al-Monitor* 24 September 2019, https://www.al-monitor.com/pulse/en/originals/2019/09/iran-hardliners-opposition-new-marja.amp.html.

Farand, Chloe, 'Marine le Pen launches presidential campaign with hardline speech', *The Independent* 5 February 2017, https://www.independent.co.uk/news/world/europe/marine-le-pen-front-national-speech-campaign-launch-islamic-fundamentalism-french-elections-a7564051.html.

Fatoohi, Louay, *Abrogation in the Qur'an and Islamic Law*, London 2013.

Feridoun, Hassan, 'The Flexibility of Shariah (Islamic Law) with Reference to the Iranian Experience', PhD thesis submitted to Glasgow Caledonian University, 1998.

Firestone, Reuven, *Jihad: The Origins of Holy War in Islam*, Oxford 1999.

Ghamari-Tabrizi, Behrooz, *Islam and Dissent: Abdolkarim Soroush, Religious Political and Democratic Reform*, London 2008.

Ghamari-Tabrizi, Behrooz, 'Women's Rights, Shariʿa' Law, and the Secularization of Islam in Iran', *International Journal of Politics, Culture, and Society* 26.3, 2013, 237–53.

Gheissari, Ali, 'The poetry and politics of Farrokhi Yazdi', *Iranian Studies* 26.1/2, 1993, 33–50.

Ghobadzadeh, Naser, *Religious Secularity: A Theological Challenge to the Islamic State*, Oxford 2015.

Gleave, Robert, 'Imami Shiʿi Legal Theory', *The Oxford Handbook of Islamic Law*, ed. Anver M. Emon and Rumee Ahmed, Oxford 2018, DOI: 10.1093/oxfordhb/9780199679010.013.31

Gould, Rebecca, 'Hijab as commodity form: Veiling, unveiling, and misveiling in contemporary Iran', *Feminist Theory* 15.3, 2014, 221–40.

Haghighatnejad, Reza, 'Khamenei dismisses hijab protesters as "insignificant and small"', 12 March 2018, http://www.trackpersia.com/khamenei-dismisses-hijab-protesters-insignificant-small/.

Haghighi, Ali Reza, 'Politics and cinema in post-revolutionary Iran', *The New Iranian Cinema,* ed. Richard Tapper, London 2002, 109–16.

Hahn, Ernest, 'Sir Sayyid Ahmad Khan's "The controversy over abrogation (in the Quran)"', *The Muslim World* 64.2, 1974, 124–33.

Hakim, Avraham, 'Context: ʿUmar b. Al-Khaṭṭāb', *The Blackwell Companion to the Qur'an*, ed. Andrew Rippin, Oxford 2006, 218–33.

Hashemi, Kate C., 'The Girls of *Enghelab* Street: Women and Revolution in Modern Iran', *Global Policy* 2018, https://www.academia.edu/37994754/The_Girls_of_Enghelab_Street_Women_and_Revolution_in_Modern_Iran.

Hoodfar, Homa, 'Veil in their minds and our heads', *Resource for Feminist Research* 22.3/4, 1994, 5–18.

Hovespian-Bearce, Yvette, *The Political Ideology of Ayatollah Khamenei: Out of the Mouth of the Supreme Leader of Iran*, Abingdon 2016

Ibn Battuta, *The Travels of Ibn Battuta*, vol. 2, trans. H. A. R. Gibb, Delhi 1999.

Iranwire, 'Iran's Prosecutor Dismisses Hijab Protesters as Childish and Ignorant', 31 January 2018, https://iranwire.com/en/features/5136.

Jahanbakhsh, Forough, *Islam, Democracy and Religious Modernism in Iran, 1953–2000*, Leiden 2001.

Jalaeipour, Zahra, *Hijab in Transition Dress Code Changes amongst Iranian Diaspora in London*, MPhil submitted to University of Sussex, May 2016, http://sro.sussex.ac.uk/72698/1/Jalaeipour%2C%20Zahra.pdf.

Jansen, Godfrey, 'Khomeini's heretical delusion of grandeur', *Middle East International* 317, 1988, 18–19.

Javadi, Hasan, 'Women in Persian satire', *The Education of Women and the Vices of Men*, ed. Hasan Javadi and Willem Floor, New York 2010.

Jeffreys, Stewart, 'Landscapes of the Mind', *The Guardian* 16 April 2005.

Kadivar, Muhsin, 'Freedom of thought and religion in Islam', *The New Voices of Islam: Reforming Politics and Modernity – A Reader*, ed. Mehran Kamrava, London 2006, 119–42, https://english.kadivar.com/2006/09/29/the-freedom-of-thought-and-religion-in-islam-2/.

Kadivar, Muhsin, 'Human Rights and Intellectual Islam', *New Directions in Islamic Thought: Exploring Reform and Muslim Tradition*, ed. Kari Vogt, Lena Larsen and Christian Moe, London 2009, 47–73, https://english.kadivar.com/2009/05/15/human-rights-and-intellectual-islam/.

Kadivar, Muhsin, 'From traditional Islam to Islam as an End in Itself', *Die Welt des Islams* 51, 2011, 459–84, https://english.kadivar.com/2011/12/11/from-traditional-islam-to-islam-as-an-end-in-itself-2/.

Kadivar, Muhsin, 'Revisiting Women's Rights in Islam: "Egalitarian Justice" in Lieu of "Desert-based Justice"', *Gender and Equality in Muslim Family Law: Justice and Ethics in the Islamic Legal Tradition*, ed. Ziba Mir Hosseini, Lena Larsen, Christian Moe and Kari Vogt, London 2013, 213–34, https://english.kadivar.com/2013/05/24/revisiting-womena-rights-in-islam/.

Kadivar, Muhsin, 'Ijtihad in Usul al-Figh: Reforming Islamic Thought through Structural Ijtihad', *Iran Nameh* 30.3, 2015, xx–xxvii, http://irannameh.org/index.php/journal/article/view/2286/3695.

Kahf, Mohja, *Western Representations of the Muslim Woman: From Termagant to Odalisque*, Texas 1999.

Kamali, Muhammad Hashim, '"Ikhtilāf": juristic disagreement in the Shariah', *Islamic Studies* 37.3, Autumn 1998, 315–37.

Kamali-Dehghan, Saeed, 'Iran arrests models in renewed crackdown on unlicensed industry', *The Guardian* 16 May 2018, https://www.theguardian.com/world/2016/may/16/iran-arrests-models-crackdown-unlicensed-industry-hijab.

Kamalkhani, Zahra, *Women's Islam: Religious Practice Among Women in Today's Iran*, London 1998.

Kara, Seyfeddin, 'Rational-analytical Tafsīr in Modern Iran: The Influence of the Uṣūlī School of Jurisprudence on the Interpretation of the Qurʾan', *Approaches to the Qurʾan in Contemporary Iran*, ed. Alessandro Cancian, Oxford 2019.

Kashani-Sabet, Firoozeh, *Conceiving Citizens*, Oxford 2011.

Kasravi, Ahmad, 'Shiʿism', *On Islam and Shiʿism*, trans. M. R. Ghanoonparvar, Costa Mesa 1990.

Katz, Marion, *Ethics, Gender, and the Islamic Legal Project*, Yale Law School, Occasional Papers, 2015.

Kavas, Serap, '"Wardrobe modernity": Western attire as a tool of modernization in Turkey', *Middle Eastern Studies* 51.4, 2015, 515–39.

Kazemi, Farhad, 'Fedāʾīān-e eslām', *Encyclopedia Iranica* IX, 2012, 470–4.

Khalaji, Mehdi, 'Becoming anti-American', *Gulf Magazine* 24 August 2015.

Khomeini, Ruhollah, *A Clarification of Questions: An Unabridged Translation of Resaleh Towzih Al-Masael*, trans. J. Borujerdi, London 1984.

Khomeini, Ruhollah, *Islam and Revolution*, trans. Hamid Algar, London 1985.

Khomeini, Ruhollah, *The Position of Women from the Viewpoint of Imam Khomeini*, Tehran 1380/2001–2.

al-Khuʾi, *The Prolegomena to the Qurʾan*, trans. Abdalaziz Sachedina, Oxford 1998.

Kian, Azadeh, 'Gendered Khomeini', *A Critical Introduction to Khomeini*, ed. Arshin Adib-Moghaddam, Cambridge 2014.

Kinberg, Leah, 'Muḥkamāt and mutashābihāt (Koran 3/7): Implication of a Koranic pair of terms in medieval exegesis', *Arabica* 35.2, 1988, 143–72.

Kister, M. J., 'The massacre of the Banū Qurayẓa: a re-examination of a tradition', *Jerusalem Studies in Arabic and Islam* 8, 1986, 61–96.

Knut, Vikør, *Between God and the Sultan: A History of Islamic Law*, London 2005.

Kuhlmann, Jan, 'Why Islam and democracy go well together' (interview with Muhammad Mujtahid-Shabestari), *Qantara* 2012, https://en.qantara.de/

content/interview-with-mohammad-mojtahed-shabestari-why-islam-and-democracy-go-well-together.

Künkler, Mirjam, 'The Special Court of the Clergy (*Dādgāh-Ye Vīzheh-Ye Ruhāniyat*) and the Repression of Dissident Clergy in Iran', *The Rule of Law, Islam, and Constitutional Politics in Egypt and Iran*, ed. Said Amir Arjomand and Nathan J. Brown, Albany 2013, 57–100.

Künkler, Mirjam and Roja Fazaeli, 'The life of two mujtahidahs: Female Religious Authority in 20th century Iran', *Women, Leadership and Mosques: Changes in Contemporary Islamic Authority*, ed. Masooda Bano and Hilary Kalmbach, Leiden 2010, 127–60.

Kurzman, Charles, 'Critics within: Islamic scholars' protests against the Islamic state in Iran', *An Islamic Reformation*, ed. Michelle Browers and Charles Kurzman, Lanham, MD 2003, 341–59.

Lambton, Ann K. S., 'A reconsideration of the position of the Marjaʿ Al-Taqlīd and the religious institution', *Studia Islamica* 20, 1964, 115–35.

Leaman, Oliver, *The Biographical Encyclopaedia of Islamic Philosophy*, ed. Oliver Leaman, London 2015.

Madaninejad, Banafsheh, *New Theology in the Islamic Republic of Iran: A Comparative Study between Abdolkarim Soroush and Mohsen Kadivar*, PhD thesis submitted at the University of Texas at Austin, 2011.

Mahdavi, Shireen, 'Reza Shah and women: A re-appraisal', *The Making of Modern Iran*, ed. Stephanie Cronin, London 2003, 181–92.

Marashi, Afshin, 'The Shah's official visit to Kemalist Turkey', *The Making of Modern Iran*, ed. Stephanie Cronin, London 2003, 99–119.

Martin, Richard C, Mark R. Woodward and Dwi S. Atmaja, *Defenders of Reason in Islam*, Oxford 1997.

Masud, Muhammad Khalid, 'Ikhtilaf al-Fuqaha: Diversity in Fiqh as a Social Construction', *Wanted: Equality and Justice in the Muslim Family*, ed. Zainah Anwar, Malaysia 2009, 65–94.

Matsunaga, Yasuyuki, 'Human Rights and Jurisprudence in Mohsen Kadivar's Advocacy of "New-Thinker" Islam', *Die Welt des Islams* 51.3/4, 2011, 359–81.

Matsunaga, Yasuyuki, 'Mohsen Kadivar, an advocate of postrevivalist Islam', *British Journal of Middle East Studies* 34.3, 2007, 317–29.

Mavani, Hamid, 'Paradigm Shift in Twelver Shiʿi Legal Theory (*uṣūl al-fiqh*): Ayatullah Yusef Saanei', *The Muslim World* 99.2, 2009.

McAuliffe, J. D., 'The wines of earth and paradise: Qur'anic proscriptions and promises', *Logos Islamikos*, ed. Roger M. Savory and Dionisius A. Agius, Toronto 1984, 159–74.

Mernissi, Fatima, *The Veil and the Male Elite: A Feminist Interpretation of Women's Rights in Islam*, Reading 1997.

Milani, Farzaneh, *Veils and Words: The Emerging Voices of Iranian Women Writers*, London 1992.

Mir-Hosseini, Ziba, 'Hijab and Choice: Between Politics and Theology', *Innovation in Islam: Tradition and Contribution*, ed. Mehran Kamrava, Berkeley 2011, 190–212.

Mir-Hosseini, Ziba, *Islam and Gender: The Religious Debate in Contemporary Iran*, London 1999.

Mir-Hosseini, Ziba, 'Islam and gender justice', *Voices of Islam*, vol. 5, ed. Vincent Cornell, Omid Safi and Virgina Gray Henry, Westport 2007, 85–114.

Mir-Hosseini, Ziba, 'Rethinking gender: Discussions with Ulama in Iran', *Critique: Critical Middle Eastern Studies* 7.13, 1998.

Mir-Hosseini, Ziba and Richard Tapper, *Islam and Democracy in Iran: Eshkevari and the Quest for Reform*, London 2006.

Moaddel, Mansoor, *Islamic Modernism, Nationalism and Fundamentalism: Episode and Discourse*, Chicago 2005.

Modarressi, Hossein, 'Early debates on the integrity of the Qur'an: A brief survey', *Studia Islamica* 77, 1993, 5–39.

Momen, Moojan, *An Introduction to Shi'i Islam*, New Haven 1985.

Monshipouri, Mahmoud and Mehdi Zakerian, 'The State of Human Rights in Iran', *Inside the Islamic Republic: Social Change in Post-Khomeini Iran*, ed. Mahmood Monshipouri, London 2016.

Mostaghim, Ramin, 'Iran: Ahmiadinejad's newspaper in fight with hardliners over hijab', 16 August 2011, http://latimesblogs.latimes.com/babylonbeyond/2011/08/ahmadinejad-newspaper-hijab.html.

Mottahedeh, Negar, *Displaced Allegories: Post-revolutionary Iranian Cinema*, Durham 2008.

Mottahedeh, Negar, *Representing the Unpresentable: Historical Images of National Reform from the Qajar to the Islamic Republic of Iran*, New York 2008.

Muhammadi, Majid, 'How Iran's Ruling Clerics Distort Facts About Hijab', *Radio Farda* 4 February 2018, https://en.radiofarda.com/a/iran-hijab-khamenei-facts/29017675.html.

Mutahhari, Murtaza, *Jurisprudence and its Principles*, New York n.d., http://www.iranchamber.com/personalities/mmotahari/works/jurisprudence_and_its_principles.pdf.

Mutahhari, Murtaza, *The Rights of Women in Islam*, Tehran 1981.

Mutahhari, Murtaza, *The Principle of Ijtihad in Islam*, trans. John Cooper, https://www.al-islam.org/al-serat/vol-10-no-1/principle-ijtihad-islam-ayatullah-murtadha-mutahhari.

Mutahhari, Murtaza, *The Role of Ijtihad in Legislation*, trans. Mahliqa Qaraʾi, https://www.al-islam.org/al-tawhid/vol4-n2/role-ijtihad-legislation-ayatullah-murtadha-mutahhari.

Mutahhari, Murtaza, *The Islamic Modest Dress*, trans. Laleh Bakhtiar, USA 1988.

Mutahhari, Murtaza, *Jihad: The Holy War of Islam and its Legitimacy in the Qurʾan*, trans. Mohammad Salman Tawhid, Tehran 1985.

Naficy, Hamid, *A Social History of Iranian Cinema*, Durham 2011, vol. 2.

Naficy, Hamid, 'Veiled vision/powerful presences', *In the Eye of the Storm: Women in Post-revolutionary Iran*, ed. Mahnaz Afkhami and Erika Friedl, London 1994, 131–50.

Naghibi, Nima, 'Bad Feminist or Bad-Hejabi?', *Interventions: International Journal of Postcolonial Studies* 1.4, 2006, 555–71.

an-Naʿim, Abdullahi Ahmed, *Toward an Islamic Reformation: Civil Liberties, Human Rights, and International Law*, New York 1990.

Najjar, Fauzi, 'Islamic Fundamentalism and the Intellectuals: The Case of Nasr Hamid Abu Zayd', *British Journal of Middle Eastern Studies* 27.2, 2000, 177–200.

Najmabadi, Afsaneh, *Women with Moustaches and Men without Beards: Gender and Sexual Anxieties of Iranian Modernity*, Berkeley 2005.

Najmabadi, Afsaneh, 'Veiled discourse – unveiled bodies', *Feminist Studies* 19.3, 1993, 487–518.

Niknam, Azadeh, 'The Islamization of Law in Iran', *Middle East Research and Information Project (MER212)*, 1999, http://www.merip.org/mer/mer212/islamization-law-iran.

Oppenheim, Maya, 'Iranian women defy threat of decade-long jail sentence by taking photos of themselves without headscarves', *The Independent* 1 August, 2019.

Osborne, Samuel, 'Iranian woman "sentenced to 20 years in prison" for removing headscarf in protest', *The Independent* 10 July 2018, https://www.independent.co.uk/news/world/middle-east/

iran-woman-hijab-protest-arrest-jailed-prison-shapark-shajarizadeh-headscarf-white-wednesdays-a8439816.html.

Paidar, Parvin, *Women and the Political Process in Twentieth Century Iran*, Cambridge 1995.

Panjwani, Farid, 'Fazlur Rahman and the search for authentic Islamic education: A critical appreciation', *Curriculum Inquiry* 42.1, 2012, 33–55.

Pilcher, Pat, 'Islamic cleric causes Boobquake', *NZ Herald* 27 April 2010, https://www.nzherald.co.nz/technology/news/article.cfm?c_id=5&objectid=10641150.

Pistor-Hatami, Anja, 'Nonunderstanding and Minority Formation in Iran', *Iran* LV, 2017, 87–98.

Powers, David S., *Zayd*, Philadelphia 2014.

Quataert, Donald, 'Clothing Laws, State, and Society in the Ottoman Empire, 1720–1829', *International Journal of Middle East Studies* 29.3,1997, 403–25.

Qudsizad, Parvin, 'The Period of Pahlavi I', *Pahlavi dynasty: An Entry from Encyclopaedia of the World of Islam*, ed. Ghulam Ali, H. ʿAdel and Mohammad J. Elmi, London 2012.

Rabb, Intisar A., *Doubt in Islamic Law: A History of Legal Maxims, Interpretation, and Islamic Criminal Law*, Cambridge 2015.

RadioFreeEurope, 'Iranian Religious Scholar Jailed on Propaganda, Insult Charges', 16 December 2010, https://www.rferl.org/a/2250328.html.

Rahnema, Ali, 'Ali Shariati; Teacher, Preacher, Rebel', *Pioneers of Islamic Revival*, ed. Ali Rahnema, London 1994, 208–27.

Rahnema, Ali, *An Islamic Utopian: A Political Biography of ʿAli* Sharīʿ*atī*, London 2014.

Rahnema, Ali, *Shiʿi Reformation in Islam*, London 2015.

Rahnema, Ali, *Superstition as Ideology in Iranian Politics: From Majlesi to Ahmadinejad*, Cambridge 2011.

Rahman, Fazlur, *Islam*, Chicago 1966.

Ramadan, Tariq, 'We must not accept this repression', *The Guardian* 30 March 2005.

Regan, Carol, 'Ahmad Kasravi's views on the role of women in Iranian society as expressed in *Our Sisters and Daughters*', *Women and the Family in Iran*, ed. Asghar Fatehi, Leiden 1985, 60–76.

Richard, Yann, 'Shariʿat Sangalaji: A reformist theologian of the Rida Shah period', *Authority and Political Culture in Shiʿism*, ed. S. Amir Arjomand, New York 1988, 159–77.

Ridgeon, Lloyd, 'Ahmad Kasravi and "pick-axe" politics', *Iran* LIV.I, 2016, 59–72.

Ridgeon, Lloyd, 'Ahmad Qabil, a reason to believe and the New Religious Thinking in Iran', *Middle Eastern Studies* 56.1, 2020, 1–15.

Ridgeon, Lloyd, *Awḥad al-Dīn Kirmānī and the Controversy of the Sufi Gaze*, London 2018.

Ridgeon, Lloyd, 'Listening for an "Authentic" Iran: Mohsen Makhmalbaf's Film 'The Silence' (Sokut)', *Iranian Intellectuals, 1997–2007*, ed. Lloyd Ridgeon, London 2008, 139–53.

Ridgeon, Lloyd, *Sufi Castigator: Ahmad Kasravi and the Iranian Mystical Tradition*, London 2006.

Rodziewicz, Magdalena, 'From Compulsory Unveiling (*kashf-e hejab*) to Compulsory Veiling (*hejab-e ejbari*) *Hejab* in the Iranian Perspective', *Politics and Society in the Islamic World*, ed. Izabela Kończak, Magdalena Lewicka and Marta Widy-Behiesse, Warsaw 2016, 228–41.

Rostam-Kolayi, Jasamin, 'Family law, work and unveiling', *The Making of Modern Iran: State and Society under Riza Shah, 1921–1941*, ed. Stephanie Cronin, London 2003.

Rostam-Kolayi, Jasamin and Afshin Matin-Asgari, 'Unveiling ambiguities: revisiting 1030s Iran's *kashf-i hijab* campaign', *Anti-Veiling Campaigns in the Muslim World: Gender, Modernism and the politics of Dress*, ed. Stephanie Cronin, London 2014, 128–48.

Rubin, Barry and Wolfgang G. Schwanitz, *Nazis, Islamists, and the Making of the Modern Middle East*, London 2014.

Rumi, *The Discourses of Rum* (*Fihi ma fihi*), trans. A. J. Arberry, London 1961.

Sachedina, Abdalaziz, 'Abdulaziz Sachedina on His Life and Scholarship', *Maydan*, 13 September 2017, https://www.themaydan.com/2017/09/interview-abdulaziz-sachedina-life-scholarship/.

Sachedina, Abdalaziz, *The Just Ruler in Shiʿite Islam*, Oxford 1988.

Sachedina, Abdalaziz, 'Woman, half-the-man? The Crisis of Male Epistemology in Islamic Jurisprudence', *Intellectual Traditions in Islam*, ed. Farhad Daftary, London 2000, 146–60.

Sadeghi-Boroujerdi, Eskander, 'Mostafa Malekian: Spirituality, Siyasat-Zadegi and (A)political Self-Improvement', *Digest of Middle East Studies* 23.2, 2014, 279–311.

Sadeghi-Boroujerdi, Eskander, 'From Etelāʿāti to Eslāhtalabi: Saʿid Hajjariyan, Political Theology and the Politics of Reform in Post-Revoultiuonary Iran', *Iranian Studies* 47.6, 2014, 987–1009.

Sadeghi-Boroujerdi, Eskander, 'The Post-Revolutionary Women's Uprising of March 1979: An Interview with Nasser Mohajer and Mahnaz Matin', *Iranwire.com* 2013. https://iranwire.com/en/features/24.

al-Sadr, Muhammad Baqir, *Lessons in Islamic Jurisprudence*, trans. Roy Parviz Mottahedeh, Oxford 2005.

al-Sadr, Muhammad Baqir, *Principles of Islamic Jurisprudence: According to Shi'i Law*, London 2003.

Sadri, Mahmoud, 'Sacred defence of secularism: The political theologies of Soroush, Shabestari and Kadivar', *International Journal of Politics, Culture and Society* 15.2, 2001, 257–70.

Sahimi, Muhammad, 'Progressive Muslim Scholar and Political Dissident Ahmad Ghabel: 1954–2012', http://www.payvand.com/news/12/oct/1157.html.

Sakurai, Keiko, 'Shi'ite women's seminaries (*howzeh-ye 'elmiyyeh-ye khahran*) [sic] in Iran: Possibilities and limitations', *Iranian Studies* 45.6, 2012, 727–44.

Samuel, Henry, 'French election 2017: Emmanuel Macron and Marine Le Pen through to presidential run off', *The Telegraph* 24 April 2017, https://www.telegraph.co.uk/news/2017/04/23/french-election-live-results-exit-polls.

Saul, Heather, 'French journalist confronts President Rouhani with picture of an Iranian woman without a hijab', *The Independent* 12 November 2015, https://www.independent.co.uk/news/people/french-journalist-confronts-president-rouhani-with-picture-of-an-iranian-woman-without-a-hijab-from-a6732001.html.

Saul, Heather, 'Iranian model Elnaz Golrokh leaves Iran with her boyfriend after sharing photos without hijab', *The Independent* 20 May 2016, https://www.independent.co.uk/news/people/iranian-model-elnaz-golrokh-leaves-iran-with-her-boyfriend-after-sharing-photos-without-hijab-a7037801.html.

Scarce, Jennifer, *Women's Costumes of the Near and Middle East*, London 2002.

Schultheis, Emily, 'Viktor Orban: Hungary does not want "Muslim Invaders"', *Politico* 1 August 2018, https://www.politico.eu/article/viktor-orban-hungary-doesnt-want-muslim-invaders/.

Segir, Fatma, 'Interview with Muhammad Mujtahid Shabistari (Part 1): "Islam Is a Religion, Not a Political Agenda"', 2008, https://en.qantara.de/content/interview-with-mohammad-mojtahed-shabestari-part-1-islam-is-a-religion-not-a-political.

Shaikh, Sa'diyya, 'Transforming Feminism', *Progressive Muslims: On Justice, Gender and Pluralism*, ed. Omid Safi, Oxford 2003, 147–62.

Shams Esmaeili, Fatemeh, 'The Iranian actress's sex tape scandal', *Free Speech Debate* 12 June 2012, http://freespeechdebate.com/case/the-iranian-actress-and-sex-tape-scandal/.

Shavarini, Mitra K., 'The Feminisation of Higher Education', *International Review of Education / Internationale Zeitschrift für Erziehungswissenschaft / Revue Internationale de l'Education* 51.4, 2005.

Shirazi, Faegheh, *The Veil Unveiled: The Hijab in Modern Culture*, Gainesville 2001.

Shirazi, Faegheh, 'Iran's Compulsory Hijab: From politics and religious authority to fashion shows', *The Routledge International Handbook to Veils and Veiling*, ed. Anna Mari Almila and David Inglis, London 2017, 97–115.

Shoard, Catherine, 'Iran news agency gives Charlize Theron a polo neck in altered Oscars footage', *The Guardian* 1 March 2016, https://www.theguardian.com/film/2017/mar/01/iran-news-agency-charlize-theron-polo-neck-oscars-asghar-farhadi-salesman.

Sirjani, Ali-Akbar Saʿidi, 'Clothing xi. In the Pahlavi and post-Pahlavi periods', *Encyclopaedia Iranica* V/8, 2011.

Soroush, Abdolkarim, 'The evolution and devolution of religious knowledge', *Liberal Islam*, ed. Charles Kurzman, Oxford 1998.

Soroush, Abdolkarim, *The Expansion of Prophetic Experience; Essays on Historicity, Contingency and Plurality in Religion*, trans. Nilou Mobasser, Leiden 2009.

Soroush, Abdolkarim, *Reason, Freedom, and Democracy in Islam: Essential Writings of Abdolkarim Soroush*, Oxford 2000.

Sprachman, Paul, 'The poetics of *hijab* in the satire of Iraj Mirza', *Iran and Iranian Studies: Essays in Honor of Iraj Afshar*, ed. Kambiz Eslami, New Jersey 1998.

Tabatabaʾi, Muhammad Husayn, *Shining Sun* [*Mihr-i Ṭābān*], trans. Tawus Raja, London 2011.

Taha, Mahmoud Mohamed, *The Second Message of Islam*, trans. Abdullahi Ahmed An-Naʿim, New York 1987.

Tahmasebi, Sussan, 'The One Million Signatures Campaign: An Effort Born on the Streets', *Amnesty International Middle East North Africa Regional Office* (no date), http://amnestymena.org/en/Magazine/Issue20/TheOneMillionSignatureCampaigninIran.aspx?media=print.

Tait, Robert, 'Iranian actor in sex video scandal says ex-fiancé faked footage', *The Guardian* 22 November 2006.

Takim, Liyakat, 'Custom as a Legal Principle of Legislation for Shiʿi Law', *Studies in Religion/Sciences Religieuses* 47.4, 2018, 481–99.

Takim, Liyakat, 'Islamic Law and Post-Ijtihadism', http://www.ltakim.com/Post-Islamism.pdf.

Takim, Liyakat, 'Maqāṣid al-Shariʿa in contemporary Shiʿi jurisprudence', *Maqāṣid al-Sharīʿa and Contemporary Reformist Muslim Thought*, ed. Adis Duderija, New York 2014, 101–26.

Takim, Liyakat, 'Privileging the Qurʾan: Divorce and the Hermeneutics of Yusuf Saniʿi', *Approaches to the Qurʾan in Contemporary Iran*, ed. Alessandro Cancian, Oxford 2019.

Tanavoli, Parviz, *European Women in Persian Houses: Western Images in Safavid and Qajar Iran*, London 2015.

Tehranian, Majid, 'Islamic fundamentalism in Iran', *Fundamentalisms in Society: Reclaiming the Sciences, the Family and Education*, ed. Martin E. Marty and R. Scott Appleby, Chicago 1993, 341–73.

Terman, Rochelle, 'The piety of public participation: The revolutionary Muslim woman in the Islamic Republic of Iran', *Totalitarian Movements and Political Religions* 11.3/4, 2010, 289–310.

Torab, Azam, *Performing Islam: Gender and Ritual in Iran*, Leiden 2007.

Ushama, Thameem, 'The phenomenon of al-naskh: a brief overview of the key issues', *Jurnal Fiqh* 3, 2006, 101–32.

Vahabzadeh, Peyman, 'Fedāʾiyān-e Khalq', *Encyclopaedia Iranica*, 2015.

Vahdat, Farzin, 'Post-revolutionary discourses of Mohammad Mojtahed Shabestari and Mohsen Kadivar: Reconciling the terms of mediated subjectivity', *Critique: Journal for Critical Studies of the Middle East* 17, 2000, 135–57.

Vahdat, Farzin, 'Post-revolutionary Islamic modernity in Iran: the inter-subjective hermeneutics of Mohammad Mojtahed Shabistari', *Modern Muslim Intellectuals and the Qurʾan*, ed. Suha Taji-Farouki, Oxford 2006, 193–224.

Vasmaghi, Sedigheh, *Women, Jurisprudence, Islam*, trans. M. R. Ashna and Philip G. Kreyenbroeck, Wiesbaden 2014.

von Schwerin, Ulrich, *The Dissident Mullah: Ayatollah Montazeri and the Struggle for Reform in Revolutionary Iran*, London 2015.

Walbridge, Linda, 'The counter reformation: Becoming a Marjaʿ in the modern world', *The Most Learned of the Shiʿa: The Institution of the Marjaʿ Taqlid*, ed. Linda Walbridge, Oxford 2001, 230–46.

Watt, W. Montgomery, *The Formative Period of Islamic Thought*, Oxford 1988.

Woodhead, Linda, 'The Muslim Veil Controversy and European Values', *Swedish Missiological Themes* 97.1, 2009, 89–105.

Zahedi, Ashraf, 'Concealing and Revealing Female Hair: Veiling Dynamics in Contemporary Iran', *The Veil: Women Writers on its History, Lore, and Politics*, ed. Jennifer Heath, Berkeley 2008, 250–65.

Zein-ed-Din, Nazira, 'Unveiling and veiling', trans. Ali Badran and Margot Badran, *Opening the Gates: A Century of Arab Feminist Writers*, ed. Margot Badran and Miriam Cooke, London 1990.

Persian sources

Abrar, Gulshan. *Jamīʿi az Pazhuhishgarān-i Ḥawza'yi ʿAmaliya Qum*, Qum 1385/2006–7.

al-Ajdad, Muhammad H. Manzur, *Marjiʿīyat dar ʿArṣah-i Ijtimāʿ va Siyāsat: Asnād va Guzārish-hā-yī az Āyāt-i ʿIzam Naʾini, Isfahani, Qumi, Haʾiri va Burujirdi*, Tehran 2000.

Anonymous, *Baḥthī dar barā-yī Marjaʿiyat va Rūḥāniyat*, Tehran 1341/1962.

Aqiqi-Bakhshayishi, ʿAbd'ul Rahim, *Yakṣad Sāl-i Mubārazah-i Rūḥānīyat-i Mutaraqqī*, Tehran 1982.

Awhadi, *Jām-i Jam, Dīvān-i Awḥadī*, ed. S. Nafisi, Tehran 1340/1961.

Ayazi, Muhammad Ali, 'Naqd va barrasī-yi adilla-yi fiqhī-yi ilzām-i ḥukumat-i ḥijāb' ['A critique and study of jurisprudential reasons of the governmental requirement [to wear] the hijab'], *Fiqh* 31 Tir 1392 / 22 June 2013.

Ayazi, Sayyid Muhammad Ali, 'Sayyid Muḥammad ʿAlī Āyāzī: Ḥijāb amri-yi ijtimāʿī nīst ki mujazat dashta bashad' ['Sayyid Muhammad ʿAli Ayazi: Hijab is not a social matter that is punishable'], *Intikhāb*, https://www.entekhab.ir/fa/news/69889/.

Basiratmanish, Hamid, *ʿUlamāʾ va Rizhīm-i Riżā Shāh: Naẓarī bar ʿAmalkard-i Siyāsī-Farhangī-i Rūḥānīyūn dar Sālhā-yi 1305–1320*, Tehran 1997.

Eshkevari, Hasan Yusufi, 'Ḥuqūq-i bashr va aḥkām-i ijtimāʿī-yī Islām' ['Human Rights and the social commands of Islam'], 7 May 2010, http://yousefieshkevari.com/?p=751.

Eshkevari, Hasan Yusufi, 'Qabil, shahrvand-i mudirn-i mūʾmin-i musalmān būd' ['Qabil was a modern, believing Muslim citizen'], 28 October 2012, *Yād-nāma*.

Hafiz, *Dīvān-i Ḥāfiż*, ed. Parviz Natil Khanlari, Tehran 1984.

Jaʿfariyan, Rasul, *Dāstān-i Ḥijāb dar Irān Pīsh az Inqalāb* [*The Case of the Hijab in Iran Before the Revolution*], Tehran 1383/2004–5.

Ja'fariyan, Rasul, *Rasā'il Ḥijābiya*, ed. Rasul Ja'fariyan, Tehran 1380/2001–2.

Kai Kawus ibn Iskandar ibn Vashmgir, *Qābūs-nāma*, ed. Ghulam Husayn Yusufi, Tehran 1345/1966–67.

Kadivar, Muhsin, 'Aḥkām-i hijāb' ['The commands of the hijab'], July 2016, https://kadivar.com/?p=10194.

Kadivar, Muhsin, *Asnādī az Mazlūmiyyāt-i Ayatollah Sharī'atmadārī* [*Documents of the Oppression of Ayatollah Shari'atmadari*], 2015, https://kadivar.com/category/1-books/17-b/b-17-0/.

Kadivar, Muhsin, 'Ayzāḥ-i naskh-i 'aqlī' ['Explaining rational abrogation'], 2015, https://kadivar.com/?p=14660.

Kadivar, Muhsin, *Bi-Nām-i Islām: Harcha Mī-Khāhad Mi-Kunad* [*Arbitrary Rule in the Name of Islam*], 2018, https://en.kadivar.com/wp-content/uploads/2018/05/English-Preface-1.pdf.

Kadivar, Muhsin, *Daghdagha-hā-yi Ḥukūmat-i Dīnī* [*Apprehension about Religious Government*], Tehran 2000, https://kadivar.com/category/1-books/b-09/0-b-09/.

Kadivar, Muhsin, *Daftar-i 'Aql* [*Book of Reason*], Tehran 1377/1998–9, https://kadivar.com/category/1-books/02-b/1-b-02/.

Kadivar, Muhsin, *Dar Mahzar-i Faqīh-i Āzādāna: Ustād Ḥusayn 'Alī Muntazarī Najafābādī* [*In the Company of the Noble Faqih: The Master Husayn 'Ali Muntazari Najafabadi*], 1392/2013, https://kadivar.com/category/1-books/14-b/0-b-14/.

Kadivar, Muhsin, *Farāz va Furūd-i Azarī-Qumī* [*The Rise and Fall of Azari-Qumi*], 2014, https://kadivar.com/category/1-books/b-18/b-18-0/.

Kadivar, Muhsin, *Ḥaqq al-Nās* [*Islam and Human Rights*], Tehran 2007, https://kadivar.com/category/1-books/b-12/b-12-0/.

Kadivar, Muhsin, '*Ḥijāb: hadd-i sharī', hadd-i qanūnī*' [The hijab: the religious limit and the legal limit] 1386/2007, https://kadivar.com/?p=2116.

Kadivar, Muhsin, 'Ḥijāb-i ijbārī fāqid-i dalīl-i mu'tabar-i shar'ī ast' ['There is no reliable sharia proof for compulsory hijab'], 1 July 2012, https://kadivar.com/?p=9381.

Kadivar, Muhsin, *Ḥukūmat-i Intiṣābī* [*Government by Appointment*], 1393/2016, https://kadivar.com/category/1-books/b-10/0-b-10/.

Kadivar, Muhsin, 'Ḥuqūq-i bashar va rawshanfikr-i dīnī', *Aftāb* 3.27, 2003, https://kadivar.com/1069/.

Kadivar, Muhsin, *Ibtizāl-i Marji'yat-i Shi'a: Istizār Marji'at-i Maqām-i Rahbarī, Ḥujjat al-Islām wa'l-Muminīn, Sayyid 'Ali Khamenei* [*The*

Trivialization of Shiʿi Marjaʿiyyat: Impeaching Iran's Supreme Leader on His Marjaʿiyyat], 2014, https://kadivar.com/category/1-books/b-20/b-20-0/.

Kadivar, Muhsin, *Inqilāb va Niẓām dar Būta-yi Naqd-i Akhlāqī* [*Testing the Revolution and the Regime with Ethical Criticisms*], 2015, https://kadivar.com/category/1-books/b-19/b-19-0/.

Kadivar, Muhsin, 'Kalām ijmālī fī sitr al-murāh' ['A brief discussion about covering women'], 2004, https://kadivar.com/?p=267.

Kadivar, Muhsin, *Majāzat-i Murtad va Āzādī-yī Mazhhab* [*Apostasy, Blasphemy, & Religious Freedom in Islam*], 2014, https://kadivar.com/category/1-books/b-21/b-21-0/.

Kadivar, Muhsin, *Majmuʾa-yi Musanafāta-yi Ḥākima Muʾassiss Āqā ʿAlī Muddaris Tihrānī* [*The Compilation of the Works of the Sage and Originator Aqa Ali Muddaris Tehrani*], Tehran 1999, https://kadivar.com/1302/.

Kadivar, Muhsin, *Mujāhidat-hā-yi ʿIlmī-yi Marḥūm Aḥmad Qābil* [*The Scientific Struggles of the Late Ahmad Qabil*], 2012, https://kadivar.com/9795.

Kadivar, Muhsin, 'Musāfaha bā ajnabiya' ['Shaking hands with foreigners'], 2003, https://kadivar.com/?p=8429.

Kadivar, Muhsin, *Naẓariya-hā-yi Dawlat* [*Theories of the State*], Tehran 1998, https://kadivar.com/category/1-books/01-b/b-01-0/.

Kadivar, Muhsin, *Nidāʾyi Sabz: Rawāyātī az Junbish-i Sabz-i Mardum-i Irān* [*The Green Call: A Narrative of the Iranian Green Movement*], 2014, https://kadivar.com/category/1-books/b-22/b-22-0/.

Kadivar, Muhsin, 'Nukātī darbāra-yi mubāḥith-i vaḥī-yi pazhūhān-i akhīr' ['Some points about the controversy of revelation by recent researchers'], 2008, https://kadivar.com/2995.

Kadivar, Muhsin, 'Pursish va pāsukh-i ḥuqūq-i bashr va rawshanfkikrī-yi dīnī' ['Question and answer about human rights and the religious intellectuals'], 1387/2008, https://kadivar.com/1066.

Kadivar, Muhsin, 'Sanjaq kardan-i hijāb-i ijbārī bi hayāt-i niẓām' ['The linkage of the mandatory hijab with the life of the regime'], 2018, http://kadivar.com/?p=16476.

Kadivar, Muhsin, 'Sharīʿat: niẓām-i ḥuqūqī yā arzish-hā-yi akhlāqī?' ['*Shariʿat*: a legal order or moral values?'], 19 October 2013, https://kadivar.com/?p=12859.

Kadivar, Muhsin, *Siyāsat-nāma-yi Khurāsānī* [*Khurasani's Political Philosophy*], Tehran *2006,* https://kadivar.com/1253/.

Kadivar, Muhsin, *Sūg-Nāma-yi Faqīh-i Pāk-Bāz Ustād Muntazirī* [*A Tribute to the Virtuous Theologian*], 2013, https://kadivar.com/category/1-books/15-b/0-b-15/.

Kadivar, Muhsin, 'Taʾamūllī dar masʾāla-yi ḥijāb' ['Reflections on the issue of the hijab'], 2013, https://kadivar.com/?p=10843.

Kadivar, Muhsin, 'Taʾamullī darbara-yi naw andīshī-yi dīnī dar irān-i muʿasir' ['Reflections on the New Religious Thinkers in Contemporary Iran'], 2015, http://kadivar.com/?p=14729.

Kadivar, Muhsin, 'Tāʾamullī darbāra-yi vaḥī' ['Reflections on revelation'], 2017, https://kadivar.com/15964.

Kar, Mihrangiz, *Khushūnat ʿAlayh-i Zan dar Irān* [*Violence Against Women in Iran*], Tehran 1380/2001.

Khamenei, Ali, Speech of 8 March 2018, http://ijtihadnet.ir/%D9%81%D8%B5%D9%84-%D8%A7%D9%84%D8%AE%D8%B7%D8%A7%D8%A8-%D8%AD%D8%AC%D8%A7%D8%A8%D8%9B-%D8%AD%DA%A9%D9%88%D9%85%D8%AA-%D8%A7%D8%B3%D9%84%D8%A7%D9%85%DB%8C-%D9%85%D9%88%D8%B8%D9%81-%D8%A7/.

Khatami, Sayyid Muhammad, *Bīm-i Mawj* [*Fear of the Wave*], Tehran 1372/1993.

Khomeini, Ruhollah, *Kashf al-Asrār*, Tehran 1943, http://www.imam-khomeini.com/web1/english/showitem.aspx?pid=-1&cid=2139.

Khomeini, Ruhollah, 'Manshūr-i baradari' ['Brotherly charter'], 1 November 1988, *Sahīfa-ya Imām*, vol 2, http://www.imam-khomeini.ir/fa/page/210/.

Khomeini, Ruhollah, 'Payām bi-rūḥāniyat, mudarrisīn, ṭullāb…' ['Message to the spiritual leaders, religious teachers and religious students'], 3 Isfand 1367 / 22 February 1988, *Ṣahīfeh-ye Imām*, vol. 21.

Khomeini, Ruhollah, *Vilāyat-i Faqīh: Hukūmat Islāmī*, Tehran 1377/1998.

Matin, Mahnaz and Mohajer, Nasser, 'Guftagū ba Ayatollah Ṭāliqānī' ['Conversation with Ayatollah Ṭāliqānī'], *Zanān-i Irānī dar Inqilāb* [*Iranian Women in the Revolution*], ed. Matin and Mohajer, *Khīzish-i Zanān-i Irān dar Esfand 1357* [*The Uprising of Iranian Women in Esfand 1357*], vol. 2, Paris 2010.

Montazeri, Ali, *Islām va Dīn-i Fiṭrat* [*Islam and the Religion of [Original] Nature*], 1385/2006–7, https://amontazeri.com/static/books/Eslam_Dine_Fetrat.pdf.

Montazeri, Ali, *Pāsukh bi Pursish-hā-yi Dīnī* [*Answers to Religious Questions*], Tehran 1389/2010–11, https://amontazeri.com/book/posesh/356.

Mujtahid-Shabistari, Muhammad, *Naqdi bar Qirāʾat-i Rasmī az Dīn* [*Criticism of the Official Reading of Religion*], Tehran 1381/2002–3.

Mujtahid-Shabistari, Muhammad, 'Qirāʾat-i nabawī az jahān' ['A prophetic reading of the world'], *Madrasa* 2.6, 2007, http://mohammadmojtahedshabestari.com/category/%D9%86%D9%88%D8%B4%D8%AA%D9%87/%D9%82%D8%B1%D8%A7%D8%A6%D8%AA-%D9%86%D8%A8%D9%88%DB%8C-%D8%A7%D8%B2-%D8%AC%D9%87%D8%A7%D9%86/.

Mujtahid-Shabistari, Muhammad, 'Rāh-i dusuwār-i mardumsālārī' ['The difficult path of democracy'], *Aftāb* 4.22, 2003.

Mutahhari, Murtaza, *Islām va Muqtażiyāt-i Zamān* [*Islam and the Necessities of Time*], Tehran 1370/1991–2.

Mutahhari, Murtaza, *Masʾala-yi Ḥijāb*, Tehran 1348/1969.

Mutahhari, Murtaza, *Niẓām-i Ḥuqūq-i Zan dar Islām*, Tehran 1370/1991.

Mutahhari, Murtaza, *Pāsukh-hā-yi Ustād bi Naqd-hā-ī bar Kitāb-i Masʾāla-yi Ḥijāb*, Tehran 1370/1990–91.

[All of Qabil's works listed below are found at: http://www.ghabel.net/shariat/books.]

Qabil, Ahmad, *Aḥkām-i Bānuvān dar Sharīʿat-i Muḥammadī*, 1392/2013–14.

Qabil, Ahmad, 'Ākharīn muṣāḥiba-yi Ahmad Qabil' ['Last interview with Ahmad Qabil'], 7 June 2012, *Vaṣiyat bi Millat-i Irān*.

Qabil, Ahmad, 'Amr ghayr-i ʿaqlānī dar sharīʿat pazīrufta na-mī-shavad' ['Non-rational acts in the sharīa are not acceptable'], *Vaṣiyat bi Millat-i Irān*.

Qabil, Ahmad, *Bīm va Umīd-hā-yi Dīndārī*, 1391/2012–13.

Qabil, Ahmad, 'Chirā libās-i rūḥāniyat-rā kinār guzashtam' ['Why I put aside the clothes of the men of religion'], *Naqd-i Khud-kāmagī*.

Qabil, Ahmad, 'Dastgīrī-hā bā imżā-yi Ayatollah Khāmeneī sūrat girifta ast' ['The arrests have taken place with the authorisation of Ayatollah Khamenei'], 31 July 2010, *Vaṣiyat bi Millat-i Irān*.

Qabil, Ahmad, 'Durānī nīst ke mānnand Gālīleh az harfam bar gardam' ['This is not the time for me to recant like Galileo'], *Vaṣiyat bi Millat-i Irān*.

Qabil, Ahmad, *Fiqh, Kārkard-hā va Qābiliyat-ha*, 1392/2013–14.

Qabil, Ahmad, *Islām va Tāʾmīn-i Ijtimāʿī*, 1383/2004–5.

Qabil, Ahmad, 'Junbish-i sabz, iṣlāhāt, rūhāniyat va vilāyat-i faqīh' ['The Green Movement, Reforms, the Clergy and the Guardianship of the Jurist'], 8 April 2011, *Vaṣiyat bi Millat-i Irān*.

Qabil, Ahmad, 'Karūbī va Mūsāwī bi jurm-i mukhālifat bā istibdād habs shuda-and' ['Karubi and Musavi have been imprisoned for the crime of opposing tyranny'], *Vaṣiyat bi Millat-i Irān*.

Qabil, Ahmad, *Mabānī-yi Sharīʿat*, 1391/2012–13.

Qabil, Ahmad, 'Mushtārakāt-i junbish-i sabz' ['The common points with the Green Movement'], *Vaṣiyat bi Millat-i Irān*.

Qabil, Ahmad, 'Nama bi-rahbar-i jumhūrī-yi Islāmī-yi Irān' ['Letter to the Leader of the Islamic Republic'], http://www.bbc.com/persian/iran/story/2005/06/050601_ahmad-Qabil-letter.shtml.

Qabil, Ahmad, *Naqd-i Farhang-i Khushūnat*, 1381/2002–3.

Qabil, Ahmad, 'Naqd-i ijmālī-yi ashghāl-i sifārat-i Āmrīkā dar Irān' ['A brief criticism of the occupation of the American embassy in Iran'], 10 Aban 1388, *Fiqh, Kārkard-hā va Qābiliyat-ha*.

Qabil, Ahmad, *Naqd-i Khūdkāmagī*, 1391/2012–13.

Qabil, Ahmad, *Sharīʿat-i ʿAqlānī*, 1391/2012–13.

Qabil, Ahmad, 'Ṭarḥ-i mawrid-i adʿā-yi "Islāmī kardan dānishgāh-hā" rāhī juz-i shikast na-khwāhad dāsht' [The plan to 'Islamicise the universities' will be a path to failure], *Vaṣiyat bi Millat-i Irān*.

Qabil, Ahmad, 'Tashkil-i shūrā az sū-yi rahbarī, iqrār bi ikhtalāf-i shadīd bayn-i qavast' ['The creation of a council by the leadership acknowledges the serious split among the powers of government'], 27 August 2011, *Vaṣiyat bi Millat-i Irān*.

Qabil, Ahmad, 'Thābit va mutaghayyir dar Qurʾan', *Fiqh, Karkard-hā va Qābiliyat-ha*.

Qabil, Ahmad, 'Vilāyat-i faqīh', *Fiqh, Kārkard-hā va Qābiliyat-ha*.

Qumi, Abbas, *Fawāʿid al-Razwiya*, Tehran 1327/1948–49, vol. 1.

Ranini, Mihdi Sultani, 'Naskh az dīdgāh-i Ayatollah Maʿrifat', *Majalla-yi Takhassusī Ilāhiyat va Ḥuqūq* 46, 1386/1997.

Rudi-Kadivar, Zahra, ed., *Bahāʾī-yi Āzādī: Dafāʿiyat-i Muhsin Kadivar dar Dādgāh-i Vizha-i Rūḥaniyyat* [*The Price of Freedom: In Defence of Mohsen Kadivar at the Special Clerical Court*], Tehran 1378/1999–2000.

Shafiʾi-Sarustani, Ibrahim, ed., *Ḥijāb: Masʿūliyat-hā va Ikhtiyārāt-i Sawlat-i Islāmī* [*Hijab: The Responsibilities and Rights of an Islamic State*], Qum 1387/2008–9.

Sharif-Razi, Muhammad, *Aṭhār al-Ḥujjah: yā Tārīkh va Dāʾirat al-Maʿārif-i Ḥawza-yi ʿIlmīyya-yi Qum*, Tehran 1953.

Suroush, Abd al-Karim, *Qabż o Basṭ-i Tiʾurīk-i Sharīʿat* [*The Theoretic Expansion and Contraction of the Sharia*], Tehran 1995.

Soroush, Abd al-Karim, 'Taḥlīl-i mafhūm-i ḥukūmat-i dīnī' ['Analysis of the understanding of religious government'], *Kiyān* 6, 1996, 32–3.

Turkashvand, Amir, *Ḥijāb-i Shar'ī dar 'Aṣr-i Payghambar* [*Legal Hijab in the Age of the Prophet*], https://academia.edu/1228672/.

Illustrations

Ahmad Qabil (left) in non-traditional garments, http://www.ghabel.net/shariat/gallery?album=1&gallery=8.

Ahmad Qabil with Ayatollah Montazeri, https://www.facebook.com/ghabel.ahmad/photos/a.766644343427892/766644333427893/?type=3.

'*Dukhtar-i Shāyista*' (worthy lady), 1967, image taken from the front cover of *Zan-i Rūz*, http://www.wishe.net/dreja.aspx?Jmare=43489&Jor=6.

Encouraging sons to join the war effort, Middle Eastern Posters Collection at University of Chicago, box 3, no. 71, Special Collections Research Center, University of Chicago Library, https://www.lib.uchicago.edu/ead/pdf/meposters-0003-071.pdf.

Fatima on the occasion of the Week of War, Middle Eastern Posters Collection at University of Chicago, box 3, no. 67, Special Collections Research Center, University of Chicago Library, https://www.lib.uchicago.edu/ead/pdf/meposters-0003-067.pdf.

'Fatima Rising, Celebrate the True Leader', 1979, Middle Eastern Posters Collection at University of Chicago, box 2, no. 30, Special Collections Research Center, University of Chicago Library, http://pi.lib.uchicago.edu/1001/scrc/md/meposters-0002-030.

Gabbeh, 1996, Photography by Mohammad Ahmadi, Makhmalbaf Film House.

Golestan, Hengameh, *Untitled* (Witness '79 series), photograph, March 1979, Anatole France (Neuphle le-Chateau) Street, opposite the USSR (Russian) Embassy, Tehran; © Hengameh Golestan, Courtesy of Archaeology of the Final Decade.

Haft Shahr-i 'Ishq, from Hamid Naficy's collection of Iranian film posters, held at North Western University, Courtesy of Northwestern University Archives, https://images.northwestern.edu/multiresimages/inu:dil-c59576a8-9545-4282-8bdd-f066521ad4d2.

'Our army does not only belong to our brothers in the armed forces', Middle Eastern Posters Collection at University of Chicago, box 3, no. 77, Special Collections Research Center, University of Chicago Library, http://pi.lib.uchicago.edu/1001/scrc/md/meposters-0003-077.

Painting of Shaykh Safi al-Din, opaque watercolour, ink and gold on paper, Shiraz, Iran, Shaʿban 990 AH / August–September 1582, © The Aga Khan Museum, AKM264.

Sevruguin, Antoin, *Studio Portrait: Man, Woman and Infant*, Myron Bement Smith Collection: Antoin Sevruguin Photographs, Freer Gallery of Art and Arthur M. Sackler Gallery Archives, Smithsonian Institute, Washington D.C. Gift of Katherine Dennis Smith, 1973-1985, FSA_A.4_2.12.GN.26.07, http://archive.asia.si.edu/iran-in-photographs/gallery.asp?set=FSA_A.4_2.12.GN&page=15.

Sevruguin, Antoin, *Studio Portrait: Seated Veiled Woman with Pearl*, Myron Bement Smith Collection: Antoin Sevruguin Photographs, Freer Gallery of Art and Arthur M. Sackler Gallery Archives, Smithsonian Institute, Washington D.C. Gift of Katherine Dennis Smith, 1973-1985, FSA_A.4_2.12.GN.02.07, http://archive.asia.si.edu/iran-in-photographs/gallery.asp?set=FSA_A.4_2.12.GN&page=3.

Sevruguin, Antoin, *Studio Portrait: Veiled Woman*, Myron Bement Smith Collection: Antoin Sevruguin Photographs, Freer Gallery of Art and Arthur M. Sackler Gallery Archives, Smithsonian Institute, Washington D.C. Gift of Katherine Dennis Smith, 1973-1985, FSA_A.4_2.12.GN.02.05, http://archive.asia.si.edu/iran-in-photographs/gallery.asp?set=FSA_A.4_2.12.GN&page=2.

Sevruguin, Antoin, *Veiled Women Boarding a Train, One of 274 Vintage Photographs*, late 19th century, Brooklyn Museum, Purchase gift of Leona Soudavar in memory of Ahmad Soudavar, 1997.3.12, https://www.brooklynmuseum.org/opencollection/objects/159273.

Sokout, 1998, Photography by Maysam Makhmalbaf, Makhmalbaf Film House.

'We created you from men and women' (Qur ʾan 49.13), Middle Eastern Posters Collection at University of Chicago., box 2, no. 45, Special Collections Research Center, University of Chicago Library, http://pi.lib.uchicago.edu/1001/scrc/md/meposters-0002-045.

Women off to war. Middle Eastern Posters Collection at University of Chicago, box 3, no. 60, Special Collections Research Center, University of Chicago Library, http://pi.lib.uchicago.edu/1001/scrc/md/meposters-0003-060.

Index